W9-ABS-160

THE COMPLETE
WOODSHOP GUIDE

HOW TO **PLAN, EQUIP** OR **IMPROVE** YOUR WORKSPACE

WITHDRAWN

POPULAR WOODWORKING BOOKS
CINCINNATI, OHIO
www.popularwoodworking.com

Read This Important Safety Notice

To prevent accidents, keep safety in mind while you work. Use the safety guards installed on power equipment; they are for your protection.

When working on power equipment, keep fingers away from saw blades, wear safety goggles to prevent injuries from flying wood chips and sawdust, wear hearing protection and consider installing a dust vacuum to reduce the amount of airborne sawdust in your woodshop.

Don't wear loose clothing, such as neckties or shirts with loose sleeves, or jewelry, such as rings, necklaces or bracelets, when working on power equipment. Tie back long hair to prevent it from getting caught in your equipment.

People who are sensitive to certain chemicals should check the chemical content of any product before using it.

Due to the variability of local conditions, construction materials, skill levels, etc., neither the author nor Popular Woodworking Books assumes any responsibility for any accidents, injuries, damages or other losses incurred resulting from the material presented in this book.

The authors and editors who compiled this book have tried to make the contents as accurate and correct as possible. Plans, illustrations, photographs and text have been carefully checked. All instructions, plans and projects should be carefully read, studied and understood before beginning construction.

Prices listed for supplies and equipment were current at the time of publication and are subject to change.

Metric Conversion Chart

TO CONVERT	TO	MULTIPLY BY
Inches	Centimeters	2.54
Centimeters	Inches	0.4
Feet	Centimeters	30.5
Centimeters	Feet	0.03
Yards	Meters	0.9
Meters	Yards	1.1

The Complete Woodshop Guide. Copyright © 2009. Edited by Jim Stack. Printed and bound in China. All rights reserved. No part of this book may be reproduced in any form or by any electronic or mechanical means including information storage and retrieval systems without permission in writing from the publisher, except by a reviewer, who may quote brief passages in a review. Published by Popular Woodworking Books, an imprint of F+W Media, Inc., 4700 East Galbraith Road, Cincinnati, Ohio, 45236. (800) 289-0963. First edition.

Distributed in Canada by Fraser Direct
100 Armstrong Avenue
Georgetown, Ontario L7G 5S4
Canada

Distributed in the U.K. and Europe by David & Charles
Brunel House
Newton Abbot
Devon TQ12 4PU
England
Tel: (+44) 1626 323200
Fax: (+44) 1626 323319
E-mail: postmaster@davidandcharles.co.uk

Distributed in Australia by Capricorn Link
P.O. Box 704
Windsor, NSW 2756
Australia

Visit our Web site at www.popularwoodworking.com.

Other fine Popular Woodworking Books are available from your local bookstore or direct from the publisher.

13   12   11   10   09   5   4   3   2   1

Library of Congress Cataloging-in-Publication Data is available upon request from the publisher.

ACQUISITIONS EDITOR: David Thiel, david.thiel@fwmedia.com
SENIOR EDITOR: Jim Stack, jim.stack@fwmedia.com
DESIGNER: Brian Roeth
PRODUCTION COORDINATOR: Mark Griffin

Thanks to Gil Russ for letting us photograph his shop for the cover of this book.

684.08
COM

About the Authors

CHARLIE SELF is a writer and photographer who first worked in the Katonah Altar Factory before he was 17, a whole lot of years ago. For the past 40 years, he's worked as a free lance writer, with more than 20 of those years devoted to writing about woodworking. Charlie is currently starting his second term as President of the National Association of Home & Workshop Writers (NAHWW). He is also a multiple winner of the Golden Hammer award presented by NAHWW for excellence in writing or photography in his field.

BILL STANKUS has been woodworking for over 25 years. Before his love of woodworking took hold, he was an oceanographer and a fine-arts photographer. He has designed and built custom furniture and specialized in museum-quality restorations of antique furniture. He has taught woodworking at the university level, given seminars throughout the United States and consulted with major tool manufacturers. Bill is the author of magazine articles, video scripts, tool manuals and woodworking books. He currently resides with his wife and family in western Washington, and continues to work on his own ideal woodshop.

DANNY PROULX shared with us his passion for woodworking through his book, magazine articles and web site advice, as well as through teaching and mentoring his students and clients. He founded Rideau Cabinets in 1989 and started building kitchens and specialty cabinets. Over time, Danny married his love of woodworking and writing with his photographic skills and wrote 15 books in 9 years. He also wrote for several magazines including *Canadian Woodworking* and *CabinetMaker* magazine. He started giving seminars in his home to new woodworkers and eventually started teaching courses at Algonquin College in Ottawa. Danny passed away on November 26, 2004.

CONTENTS

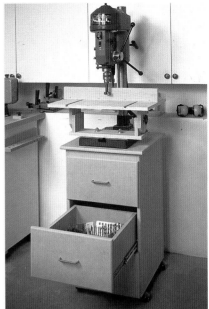
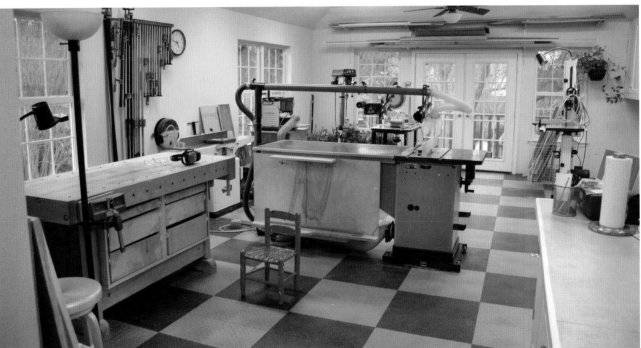

INTRODUCTION

EACH OF US HAS A DIFFERENT STARTING PLACE
WHEN SETTING UP A SHOP.

Some of us have advanced woodworking skills and some of us have basic or even beginning skills. No matter. Start where you are — whether you live in an apartment, house, condo, farm or if you are presently in prison (yes, you too can do some minimal woodworking).

Budgets vary also, from those with almost unlimited funds to those with tight budgets. Some us have inherited tools from our parents, grandparents or even our great-grandparents. There are those that have a hammer, screwdriver and a few wrenches — but they have a great desire to start working wood.

SO, THE BIG QUESTION IS, "WHERE CAN I FIND ADVICE AND INSTRUCTIONS ABOUT SETTING UP SHOP?" THE ANSWER IS IN YOUR HANDS — THIS BOOK!

We, the editors of Popular Woodworking books, have compiled the best of the best from three woodworking experts who are also good writers: Bill Stankus, Charlie Self and the late Danny Proulx. Plus, we've included some great information from the pages of *Popular Woodworking* magazine.

Bill has combed the country to find a wide range of woodworking shops — from closets (literally) to large shops that stand as buildings separate from the owner's house. There's even a shop in a van. He also offers top-notch advice about shop safety, electrical and dust collection issues.

Charlie is a woodworker and writer who has built and helped build a lot of woodworking shops and he knows what works and what doesn't.

Danny was a woodworker, cabinetmaker, teacher and author. He offers some of the best woodshop projects to outfit your shop. You can build the projects as you need them or take the plunge and build them all as a set. They are all built to the same heights, so using them as extra work surfaces is easy if the need arises.

If your needs are few and/or your budget is tight, you will learn what others have done to make their woodworking come alive, no matter what their means.

Woodworking is a hobby and profession that will keep your mind and hands busy. In times of stress or when you want to relax and take your mind somewhere where you can do things your own way. Going into your shop, whatever form it might take, you enter a world that you have created and where you create. Whether you carve, turn, make scroll saw puzzles, rout signage, build cabinets, make furniture or toys or just want to make shop projects, you will find great satisfaction and a feeling of accomplishment.

So, read on and discovery what others have already learned and turn it to your own benefit. Find a place to work and learn how to outfit it with electricity, dust collection and what safety features you need to include.

CHAPTER 1

BUILDING SAFETY INTO SHOP DESIGN

Before setting out to design your ideal woodshop,

safety should be foremost in your mind,

since safety is a factor that has extraordinary

consequences in both the present and future.

Is your woodshop a safe place? Think about this: Some of the most dangerous objects and materials that you will ever come across are in the woodshop. This includes just about everything that is used in the woodshop: machines, hand tools, solvents, wood and sawdust. The physical activity of lifting or moving heavy objects, breathing solvent fumes, touching various chemicals, listening to high-decibel sounds, holding vibrating electrical tools and climbing on stepladders are some of the obstacles that need to be safely managed. In fact, they are at the core of how you should design and build your woodshop.

There is a certain disconnect most beginners have regarding today's woodworking. Most beginners have never had years of instruction or the hands-on traditions of trade schools or apprenticeships. But let's assume that the beginner has the desire and abilities to set up a woodshop, and that person comes from some unrelated background: computer programming, business, sales and so on. Where does this beginner get the information necessary for woodworking? Most likely from books,

magazines, videos and hardware store salespeople. But is that enough to really understand the relationships of the many facets of woodworking and safety? Does the beginner have the correct information necessary to judge appropriate products? Is the salesperson or magazine writer or video personality free of vested interests? Probably not. If the information is from a company, you can bet their legal and advertising departments have influenced their information. If the information is from a magazine or store, the information is potentially biased by advertiser or supplier influences. And, product review magazines rarely deal with the interrelationships of diverse products.

The essential question of safety is often obvious and also it is more than likely to be very subtle. Furthermore, there are other complications to essential safety that historic woodworkers never dealt with: an array of plastics, man-made building materials, volatile liquids, environmental issues, building codes and regulations and so on. Today, it is not enough to know how to cut dovetails: Do you understand the complexities of mix-

ing heat, chemical and dust fumes, synthetics, sharp things and electricity with flesh and blood?

It's possible that we could one day see the advent of safety inspectors for the home woodshop. Woodworkers, especially those with home woodshops, have had a long history of not being monitored by the agencies that scrutinize commercial woodshops. However, if you notice modern safety trends, there probably are (or will be) people and organizations that want to codify what goes on in home woodshops. While there has been a trickling down of valuable safety products to the home woodshop, I can't imagine that many people want to have outside groups dictating home woodshop procedures and necessities. Having said that, most woodworkers are doing a good job of learning how to do woodworking, and they are generally buying tools and machinery that have been tested for safe use. Of course, there are many old, worn-out or poorly modified tools sold at garage sales or passed down through families. And these should be identified and gotten rid of so that accidents won't happen. However, in addition to operating machinery safely, we should also improve our handling of heavy materials (thus reducing bodily sprains and strains) and our use of chemicals (solvents and finishing products). More or less, the amateur woodworker and the one-person small-business woodshop want the best of two different worlds: the freedom of the hobby and craft world, and the tools, materials, techniques and business of the professional and commercial world. While this may seem fair if you are a home woodworker, the problem is that there are potentially unsafe woodshop situations not being corrected.

It is up to each of us to be individually responsible for having safe woodshops. Don't pretend that your woodshop is safe or that it's too expensive to do the right thing, or don't come up with some other rationalization that keeps you from upgrading questionable situations. Make your woodshop safe, learn proper woodworking techniques and never attempt to use tools or supplies in unsafe ways. Stay current on new tools, accessories and supplies. For example, router bits are now available in bright colors that are visible when the router is operating. Manufacturers often improve their products to comply with new safety guidelines. A few manufacturers actually make their products safer because of consumer demands.

SAFETY CHECKLIST

The initial steps toward woodshop safety begin with the idea that you have to be aware of your surroundings.

- Always look for the accident that's about to happen.
- Don't ignore potential accidents or dangerous conditions.
- Always evaluate the situation and ask yourself, "Is this the best way of doing something or is there a safer way?"
- If there's a potential safety problem, take the appropriate steps to correct it.
- Periodically review all woodshop safety considerations.
- If you have older machines, compare them to their modern counterpart's safety features.

General Safety Concerns

This list, though not definitive, is meant as a basic overview and a start-

ELECTRICAL HAZARDS
CHECKLIST

Make a copy of this list and check your woodshop for the following electrical hazards:

- ☐ Comply with local electrical codes concerning wiring type, conduits, hookups, service panels and other electrical features.
- ☐ Have the correct amperage and type fuses or circuit breakers installed in the electrical service.
- ☐ Light fixtures should have bulbs with the correct wattage.
- ☐ Halogen type lights generate considerable heat and should be kept away from accidental bumping and flammable materials.
- ☐ Electrical motors, power tools and machines should have their technical information plates attached.
- ☐ Electrical motors, power tools and machines should have labeling indicating that the product has been tested by a nationally recognized testing laboratory.
- ☐ Replace frayed or worn electrical cords.
- ☐ Replace electrical cords that have worn or bent plugs.
- ☐ Replace electrical cords nicked by sharp tools.
- ☐ There should be no standing water or moisture where electrical devices are used.
- ☐ Don't use unnecessary or overloaded extension cords.
- ☐ If extension cords are used, be sure to use correct wire gauge.
- ☐ Don't use modified adapter plugs: All three prongs should be intact.
- ☐ Don't use adapters that have a missing ground prong or grounding wire.
- ☐ Electrical cords shouldn't be placed in walkways or traffic areas.
- ☐ Don't have heavy objects resting on electrical cords.

- ☐ Electrical cords should be positioned well away from spinning or operating machinery.
- ☐ Unplug electrical cords when adjusting or performing maintenance on machines and power tools.
- ☐ Electrical cords shouldn't be fastened down with nails or staples.
- ☐ The woodshop should have a sufficient number of well-placed electrical receptacles.
- ☐ All outlets must work properly.
- ☐ Unused outlets should have safety covers placed in receptacle openings.
- ☐ GFI (ground fault circuit interrupters) outlets should be installed near sinks or other wet areas.
- ☐ Never use sparking electrical motors or tools near dust, oily rags or solvent fumes.
- ☐ Ventilation fans must be non-sparking and certified for ventilation of flammable fumes.
- ☐ There should be air circulation around electrical tools.
- ☐ Portable heaters must be listed as tested and approved for use in woodworking environments.
- ☐ Never use portable heaters near flammable materials such as rags, dust, scrap wood, finishing supplies, paper and drapes.
- ☐ Position approved portable heaters so that they can't be tipped over.
- ☐ Check for unnecessary machinery vibrations that can cause wear or stress on electrical wiring.
- ☐ Never leave woodburning tools, soldering irons, hot-glue guns, heat guns or other high temperature tools unattended, and unplug these tools immediately after using them.

ing point for your own quest for a safe woodshop.

- Never work when you are tired.
- Never use tools and machinery when under the influence of alcohol, drugs or medications.
- Wear suitable work clothing that is not loose fitting or with floppy or dangling sleeves, ties, etc.
- Remove all jewelry, ties and scarves, and tie up long hair.
- Wear safety goggles or safety glasses that have side guards.
- Wear hearing protection when operating machinery and power tools.
- Have approved and fully charged fire extinguishers in the woodshop.
- Don't wear gloves while operating tools and machinery.
- Keep up-to-date insurance information on yourself, others using the woodshop and the woodshop itself. Check with your insurance company on policy coverage relating to accidents and other woodshop misfortunes.
- Keep a list of emergency telephone numbers near the telephone.
- Know where to go for emergency medical treatment.
- Stay current on codes, laws and other regulations pertaining to safety and hazardous materials, equipment and procedures.

Safety Preparation and Maintenance

- Read, understand and follow all instructions in the owner's manual for all machines and tools.
- Keep all owner's manuals in a handy location.
- Maintain all machines and tools to the manufacturer's recommendations.
- Use machine safety guards provided by the manufacturer.
- Don't modify safety guards or other safety-related equipment.
- Be sure that any modification to a tool or machine is either approved by the manufacturer or within the design limits of the tool.
- Before adding any accessory to a

tool or machine, be sure that it is both acceptable and safe.

- Use tools and machines for their intended purposes.
- Periodically review owner's manuals for safe operating procedures.
- Periodically inspect cutting tools, such as tungsten-carbide table saw blades and router bits, for damage or cracks. Replace as necessary.
- Keep cutting tools sharp.

Work Area Safety

- Do not work with a cluttered floor or with unstable piles of tools and materials.
- Wheels on mobile bases must be secured before using the machine.
- Prevent unauthorized use of the woodshop by installing lockable on/off switches on all machines.
- Have proper lighting and ventilation.
- Read and follow label information, including all warnings and cautions, prior to using solvents, finishing products or other chemicals, and follow all recommended use and safety procedures. If you have any concerns about products, call the manufacturer, your own physician or health agencies of the EPA.
- Not all rubber gloves are the same. Use the correct type when working with solvents, finishing products, paint strippers, etc.
- Never dispose of oily rags in sealed trash cans that will be exposed to heat or direct sunlight.
- Store solvents and other flammable materials in approved storage units.
- Never use flammable solvents or other flammable finishing products near water heaters or any other high-temperature device or open flame.

Equipment Safety

- Use vises, clamps or other safe holding devices to firmly hold work material.

TREATING CHEMICAL BURNS

Numerous solvents, oils, paint strippers, bleaches and dyes are dangerous, and their labels offer information regarding their uses and side effects. The following is the standard first aid procedure for treating chemical burns.

1. Immediately call for medical aid and rescue. If possible, tell the operator what kind of chemical has caused the burns.

2. As quickly as possible, flood the affected chemical burn area with water. Continue with the water for at least 15-30 minutes so that all traces of the chemical are removed.

3. If the chemical has gotten into the eyes, gently spray clean water into the eyes. If a water spray is unavailable, have the victim lay flat and then gently pour water into the eyes. Continue the eye washing for a minimum of 5 minutes.

4. Clothing can absorb spilled chemicals so remove the victim's clothes.

5. If available, place a clean pad over the chemical burn area.

- If you are considering buying used equipment, be very cautious about missing parts, modifications, wobbly shafts and belts, and any other loose, damaged, bent or out-of-the norm condition. When possible, ask for owner's manual and parts list.
- Don't buy used air compressors. The problem is that you can't see rust and corrosion inside the air tank.
- Absolutely never consider buying an air compressor that has patched pinholes in the air tank.

Safety with Chemicals

I feel compelled to repeat myself: Read the labels on all finishing products and follow all recommended use and safety procedures. If you have any concerns about products, call the manufacturer, your own physician, health agencies or the EPA. Take no unnecessary risks relating to the handling and use of chemicals; design your woodshop to be user-friendly and safe.

Working with Hazardous Materials

- Read product labels and understand their implications.
- Have operational smoke detectors within the woodshop.
- Most vapors are invisible. And it is difficult to know how much vapor is too much. Ventilate the room.
- If the woodshop is located within a garage which has a gas water heater and parked automobiles, install a carbon monoxide detector and natural gas and propane gas detectors.
- If the woodshop is located in a garage or basement which has cracked concrete floors, then you should periodically use a radon detection kit.
- Have fully charged fire extinguishers rated ABC or BC and know how to properly use them. Consult with your local fire department for fire extinguisher training classes.
- Do not pour water on chemical fires.
- Never mix ammonia with household bleach. The resulting solution produces a deadly gas.
- Use safety goggles, dust masks, multi-purpose respirators and rubber gloves.
- Be aware that standard clothing can retain vaporous fumes.
- Know the telephone number and location of a local Haz-Mat office.

FIRST AID

I have visited with manufacturers and their lawyers enough to realize that there are quite a few people who have gotten hurt by doing things that perhaps they shouldn't. A standard knowledge of first aid should be a priority for you, both in and out of the woodshop. But within the shop, you'll most likely face two types of trauma — cuts and electrical shock.

Treating Severe Cuts and Bleeding

Steel is indifferent to flesh. Neither minor nor major cuts should be taken lightly. Severe bleeding can result in death. I suggest that, at the minimum, you read a first aid book and that the appropriate techniques for cut treatment are understood and practiced. I purchased a useful first aid book at a local community college titled *American Red Cross First Aid, Responding to Emergencies* by American Red Cross, Health and Safety Services (Mosby Lifeline 1996). I know from experience about the blink-of-the-eye speed in which accidents occur and about the trauma of bleeding cuts. Believe me, that is not the time to wonder "Gee, what do I do?" I still have all my fingers, but there are a few scars left over from unnecessary accidents.

MAKING A FIRST AID KIT

To make a first aid kit, get yourself a sealed container, such as a tool box, and paint the red cross symbol on all sides so that it is easily identified by anyone. Remember to replace all supplies as they are used. Include the following:

- 5" x 8" card, preferably laminated, with street address and driving directions to the woodshop. This saves time when speaking with an emergency operator. This card should also include any medical conditions, such as diabetes, heart disease, allergies, reactions to medications and so on. Include name of personal physician.
- Box of assorted bandages
- 12 each 2" x 2" sterile pads
- 12 each 4" x 4" sterile pads
- 2 each 2" roller bandages
- 2 each 1" roller bandages
- Roll of 1" adhesive tape
- 6 each 3" to 6" wide elastic bandages
- Scissors
- Tweezers, a nice version has an attached magnifying glass
- Safety pins
- Box of alcohol swabs
- Several pairs of latex gloves
- Antiseptic solution and wipes
- Eye goggles
- Resuscitation mask or face shield

Other useful items:

- Hand soap
- Flashlight
- Additional sterile or clean strips of cloth
- Plastic quart or liter bottle filled with water
- Survival blanket — it compacts to size of a fist, but will give warmth to shock victim
- Ice bag or chemical ice pack

Treating Electrical Shock

- Never put yourself in danger when considering the rescue of a person endangered by electrical current.
- If the victim is immobilized by live current, knock him free using a stout wooden implement.
- Monitor the victim's life signs.
- Have someone immediately call for medical support.
- Locate any burns where the electricity entered and exited the victim. These burns are often found at jewelry locations, belt buckles or where there was contact with the electrical wire.
- Treat entrance and exit burns as third-degree burns.
- The victim should be lying down and with the feet slightly raised.
- If the victim has no pulse, or the pulse is weak or irregular, a qualified person should administer CPR (cardiopulmonary resuscitation).
- If the victim is not breathing, or has uneven or very shallow breathing, administer artificial respiration.
- Keep the victim warm with blankets or jackets placed on top and under so that body heat loss is minimized.

WOODSHOP SECURITY

I am not someone who wants to live in a bunker. But I also know we live in a tough world. Prudence is an important value, and it is wise to at least review your work area's current security. The following list also is an approach for reviewing the windows, doors, lighting and safety procedures of your woodshop.

Inexpensive Security Devices

- standard dead bolts
- dead bolts with attached alarmed rim; a battery-powered unit that will sound when the locked door is forced
- wide-angle door viewers
- keyed security bolt for sliding door
- any of a variety of window locks designed for different-style windows
- security bar for sliding doors and sliding windows
- metal lock reinforcers which fit on both sides of the doorknob and dead bolt areas
- a third hinge added to doors
- a rechargeable flashlight kept near a door or in an easy-access location
- for increased fire safety, lock sets can be installed to interconnect the doorknob mechanism with the dead bolt
- night lights can be installed at appropriate outlets
- three-way wall switches can be installed so that lights can be turned on and off at the top and bottom of stairs or at opposite sides of a room
- telephones programmed with emergency numbers
- inventory your tools and accessories and keep a record of their models and serial numbers in a location other than in your woodshop
- have a proper insurance policy, including coverage for loss, accidents or disasters; ask your insurance agent about riders for additional coverage

Advanced Security Methods

- Replace basement windows with glass blocks. These will create a

USING FIRE EXTINGUISHERS

Fire extinguishers give the appearance of something that is self-evident and as easy to use as "pull the trigger and spray." The truth is, there is more to it than that, and I recommend that you read further about the use of fire extinguishers and talk with your local fire department about instructions in the proper use of fire extinguishers. Imagine this scene — a shop fire being spread further by incorrect use of a fire extinguisher.

Install fire extinguishers that have a gauge and use the PASS technique:
- P—Pull the pin on the fire extinguisher.
- A—Aim the fire extinguisher at the base of the fire.
- S—Squeeze the handle of the fire extinguisher.
- S—Sweep the fire extinguisher back and forth repeatedly to cover the base of the fire.

(From: Kidde Safety, Mebane, NC)

PLANTS THAT PROVIDE SECURITY

Holly
Hawthorn
Rose
Barberry
Blackberry
Oregon Grape
Flowering Quince
Cactus
Yucca
Locust
Bougainvillea
Red Currant or Gooseberry

distorted image to anyone attempting to look in from the outside.

- Windows can be covered with a specialized security film that laminates glass with a tough transparent coating. This film resists penetration and will hold broken glass, more or less in place — a jagged window hole.
- There are many types of sophisticated alarm systems that can be customized for woodshops.
- Monitor the woodshop via closed-circuit TV. If you work alone and the woodshop is distant from the main living area, this allows a family member to periodically check that all is well.
- Install an intercom system for instant communication with remote areas.
- If you spend sufficient time working while it is dark, install sound- or motion-activated light switches.

Exterior Security

Many security experts recommend using exterior devices and systems for home security simply because they are meant to keep trouble from entering your house and woodshop. There are far more choices than this list — these are meant to be suggestions of possible methods of securing your property.

- Install fencing around the grounds or yard. A minimum height of 40" is recommended.
- Do you like dogs? Dogs have keen hearing and are protective of their turf. They offer some protection against prowlers and thieves.
- If you don't own a dog, you can still install "Beware of Dog" signs or place a dog water bowl and resting pad outside on a porch or walkway.
- There are alarm systems that respond to motion detection with the sound of barking dogs. The sensors track any motion, and once the motion ceases, the barking stops.
- Have bright exterior lighting at doors, driveways and walkways. Place lighting on sides of buildings, on posts, under eaves or under windows.
- Motion detection lights will give visual warning that someone is outside.
- There are a variety of plants that have thorns or sharp leaves that can be planted under windows or near fences and walkways — consult your local nursery or garden center for plant hardiness in your climate zone (see "Plants That Provide Security" sidebar).

CHAPTER 2

POWERING AND LIGHTING THE SHOP EFFECTIVELY

There's no denying the fact that electricity is the fundamental necessity of the modern woodshop.

WARNINGS ABOUT ELECTRICITY

Before you begin to do anything with electrical wiring there are a few cautions. Never attempt any electrical work if you have doubts about the wiring layout or the consequences of your effort. The two agencies you should be aware of are your local building departments (usually city and county) and the utility company. The building department has electrical inspectors who can explain local codes and requirements concerning permits for the work and any necessary inspections. Requirements, regulations and amended versions of the National Electrical Code (NEC) vary from area to area. It is very important to follow the codes and guidelines established for your area. The utility agencies can assist in the location of underground cables and will recommend the correct approach to any electrical service upgrades. Often, it's less time-consuming, more economical and safer to hire a licensed electrical contractor to install new wiring, electrical service panels or other custom work. Electrical work is similar to woodworking: Both require specialized tools and supplies. If you don't have the correct tools, be prepared to rent, buy or borrow them. A visit to an electrical supply store is enough to make you realize that there are scores of supplies, many of which have to meet your local electrical codes.

EVALUATE YOUR ELECTRICAL NEEDS

There are several starting points in the evaluation of electrical requirements for a woodshop. The first, and most obvious, is that if the existing room has a single overhead light with a pull chain and only one or two outlets, the room is underpowered for woodworking machinery. Check the electrical service panel for the circuit breaker to the potential shop location; if there is only one 15- or 20- amp circuit, the service will need upgrading. If you start up a table saw and the lights dim, perhaps you should stop woodworking and upgrade the electrical service.

How you upgrade or install adequate electrical service for a woodshop location is dependent on whether you're remodeling or building a new room. It's certainly more straightforward installing wiring and outlets in a new construction. Routing cables through open framework is much simpler than when walls, doors and ceilings are in place.

Electricity Essentials

There are many comprehensive books on basic wiring that detail all of the various electrical requirements and upgrades for a house. Many of these books are written for do-it-yourselfers, so they're easy to read and follow.

What I want to address are the specific electrical essentials of the woodshop. These essentials are:

- safety
- adequate electrical supply
- 110V and 220V service
- sufficient outlets
- proper lighting

SAFETY RULES

There are two main safety considerations: the type required when actually upgrading a system and the safety of having the correct amperes, cables, outlets, etc., once the upgrading is done. While these may seem similar, they're distinctly different.

Proper upgrading generally consists of knowledge, information, common sense, proper tools and supplies. To safely complete an electrical upgrade requires knowing the machinery and tool electrical requirements, code-compliant installation of outlets, use of the proper types and sizes of cables, outlets, etc. If you have any reservations about any of these points, it might be best to call in an electrical contractor. After all, electrical current is invisible until there is electrical shock or electrical fire.

Never work on a live circuit. Always disconnect the circuit at the service panel. That means switching the circuit breaker to an 'off' position or removing a screw-in fuse. Remember that the electrical power will still be live to the service panel from the power utility lines (either below or above ground). So even if you switch the main power off, the power will still be live to the service. It's sort of like closing a dam's spillway: Water may not be leaving the dam, but there is water on the other side of the dam.

Be certain that the circuit is off by first turning on a light that's plugged into that circuit. If it goes out when the circuit is switched off, then you may proceed with the next step.

It's always a good idea to tell others that you are disconnecting a circuit. This is especially important when working at some distance from the service panel. You might even tape a note to the service panel warning others that you are working on the service.

Never work on any electrical fixtures, the service panel, the wiring or anything else electrical when there are wet spots, moist conditions or standing water. Dry the area as much as possible. Open windows and doors to aid in drying damp basements. If there is moisture on the floor, construct a platform of dry boards over the wet areas.

USE THE CORRECT TOOLS

Common tools that you probably have in the woodshop that are useful for electrical work:
- mat knife — for cutting wallboard and, with the blade barely exposed, cutting sheathed cable
- hammer — the obvious
- screwdrivers — also obvious
- Allen wrenches — fittings and terminals often are secured with hex screw heads
- square-drive screwdrivers — many electricians now use screws with square holes instead of slot or Phillips heads. Square-drive screws are fast and easy to use.
- tape measure — the obvious
- keyhole saw — for sawing holes in walls and hard-to-reach locations prior to installing boxes or cables
- hacksaw — for sawing conduit to length
- cordless drill with drill bits — the perfect drill when the power is off

Specialized Tools
- engineer's or lineman's pliers — used to twist bare wires together and then cut the last ⅛" off so that the twisted wires fit into a wirenut; large serrated jaws can bend flat metal
- diagonal cutting pliers — for cutting wire; fits in confined locations
- needle-nosed or snipe-nosed pliers — for picking up and holding small parts in confined locations
- wire strippers — adjustable to different wire gauges for removing insulation
- multipurpose electrician's wire strippers/tool — several features: wire stripper, wire cutter, crimper and bolt cutter
- insulated screwdrivers — entire screwdriver, except blade tip, is coated with insulation
- conduit bender — long-handled device for bending metal conduit to various angles
- fish tape — thin metal line for pulling cable through enclosed areas; i.e., walls and ceilings
- cable ripper — a cutting device for slitting the sheathing on cable
- electronic metal and voltage detector — a device similar to stud finder that locates any metal object and detects AC voltage within a wall
- continuity Tester — used to determine whether an electrical path is complete. Simple to use when checking fuses, switches and plugs. It has a battery and indicator light and is only used when the power is off! Handy to have, even if not an electrician.
- voltage Tester — used to determine if power is present. The probes are touched to a hot line and the ground thus causing the indicator to light. It is used with the power on. Useful for checking DC/AC voltage, outlets, motors, appliances and fuses. Useful if you have some experience working with electricity.
- volt-ohmmeter, or multitester — used for testing a variety of conditions, including voltage, low-

voltage current, resistance to ohms and continuity. Useful for checking outlets, fuses, wires, plugs, motors and electronic circuits. Useful if you have some experience working with electricity.
- circuit analyzers — look like an oversize electrical plug. The simplest version can determine if there is power to a receptacle, whether it is properly grounded and whether the wiring is correct. There are more sophisticated circuit analyzers that can check from the receptacle back to the service panel for voltage drops or for current leaks. Handy to have, even if not an electrician.

ELECTRICAL SUPPLIES
Be certain that the electrical supplies you select are approved or meet local building codes. If you aren't sure about this, then it would be best to consult certified experts. There are too many choices — guessing which part or wire size to use is the wrong approach.

Wire is a single strand of conductive metal enclosed with insulation. Cord is stranded wires protected by insulation. It can consist of two or three stranded wires within the insulation and is used for appliances, lamps, etc. Cable has two or more color-coded insulated wires that are protected by sheathing.

In the United States, the colors of the individual wire are agreed upon: Black or red is the power or hot wire, white or gray is the neutral, and green or green with a yellow stripe is the ground wire. Sometimes ground is a single uninsulated copper wire.

Wire Type and Size
It's very important to use the correct wire size and type when upgrading an electrical system. Local codes will specify what sorts of cable and cable conduits are permitted in your area.

Wire Types
TYPE NM has a thermoplastic insulation and is capable of withstanding a

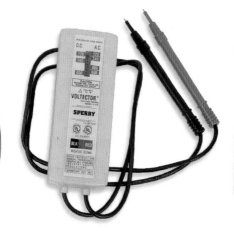

Handy electrical test equipment includes (from top left, going clockwise) a continuity tester, a voltage tester, a multitester and a circuit analyzer.

TIP It's a good idea to have insulated handles on pliers and other metal tools. Don't rely on insulated tools as the only safety precaution, always turn circuits off before working on them.

wide range of temperatures. It's used for most household circuits.

TYPE UF (underground feed cable) is waterproof and is used for damp and outdoor locations.

TYPE USE (underground service entrance) is used for underground or overhead service entrance and direct burial to garages and woodshops.

TYPE THW is used for outdoor hanging or indoor conduit as service entrance cables and for conduit to a subpanel.

Nonmetallic (NM) cable is the most common plastic-sheathed cable. It's often referred to as Romex, which is a trade name. The sheath is usually moisture resistant and flame retardant. Normally, there are insulated power wires and a bare ground wire inside of the sheath.

Armored cable, referred to by the trade name BX cable, has an outer armored layer, usually flexible galvanized steel, that often contains two or three wires wrapped in paper.

Conduit is usually galvanized steel or plastic pipe. It's generally available in $\frac{1}{2}$", $\frac{3}{4}$", 1" and $1\frac{1}{4}$" diameters. The correct size to use depends on the diameter and number of wires inside the conduit.

Wire Size

Wire size, basically the diameter of the wire excluding insulation, is extremely important when upgrading an electrical system. There are standard reference numbers, usually printed on the outside of wire insulation, that are based upon the American Wire Gauge (AWG) system. Gauge numbers are inverse to their size; that is, the smaller the number, the larger the wire diameter. The maximum current that a wire can safely manage is stated in amperes (amps). Wire diameter and the amount of amperes are directly related. Smaller diameter wires have greater resistance to electrical current flow; consequently, as the current flow increases so do friction and heat. To avoid melting wires and electrical fires, use larger-diameter wires for heavier electrical needs.

CALCULATING ELECTRICAL USAGE IN THE WOODSHOP

No matter what electrical circuits or subpanels are added to the house's electrical service, the total house load must not exceed the service rating. Generally, older homes having no electrical modernization have 100-amp services. Newer homes generally have 200-amp services. If you are not certain about the service, look at the main circuit breaker in the service panel — it should be labeled. If you have 100-amp service, consult with both the utility company and a licensed electrician about upgrading to a 200-amp service.

The woodshop is probably going to have machines and power tools, unless, of course, you're taken with the joy of only working with hand tools. Generally, woodshops will have one woodworker using no more than two machines at one time (table saw and dust collector, drill press and vacuum). The advantage of this is that the electrical system isn't going to need to support the simultaneous operation of all the woodshop's machinery. As you plan the electrical layout, make a best guess as to the frequency of use of tools and machines. Not only will this aid in determining circuit requirements, but it will also aid in planning the placement of outlets. The reality of upgrading woodshop electrical systems is that it's often easier to install separate outlets on separate circuits than to have one circuit with multiple outlets. For example, in my woodshop I have three machines requiring 220V service: the table saw, jointer/planer and band saw. Rarely, if ever, are two machines running at the same time. So it's possible for the three machines to have their outlets wired to the same circuit. However, these machines are located in different areas of the woodshop and it was much easier to install outlets at each of the machine locations and route wires through one or more conduits. Since there was adequate space in the subpanel, it was a straightforward addition of circuit breakers and wire. The exception to this is the dust collector, which is also 220V. Because it's operated simultaneously with each of the stationary machines, there was no choice — it required its own circuit.

The National Electrical Code sets minimum capacities for circuits regarding use and amperage:

- Small appliances — 20 amperes
- General lighting — 15 or 20 amperes
- Stationary tools — multiply the machine's amperage by 125%. The 125% factors the electrical surge that occurs when a machine is first switched on. For example, a 12" planer rated at 15 amps (1.25 × 15 = 18.75) will require a 20-amp circuit.

OUTLETS, SWITCHES AND PLUGS

Until the day comes that we can use tools powered by wireless telemetry, woodshops will need outlets and switches. When designing a new electrical layout, placement of outlets and switches requires planning, guesswork and a bit of luck. The reality of woodshops is that work projects, new machines, relocation of cabinets, stacks of lumber and other fluctuating events will block existing outlets

Number of Wires in a Conduit*

WIRE SIZE	1/2" CONDUIT	3/4" CONDUIT	1" CONDUIT	1 1/4" CONDUIT
14	4	6	9	9
12	3	5	8	9
10	1	4	7	9
8	1	3	4	7
6	1	1	3	4

*Actual number is also governed by local codes

and switches from access. Often, well-thought-out locations aren't that handy once the woodshop is used. The ideal situation is never having to use extension cords because you have outlets wherever you work. This can be accomplished simply by locating outlets three to five feet apart throughout the woodshop, including the ceiling. This may seem excessive, but it's not. There are too many work conditions that occur away from the workbench area: Using a vacuum, sander, plate joiner, rotary carving tool or heat gun are but a few of the applications possible.

Two scenarios for installing outlets: If the woodshop area is a new construction, wires should be installed within the wall framework. If wall coverings are already in place, outlets can be installed on the outside of the wall surface if metal conduit and metal outlet boxes are used. Always check your local electrical codes concerning this type of installation. External conduit adds flexibility to designing and locating outlets, simply because conduit can be routed just about anywhere. Metal conduit pipe is easily bent to a variety of shapes and angles with a conduit bender. One option for the 90° bend at corners is to use short prebent right-angle conduit pieces. These are attached to the straight conduit with sleeve connectors. Conduit pipe can be cut wherever necessary and outlets installed.

Common Copper Household Wire (By Gauge) & Its Ampere Rating:

GAUGE	AMPERE RATING
No. 18	7 amperes
No. 16	10 amperes
No. 14	15 amperes
No. 12	20 amperes
No. 10	30 amperes
No. 8	40 amperes
No. 6	55 amperes

Steven Gray has an unusual (for the home woodshop, that is) electrical system. His woodshop features overhead electrical rails. These feed rails are connected to the main power panel. What is unique is that trolleys slide within the rails, and lights or AC switches can be attached to the trolleys. The feed rail is both 110V and 220V. Both voltages are usable depending upon how the contact trolley wheels are aligned within the feed rail. It's a very neat system, with movable electrical items all in one track, both 110V and 220V outlets and different types of lighting.

Acceptable Outlets

- Grounded three-prong, 120V, 15 amp
- Grounded three-prong, 120V, 20 amp
- Ground fault circuit interrupter, 120V, 15 amp and 20 amp
- Grounded three-prong 220/240V
  Note: Ungrounded two-prong 120V receptacles are unacceptable for shop use.

Typical Machine & Tool Ampere Ratings

Note: Machines and tools are 110V-120V with exceptions noted.

MACHINE/TOOL	AMPERAGE
10" Table saw	8.3 @ 230V
10" Contractor's table saw	12.8
14" Band saw ($\frac{1}{2}$ hp)	9
10" Radial-arm saw	11/5.5 @ 120/240V
12" Miter saw	13
6" Jointer	9.5
12" Planer	15
Drill press	6
6" x 48" Sander	8.4 @ 240V
2-hp Shaper	16/8 @ 110/220V
12" Lathe ($\frac{3}{4}$ hp)	11.4
Scroll saw	1.3
Dust collector (2 bag)	16/8 @ 115/230V
Dust collector (4 bag)	17 @ 230V
20-gallon Shop vacuum	10.5
3$\frac{1}{2}$-hp air compressor	15
Router, 1 hp	6.8
Router, 3 hp	15
Belt sander, 4" x 24"	10.5
Plate jointer	6.5
Finish sander	1.7
Spindle sander	3.5
$\frac{3}{8}$" Hand drill	4
Bench grinder	6
Strip sander, 1" x 30"	2.6
Jig saw	4.8
Circular saw	13
Heat gun	14
Benchtop mortiser	6
HVLP spray gun turbine	11.5

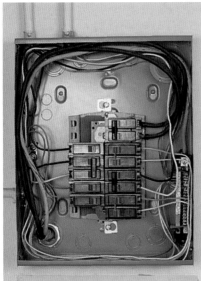

Above is a typical subpanel installed above the main circuit breaker panel. Below the main panel is a Gen/Tran unit — used for connecting a portable generator to the main panel in the event of a power outage. At left, you see the subpanel cover removed for a better look at the breaker switches and wiring.

Use grounded three-prong 20-amp outlets in the woodshop. This will accommodate most woodworking tools (see the tool amperage chart on page 77). If an existing woodshop has ungrounded two-prong outlets, turn off the main power and replace the old outlets with grounded outlets. If there isn't a ground wire to the outlet, attach one from the outlet to the receptacle box or the nearest cold water pipe. Check that the ground is functional by using a ground tester.

Ground fault circuit interrupter outlets (GFI) are designed to protect you from shock. GFI outlets monitor current; if the incoming and outgoing currents aren't within 0.005 amps, the GFI instantly cuts off the electricity (in 1/40 second). GFI outlets are found in newer houses, generally in bathrooms and outdoor locations where someone may have wet hands and feet. If you are installing outlets in damp basements or around sinks, you should install GFI units. As with all electrical installations, check local codes or hire a licensed electrician if you have any questions regarding the installation.

Switches

Switches are rated according to amperage and voltage, so it's important to choose the correct switch for compatibility with circuits, wire and outlets.

There are four basic types of switches:

- Single-pole switches have two terminals, one for the incoming hot wire and one for the outgoing hot wire. The switch toggle is imprinted with ON/OFF.
- Double-pole switches have four terminals and are used primarily for 240V circuits. The switch toggle is imprinted with ON/OFF.
- Three-way switches have three terminals. One terminal is labeled COM (common), and the hot wire is connected to this terminal; the other two terminals are switch leads. Two three-way switches are used to control a circuit from two different locations. The toggle has no ON/OFF imprint.
- Four-way switches have four terminals and are used with two three-way switches to control a circuit from more than two locations. The toggle has no ON/OFF imprint.

Plugs

Despite the proliferation of battery-powered tools, there are still many tools and machines that have AC plugs. Usually these plugs receive quite a lot of use and wear, often because of the neglectful act of pulling the cord and bending the prongs. When plugs need replacing, replace them with dead-front plugs. This type of plug has no exposed wires or

screws and the prongs are surrounded by smooth plastic. If there are screws on the plate surrounding the prongs, they are recessed and are only for securing the plug body together.

If you are attaching wires to a 125V plug with three prongs, connect the black wire to the brass terminal, the white wire to the silver terminal and the green wire to the green or gray terminal.

Polarized plugs are identified by having one brass prong (hot) and one silver prong with a wider tip. The plug is designed to fit into an outlet in only one direction. This plug is commonly installed on smaller appliances and woodworking tools.

LIGHTING THE WOODSHOP

There are two distinct types of lighting in most woodshops: fluorescent lighting and minimal use of all other types of lighting. Fluorescent lighting fixtures are probably used the most because they are inexpensive and commonly available. Other lighting types are thought to be useful as house lighting and not for woodshop lighting. While there is some truth to the generalization that fluorescent lights are useful in the woodshop, perhaps their limitations are overlooked.

Woodshop lighting is woefully neglected in today's woodworking. There's a cornucopia of aftermarket improvements to almost everything

Overhead electrical feed rail system in Steven Gray's woodshop.

Close-up view of the electrical feed rail. Each rail is on its own separate 30-amp circuit. The rail accepts any combination of outlets and lights. Both 110V and 220V can be used simultaneously.

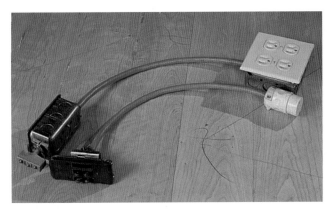

Switches and plugs are installed on the electrical feed rail system.

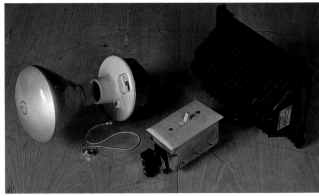

Various lights are installed on the electrical feed rail system.

electric within the woodshop except lighting. Lighting stores and hardware stores usually have jumbled lighting displays, making it nearly impossible to view and judge lighting fixtures one at a time. The one exception I've found is a GE display of different fluorescent lamps. This display is a set of identical photographs, individually set in a series of recessed boxes, each lit by a different fluorescent lamp. This display nicely reveals the color-rendering differences of fluorescent lamps.

Unfortunately, few light fixtures seem to be designed specifically for woodshops. Those that are tend to be either sterile-looking white metal devices or cheap-looking clip-on reflector hoods. This simply means that it's up to the woodworker to solve shop lighting questions through both personal experience and research. Trial and error may seem like a difficult path to follow, but it does allow you to customize your woodshop.

When evaluating lights and fixtures, consider that there are several key elements to using light: color, shadow, contrast and reflection. These are the products of lighting that we

TIP The amount of light required by a person to perform a task is directly related to age. At the age of 40, the requirement is three times greater than that for a 10-year-old. At the age of 60, the need is 15 times that for a 10-year-old.

see in both dynamic and subtle ways. They give usefulness, meaning and emotional connection to woodworking. Many artists refer to the process of their work as "painting with light." Woodworkers should also control and use light for both acceptable room lighting as well as artistic and aesthetic reasons.

Color is perhaps the most subjective and difficult aspect of light. A simple request proves this point: Define "red." We may generally agree upon the notion that tomatoes and apples are red, but it's extremely difficult to describe a particular color and have agreement on it: Color perception is in the eye of the beholder. Furthermore, location, situation and light source will change color. For example, if a person is holding an apple and standing in the glow of a sunset, the apple will look different (warmer) than when it's sitting on a workbench situated under fluorescent lights (cooler). If the apple is placed under a green light, it will change color again — it will appear grayish. Imagine the effect that lighting will have if a dark cherry workpiece is subjected to warm or cool lights. Will that "golden oak" stain look yellowish or greenish?

Elements That Offer Some Control Over Color

The problem isn't just that color perception is subjective, it's often that a woodworker and client can't see the same color. Suppose that you restore a Stickley chair using only fluorescent

lights and the client places the chair so that it's lit by an incandescent lamp. Color for a Stickley piece is very important. In fact, collectors pay such close attention to the color that it and value are connected. The chair will appear different under those various lights — and the client probably won't be happy. This difference of color is a function of wavelength variations. Different lighting will have warmer or cooler colors with many different combinations of spectral differences.

Warmer light is often thought of as the daylight at sunset or the light from an incandescent bulb. Cooler light is the light of noon, an overcast sky or fluorescent light.

One commonly used term that describes the differences in light is temperature, expressed in degrees Kelvin (K). This scale is invaluable for selecting light to match your needs. Generally, lower degrees Kelvin represents a warmer appearance and higher degrees Kelvin represents a cooler look.

Note: The Kelvin reference, while useful, is somewhat of a "ballpark" number. The visual color of an object will be influenced by such things as the age and darkening of a bulb or by the fact that two different lights (natural and warm) may have the same Kelvin value but different color renderings.

If your work demands color-balanced conditions so that the workpiece color is true, the woodshop lighting system must be designed accordingly. The most obvious solution is to have windows and skylights so that natural light floods the work area. If that's impossible (in basements, garages and interior rooms), a mixture of different fluorescent and incandescent lights might be the solution.

Shadow, Reflection, Contrast

One of the most vexing lighting assignments I had in art school was to place an egg on a white surface that also had a white background and, using a single photoflood lamp, light the egg so that there was complete definition of the egg and no bleeding of white from the egg to the surface or background. After more than a few hours, I thought that I had a workable scene. The problem was one of degree, too much or too little shadow, too much or not enough reflection and too much or too little contrast. Lighting focused straight on from the camera produced flat light; lighting from the side produced strong shadows; and diffuse lighting softened the image but at times produced no tonal separation. And all of these lighting setups were further changed if the light was close to or far from the subject.

In the woodshop, the location, type and intensity of lights will produce a continuum of unacceptable and acceptable lighting conditions. Work area illumination requires careful light placement so that the area is shadow-free. Obviously it's possible to cover every square inch of ceiling with lights, but that's very inefficient. A better method is using the correct lights at their correct location. Flat lighting can be beneficial to a cabinetmaker wanting to see dovetail layout lines clearly. However, flat lighting isn't very useful for woodcarving. Lighting that is 45° to 90° to the carving will create better and more useful shadows that enhance the carving process. The texture and incisions from carving tools are very visible and the carver can use the shadows to enliven details.

If a carver knows the location and lighting conditions of the site a large carving will finally reside in,

lights can be temporarily placed in the woodshop to duplicate that lighting. This preparation can spare the carver future problems. For example, a large statue of a Greek warrior will be permanently lit by two overhead spotlights. Knowing this, the carver can dramatize specific features, such as the helmet against the skin or the shape of a flowing cape. The carver can also shape facial features, such as the nose and eyebrows so that the face isn't ruined by ugly shadows.

Generally, it's best to locate light fixtures so that light falls directly over a work area. If there are numerous fluorescent lights throughout a work area, the diffuse light should limit shadowing. If, for example, there's a fluorescent light positioned above and behind someone at a workbench (or table saw), there will be shadows in the work area. This will occur even with the diffuse lighting of numerous fluorescent lights. To avoid this problem at the workbench, I have placed one double 8' fluorescent light fixture above the workbench and I have three double 8' fluorescent light fixtures positioned perpendicular to the workbench and slightly behind and above the work side of the bench. These fixtures are approximately 5' apart and the ceiling height is 9'. The result is that I have diffuse, shadow-free lighting at the workbench. When I need more light intensity at the workbench, I clamp an incandescent Luxo articulated lamp on the corner of the workbench. This gives a spotlight effect, ideal for carving and seeing very fine drawing lines.

Ceiling height, or the distance from the light to the work area, is also important. The general rule is that for any type of light (direct or diffuse, incandescent or fluorescent), the closer to the

work area the stronger the shadows. The opposite is also true: The more distance between light and work area, the weaker the shadows.

Types of Lamps

There are three main types of lights for use in the woodshop: tungsten-filament lamps, halogen lamps and fluorescent lighting.

TUNGSTEN-FILAMENT BULBS Tungsten-filament bulbs are the most common bulbs found in homes. These are made of clear, frosted or tinted glass. Tungsten lamps are the most common lamps because their light is similar to the warm tone of natural light and because they have history on their side — this is the bulb that Edison invented. Tungsten bulbs are everywhere, and it's easy to change lighting conditions by simply replacing one bulb with another type of tungsten bulb. Clear bulbs produce a bright and more contrasting type of lighting. Frosted bulbs produce a diffused lighting; tinted bulbs can add a diffused warmth to the environment. Spotlights and floodlights are also tungsten bulbs. These have body shapes and front lenses that either focus or diffuse the light. Generally,

Degrees Kelvin Ratings

LIGHT SOURCE	DEGREES KELVIN
Daylight at sunrise	1,800 K
Incandescent lamp (tungsten)	2,600 K
Halogen lamp	3,200 K
Warm white fluorescent lamp	3,000 K
Cool white fluorescent lamp	4,200 K
Daylight at noon	5,000 K
Photoflood lamp (tungsten)	3,200 to 3,400 K
Photoflood lamp (daylight)	4,800 to 5,400 K
Photo strobe (electric flash)	5,200 to 5,400 K
Daylight-balanced film	5,000 to 5,400 K
"Sunshine" fluorescent lamp	5,000 K
"Daylight" fluorescent lamp	6,500 K

Degrees Kelvin is also useful if you are photographing your woodworking. The type of lights or strobes and film used will warm or cool the subject.

the beam angle is 15° to 25° for spotlights and 30° to 75° for floodlights.

HALOGEN LAMPS What we refer to as halogen lamps are actually tungsten-halogen lamps. There are two basic halogen lamp types: low voltage and standard line voltage. Low-voltage halogen lamps require a transformer and operate at both lower voltage and lower wattage than standard line-voltage halogen lamps. They are usually designed as reflectors, allowing them to be directed at specific work areas. Low-voltage halogen lamps are relatively small and lend themselves to use in recessed fixtures. Generally, the beam angle from the reflector is 5° to 30°.

Standard line-voltage halogen lamps are more efficient than standard incandescent tungsten lamps, but they have the disadvantages of expense and high temperatures. Light fixtures must be capable of dissipating heat, and line-voltage halogen lamps should be kept away from any flammable materials — not a simple task in the woodshop. Recently, there have been safety notices regarding fires being started from certain styles of line-voltage halogen lamps, and screens have been made available for retrofitting on the lamp housing to keep cloth, paper and other flammable materials from touching the bulb. Furthermore, avoid touching the bulb with your bare hands because skin oil will affect the bulb and shorten its lifespan.

FLUORESCENT LAMPS There is a distinct division between home and commercial lighting: That is, most homes have tungsten lighting and most businesses use fluorescent lighting. The reasons for this difference are both historical and economical. Simplistically, houses have always been built and designed with incandescent lights as the principal lighting. What we can learn from commercial use is that fluorescent lighting is a source of low-cost, efficient, diffused lighting. As a dramatic comparison, tungsten bulbs have an average life of 750 to 1,250 hours; fluorescent lights have an average life of 20,000 hours.

Fluorescent lamps are available in a variety of lengths, shapes and colors for any woodshop requirement. There are different color sensitivities, ranging from cool to warm white. Before purchasing the different varieties of fluorescent lights, make sure that the lamp and the fixture are compatible by checking the lamp's wattage with that of the ballast.

Poor-quality fluorescent lights have created a bad reputation for better quality fluorescent lights. Typical problems associated with low-quality fluorescent lights are leaking ballasts, humming or vibration noise and pulsing light. These are generally not problems in better made units, at least not until they've been in service for very long periods.

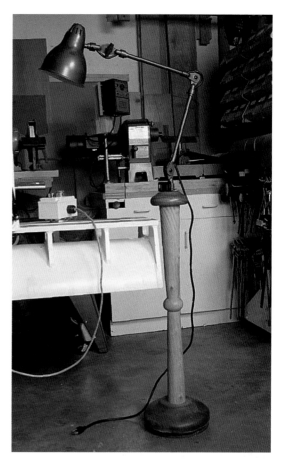

This is Earl Bartell's custom-made light stand with attached lamp. The base is heavy and sturdy enough to be used at any location.

One problem that occurs in woodshops is that of long boards reaching fluorescent lights. Lights above workbenches and table saws are often hit, showering the woodworker with glass particles. Avoid this by using clear plastic sleeves or tubes which fit fluorescent lamps. If the lamp is hit and breaks, the glass shards remain in the plastic sleeve.

TYPES OF FLUORESCENT LAMPS When shopping for fluorescent lamps, find a hardware or electrical supply store that stocks a full array of lamp types. There are at least eight different types of fluorescent lights. Store displays and product packaging should furnish lamp designations, including references to color rendering, degrees Kelvin, watts and lumens. Product names, such as "cool white" or "warm white," are older designations. To comply with newer U.S. government

CHOOSE YOUR LIGHTING CAREFULLY

It's expensive to illuminate a woodshop, so carefully choose the best for yours.

- Use long-life, reduced-wattage bulbs whenever possible.
- If color is important, use bulbs that approximate daylight.
- Have zone lighting so that areas not in use can be unlit.
- Paint walls, ceiling and other surfaces such as pegboards, light colors.
- Use light colors for the maximum light reflection.
- Use incandescent spot lamps at drill press or band saw.
- Use droplights over workbench if you need more of a spotlight effect and less diffused light.

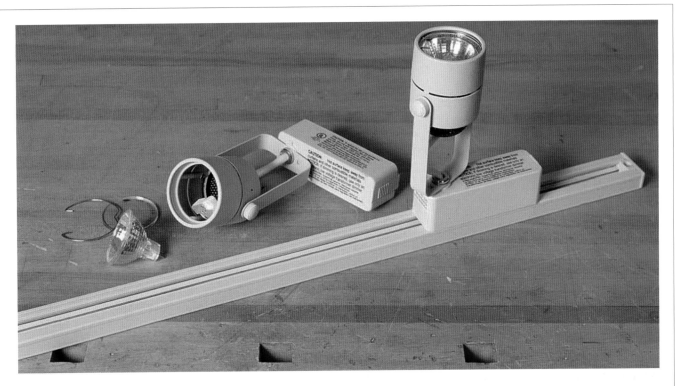

standards regarding fluorescent lights, companies have had to redesign lights. Since the newer versions of "cool white" are different from the older products, newer product names were necessary. Hence, "Sunshine or SP-41."

HIGH-INTENSITY-DISCHARGE LAMPS This lamp wasn't mentioned earlier because they are a fairly new type of lamp and are not commonly used. High-intensity-discharge (HID) lamps include metal halide lamps, mercury lamps and high-pressure sodium lamps. These have primarily been used for industrial purposes but are slowly being accepted for other uses (mostly for architectural and security purposes). There are disadvantages to using HID lamps: They require warming up and cooling down periods when they are turned on and off, and they produce a bluish light that gives an unfamiliar coloring to most things, including woodworking projects. Currently, the metal halide lamps are the only HID lamps that approach normal colorization. HID lamps, even though they are energy efficient, aren't useful for the woodshop because of their color rendering and fixture configuration.

In those locations that need more direct and less diffused light, I have replaced fluorescent lights with this type of halogen track lighting. This type of light gives a brilliant white light, lasts about three times longer and uses about 65% less energy than a standard incandescent light. This particular halogen light requires a 50-watt reflector bulb that is equivalent to the light of a standard 150-watt reflector bulb. It has a built-in transformer which converts 120V to 12V.

Typical Fluorescent Lights (48" tubes, GE products)

BULB NAME	°KELVIN	LUMENS*	WATTS	CRI**
Sunshine	5,000 K	2,250	40	90
Daylight Delux	6,500 K	2,250	40	84
SP-35, moderate white	3,500 K	3,200	40	73
Kitchen & Bath	3,000 K	3,200	40	70
Residential/Shoplight	4,100 K	3,150	40	72
SP-41, cool white	4,150 K	3,200	40	42

*Lumens is a unit of measurement that expresses the total quantity of light given off by a light source. For practical purposes, if comparing incandescent and fluorescent light, fluorescent lights use much less energy than incandescent bulbs and still produce similar or better light levels.
  · 100-watt incandescent bulb is 1,710 lumens
  · 75-watt incandescent bulb is 1,190 lumens
  · 20-watt fluorescent light is 1,200 lumens
  · 32-watt fluorescent light is 2,850 lumens
  · 40-watt fluorescent light is 3,050 lumens

**Color rendering index (CRI) is a measurement of color shift when an object is illuminated by a light. CRI ranges from 1 to 100, with natural daylight and incandescent light equal to 100. Therefore, lights with a higher CRI produce more natural colors.

Note: Foot-candles is a measure of lumens per square foot, as measured on a working surface or floor area. For an office, the general working range is 15 to 70 foot-candles. If you are doing precise work, such as woodworking or drafting, 100 to 200 foot-candles is usually recommended. And if you think that is bright, on a cloudless sunny day, the sun gives off 1,000 foot-candles!

CHAPTER 3

IMPLEMENTING YOUR DUST-COLLECTION SYSTEM

If you are using machines and sanding materials for woodworking, then you are making a mixture of waste products: chunks of debris that fall in a large radius area and airborne particles which permeate the entire woodshop.

If you work exclusively with hand tools — hand saws, hand planes, chisels and scrapers — the principal waste will mostly be solid chunks deposited on the floor where you stand.

MANAGING SHOP WASTE

1. Remove floor debris with a broom or shop vacuum.
2. Capture machine-made dust and chips at the source with a dust collector.
3. Filter airborne particles with an air filtration system — or wear a filter mask.
4. Work in a wind tunnel so that all debris is blown out the door and into the neighbor's yard.
5. Ignore the problem and work in piles of chips and clouds of dust.

I have seen few totally chip-and dust-free woodshops. Most woodworkers make some effort to remove most of the debris. Although many woodshops have some sort of dust collection system, very few have air filtration systems. And even with operational dust collectors, there is dust in most woodshops. Surprisingly, few woodworkers use filter masks, and

I've even found several woodshops that rely on air flow from open doors and windows to minimize air-suspended particle dust.

There are many sizes and types of dust collectors and air filtration systems. There are readily available dust collectors powerful enough to have three separate 25'-long ductworks and to simultaneously remove debris from three separate machines. Additionally, there are many magazine articles detailing how to build everything from collector ductwork systems to air filtration systems. Over the past 10-plus years there has been considerable interest in the process of ductwork collection and air filtration.

Why are Woodshops Still Dusty?
The curious reasons why there are so many dusty woodshops:

• There are those who still don't care about the hazardous or unsafe nature of dust. It's a strange mindset, based on a perception that since woodworking tools and machines make chips and dust, the woodworker should just let the stuff fall where it may. This false perception equates productivity with the amount of dust

and chips on the floor (and everywhere else). The myth that a busy woodshop is a dusty woodshop still exists.

• Another erroneous notion about dust collection is that home woodshops don't have the same volumes of productivity as professional woodshops, hence there is less dust. The Occupational Safety and Health Administration (OSHA) has rules and standards for dust levels in commercial woodshops, and they have standards about air quality, safety equipment, proper installation of dust collectors and many other issues relating to the hazardous nature of dust because dust is unsafe. It is wrong to think that since the home woodshop is not regulated by OSHA, the need for proper dust management equipment isn't necessary.

• Collectors and filtration systems are not purchased because they aren't primary machines such as table saws or routers. Dust collectors don't directly help cut better edges or make better dovetails. It is also easy to think of dust collectors as something that we own but aren't overly enthusiastic about. Most woodworkers don't wake up in the morning thinking, "I can't wait to go to the woodshop and turn on the dust collector!"

• Dust collection systems aren't cheap. A basic dust collector costs from $300 to $1,000. 4"-diameter ductwork costs approximately $2 to $4 per foot. Fittings, such as elbows, reducers, shutoff gates and Y- and T-fittings cost $10 to $20 each, and replacement filter bags cost $25 to $75.

• Cost is often the only factor considered when purchasing a dust collector. There are numerous low-priced collectors that are popular simply because they are inexpensive. To be fair, some of these units probably are adequate if they only have 6' of hose and are hooked to a single machine. In order for manufacturers to make low-cost collectors they often simplify the collector's frame size, use low-quality impellers, include small-capacity filter bag sizes (and also use low-quality filter material), and install inexpensive (and lower hp) motors.

• Dust collection and air filtration systems are frequently either installed incorrectly or are inadequate for the volume of debris produced. Very often the technical specifications of dust collectors aren't well understood. It's critical to understand certain technical information when purchasing a dust collector.

DUST COLLECTION BASICS

There are a few noteworthy technical considerations specific to dust collection:

- SP (static pressure) is resistance to air in a ductwork and is measured in inches of water. Resistance is often referred to as friction.
- CFM (cubic feet per minute) is air volume.
- FPM (feet per minute) is air velocity.

The question is: How do you know if a dust collector is right for your woodshop, if it is installed correctly and if it can efficiently remove debris? Several important variables affect the performance of any collector:

- technical specifications (hp and CFM)
- distance from the collector to a given machine (ductwork run)
- number of fittings
- smoothness within the ductwork system
- diameter of ductwork
- number of machines

Dust System Considerations

Dust collectors and air filtration systems need to be integrated into the entire woodshop. In fact, a case could be made that the dust collection system should be one of the first installations within a woodshop, and all machines and other features should be installed subsequently. Consider that when a new house is being constructed and the framing is finished, plumbing and electrical components are installed. Ideally, that is how dust collectors should be viewed. However, most woodworkers usually purchase a dust collector after they start generating mounds of debris from their machines. Then the dust collector is retrofitted to the woodshop.

Very few machines are adequately designed for dust control. To make a dust collection system functional, it must be fitted to machines so that all dust and chips are collected. This is a fundamental weakness of any woodshop collection system. Few factory machine hookups are efficient. It seems that manufacturers, in general, view dust collection as an afterthought. Consider the power tools that produce dispersed dust: planers, routers, all sanders, scroll saws, plate jointers and table saws. How many of these machines are designed with high-quality connections for dust collecting? For example, an efficient table saw dust collection should have two collection areas: The area below the table should have a collection enclosure close to the saw blade, and there should also be collection above the saw blade, preferably integrated with the blade guard. Unfortunately, these features mostly exist on the more expensive table saws.

Most experienced woodworkers eventually construct collection hookups for their machines. Well-established woodshops often have all sorts of shop-made fittings and specialized hookups on machines. These are usually made of plywood or particleboard, and sometimes acrylic-type plastics, and they are characterized

In order to collect dust at the sanding machine, I built a plywood housing that encompasses both disc and belt sanding ports. The housing also encloses the belt beneath the table. Plastic fitting for the dust hose is available at most hardware stores.

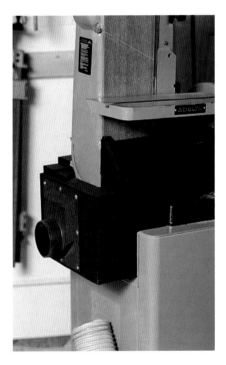

Here is a close-up of the sanding machine's dust hose housing.

The drill press table in my woodshop features different table inserts for different-diameter sanding drums. The fence has a holder for a vacuum hose.

Here's the sanding drum lowered into the table; the vacuum hose is mounted on top of the table.

Here's the sanding drum lowered into the table and the vacuum hose mounted to the lower box.

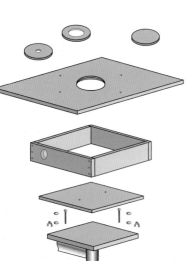
This is an exploded view of the drill press table above: The frame has a hole for the vacuum hose. The top surface has a center hole with a rabbeted edge for the holding discs. The discs have different-size cutouts to accommodate sanding drums.

by form-fitting the machine's cutting area, dust chute or wood ejection area.

Locating the Dust Collection and Air Filtration Systems

As an analogy, most woodworkers locate dust collectors much like the antiquated houses that were built before indoor plumbing and electricity. When these new conveniences were first installed in houses, they were attached to the outside of walls. (Antique tool collectors now prize the hand planes used to make channels in moulding for the exterior attachment of electrical wires.) A modern person would never consider having electrical wires exposed and running around the outside of doors and moulding, nor having water pipes visible in a kitchen or bath. Yet, that same modern person will generally not think that retrofitted and exposed dust collection ductwork is inappropriate. I realize that there are many reasons for exposed ductwork systems:

- basement woodshops with concrete walls
- using portable collectors with short hoses
- ease in suspending ductwork from rafters (joists, etc.)
- exposed ductwork is less expensive to install

New woodshops are being constructed that integrate ductwork systems into walls and under flooring. This approach requires the same mind-set that's used to install water pipes and electrical wiring. That is, there must be precise design planning of the system. Like an electrical circuit box or water heater, the dust collector must have a fixed location. This location should be somewhat removed from the general work area of the woodshop, and it should be accessible for cleaning. Furthermore, the number and location of machines should be determined prior to building the system.

I suppose it's reasonable to ask, "What's the gain of having a ductwork system built into walls and flooring?" The answer is that an internal ductwork system is out of the way, and consequently, wall and floor space is freed up and made available for other uses. Most woodshops are small, and every visible surface is used for some sort of storage. Long expanses of 4"-diameter, horizontally mounted cylinders complicate the placement of cabinets, lumber storage, lighting and everything else required in the woodshop. Second, machines that are located in the central woodshop area and away from any wall create a complication regarding ductworks. For example, a table saw in an open area that is hooked up to an exposed ductwork system will have a ductwork or hose resting on the floor. This not only makes maneuvering large or heavy objects difficult, but walking over exposed ductwork is one hazardous step away from tripping.

Furthermore, the ductwork itself will eventually be damaged by being stepped on or by heavy objects falling on it. In fact, having ductwork or hose located below floor level for a table saw is enough of a justification for such a system. Of all the principal woodshop machinery, the table saw probably has the most awkward ductwork or hose arrangement. This is due to the fact that table saws have dust fittings at floor level, and the saws are generally situated in open areas, away from walls. When machines are located near walls, machines then have a back (unused) side, making it easier to install ductwork that is out of the way. It's also difficult to have ductworks and hose connections that drop from ceiling

John MacKenzie has underfloor dust collection ductwork.

areas to the centrally located table saw. These perpendicular hoses will be in the way of lumber, and they create safety problems (the material being cut can bump into the ductwork and back toward the blade and the operator).

Requirements for An Internal Dust Collection Ductwork System

• Existing woodshops may be impossible to retrofit with an internal dust system unless there is extensive remodeling or there is a sufficiently large underfloor crawl space. Ductwork is usually from 4" to 10" in diameter and this means that systems destined for walls, ceilings and floors require sufficient open areas to accommodate these dimensions.

• If walls are not to be remodeled, wood enclosures can be made so that ductworks are enclosed within. This wood box can be located either at the wall/ceiling interface or the wall/floor interface. At either location, the ductwork is enclosed and safe from bumps and damage. Furthermore, these wood enclosures can be easily integrated with cabinets and other storage units.

• Ductwork systems that include drop-downs from the ceiling area are somewhat easier to install if there is sufficient room above joists or there is attic space. Install metal ductwork systems similar to central heating and air conditioning ductworks. However, ductwork drop-downs in the middle of a room should always be considered a nuisance; that is, drop-downs probably will be in the way of other woodshop functions (moving lumber, etc.).

• In-the-floor ductwork has the most to offer in both usefulness and in the degree of difficulty in installation. If there is sufficient floor-to-ceiling height in the woodshop, the most straightforward solution is to construct a subfloor; that is, build a new floor above the existing floor so that there is space for the ductwork system. The new subfloor should be stoutly constructed to support the heavy loads of machines and lumber. The real bonus is that ductworks can be brought up through the floor next to a machine, or even within a machine's cavity. This minimizes tripping over and/or bumping ducts and hoses.

If a new woodshop is being constructed with concrete floors, there are several considerations for ductwork below the floor. The basic room design must include adequate floor thickness and floor-to-ceiling height. Ductwork channels must be created with forms and poured cement.

Instead of a single continuous floor surface, it will be necessary to carefully pour cement in different areas between forms and to ensure those areas are flat and true to each other. Once the concrete is hard, ductwork is placed in these channels and the open channel is then covered with wood, brick or concrete blocks.

The very nature of woodshop design is constant change and the incorporation of new ideas, products and evolution. Although the marketplace is now filled with a variety of similar dust collectors, the use and setup of those dust collectors is changing. It wasn't that long ago that few woodshops had any dust collection whatsoever. Now we are using dust collection systems and are attempting to customize them to our individual woodshops. Presently, it may be adequate to use dust collectors in the familiar way, using metal ductwork attached to walls and ceilings with a short length of flexible hose attached to a machine. In the near future, more and more woodshops will be set up with more efficient ductwork systems hidden in walls, ceilings and floors. Just as there was no interest in air filtration systems 20 years ago, the integrated ductwork system will undoubtedly be part of future woodshops.

SETTING UP DUST COLLECTION AND AIR FILTRATION SYSTEMS
Gather Information

Use magazine advertisements as the first source of information, and request technical information from the manufacturers and retailers that supply the collection and filtration systems. Request information about dust collectors, filtration systems, ductwork, flexible hose, remote on/off devices, high-efficiency filter bags and grounding kits. Once you have gathered your information, make comparison charts that include:

• model
• motor hp
• motor repair service location
• amperes

- voltage
- CFM (maximum)
- static pressure
- dBA at 5 ft. (dBA is a unit of measurement that expresses the relative intensity of sound. The least-perceptible sound to pain-level sound ranges from 0 to about 130 dBA.)
- hose-diameter hookup at collector
- number of hose outlets on collector
- bag capacity
- type of bag material (traps what micron size of dust particles?)
- drum size
- cost of basic unit
- cost of add-on accessories

Choose a Type

There are three basic types of dust collectors: single-stage, two-stage and cyclone. Each type will collect dust. Aside from design differences, the main considerations for choosing which type to use are the number of machines and amount of dust and debris created, length of ductwork, ease of removing captured waste from bags or barrels, noise level and cost.

SINGLE-STAGE DUST COLLECTORS Single-stage collectors are visually characterized by having two or four filter bags. The bottom bags collect larger debris, and the top bags filter the finer dust and return air back into the wood-shop. This type is usually the most portable and affordable in the market-place. There are two common draw-backs to the single-stage collector, both of which are easily remedied. It is often stated that, because the debris travels directly through the impeller housing, there is unnecessary wear on parts. Manufacturers of better-quality units often make heavy-duty impellers or design the impeller so that a bent fin can be easily replaced. Optionally, an in-line separator can be installed before the collector in order to separate out larger debris. These inexpensive units are installed between the woodworking machine and the dust collector. They simply replace the lid

This table saw has a portable dust-collector hookup. Jon Magill plans on replacing this stiff hose with a more flexible type. He works with one machine at a time and he isn't bothered by moving the dust collector to another machine when changing operations.

Doug Matthews keeps his dust collector tucked behind an unfinished interior wall. The planer and jointer are easily hooked up to the collector when they are used. Note how he has also used this area for clamp storage.

on a garbage can. Chips are then deflected via baffles into the garbage can and only very small debris and dust continues through to the main dust collector.

I have used this style with four bags for over 15 years and have never had mechanical problems. However, I strongly recommend that no large wood fragments or cutoff pieces be vacuumed into the impeller — that would probably cause damage. I don't have a floor sweep, a floor-level debris pickup attachment, connected to the system because I don't want large, heavy objects zooming through the ductwork and slamming into the spinning impeller. The second serious drawback of the single-stage collector is the blowing of fine dust through the filter bags and back into the woodshop. The filter bags that come with most collectors are porous enough to allow fine dust through the bag weave. As a consequence, larger debris is caught in the bags and fine dust migrates throughout the woodshop, creating unpleasant and unnecessary air pollution. Replacement filter bags that filter down to 1 micron particle size are recommended.

TWO-STAGE DUST COLLECTORS Two-stage collectors are characterized by a blower motor on top of a collector drum (35 or 55 gallons) with a side-mounted filter bag. Generally this type is mounted on wheels. These are designed so that larger debris settles into the drum, and fine dust is captured in the filter bag. The significant drawback is that the motor housing is heavy and it has to be lifted off in order to empty the collector drum (which is also heavy when it's full). This is a tiresome process, especially if you need to frequently empty the drum. Those that use this type often use ropes and pulleys to raise the housing off the drum.

CYCLONE DUST COLLECTORS Cyclone collectors appear to be industrial; it's a tall steel cylinder with a funneled

midsection and a 35- or 55-gallon collector drum. Debris enters the upper chamber and is cyclonically separated. Larger debris spirals downward into the collection drum, and the fine dust is caught in filters located within or near the cyclone unit. The exterior filters, called shaker bags, are a series of tall, thin bags, that effectively trap dust particles and filter the exiting air. Most of the cyclone units are fairly quiet when operating. This is due in part to having a muffler for quieting the exiting air. Interestingly, there are two types of cyclone systems: commercially made units and do-it-yourself units (*WOOD Magazine*, Issue 100, November 1997).

Stay Within Code
Check local building codes concerning the placement of collectors. Certain types of collectors may need to be located outside of the main woodshop.

Lay Out Your System
Draw a layout for your woodshop. Locate the collector so that it's out of the way without requiring unnecessary ductwork lengths. As a reference, consider the vein pattern in a leaf. Determine the length of the ductwork, the number of fittings (elbows, etc.) and the diameter of the ductwork.

Note that the length of ductwork and its internal smoothness, as well as the shape and number of fittings, all increase frictional resistance to air flow. Any internal friction and/or air turbulence decreases collection efficiency.

Ducts and fittings that have gradual directional changes will help make a system more efficient. Avoid ductwork runs having abrupt angles or turns. If possible, avoid using 90° T-fittings; instead, use 45° to minimize

The Oneida cyclone dust collector, shown above in Charles Caswell's shop, has the air filter within the cyclone. It also features a muffler (protruding horizontally just below the motor), 5" ductwork, 35-gallon fiber barrel and a remote on/off switch located on the combination machine.

For this cyclone dust collector, the filter bags are suspended in a closet. The cyclone unit is located outside of the woodshop, behind the closed door, visible through the window.

Typical Air Flow Requirements for Various Machines

MACHINE	CFM
Table saw	300-350
Band saw	400-700
Disc sander	300-350
Jointer	350-440
Planer	400-785
Shaper	300-1,400
Lathe	350-500

CFM Requirements for Duct Diameters

DUCT DIAMETER	CFM@3500 FPM
3"	170
4"	300
5"	475

Static Pressure by Duct Diameter

DUCT DIAMETER	INCHES OF STATIC PRESSURE*
3"	7.5
4"	5.5
5"	4.2
6"	3.5

*3,500 FPM per 100' of duct

turbulence. If different diameters are required, use tapered connectors for smoother transitions between the ductworks.

Companies such as Air Handling Systems by Manufacturers Service Co., Delta Machinery Corp. and Oneida Air Systems, Inc., all provide excellent information regarding how to determine CFM for the system, ductwork air velocity, system resistance, and the proper size of ductworks and fittings. If you send Oneida Air Systems a blueprint of your woodshop, they will design the correct ductwork for your woodshop — free.

Consider Your Needs

The diameter of the ductwork will affect air flow. Wood dust requires a minimum velocity of 3,500 FPM within the main ductwork or debris can settle out of the airstream, leading to blockage problems. The two variables that relate to ductwork diameter are velocity and static pressure. Larger-diameter ductwork increases static pressure and reduces air velocity; as ductwork diameter decreases, static pressure decreases and air velocity increases. The main consideration is to minimize static pressure loss. To accomplish this you must measure each ductwork run; that is, the length from the machine to the collector. Also, each fitting causes a reduction in air velocity, so fittings must also be factored into the length measurement. The common practice is to assign an equivalent length for a fitting. For example, a 90° elbow is equivalent to 6' of duct, or a 45° elbow is equivalent to 3' of duct. Therefore, a ductwork run that consists of 20' of straight 4" ductwork, three 90° elbows and one 45° elbow is equivalent to 41' of ductwork.

To use this value, there is another step to calculate the actual static pressure for the ductwork run. Static pressure is usually based upon 100' of ductwork. 4"- and 5"-diameter ductwork are the most commonly used sizes.

For the example of 41', multiply 0.41 (41' of 100') by 5.5, equaling 2.55" of static pressure ("inches of water"). If the filter bags are dirty, an additional static pressure loss should also be added to the value. As a generalization, add a value of 1, thus

equaling 3.55". Note: This is for one ductwork run without any branch runs. If several machines are hooked up to the collector but are operated one at a time, the ductwork diameter will be dependent on the machine with the greatest CFM requirement.

If you are creating a complicated network of ductwork and fittings, careful calculations of ductwork length and all fittings is required. Determine the static pressure value for the entire system and compare that value with those of the various dust collectors in the marketplace. This value isn't absolute: there are a number of factors that influence the actual rating. Air leaks, ductwork crimps and rivets, ductwork interior smoothness, corrugated flex hose, dirty filter bags and machine hookup attachments are only a few of the variables influencing dust collector efficiency.

Metal Ductwork

Metal ductwork is slightly more difficult to install than plastic (PVC) pipe, but it is easier to ground against static electricity. Oneida Air Systems recommends using 26- to 24-gauge, or heavier, galvanized straight pipe for small custom woodshops. Heating and ventilation ductwork (usually 30 gauge) is too thin for dust collection because it can be easily dented. This causes disruption in the air flow; also the thin walls can collapse under dust collector fan pressure.

Flex hose should be used for connecting metal ductwork to a machine. Keep the lengths to a minimum because of the increased air resistance within the uneven hose.

Plastic Pipe

The common method for grounding plastic pipe is to run a ground wire inside the entire length of the pipe and then attach it at either end to the machine and the earth ground. The disadvantage of this method is that wood debris can break the internal wire unbeknownst to the operator. Debris can also lodge around the

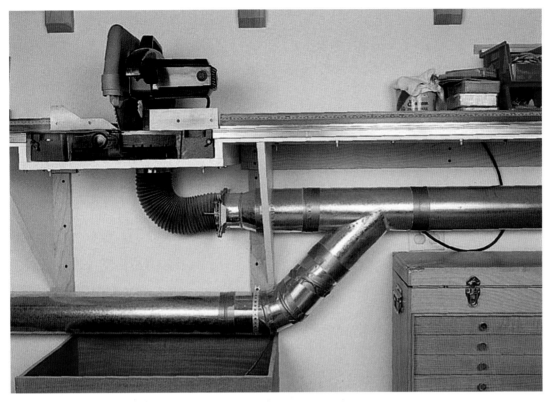

Tidy metal ductwork. There's a blast gate at the flex hose to the chop saw with the other duct going to the combination machine in the Caswell woodshop.

wire and eventually cause a blockage. I won't use plastic pipe because static electrical charges build up as dust travels rapidly through it — and airborne dust has the potential to be highly combustible. I talked with one woodworker who thought he had done all the correct hookups and grounding for using plastic pipe. Yet, late one night, when no one was using the woodshop, there was a static discharge within the pipe which sparked into residual dust and his woodshop was lost to fire. Another person told me his story of attempting to add more PVC pipe to an existing system. The PVC pipe was grounded and the system was off. When he hand sawed into the pipe, there was a static discharge powerful enough that it knocked him across the room.

AIR FILTRATION
Air filtration is perhaps one of the most important features that relate to a woodworker's health. Fine dust particles will stay in air suspension for hours. These particles are so small that they are almost invisible. However, a person in the woodshop will breathe these particles into the nasal

and throat passages and lungs. There is much evidence as to the health risks of breathing dust, so the ideal woodshop should have a method of removing these particles. As a doctor woodworking friend once said, "You don't breathe the large chips that settle out on the floor, you breathe the tiny airborne particles that you can't see."

I had numerous woodworkers tell me they think that their woodshops got dustier after they installed dust collectors. So, the first thing to do before using a new dust collector is to make the dust collection system free of dust leakage. Leakage can occur at the machine and the filter bags. Well-fit hookups at the machine are mandatory. If the machine's factory-made hookup seems inadequate, make your own. Second, most dust collection bags are susceptible to dust migrating through the fibrous weavings. Most standard-issue bags capture dust sizes of 10 to 50 microns; smaller sizes escape back into the woodshop environment. The best solution is to check with the dust collector manufacturer about replacing the bags with high-efficiency filter bags, which will filter particles down to 1 micron in size.

PLASTIC PIPE GUIDELINES
If you are determined to use plastic pipe for dust collection because "Old George at your woodworkers' club uses it," you should at least do the following:

1. Ground the pipe by installing a taut ground wire inside of it.

2. Also ground the plastic pipe by wrapping a ground wire spirally around the outside of it. Both types of grounding should be done to all pipes in the system, and the wires should be properly attached at either end to machines and a proper ground location.

3. Assemble the plastic pipes so that they can be unassembled for cleaning out chip blockages (use pipe connectors and ductwork tape).

4. Occasionally check for any internal blockage and for continuity in the internal ground wire (look for chip buildup around the wire and for wire abrasion).

Air filtration units are also becoming popular. These units are hung from the ceiling in the room's air circulation pattern and filter the air. By using a continuous-duty fan and a series of filters, very fine airborne dust (1 to 5 microns) is trapped and clean air is circulated back into the woodshop. The air filtration unit is not meant to be a dust collector. Rather, its purpose is solely to filter the finest dust from the air. Commercially made units cost approximately $250 to $700. However, it's fairly easy to make your own air filtration unit by building a plywood box (approximate size would be 12" × 24" × 36") and installing a furnace-type fan ($\frac{1}{4}$ hp) with several high-quality slide-in furnace type filters. Carbon filters can be added to the air filtration unit so that fumes and odors are also filtered out of the woodshop.

The ideal solution for dust collection, especially if your woodshop is attached to your house, is to have an efficient unit that is both quiet and powerful enough to use with several machines operating. For most woodshops, suspend metal ductwork from the ceiling and make certain that the ducts are properly sealed, free of leaks and properly grounded against static electricity buildup. The hookup fittings should be well made and fit tightly on the machines. The dust collector should have high-efficiency filter bags and a manageable system for removing the drums or bags when they are filled. Finally, an air filtration unit should be hung from the ceiling so that fine dust is also captured. If that doesn't make a dust-free woodshop, open a window and the door.

Accessories

I suppose that anything purchased separately from the basic dust collector is considered an accessory. But several noteworthy items will definitely improve dust collectors. Check for availability — or adaptability — with specific models of dust collectors. Accessories include:

(left) Here is a Delta air cleaner suspended from a ceiling.

(below) A small blower fan is used to vent the shop of very fine airborne dust.

• high-quality filtration bags — look at the specifications of these bags and be certain they offer at least a 99% efficiency in filtering 1-micron particles

• in-line separator — this item is installed between a machine and dust collector and looks like a garbage can lid; it has no moving parts and simply sits on a standard garbage can; an inexpensive improvement for most dust collection systems

• positionable vacuum hose — Lockwood Products makes the Loc-Line vacuum hose, a nifty articulated self-supporting (up to 3') ball-and-socket type of hose that is ideal for dust pickup at the drill press or the router table; a 2$\frac{1}{2}$" vacuum hose — the typical shop vacuum; the Loc-Line system has many different fittings, including both a round and a rectangular nozzle, slide valve (blast-gate), 3" PVC adapter and shop vacuum adapter

• automatic blast-gates — Ecogate manufactures a system of computerized blast-gates that automatically open or close when a machine is either turned on or off; control box allows you to set the sensitivity of the sensors, and can be programmed to

keep one or more gates open; this system reduces the time of manually working blast-gates, saves electrical energy and actually assists in woodshop cleanliness; plus, not a complicated installation

A TYPICAL DUST COLLECTION SYSTEM

The most confusing aspect of setting up a dust collection system is understanding the relationships of air volume or CFM (air measured in cubic feet per minute) and static pressure (the resistance to air at rest in a ductwork) to the length and diameter of ductwork and the number of machines in the woodshop.

Let's assume that your woodshop is in either a garage or basement and you are the only person operating machinery. Your plan is to connect the dust collection system to a table saw, band saw, jointer, planer, disc/belt sander, lathe and drill press:

1. After you have reviewed the specifications of all potential dust collectors, select the one that has the greatest horsepower (at least 1½ to 3 hp) and is rated greater than 700 CFM at 5" to 6" of static pressure. For example:

- Grizzly model G1029, 2 hp, 1,182 CFM at 5.00" of static pressure
- Oneida air blower, 2 hp, 900 CFM at 8.00" of static pressure
- Delta model 50-181, 2 hp, 1,100 CFM at 8.50" of static pressure
- Bridgewood BW-003, 3 hp, 1,950 CFM at 5.80" of static pressure
- Oneida air blower, 3 hp, 1,350 CFM at 8.00" of static pressure

2. Determine the filter bag area. Typical bag sizes range from 10 to 40 square feet. As a guide, have at least 1 square foot of filter bag area for every 10 CFM. For example, a 10 square foot filter bag is useful for a 1,000 CFM collector. If the filter bag area is less than the rated CFM, install larger bags.

3. Install metal 6" and 5" main ductwork going out from the collector. Generally, 6"-diameter ductwork is used nearest the collector and then it's reduced to a 5"-diameter ductwork further from the collector.

4. Please don't use plastic pipes. Plastic pipes can be dangerous because of the significant static electricity charges that are generated when air, wood dust and chips travel through the pipes.

5. Securely assemble the ductwork system with pop rivets, sheet-metal screws or ductwork tape. Seal all duct-

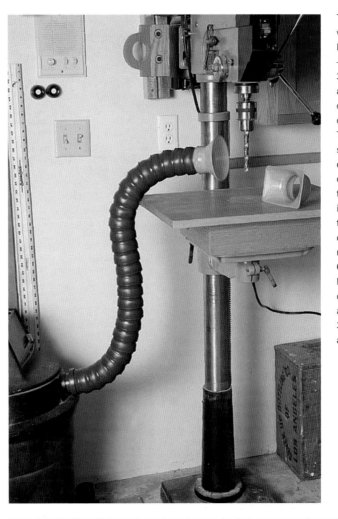

The Loc-Line flexible vacuum line (2½" I.D.) is self-supporting — to approximately 36" — and with an adapter fits the 2¼" connector hose hole of a shop vacuum. This is a long overdue solution for collecting dust at the drill press or other machines that don't have built-in collector capabilities. Shown are 36" of Loc-Line, the 4½" round nozzle and the 6" × 3½" rectangular nozzle. Various other accessories are available, including a 3" sheet-metal duct adapter.

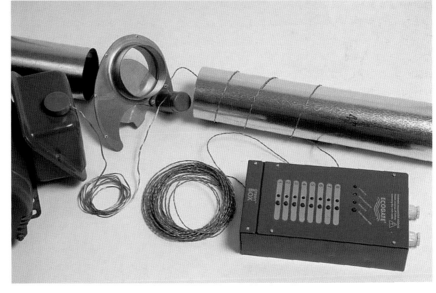

The Ecogate electronic blast-gate has sensors to detect which gate to automatically open or close when debris is moving within the ductwork, thus saving the operator time, and lowering electrical operation costs. I have laid out the basic configuration (from left to right): a woodworking machine motor, sensor pad with wiring to the Ecogate, ductwork with the spirally wrapped connector wire from the gate to the electronic control box.

work with silicone sealer, and be sure there are no small openings or cracks, which cause air loss.

6. Minimize the use of elbows and turns. Use large-radius elbows when branching off of the main ductwork to the individual machines; don't use 90° T-fittings. Also, use 45° Y fittings for any turns off of the main ductwork line. If it's necessary to use smaller diameter hose, use reducer fittings on the machine side of the elbows. Use metal ductworks up to within approximately 3' of the machine. Then, use flexible hose as the 3' connector to the machine. Properly ground the flexible hose by wrapping the ground wire around the hose and attaching one end to the metal ductwork and the other to ground.

7. Use gates (blast-gates) at all machines to control air to each machine. Place the gate between the metal ductwork and the flexible hose.

- When using the dust collection system, keep blast-gates closed at unused machines.
- If the dust collector is in an out-of-the-way location, install a remote control device for wireless on/off operation. These units are available from most sellers of dust collectors.

CONSIDER WOOD TOXICITY

Perhaps after the discussion of machines and collectors, there is another topic that needs to be mentioned — toxic woods. While dust collectors will remove the majority of dust and chips, it is inevitable that some dust is going to fall on your skin and be breathed into your lungs.

Sometimes I think that working with wood is like having a tiger for a pet — it looks great, but it can bite your hand off. While everyone has different sensitivity levels, wood is known to cause skin and eye allergies as well as respiratory and cardiac problems. Some woods are classified as primary irritants because they are highly toxic (West Indian satinwood, for example). Other woods are classified as sensitizers because they may

WOOD TOXICITY
SAFETY GUIDELINES

· Always wear some form of face mask or respirator. Disposable masks are often form-fit around the nose and mouth; reusable respirators have replaceable filter cartridges. If these are inadequate for your needs, there are space-age-looking air purifying respirators. These have a hard hat with a clear plastic face shield. The shield form-fits the entire face, and at the back of the hard hat is a fan unit that blows filtered air over the top of the head and down across the face. Note that you are breathing filtered air — and not breathing through a filter. While these units are expensive, they offer features not found in standard filter masks, such as full-face protection from flying debris (they are popular with lathe turners) and comfort for woodworkers with beards or eyeglasses (standard filter masks and respirators don't fit well on beards and under eyeglasses).

· Wear long-sleeved shirts to keep dust off your arms. Don't wear loose or unbuttoned shirts because loose clothes and machinery are a disaster waiting to happen. Long-sleeved T-shirts are a better choice.

· If you are sanding, create air circulation away from the work area. Place a portable fan at one end of the workbench and sand at the other end. The fan should blow dust away from you.

cause physical reactions after repeated exposures (such as cocobolo).

One of the toxic conditions that is often difficult, if not impossible, for consumers to know about is wood contaminated with pesticides and preservatives. Treated lumber in the United States is labeled as such, and the manufacturers post handling guidelines for their products. Unfortunately, while there are many chemicals banned from use in the United States, those chemicals are often used by foreign companies with no posted notices or guidelines.

If you have questions about wood toxicity, consult your own physician, the Occupational Safety and Health Administration (OSHA), your local city health department, and/or textbooks on poisonous plants.

A Partial Listing of Woods and Their Potential Hazards

WOOD	REACTION LOCATION*
Arbor Vitae	respiratory
Bald Cypress	respiratory
Balsam Fir	skin, eyes
Beech	respiratory, skin, eyes
Birch	respiratory
Black Locust	skin, eyes
Blackwood	skin, eyes
Boxwood	respiratory, skin, eyes
Cashew	skin, eyes
Cedar, Western Red	respiratory, skin, eyes
Cocobolo	respiratory, skin, eyes
Ebony	respiratory, skin, eyes
Elm	skin, eyes
Goncalo Alves	skin, eyes
Greenheart	respiratory, skin, eyes
Hemlock	respiratory
Mahogany, African	respiratory, skin, eyes
Mahogany, American	skin, eyes
Mansonia	respiratory, skin, eyes
Maple, spalted	respiratory
Myrtle	respiratory
Oak	skin, eyes
Obeche	respiratory, skin, eyes
Oleander	respiratory, skin, eyes
Olivewood	respiratory, skin, eyes
Padauk	respiratory, skin, eyes
Pau Ferro	skin, eyes
Purpleheart	nausea, malaise
Redwood, Sequoia	respiratory, skin, eyes
Rosewood, Brazilian	respiratory, skin, eyes
Rosewood, East Indian	respiratory, skin, eyes
Satinwood	respiratory, skin, eyes
Sassafras	nausea, malaise
Snakewood	respiratory
Spruce	respiratory
Teak	respiratory, skin, eyes
Walnut, black	skin, eyes
Wenge	respiratory, skin, eyes
Willow	respiratory, nausea, malaise
Yew	nausea, malaise, cardiac
Zebrawood	skin, eyes

*This does not represent the order in which any ailments or problems occur.

This information on wood toxicity is from "Health Hazards in Woodworking" by Stanley N. Wellborn, *Fine Woodworking*, Winter 1977, *American Woodturner*, June 1990.

CHAPTER 4

PLANNING YOUR IDEAL WORKSHOP

Your woodshop will reflect your type of woodworking. Usually that means you're either a generalist or a specialist. Whether you are setting up a new woodshop or enhancing an existing shop, it is of

utmost importance to maintain a realistic goal, similar to when buying or remodeling a house. Having expectations and making subsequent changes in design often result in unforeseen adventures.

There are several principles that motivate and drive the desire for a woodshop. First is wanting to build something. Second is having the finances to set up the woodshop. Third is having a location for the woodshop. What is often missing is having some background or experience that forges and shapes the generalizations we think are the foundations of woodworking. Unfortunately, many of us reinvent the wheel when we are attempting to design and set up a woodshop. Sometimes it's impossible to separate the wheat from the chaff when your own reference points are vague. And sometimes it's difficult to ask the right questions simply because you haven't learned the vocabulary. Consequently, we are often making do or working with the wrong equipment in an inappropriate space.

Many of us set up woodshops without a reference point, such as that provided by a trade school or a master craftsman. The advantage of not having had years of training from a master craftsman is being free to pick and choose everything from adzes to zebrawood — and using them for whatever seems appropriate. The disadvantage is that we don't have someone's hard-earned experiences to guide us. Being self-taught, we can't call upon traditions to specify project design or answer questions such as, "Should I buy a table saw or a band saw first?" And therein is the crux of the problem. How does one design and organize a woodshop? It's a tough question that, when answered, can lead one through the full spectrum from happiness to misery.

If you are fortunate, you will have friends with useful woodshop experiences and you will have ideas about what you want to do in a woodshop. Most areas have clubs or guilds that are a great resource center because their main purpose is advancing woodworking knowledge. Their members are motivated by an interest in woodworking and a desire to socialize with other woodworkers. While there are clubs which focus on general woodworking, there are also specialized clubs for carvers, lathe turners, model makers and other unique endeavors. Visit these clubs both for problem-solving information and for camaraderie.

FINDING THE PERFECT WOODSHOP

The thorny issue of using master woodworkers as sources of information must be addressed. There is no question that a skilled craftsman can inspire, motivate and educate. I can think of no better person to go to for learning about cutting dovetail joints, applying lacquer, carving or lathe turning. These individuals have spent a lifetime learning the skills that most of us cherish. However, some caution is in order when looking at their woodshops. I would suggest that the woodshop of a seasoned craftsman or master woodworker is akin to a comfortable, but worn, pair of leather shoes, which fit only one person. Anyone else who tries to wear those shoes will get pinched toes, sore ankles or fallen arches. So, too, is the woodshop of the craftsman: The shop is an extension of that person. The layout, the equipment and the open space all reflect personal interests, habits and projects. Additionally, the temperament, rationalizations and judgments of a craftsman are imperfect. Even the masters have learned from a limited sampling of woodworking experiences. A person taught to use computer-controlled machines in a German trade school probably hasn't experienced the portability of a traditional Japanese craftsman's tool chest. Nor is the proponent of wooden planes necessarily interested in using an air gun nailer.

Setting aside the meticulousness of engineers and patternmakers, I don't know of any woodworker who approaches woodshop organization using the scientific method. Nor do I know of anyone using a consumer's research system or product review method to identify woodshop organization in a precise and controlled way. Instead, we organize in a facile and casual manner and let our pocketbook and free time steer us into tools, storage and gizmos. However, because we are spending our hard-earned time and money, we should try to be somewhat methodical and logical when organizing the woodshop. Ignorance might be blissful, but it's not the best approach when organizing the woodshop.

The old expression "jack of all trades and master of none" does indeed apply to woodshop organization. Typically, the novice woodworker thinks that there is a particular set of tools and equipment that should be in any woodshop. The scenario develops something like, "I need a table saw, band saw, jointer, planer, drill press, router table or shaper, dust collector, air compressor, disc and belt sanders, workbench, tool chests, all portable power tools (including three routers) and every clamp known to mankind. After all," you say to yourself, "there must be a reason for a hundred different router jigs and templates being in the marketplace and don't the toolmakers and sellers know more about all of this than I do?" My advice is to show restraint and buy tools and equipment with caution and prudence. In fact, if you want to include a tool in your woodshop because it was used on a TV woodworking show

or demonstrated at a woodworking seminar, be wary, that tool might have been shown simply as a sales and marketing ploy.

The media has also fostered the notion that there is a "perfect" woodshop complete with stationary and portable tools, uncluttered storage and room left over for the car, water skis and a winter's worth of firewood. There are so many references to the ideal positioning of equipment and workbenches, and the systematic flow of work from machine to machine, that it seems the goal is to have an efficient production business instead of a neat and useful woodshop. I have never seen a woodshop plan that matches my woodshop with regard to type of machines, size of workbench, available wall storage or family cooperation about not parking their bicycles in the shop. However, we do need to begin the planning and organization of the woodshop with some type of personal perspective; otherwise, the woodshop might end up looking like a hardware store. There should be a reference back to the three guiding principles: woodworking inclination, money and space. Ask yourself these questions: "What do I want to build? What do I want to spend? Where will I do the work?"

TYPICAL WOODSHOPS

Some of the basic requirements for a woodshop are sufficient room size, machines, hand and power tools, workbench, lumber storage, tool storage, assembly area, dust collection, air circulation and ventilation and proper lighting. Each of these requirements has some application to all woodworking endeavors. How these requirements apply are a function of your woodworking interest. Tool storage, for example, is different for carvers and turners. And side lighting, although useful for carvers, isn't generally useful when making cabinets. One more thought before I outline the various types of woodworking and woodshop peculiarities: The majority

of tools are designed for general-purpose use. Everything from band saws to mallets has to be reviewed as it applies to your needs.

The Cabinetmaker's Woodshop

If there is such a thing as a general-purpose woodshop, the furniture or cabinet woodshop might be it. Here is where we find the most general-purpose machines, tools and accessories. Why? Because furniture-making and cabinetmaking require basic cuts and joinery that are thought to be the domain of the basic power tool group (whatever that is). It's worth noting that tool and machine manufacturers rarely state that their products are designed for specific constructions. Their product information emphasizes the general nature or usefulness, accuracy or precision of nonspecific functions. That is because companies deliberately design these products for general use. The exceptions are the tools designed for a specific function, such as biscuit joiners or dovetail jigs. Generally, someone who has been building furniture or cabinets for years has a repetitive woodworking style and probably has a basic collection of tools to match that repetition. For example, I like to make table legs that have 1" × 2" round tenons that fit 1"-diameter through-mortises in the tabletop. To simplify cutting the round tenons, I made a jig out of plywood to use with a router. The set up is fast and easy and it takes very little time to make a set of legs. Consequently, I find it natural to design furniture using the round-tenon jig and I use it frequently. Thus, the woodshop becomes simplified through the process of repetition.

ROOM SIZE Furniture and cabinet work require a room that permits the safe operation of machines and other tools. There should be safe zones around machines such as table saws, so that the operator and anyone else in the woodshop can stand in an uncluttered and safe location while the machine is running. It is also necessary to allow enough space to move any workpiece to and from a machine without being obstructed. Yellow or orange safety tape stuck to the floor can be used to define this safety zone.

The furniture and cabinet shop should be large enough to accommodate typical machines, a workbench, storage cabinets and lumber storage. Mobile bases can be attached to machines so that they can be stored out of the way when not in use, but remember, even mobile machines require floor area for storage. Although a machine can be moved to create an open area, it still must be stored somewhere. Consider this point when arranging the work area.

An assembly area, or open space, is necessary for putting things together. Think of open space as an object, similar to a workbench or table saw. When designing your woodshop be certain to include enough room for assembling the largest piece of furniture to be built. Factor in the following: moving workpieces for assembly; access to, and positioning of bar clamps; flat and even flooring; and whether the workpiece can be left in this location while other tools or machines are used. Ideally, this open space should be away from stationary machines and near the workbench and clamp storage. And if the workpiece will have finishes applied at this location, the space should be away from any heat sources (e.g., water heaters, furnaces or sparking motors) to avoid fire danger.

LUMBER STORAGE Lumber storage is typically very low-tech in the furniture woodshop. The most common storage technique is to pile it on the floor or lean it against a wall. Lumber is heavy and, for safety reasons, shouldn't be stored at too great a height. If wall racks are used, care must be taken to build the racks sturdy and strong. There are several commercial wall racks suited for lumber storage. How-

ever, suitable storage can be made from 2×4s at a fraction of the cost. A simple storage rack need be nothing more than an open frame structure. If you need to store short lengths, the structure can be shelved in with plywood or particleboard. Another simple lumber storage system consists of 2×4s or 4×4s vertically bolted to wall studs with sturdy dowels or metal rods inserted into holes. Remember not to place heavy loads at the ends of the dowels.

A very real option for the hobby woodworker is to let the lumberyard store the wood. Purchase what you need prior to starting a project. If the environment of your woodshop is significantly wetter, drier, hotter or colder than the lumberyard, purchase the lumber a month or so before you plan to start construction to allow the wood to acclimate to the woodshop. Small pieces of wood (good scrap pieces and cutoff pieces) usually are stored in boxes, bins and on shelves. I believe that there is a Murphy's Law concerning these pieces: "If they are left alone in a box on a shelf, their numbers will multiply and they will never go away!" Some woodworkers actually burn scrap wood in wood-burning stoves.

MACHINERY Never before in the history of the world has there been such a variety of woodworking tools. It would take several football stadiums to display one of each machine model from all of the world's manufacturers. Today's woodworker can own an infinite combination of machines for making furniture. Selecting the machines that best satisfy your requirements is time-consuming and difficult. Most experts suggest the basic furniture-making machines: table saw, radial-arm saw, band saw, lathe, shaper/router table, drill press, jointer and planer. While this a predictable (and expensive) answer, there are other approaches for determining the machinery you need.

Keep in mind what you are planning to build, and avoid the notion

that a general-purpose tool might be useful at a later date. Create a budget for machinery and set high and low dollar amounts. Next, visit with friends and acquaintances who enjoy woodworking. Ask questions about favorite machines, warranties, accuracy, maintenance, durability, accessories, spare parts and other concerns of this sort. Obtain specification and price sheets from manufacturers. Use caution when visiting retail stores selling machinery. Using the table saw as an example, no store is large enough to display all of the models from one manufacturer, let alone all of the table saws from all of the manufacturers. Most retail stores are going to attempt to sell you whatever is in stock — but the saw that they don't sell may be the perfect one for your needs.

Once you have a list of potential machines, add up the costs and look at your budget. But don't get discouraged and go out and buy a new truck instead. If the cost exceeds your budget, ask yourself, "Do I need that machine? Is there an alternate way to do the work? Can I use machines at the local school? What about combination machines? Hand tools?"

If you are a beginning furniture or cabinet maker, start with good-quality and reasonably priced machines such as a contractor's 10" table saw, a 14" band saw, a 6" or 8" jointer and a portable 12" planer. Look for sale prices or buy used (but not worn-out) machines. Work with these machines for awhile until you understand their functions, foibles and how they apply to your own work. In time, as your skills improve, you can sell them (there's always a market for used machines) and move up to better or more specialized machines. If you have a limited budget, selling your older machine to buy a newer one is a great way to afford better tools.

Take your time when buying machines. There is nothing wrong with having a five- or ten-year plan. That is, use your machines, complement them with hand tools and plan for future purchases based upon your current woodworking interests. Perhaps a mortising machine or dovetail jig or wide-belt sander might suit your needs once you have spent time making furniture without them. Doing without is a wonderful woodworking process, because it allows you to problem solve and appreciate the real value of a woodworking machine.

HAND TOOLS AND POWER TOOLS Selecting hand tools and power tools requires the same process as that for machinery. The appealing nature and cost of these tools make them easier to purchase and store away. The problem is that, after reading a typical tool catalog, it seems that every tool is necessary for the woodshop. The reasonable thing to do is look at the construction process for your work and then decide whether a monster miter saw or battery-powered router is really necessary. The new home improvement centers (the modern version of hardware stores) are great for browsing and handling tools. It's important to touch hand tools and to experience their heft, balance and physical nature. But remember, don't buy a tool unless you need it — and need it for more than one work project.

WORKBENCH Furniture and cabinet makers require a workbench. Size, shape and number of vises are matters of personal taste. I know of woodworkers who use their bench as a catch-all surface and others who treat the workbench as a piece of fine furniture. The workbench may be positioned against a wall or located so that it can be accessed from all four sides. The workbench should have the flattest reference surface in the woodshop so that it can also be used as a clamping surface. In my opinion, a traditional workbench is OK for building furniture with traditional hand tools, but if you are using routers, portable belt sanders and other modern tools, the workbench should be designed with those tools in mind.

TOOL STORAGE The shops of furniture and cabinet makers probably have the greatest array of tools, accessories, jigs and fixtures of any woodshop because this type of woodworking requires assorted layout and measuring tools, chisels, saws, sharpening equipment, mallets, hammers and accessories for all the power tools. Generally, these items are stored in chests or drawers. or are hung on walls.

Some potential furniture makers and cabinetmakers get distracted from their goal of making furniture and instead pursue the notion of the "perfect" woodshop: Drawers and cabinets are designed to store (or showcase) pristine tool collections. While there is nothing wrong with collecting, functional storage should be the goal if you plan to use the tools.

DUST COLLECTION Until recently, woodshops with piles of sawdust mounded around table saws and jointers were the norm. Heaps of chips were a sign that something was being made in the woodshop. Thankfully, times have changed. Furniture and cabinet shops can now be reasonably free of chips and dust because numerous types of dust collection units are available. The portable units take about the same amount of floor space as a band saw; built-in units can be as large as you want or need. Most dust collectors are affordable, so there is no reason to have potentially dangerous and unhealthy dust in the woodshop.

AIR CIRCULATION AND VENTILATION Woodshops need adequate air circulation. Windows, fans, open doors or any other system of venting the room to provide fresh air is a must. If the woodshop is located in a basement, humidity and lack of fresh air can rust tools and cause finishing products to set up poorly. And as the basement environment cycles between dry during the winter when the furnace is operating, and the warm humidity of summer, wood that is stored there will react accordingly. For example,

drawers that work smoothly in the winter may swell with the summer's humidity and not open.

Another air-quality problem is radon radiation not dissipating due to poor air circulation. Radon is most commonly found when rooms are located over shale and the radiation seeps upward and into rooms through cracked floors and leaky foundations.

Fumes from finishing products and solvents, when confined to a closed room, are another potential hazard. Furthermore, many finishing products that evaporate into the air are flammable either as a liquid or as a vapor. Using flammable products in a closed room with a furnace or water heater or other heat source near by is a good way to end up with TV coverage of firemen hosing down the rubble of what was once your woodshop.

LIGHTING Ideal lighting should be glare-free, color-balanced and visually comfortable. If it were possible, I would like my woodshop to have every lighting source possible: windows, a skylight, incandescent lights and fluorescent lights. If windows and skylights aren't possible, the best artificial lighting is a combination of incandescent and daylight-balanced fluorescent lights. The fluorescent lights cover the overall woodshop, and incandescent lights enhance specific work areas (e.g., above the workbench and at machines).

The Carver's Workshop

ROOM SIZE Woodcarvers are very fortunate when it come to choosing work areas, as the possibilities are almost unlimited. Carving tools can be packed up in a shoe box and taken to a vacation locale, so a seat under a palm tree becomes the workshop. Or woodcarvers can have beautiful state-of-the art woodshops with room to carve old-fashioned circus wagons. But most woodcarvers work in modest-size shops in garages, spare bedrooms or basement corners. Compact work areas (50 to 100 square feet) are common.

MACHINES The diversity of woodcarving makes it difficult to generalize about the typical machines used. With that said, a modest-sized band saw, scroll saw, drill press and motorized grinding wheel (for sharpening) are the most commonly found machines. Woodcarvers do more rough shaping of wood than the precise type of cutting found in a cabinet shop. Also, carvers can work on thicker or smaller workpieces than are found in a furniture shop. If power rotary carving tools are to be used frequently, a small dust collector or shop vacuum should be included in the woodshop.

HAND TOOLS AND POWER TOOLS Woodcarving tools are generally either traditional chisels and mallets or power rotary tools. And rarely does a woodcarver use only one carving chisel. Generally, chisels are grouped as a complementary set (10mm No. 5 straight, 20mm No. 31 spoon, 12mm V-tool and so forth). Chisels are also long, short, stubby and microsize. Some are meant to be hand pushed; others are to be hit with a mallet. Rotary tools require AC, battery or air power. And there are hundreds of carving burrs and abrasive points from which to choose. What this means is that the carver's shop requires thoughtful storage for easy access to potentially hundreds of tools that vary in size from 1" to 18". Furthermore, there are mallets, sharpening tools, drill bits and assorted knives to use and store.

WORKBENCH One key requirement of a woodcarver's bench is that it must be capable of holding a workpiece rigid. When carving a statue, the workpiece is typically held vertically, and carving is done 360° around the piece. As work progresses, the workpiece needs to be moved so that work proceeds evenly around it. To do this, the workpiece must constantly be clamped, unclamped, repositioned and reclamped. Typical front and end vises are not designed for this type of holding. However, specially designed workpiece holders that mount directly to the workbench and can be rotated 360° are available for carvers.

Typically, woodcarvers use smaller benches than those of cabinetmakers. Some workbenches are about the same size as a bar stool. If using mallet and chisels, the workbench must be heavy enough to absorb the constant vibrations from the mallet blows. Power carving also requires working 360° around the workpiece, but since it doesn't produce heavy mallet hits, it doesn't have to be as stout.

For smaller carving projects (that is, the bird-in-the-hand size), the workbench probably will be used as a place to rest tools while working. A TV tray is actually adequate for small carving work. If you are sitting down, it's large enough to hold a few tools and catch the workpiece chips.

For carvers, the workbench is the assembly area. Carved workpieces are not usually the size of furniture, so a separate area is not required.

WOOD STORAGE I haven't seen many woodcarvers' woodshops that have racks of long lumber. Instead, woodcarvers tend to have boxes and bins of small wood pieces: cutoff pieces, firewood-size chunks, limbs and slabs of wood. Generally, the reasons for racking lumber (flatness, moisture control, etc.) aren't as necessary for woodcarving. Shelves and bins are perfectly acceptable for storing woodcarving wood.

TOOL STORAGE The woodcarvers I have known all have had a similar work environment in one respect: Their work area is like that of a piano player; that is, most of their tools are within easy reach when sitting or standing at the workbench. Consequently, tool chests with plenty of small drawers, tool racks behind the workbench or even coffee cans filled with tools sitting on the workbench are common types of storage. Power carving tools are generally suspended over the workbench or hung on a nail next to the bench, and the grinder for sharpening is equally close at hand.

DUST COLLECTION It's difficult to remove wood chips while carving. The old expression "let the chips fall where they may" still applies. The great thing about using a mallet, chisels and knives is that the chips do fall to the floor and you aren't breathing dust. However, when using power tools, the dust flies through the air and into faces and lungs. It's not uncommon to watch a power carver, using a rotary tool, doing detail work fairly close to the face. Obviously, safety goggles and dust masks should be used, but a dust collector for drawing the dust away from the work area would be ideal.

AIR CIRCULATION AND VENTILATION Several conditions make air circulation and ventilation very important. Paints and other finishing products should be used in a well-ventilated area. Again, many finishing products are potential fire hazards. But even if the finishing products are not flammable, it's best to vent the room so that you (and others) don't have to breathe the chemical fumes. Carvers also enjoy working with unusual and exotic woods, like applewood or cocobolo, that can cause skin irritation, so efforts should be made to work as cleanly as possible.

LIGHTING Since most carving work is done in centralized areas, fewer lighting fixtures are needed than in a cabinet shop. Ideally, the carver's shop should have both incandescent and fluorescent overhead lighting with separate on/off switches. Side light is very useful for the carver. By turning off the overhead lights and using side lighting from a tabletop gooseneck lamp or other type of lamp, the workpiece will have different shadows which helps to visually reveal textures.

The Lathe Turner's Woodshop
Woodturning is aptly named, because every time you turn around there are

new lathe and tool innovations and new lathe techniques. The past 20 years have seen incredible developments in woodturning — new lathe designs for turning bowls, spindles and miniatures, new shapes in turning tools and an armada of work-piece-holding devices — and to make it even better, a new generation of woodturning instructors, instructional videos, magazines and woodturner's clubs as sources of information.

ROOM SIZE The basic lathe turner's woodshop can be compact, with enough room for a lathe, other tools, machines and storage. The basic nature of woodturning allows the work project to be started and finished on the lathe, which means there is little need for additional room space for other types of wood processing. Because the lathe is usually located against a wall, with the operator in a more or less static position, the woodturner can easily set up a woodshop in a garage or basement.

MACHINES The traditional wood lathe has undergone considerable design changes because of the heightened interest in bowl turning. In the old days, lathes had long beds with 36" to 48" distances between centers and were mostly used for turning stair spindles and other long pieces. These lathes generally had a 6" distance from centers to bed surface which meant that a 12" bowl was the maximum capacity over the bed. Bowls of greater size were meant to be turned "outboard" on the opposite side of the head stock, if the lathe had that capacity. Today's turners often use both the head and tail stock for support while turning bowls. That means that the distance from centers to bed should be adequate to turn larger diameter bowls. Many lathes now have this capacity and other useful features, such as DC motors, which permit variable turning speeds starting at zero RPM. AC motor variable speeds usually begin at about 500 RPM.

Hobbyist John MacKenzie enjoys lathe turning and having a large air compressor.

Other machines common to woodturner's woodshops are band saws, dust collectors and grinders. Table saws, jointers and planers can be useful for wood preparation, but they aren't a necessity.

HAND TOOL AND POWER TOOLS There are many tools and accessories that aid in woodturning. A few of the more important power tools are a cordless drill for attaching face plates, a finish sander for sanding the workpiece while it's still mounted on the lathe, a rotary tool for detail work and sanding, and a jigsaw or saber saw for preliminary shaping. There are many useful measuring devices, such as inside and outside calipers and center finders. If hand tools are used, it's probably for preliminary wood removal or for some detail design work.

WORKBENCH In a sense, the lathe is the workbench. Once the preliminary shaping of the workpiece is done, just about everything else is done at the lathe. The other ongoing activity while turning is sharpening. For convenience, most turners install a grinder next to the lathe. A small workbench or countertop is useful for the odds and ends of setup or takedown work. The workbench is also

used for sorting wood and other miscellaneous tasks.

LUMBER STORAGE Depending upon your zealousness, storing wood can range from a few pieces to filling garages, decks and barns with chunks of wood. If you are collecting wood and searching for downed trees in orchards, yards, parks and forests, you will need adequate storage. Not only will you need room to store the freshly cut (often referred to as *green* or *wet*) wood, but you will also need storage areas for the drier pieces. To further complicate the picture, there should be a functional inventory system so that different species can be identified — without leaves, one chunk of wood is difficult to tell from another.

TOOL STORAGE Lathe turning, billiards and golf have one thing in common: They all require easy access to long, thin tools. Neat and tidy storage for lathe tools is indeed similar to racks designed to hold cues. But don't make a rack for 12 tools and then buy 13. One possibility is to make a wall rack that can accommodate a growing tool collection. Another easy storage solution is pegboard-covered walls near the lathe. A roll-around cart also permits easy access to lathe tools, and it's less limited in the number of tools it can hold.

ASSEMBLY AREA The assembly or construction area is at the lathe itself. Off-lathe work consists of activities such as tool sharpening, wood preparation and detailing and finishing work.

DUST COLLECTION Depending on whether dry or wet wood is turned, the debris will come off the turning as long stringy pieces or as smaller bits and dust. A good dust collection system will not only make the lathe work neater and easier, but also keep the debris from traveling many feet away from the lathe. Without dust collection, the debris field (especially that of green or wet wood) looks like a confetti celebration — of carrot peelings. Ideally, a dust collection port should be positioned behind and near the turning area. Articulated ductwork with a port is especially useful when it can be repositioned for any work angle or location. In truth, most turners will let wet wood peelings pile up on the floor because their dust collectors cannot handle the volume and weight of the debris. If a duct port is positioned at the lathe it is for dust control.

AIR CIRCULATION AND VENTILATION Moving dust and chips away from the work area also means cleaner air for the lathe operator. A simple solution is to position an electric fan near the work, so that it moves air (and dust) away from the operator, preferably toward a window or door.

Many turners use helmets with face guards that have built-in fans and filters. These battery-powered units filter air at the back of the helmet and move clean air across the face area.

LIGHTING Pleasant overhead lighting is a necessity in the wood turner's shop. It's advantageous to be able to turn different lights on and off so that wood surface textures and features can be easily viewed from different lighting angles. Isolated spotlights

Earl Bartell keeps a small take-apart table near his lathe. The table has rows of holes around its perimeter for holding lathe tools. The type of tool is identified by different colors and numbers of rings on the handles. The table is assembled with oversize knobs for quick assembly. He also uses this table when teaching lathe classes at locations other than his woodshop.

Also in Earl Bartell's shop is this oversized shelf and wall pegboard, located near the lathe. Frequently used chucks, tools and other accessories are within arm's reach of the lathe.

aimed at the work area are also useful for watching how cutting tools perform against wood.

The Furniture Restorer's Woodshop

Furniture restoration and repair woodshops have to be more versatile than the typical furniture-making, lathe turning or carving shops. That's because the restorer has to be able to set up the woodshop so that almost every woodworking skill can be performed. For example, replacement chair rungs must be turned on a lathe, broken decorations must be carved, or drawer sides and bottoms must be cut to a specific size and thickness. Even if you specialize in one particular item (chairs), it's difficult to know what demands the next broken piece will make on the woodshop.

ROOM SIZE The type of furniture being restored determines the necessary size of the room. For example, a dining room obviously requires more space than an antique jewelry box; a drop-front desk requires more space than a hall mirror.

The woodshop has to have enough room for three functions: storage of broken pieces, space to fabricate replacement pieces using tools and machines in a woodshop filled with workpieces, and finally, space for cleaning, disassembly, gluing up and reassembly. I spent many years restoring turn-of-the-century Arts and Crafts (mission-style) furniture, and the sizes of those pieces was always a problem. Sideboards and settles (benches) are large, heavy and difficult to move. If several pieces were brought into my woodshop, suddenly the room got smaller. So plan enough space to store works-in-progress as well the machines to work on them.

MACHINES Unlike furniture and cabinet shops where machines are required for a significant portion of the construction process, the same machines are minimally used for restoration. The chair or table is already made, it

Earl Bartell uses an auxiliary tray mounted to the lathe bed for frequently used tools. The tray is easily repositioned or removed when necessary.

just needs a part or two. The emphasis thus shifts to the need for high-quality machines to make occasional replacement parts. If I could assign a proportional value to the need for machines in restoration work, I would say that need is less significant than other factors. Far more important is understanding how to use various joinery techniques, using chemicals or gluing up odd-shaped pieces.

You may use a lathe to make bowls (for your own enjoyment), but very rarely do you need a lathe to restore bowls. Instead, the restorer's lathe will be used to turn replacement spindles, posts and rungs, so its main feature should be bed length (distance between centers).

A high-quality saw blade is the most important feature of a table saw for restoration work, because it's often necessary to make tear-out-free and odd-angle cuts through antique wood. The aim is to waste as little as possible of the irreplaceable original wood.

Band saws should have ⅛" or ¼" smooth cutting blades so that clean radius cuts can made easily.

The same kind of careful evaluation should be applied to other machines as well. For example, a planer with a slow feed rate is preferred for planing highly figured wood.

HAND TOOLS AND POWER TOOLS I firmly believe that successful restoration work requires the use of an array of traditional hand tools and power tools. For example, a desk or cabinet from the early 1800s probably was built with hand-cut dovetails. If the piece has boards that are damaged beyond repair, the replacement wood will need hand-cut dovetails made to match the original. That means using a tenon saw, chisels, a marking gauge and a mallet. Or there may be hardened glue in a dowel hole that resists being picked out. Using a rotary tool with a round burr might be the only method of removing the dried glue.

Here's a view of Doug Matthews' woodshop. The sliding glass doors are often left open in good weather.

The tool selection for restoration work is eclectic due the variety of potential repairs. Bench planes, moulding planes, routers with specialty cutters, scrapers, chisels, wire brushes, screw extractors, band clamps and putty knives are but a few of the tools that make work easier.

WORKBENCH The traditional workbench with front and shoulder vises is useful to the restorer simply because that prized antique now being restored was originally built at such a bench. And duplicating the original construction process will lead to a better and more valuable restoration. However, if you have the room, a low workbench (approximately 12" to 24" high) is also very useful. A 4' × 8' sheet of $^3/_4$" particle board laminated with melamine resting on low sawhorses is ideal for general cleaning and disassembly. Melamine cleans easily, resists most glues and can be turned over for another clean side if it becomes scratched.

LUMBER STORAGE Just what is the lumber in a restoration woodshop? I like to have bins of wood pieces sorted by color — dark, light, reds and tans — so that colors can be quickly matched with the workpiece. And I have storage for pieces from discarded furniture and other devices. I once had to replace a spindle in a Windsor chair that dated to approximately 1795. I searched for months to find a piece of ash that had a similar color and grain pattern. My search ended when I found an old garden rake handle that was a perfect match. Now I save all sorts of wood simply because I never know when it will be useful. I also like to keep veneer pieces stored between plywood covers, an arrangement resembling a scrapbook. Full rolls of veneer should be kept rolled and wrapped in paper to keep it clean and out of the woodshop air.

FINISHING PRODUCTS AND STORAGE Don't be casual about storing finishing materials, finishing products and solvents.

Specialized metal cabinets for storing hazardous and flammable materials are available, and there are specialized trash cans for oily rags and other flammable products. Check in the telephone yellow pages under "safety equipment" for a source of storage cabinets. All finishing materials and products should be stored a safe distance away from any heat source or direct, all-day exposure to sunlight. Finally, keep all finishing supplies away from those who aren't trained in their usage.

AIR CIRCULATION AND VENTILATION If you have done any paint stripping or furniture repair, the words methylene chloride should speak volumes to you. Also, lacquer thinner, paint thinner, benzene, MEK, alcohol, turpentine and wood bleach are all dangerous and should be handled with extreme care. Since the earliest days of the industrial revolution, chemicals have been both a blessing and disaster to man. The phrase "mad as a hatter" referred to those who made hats with poisonous chemicals. The early-day photographers worked with their faces directly over mercury-coated glass plates while developing film plates. These photographers didn't live long; old-time restorers who worked for long periods breathing formaldehyde and other toxic chemicals didn't live to ripe old age either. If having a long and healthy life is important to you, avoid chemical risks and work with intelligence and caution. Know the chemicals that you are using and follow all product safety notices. Store and use all finishing products as if they were the most dangerous liquids in the house (they probably are). Think of your skin and clothes as if they are sponges, ready to absorb any oil, solvent, bleach, dye or stain. Build and set up the woodshop with whatever it takes to be safe.

LIGHTING Restoration work should be done with proper lighting. Ideally, the lighting should be color balanced to simulate the room where the repaired piece will eventually reside in. It is worth asking the question about the room light before starting on any repair/restoration projects. Since there are a variety of different color-balanced fluorescent lights, keep a supply of these available. The lighting tubes can then be replaced according to need.

Restoration work also benefits from side lighting. That is, a strong light source angled from a horizontal location will cast shadows on the work area. These shadows that are created will enhance the wood grain and carved surfaces, and therefore make detailing the work easier.

COMMONLY FOUND WOODSHOP MISTAKES

- Floor clutter
- Poor ventilation & poor air circulation
- Poor dust collection design, including collector size, type of pipe and pipe configuration
- Improper storage and handling of volatile and hazardous materials
- No provision for chemical spills
- No provision for disposal of unwanted hazardous materials
- Heavy lumber stored at too great of height
- Removal of safety guards from machines
- Ignoring appropriate use of hearing and eye protection
- No first aid supplies or fire extinguisher
- No contingencies for accidents or emergencies
- Not reading operator's manuals
- Poor quality lighting
- Insufficient electrical supply
- Insufficient number of electrical outlets
- Reliance on electrical extension cords
- Space is too small for the number of machines, benches, etc.
- Little or no open space
- Poor access for moving large and heavy objects into woodshop
- Unrestricted humidity, especially in basement and garage woodshops
- Far too much reliance on the concept of "assuming," as in, "I assumed that it was OK."

CHAPTER 5

MAXIMIZING YOUR SHOP SPACE

Imagine 100 empty college dormitory rooms. Each of those rooms has the same dimensional configuration, and each has the same furniture. Now fill those rooms with college students and wait a

month or two and those rooms will no longer resemble each other. The unique personalization process will make it difficult to imagine the original sameness of the rooms. Individualism, personal interests, budgets, creativity and experience are just some of the factors that shape those rooms. The same is true in the woodshop. If 100 woodworkers were given the same size room in which to create woodshops, there would be 100 variations on woodshop layout. Be comfortable and enjoy the locale. Personalize your woodshop.

DESIGN WITH YOU IN MIND

Fundamentally, the layout of your shop should be safe, comfortable and reflect your personal style of woodworking. While it's interesting to study another woodworker's woodshop, you must always relate what you see to your own needs, tools, materials and room location. Ultimately, the ideal woodshop is the one in which you are comfortable. Personal satisfaction is one of the main reasons for woodworking. There are too many references to the perfect woodshop

in books and magazines; when I see these woodshops, I always feel that they are impersonal and lack character and individuality. Truthfully, when only you know what's on cluttered shelves and in boxes of odd and ends, or what a curious jig-type object is for, you have achieved that unique woodshop that is yours. The perfect woodshop is a concept, not a real place.

USING THE WORK TRIANGLE

A designer fad that surfaces occasionally is the work triangle. The triangle concept is based on the notion that there is a maximum efficiency pattern to a work area. It is frequently applied to kitchen layouts; that is, the work pattern between sink, refrigerator and range. The best work triangle configuration is when the sides of the triangle are equal (or nearly equal) and the total length of the sides is 14 to 22 feet. This preliminary design layout tool has some merit when it is applied to the woodshop, if for no other reason than to determine principal work areas and efficient placement of workstations and storage locations. If the work triangle becomes too large or

strangely shaped, it may be necessary to reorganize the work area layout. For example, it's of little value to have hand tool storage too far from the workbench or to have tools in an awkward location. Likewise, certain tools, machines and accessories should be located so that the operator can comfortably use them in interrelated processes (for example a bench grinder and a lathe).

In the woodshop, it's important to create a layout that is both comfortable for the woodworker and efficient. However, the work pathway might be circular, triangular or another shape. What is important is to design a layout in which there's a relationship among various work areas, traffic patterns, windows, doors and all the other features of a room. For example, many woodworkers think the workbench is the principal focal point in the woodshop. If that is so, machines, tools and accessories that are used the most should be in a direct pathway to the workbench. In this case, in addition to a conveniently placed hand tool storage area, a drill press, miter saw and band saw, which are the significantly used machines, should be located 5' to 10' away from the workbench. The secondary machines — a jointer, table saw or joinery machine — would be slightly further from the workbench. Overlaying the primary and secondary work patterns are factors such as being

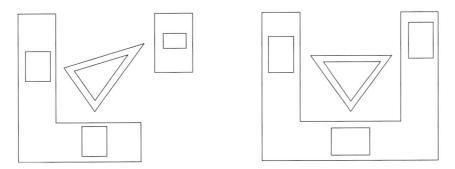

Here are some typical work triangles showing work area layout and the triangular pattern of motion between work locations.

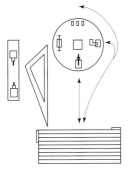

This work triangle includes a workbench, a lathe and round work surface mounted on a post.

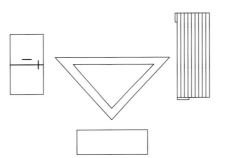

This is a work triangle between a workbench, a cabinet and a table saw.

able to move lumber freely or to avoid stepping on cables, air hoses and dust collector hoses.

BASING LAYOUT ON SEQUENTIAL WORK FLOW

Often, the experts refer to the notion that work should be done sequentially; that is, woodworking procedures can and should be done in a methodical, step-by-step sequence:

1. Rough lumber is cut to length with a radial-arm saw.
2. Rough lumber pieces are flattened, smoothed and thicknessed with a planer.
3. Rough edges are smoothed and straightened with a jointer.
4. Semifinished lumber is resawn with a band saw.
5. Resawn wood is smoothed with a jointer and planer.
6. Smoothed pieces are cut to specific lengths and widths with a table saw.
7. Joinery is done to workpieces with hand tools, router and so on.
8. Workpieces are glued and clamped.
9. Glued-up assembly is sanded.
10. Finish is applied.

If this sequence is properly followed, the layout of machines, tools, accessories and work areas would be ranked (or used) in this order:

1. Radial arm saw
2. Workbench
3. Planer
4. Workbench
5. Jointer
6. Workbench
7. Band saw
8. Jointer
9. Planer
10. Workbench
11. Table saw
12. Workbench
13. Joinery tools
14. Workbench
15. Assembly and gluing
16. Sanding
17. Finishing

RELATING MACHINE FUNCTION TO LAYOUT CONSIDERATIONS

The recurring feature of this sequential-use list is that the workbench is used repeatedly and most machines are used for unique (limited) functions. The radial arm saw is used for cutting lumber to length, the planer is used for thicknessing and smoothing boards, the jointer is used for squaring edges, the band saw is used for making different thicknesses of lumber (resawing), the table saw is used for the final sizing of boards and joinery machines are used for cutting joints (i.e., dovetails or mortises and tenons). If this process is followed as a regular routine, it can be used as a template for woodshop layout.

Start With Initial Cutting

Begin with the premise that lumber and sheet materials should be near the woodshop entry door; that way it won't be necessary to move heavy and awkward materials through the woodshop. Station the initial cutting machine — probably the radial arm saw, panel saw or sawhorses and a circular saw — near the lumber and sheet material storage.

If a radial arm saw is set up on a long table placed against a wall, the area beneath the saw is often used for storage. I have seen several useful adaptations of this space: storage for roll-around cabinet modules, fixed cabinets and drawers and open-shelf storage for shorter pieces of wood. The size and shape of the woodshop affects which style of storage is used. In large rooms the radial-arm saw is usually some distance from the main work area. This generally makes fixed cabinets and drawers less appealing, because of the walking distance, and makes open-shelf storage more attractive. If the woodshop is small and compact, the use of modular cabinets maximizes storage and tool usage.

Facing Materials

Once lumber is cut to a manageable length, the planer is used. The planer requires an open workspace on either side. The open area is defined by the length of the longest lumber entering and exiting the planer. The traditional stationary planer is large and heavy and is usually oriented on the long axis of the woodshop. The new suitcase (or lunch box) size planers are lightweight, portable and easily moved to an open area. Since the concept of a portable planer is relatively new, most traditional woodworkers haven't gotten accustomed to the idea that the planer can be stored on a shelf when it's not being used. Newer woodworkers, however, are beginning to use the planer somewhat like a router or circular saw, that is, taking it from the shelf when it's needed and then storing it away.

The jointer is often located against an uncluttered wall because, like the planer, it requires an open area for infeed and outfeed clearance. The most common jointers have 6"-wide cutter heads and 3' to 4' bed lengths. Both planer and jointer are far more efficient if the machines have cutter heads that are the same width. Oddly, very few planers and jointers are made this way, even when they are from the same manufacturer. This is based upon the (relic) premise that jointers are used for edges and planers are used for surface widths. In reality, the best method for preparing boards (to make them flat) is to first smooth and flatten one board surface on a wide jointer. Once the surface is flat, place the flat surface against the planer's flat surface and feed

This is the Inca combination jointer/planer with 10¼" knife head.

the board into the planer so that the rough side is smoothed by the cutter. This produces dimensionally flat wood, free of twists, cups and distortions. If rough lumber is fed directly into a planer without having one flattened surface, the surfaces will be planed smooth, but the board will have any twists or cups originally found in the rough lumber. The only machine solution for this woodworking dilemma is to have a wide-surface jointer.

Realistically, these machines are rather heavy, large and expensive. A

worthwhile alternative is the combination jointer/planer. The advantages of this type of combination machine are twofold. First, you have one machine instead of two. Second, a variety of combination machines with cutter head widths from 10" to 24" are available, making it much easier to work with wider boards.

The basic design of the jointer/planer machine incorporates over and under the cutter head use. Jointing and flattening work is done on the top surface of the machine, as on a

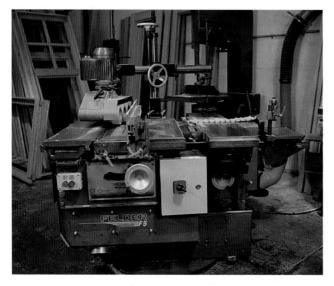

Hannes Hase has a commercial business making windows and doors, and his woodshop is in an odd-shaped and odd-sized room. He uses a Felder combination machine that includes a table saw, a jointer and a planer.

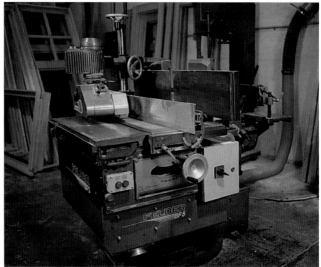

The Felder machine rotates upon a swivel base so that each function is easily accessible. Note that the planer tables are raised.

standard joiner; planing is accomplished by feeding the board under the table and into the lower area of the cutter head. I strongly recommend the combination jointer/planer, especially if woodshop space is limited and you want dimensionally flat and stable boards.

BAND SAWS The band saw has numerous and valuable applications, including cutting curved edges and resawing. Resawing is possibly the most useful application if only because it is nearly impossible with any other machine. Resawing lumber requires adequate space for the lumber to enter and exit the band saw. Typically, the band saw is positioned near a wall so that the cutting direction is parallel to the wall. However, if the band saw is too close to the wall, it's difficult to use the machine for cutting curves because the workpiece will most likely rotate into the wall.

One interesting solution is locating the band saw in front of a door. When resawing long lumber is necessary, the door is opened and the cuts are made.

Secondary Cutting and Shaping

PLACING A TABLE SAW The location of the table saw requires careful consideration. The table saw is generally used as both a primary and secondary processing machine. Primarily, it is used to cut long, wide boards to smaller lengths, or to cut full-size sheets of man-made materials to smaller sizes. Secondary work consists of the final shaping of boards, cutting joints, grooves, dadoes and moulding profiles. Each of these elements has specific design requirements. Primary processing requires adequate area around the table saw to permit the handling of large boards and sheets. This means that there should be both infeed and outfeed space for the safe handling of materials. Under no circumstances should material bump, or be deflected by, surrounding tables, cabinets or other

In this placement, notice the doors behind the band saw. They can be opened when the saw is being used for resawing long boards.

Tom Dailey's table saw features a mobile base and fold-down extension table.

woodshop items. The operator should have absolute control of large pieces while using the table saw. Many experienced woodworkers attach support tables on either side and on the outfeed side of the table saw to support oversized boards and sheets. Never attempt to cut a full-size sheet of plywood or particleboard on a table saw that doesn't have ancillary support tables. The sheer weight of plywood held suspended in air over the back of the table saw by the operator, plus the spinning saw blade, is an accident waiting to happen. Furthermore, using the table saw to crosscut the ends of long boards is also foolhardy.

DO YOU NEED A SHAPER? Ten to twenty years ago it was fairly common to find shapers as part of the standard woodshop machinery. However, many new woodworkers think that the router table replaces the shaper. I don't think that the router table actually replaces the shaper, but many woodworkers rely on the router table as the principal machine for making dadoes and grooves, shaping edges, joinery and frame and panel constructions. Part of the reason for this popularity is that there are many magazine articles featuring router tables: The router is a very popular tool and there are hundreds of different router bits. The sophistication of the router is a modern success story. Plunge routers with variable speeds and 2 to 5 hp are now very common. And there are now routers specifically designed to work upside down under a router table.

The shaper as a machine of choice has fallen out of favor due to several factors. The shaper hasn't changed all that much during this time of the router table development, and many hobby woodworkers feel that the shaper is more dangerous than a router table. This fear, distrust and rejection of shapers is, I think, based upon several perceptions: Shapers have large cutters that make large cuts, thus appearing more aggressive (i.e, more dangerous); shaper cutters

The Inca saw has a shop-made router table inserted between the saw's main table and extension. The router table compartment is sealed, with a dust collection port mounted on the back side.

Dean Bershaw's cabinetmaker's table saw features an oversize table area. This permanently installed table makes the handling and cutting of sheet materials much easier. The table is large enough to also support a planer machine.

Doug Matthews added a modest-size table to his table saw. Note how the Workmate holds an outfeed roller at the back of the table saw.

are more expensive than router bits, and shapers are more expensive than routers; common router functions are improved and made easier when done with router tables; and shapers haven't really been marketed to hobby woodworkers.

Actually, there are several important and real differences between the two machines. One of the main differences is that, excluding special adapters, shaper cutters are designed to cut board edges. Shapers operate in the 6,000 to 10,000 RPM range; while variable-speed routers run at 8,000 to 24,000 RPM. Also, the more professional shaper models have tilting spindles, forward and reverse switches and interchangeable $\frac{1}{2}$", $\frac{3}{4}$", 1" and $1\frac{1}{2}$" spindles.

WILL A ROUTER TABLE DO? Router tables allow both edge work and board surface work. However, in spite of the large-diameter router bit trend, routers are limited to $\frac{1}{4}$", $\frac{3}{8}$" and $\frac{1}{2}$" shanks. Even with a router set at 8,000 RPM, I have never felt comfortable using 2" (or greater diameter) router bits. If I do use a larger router bit, I make many light passes, raising the bit ever so slightly until the final cut is made. In my opinion, router tables are very useful with piloted bits and for cutting dadoes, grooves, rabbets, finger joints and other light cuts requiring cutter bit diameters of $\frac{3}{4}$" or less. The general safety rule is: Use lower RPM speeds for heavier and larger diameter cutters.

PLACING A SHAPER OR ROUTER TABLE Whether it's a shaper or a router table, there are several essential layout considerations. Both of these machines require space for moving wood in and away from the machines. And they both require rock-solid stability: Under no circumstances should these machines be unbalanced when they are used. Many shapers feature right-angle feet attachments so that they are easily bolted to the floor. I have seen few router tables bolted

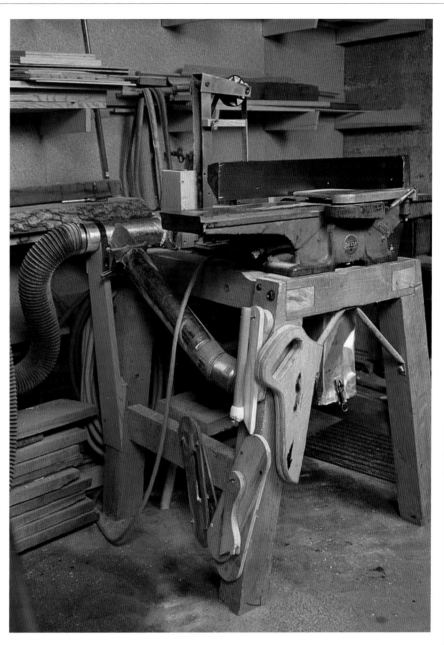

A custom stand for a jointer and a sander is in the Dailey shop. Note the dust collection system.

to the floor, and yet, they are used to cut grooves in 8' lengths of plywood. Just imagine the suspended weight of this wood as it exits the cutter and is hanging on the outfeed side of the router table. Shapers are generally constructed with the motor located in the lower areas of the body, creating a lower center of gravity that helps to stabilize the machine. In order to stabilize router tables, the framework or body should be as large as possible. If you are making a router table out of plywood, adding drawers near the floor (and filling them with tools) will enhance stability. Tim Hewitt at HTC

(makers of metal mobile bases) has sold many bases for both shapers and router tables. His product stabilizes these machines because the mobile base has three wheels externally located on a welded metal frame. The location of the wheels is important because being outside of the machine and frame increases the footprint size of the machine. HTC has had no complaints or problems relating to shaper or router table stability.

Both machines have three active sides — the infeed, the outfeed and an open side. All three require that the adjacent areas be clear of obstructions. The fourth side, the side behind the fence, is usually positioned near a wall. Shaper and router table space requirements are determined by the length of workpieces. If, for example, frame-and-panel cabinet doors are the only thing made, the clear area should be no less than 4' on the three active sides. However, if you are shaping or routing entry door pieces or floor-to-ceiling cabinet sides, the clear area for the infeed and outfeed directions should be at least 10'.

Using a Joinery Machine

The compact joinery machine is relatively new to the woodworking world, but because of its usefulness, it's being found in more and more woodshops. This machine has a router mounted horizontally and permits cutting action along X, Y and Z axes. That is, the horizontal router can be moved up and down, and the table holding the workpiece moves in and out and side to side. These machines allow for the efficient cutting of mortises and tenons, dovetails, finger joints and such.

Because this machine is used for joinery, the workpieces are shorter and smaller, thus not requiring large open areas around the machine. I use a Multi-Router joinery machine mounted on a mobile base, and when I need it, I move it from a storage area to a suitable work area. In use, a joinery machine probably is easier to manage when it's near the workbench. For example, if you are making a set of six ladderback chairs, that translates into 102 pieces, 156 mortises and 156 tenons. That's quite a few pieces to keep tidy. The workbench is ideal for sorting, organizing and keeping track of all the pieces and their joinery situations. The only drawback to this machine is that the horizontally mounted router flings dust and chips over a wide area, like a geyser of dust.

If you plan on using this machine near clean areas, I would suggest that you construct some sort of dust col-

Here is the Multi-Router joinery machine with a custom-made dust hookup.

lection device. Factor the location of a joinery machine into your layout and provide for a 4" or 5" flexible dust collection hose to dangle directly over the router bit area. That way, the discharged debris will be caught while it's airborne. Normally, dust collector ductwork is attached to specific machines and is rarely dangled near the workbench. If you do place a dangling collection hose near the workbench, be certain to add a open/close gate or a large plug at the end of the hose: There is no reason to have an open hose anywhere in the woodshop, especially near the workbench.

MOVING AROUND THE SHOP

Once the sawing, planing and joinery are finished, all that is left are the final stages of woodworking: assembly, gluing, sanding and finishing. These stages all require space — both

for your movement while working and calm space while the workpiece is glued, clamped and finished.

Open Up Space With Mobile Tools

Most small woodshops are tightly organized, with walkways, and little open space. Yet, assembly and finishing require open space. Generally, the solution is to move equipment out of the way to open up space; moving equipment can be facilitated if machines are mounted on mobile bases. However, heavy machines without mobile bases probably shouldn't be moved. Dragging a machine across the woodshop will most likely injure you and damage the machine and floor. Commercially made mobile bases are available for just about any machine. HTC has a catalog offering a comprehensive supply of well-made bases for any type and brand of tool.

They also will make customized bases for older or unique machines.

If you decide to make a mobile base, don't make it so that the machine is easily tipped or the wheels are too large. It's very easy to make custom stands, just make the wood frame as low to the floor as possible, use lockable caster wheels, and design it so the wheels are off the floor and out of the way when the machine is used.

Harry Charowsky has a modest-size woodshop and all his machines, tables and workbench are on mobile bases of his own design. He uses an outdoor covered area adjacent to the woodshop to move the machines into when he's not using them. Harry installed a removable threshold to make it easier to move heavy machines through the door. The threshold is a wide board with an attached standard-size threshold. It simply rests on the concrete and tightly seals the room from outside air when the door is closed. When he needs to move things, he just lifts it out and then there is no bump to impede moving things in and out.

Here are simple work stands for a planer and a drill press.

Focus on the Workbench to Save Space

Another common assembly solution is to use the workbench for the final woodworking steps. The problem with using the workbench for assembly, gluing and finishing is that workbenches aren't necessarily wide enough for some furniture and cabinet constructions. And the workpiece is usually too high for comfortable work. A workbench height of 12" to 24" is ideal for assembling furniture; however, a bench at this height is useless for many other projects. A simple solution is to have low sawhorses to temporarily support a sheet of plywood, particleboard or MDF. Assembly and clamping require a perfectly flat surface, so the sheet material should rest as flat as possible on the sawhorses. I've seen many woodshops that have the sheet material attached

with screws to a simple frame, which is nothing more than four edge pieces and several cross-frame pieces. When it's not in use, the flat-surfaced assembly is leaned against a wall or used as a catchall for general woodshop use. Once the sheet material is worn out (chipped, gouged, dried glue spots, etc.), simply flip it over and use the other side until it too is hopeless, and then replace it with a fresh sheet.

Plan for Glue-Up and Assembly Space

I have bruised myself more during the slow time that occurs while a workpiece is clamped than during the entire construction process. Why? I think it's because I've lowered my guard. While sawing, planing and so on, I am very focused on what I'm doing. But after the workpiece is clamped up and just sitting there, I'm usually cleaning up, putting tools away and not paying much attention to that clamp handle protruding out into the walkway. Therefore, leg and hip bruises. The moral of this tale is that clamped workpieces require an out-of-the-way place because of their disruption of normally open spaces. Or, you could simply leave the room while the glue dries.

Don't Forget About Ceiling Height

So far, woodshop layout has mainly focused on floor area. The other dimension that should be factored into layout plans is floor-to-ceiling height. While it may be impossible to increase the height within an existing woodshop, there are several things that you can do to maximize floor-to-ceiling height.

The most troublesome feature of woodshop height is the difficulty involved in moving long boards. Even if you are primarily lathe turning, carving or doing other small-scale projects, there will be times when lifting lumber is required. Lifting and transporting lumber is further complicated by the location and height of machines, workbenches, hanging objects and storage units. Furthermore, light fixtures are often lower than the ceiling. Moving an 8' board can make you feel as if you are jousting with the dark knight or battering down the castle wall!

Obviously, if you are designing a new woodshop, the simplest thing to do is to increase the floor-to-ceiling height. Ceiling heights of up to 12' will make almost any woodworking easier. When a new house is being built over a basement of concrete blocks, inquire about having one or two additional rows added to the basement walls so that there will be more overhead room. (I'm sure the additional construction expense will be negated when you use the basement woodshop, plus the additional height will probably increase the value of your house.)

Dealing With Low Ceilings

If you are setting up your woodshop in an existing garage or basement, there are several methods of dealing with standard room height.

1. Recess all light fixtures flush to the ceiling.
2. If fluorescent lights are suspended below the ceiling, install the fluorescent lights in commercially available clear safety tubes (if the light is broken, the glass shards remain in the plastic tube).
3. Remove or minimize all objects that hang from the ceiling (unnecessary light cord and so on).
4. Position machines and storage units next to a wall when moving long items. Having an open center area in the woodshop will facilitate moving long lumber.
5. Rough cut long lumber outside the woodshop.
6. If there's a window, use it for negotiating long lumber into the woodshop.
7. If the ceiling is paneled or finished, consider removing the ceiling material so that the rafters are exposed. The open area between rafters, especially above the workbench area is useful for maneuvering boards. The exposed rafters also permit additional storage and places to hang items. Dust collector ducts, air lines and wiring can be routed above rafters.
8. Work within your limits. If you do have a small and cramped woodshop, be realistic and build things that fit in the room. It is dangerous and frustrating attempting to build large items when the room size is more suited to small, handheld-size items.

Planning for Dust Collection

No matter how the final woodworking stages are done, it is a process that effects the entire woodshop — and sometimes the nearby living quarters. The most obvious by-product of this stage is sanding dust and finishing product fumes. Additionally, the woodshop may even be more cramped while a finish is drying. These factors affect woodshop layout in the following manner: Since dust and fumes can be controlled by proper collection and ventilation, it makes sense to arrange the woodshop accordingly. Set up the dust collector and sanding and finishing areas away from doors and windows — there is no need having air currents spreading dust over a wider area. Design the layout so that dust doesn't travel more than 1' to 2' from the work area. If possible, have the dust collector hidden behind a partition or screen. Even the ceiling-mounted air filtration units can circulate fine dust, and it may be necessary to reposition it until a minimum circulation of dust is determined. By minimizing dust, there is less work when applying finishes. Cleaning the entire woodshop is a tedious chore complicated by waiting for airborne dust to settle before being able to apply a finish. In fact, oil finishes are probably popular simply because they don't need a dust-free woodshop. Varnishes and, to some degree, lacquers, don't take kindly to fine dust. If you do have a dust contamination problem associated with varnish applications, there are many finishing books with instructions on how to rub out rough varnish finishes.

CHAPTER 6

CUSTOMIZING YOUR WOODSHOP

There isn't a formula for the ideal woodshop. There is you, your requirements, your budget and your expertise. Don't get sidetracked by the unnecessary.

Sam Maloof, a great American woodworker, tells the story about being approached many years ago by several very earnest engineers. They had slide rules (definitely pre-calculator), protractors, tape measures and clipboards filled with charts. Their quest was to determine the proper heights, widths, lengths and shapes to construct the ideal chair. They wanted to interview Sam about his chairs, because Sam made the most comfortable wood chairs around. (In my opinion, they are even more comfortable than upholstered and pillowed chairs.) These bright and well-meaning engineers were looking for a formula, a template, or a system of shapes and angles for building something that would apply to everyone. Sam was amused by their questions, because he didn't have a formula or a chart for building his chairs. He told them that he built a chair by feel: He sat in it, and if he was comfortable then the chair's owner would also be comfortable. The young engineers left, scratching their heads and pondering this natural approach to chair design.

NO TWO SHOPS ARE ALIKE

This story relates to designing woodworking shops because I've never met two woodworkers that have woodshops of the same shape or size. Nor have I met two woodworkers that have the same tools, machines, lumber pile or specific woodworking style. And these differences exist even though woodworkers tend to read the same books and magazines. There are simply too many personal features, budgets, locations and room configurations for there to be significant similarities between woodshops — or for me to say there is a uniform woodshop design. I know a lathe turner who specializes in turning miniature objects, and yet her woodshop is large enough to park an airplane in it. I also know woodworkers who have full shops in single-car, low-ceiling garages and are building plywood cases and cabinets. To illustrate one very simple problem in generalizing woodshop design, suppose that two woodworkers have bought exactly the same tools and plan on setting up a woodshop in order to build exactly the same wood projects. The only difference is their woodshop configuration: One is a 12' × 30' rectangle with two doors and

Luthier Robert Girdis had used a small room for many years to make beautiful guitars.

Let's say you just purchased a house with an extra building, such as the one shown in the three photos on this page. How would you design both the ground-level and loft spaces into a woodshop?

This is the ground-level view of your imaginary new building.

windows on three walls; the other is a 19' × 19' square with no windows and one door. Even though both woodshops have approximately 360 square feet, it doesn't take much to visualize that wall storage, machine placement and overhead lighting will be very different for the two woodshops. Windows and a second door create such limitations that only creatively designed storage units are effective.

What is appropriate for designing a woodshop is considering a standard set of variables that more or less apply to every woodshop. Sort of the "food, clothes and shelter" basics of the woodshop. For woodshops these elements would be: woodshop location, interest, finances, machinery, tools and storage.

Study existing woodshops. In spite of the inevitable differences with your future woodshop, existing woodshops do offer ideas and potential problem-solving solutions. Study machine locations, especially their relationship to other machines and open space (work areas). Note the locations of workbenches and storage areas for frequently used tools. Other principal concerns are lumber storage, finishing supply storage, finishing areas, clamp storage, electrical outlets, dust collection ducts and openings. Ask "Why did you do that?" and take note of the response.

START WITH PEOPLE YOU KNOW

To find woodshops, first talk with friends and neighbors who do woodworking. Because they are friends and neighbors, you probably can trust their advice. Joining local woodworking clubs and guilds is also a great source of information. Generally, woodworkers join these clubs to share information. And you will find that, because most of them have gone through the struggle of designing woodshops, they aren't shy about sharing their solutions.

Look at Schools and Pro Shops

Schools and professional woodworking shops, although they are tempting as sources of information, aren't necessarily useful for home-woodshop applications. That's because schools and professionals don't have the same purposes, room sizes, machines and tools, budgets and interests as the home woodworker. A school might be a repository of machinery valued by teachers with specific points of view; the professional woodshop might rely on expensive processing machines with no hand tool applications whatsoever. Having said that, if the opportunity arises for you to visit these woodshops, do it, and then use the information as a benchmark of a different woodworking evolution.

This is the loft of your space.

Additional Shops to Check Out

Other woodshops that might offer some value, if for no other reason than studying storage solutions, air filtration and workbenches, are those used by artists, jewelers, painters and auto mechanics. These woodshops will have single-purpose applications, yet each offers unique problem-solving solutions. As you study these shops, remember that your woodshop will be generalized in nature, but how a sculptor or mechanic stores tools can be invaluable information.

MAKE YOUR MASTER PLAN

All designs evolve from somewhere. There are historical and personal factors in how we perceive environmental needs. The woodshop is not some haphazard, all-of-a-sudden wild card sent to you from Mars. Typically, home woodshop design is developed from:

- what others have done
- what magazine and book editors think is important
- movies and TV
- how schools design classroom woodshops
- how commercial businesses set up for efficiency
- having a space and randomly setting up shop

Because woodworking seems like a "practical" craft, the woodshop is often set up and arranged as if it were an antiseptic, nonpersonalized room. Consider this: How many woodshops have you ever seen that have an individualistic flare? And, I don't mean handmade benches, cabinets and such. How often are there pictures of family, a bulletin board with drawings or even a potted plant? How different is the layout or how creative is the use of space?

I have visited many woodshops and have come to divide woodshops into two camps: the utilitarian and the artistic. The particular woodworking emphasis is not important in this observation. Carvers, turners and furniture makers are all subject to the same two divisions. What is important is the attitude and personality of the woodworker.

The utilitarian woodshop relies on a no-nonsense approach to work. Machines and cabinets are rigidly

Before construction ever began, Robert Girdis built a mock-up of his ideal woodshop.

Here's the Girdis woodshop under construction. The woodshop is located on the house property.

arranged, there is a formality to tool location and the woodworker has to adapt to the limitations of the room. These woodshops seem to be extensions of the machines and the work materials and less of the owner. Well-crafted cabinets, workbenches or other man-made shop aids, while usually lending an air of the owner's skill, aren't the issue. I'm referring to the overall nature of the woodshop. Stuff is organized, and there is a sense that anyone visiting for the first time

could quite easily use the woodshop. The emphasis is on production or, arguably, on conformity. That is, "Everyone else has a woodshop that looks like this, so I will do the same."

I feel that the "practical" and "production" part of woodworking is greatly overdone. While it is true that there is a need for organization and step-by-step construction methods, unless you are in a 40 to 60 hours per week woodworking business, you are building things for other reasons

You see here the corner and the workbench in the finished Girdis woodshop.

This is the completed Rob Girdis woodshop. The main building measures 24' × 24', and the attached secondary room measures 20' × 20'. The side walls are 13' high, and it is 21' to the roof peak.

than production. Yet, woodworking is steeped in the lore of thousands of years of woodworking with the interpretation that objects were made for practical reasons. Everything we know and use has some historic connection to wood. There is little doubt regarding the usefulness (practicality) of most historic wooden objects and the tools used to make them. But we are now in a different time, with very different values than people had in 1940, 1840 or 1240! As a result of today's large population there certainly are quite a few woodworkers. However, in terms of the actual percent of careers, there are few people earning a livelihood at plane-and-saw woodworking. There is a large contingent of hobby woodworkers and more artist woodworkers than ever before. Leisure and hobby are now integral facets of woodworking.

Few machines and tools are really as cost effective as would be necessary in a competitive business. Certainly, the nostalgia for a "traditional" woodshop is appealing, but it should not be the sole element for designing a woodshop. For the most part, we make things with wood because we like to make things with wood. But we still attempt to design our wood-

Dave Buck's in-the-forest woodshop measures 24' × 32' with a 6' roof overhang for working outside — and staying dry.

shops from two different styles. The first interpretation is that the woodshop should look somewhat like an early American or Arts-and-Crafts-era woodshop. The second design notion is that the woodshop should look like an Early American or Arts-and-Crafts-style woodshop, but it should also include the ability to turn out thousands of widgets a day!

The artistic woodshop is more of an interpretation of the owner's viewpoint and lifestyle. There is use of paint, other than white, and the use of decoration. These woodshops are rare, but they are delightful. It's amazing what a few drawings, pictures or small objects can do for a room. Not all woodshop time is devoted to pushing wood through a machine, and the artistic woodshop offers objects for reflection or visitor curiosity. There is a definite sense of the woodworker in these woodshops.

My sense is that these rooms have evolved from conceptualizing the

John MacKenzie rescued an old chicken coop and brought it to his home property. After rebuilding it, he landscaped and decorated the woodshop exterior so that it became part of a pleasant backyard.

Doug Matthews built a barn-shaped woodshop to visually fit the rural setting where he lives; note his home is located near the woodshop. Doug restores and repairs antique furniture and has just set up a showroom in the woodshop's second floor area to display and sell antique furniture.

work spaces of fine art painters, sculptors or interior designers. Often, there is less reliance on having excessive tools. Instead, there are enough tools and machinery for the purpose of the owner. What I have seen and heard from this type of woodworker convinces me that they have very specific intentions for using their woodshop, while at the same time, they have the woodshop reflect their ideas and sensibilities. And they aren't distracted by the newest gizmo and accessory — unless it fits a need. In fact, some actually have an indifference to tools because they prefer to concentrate on the things they make. The emphasis is on making objects and less about having "one of everything." Functionally there is often more open space and better lighting. Since there is less stockpiling of tools, there is less premium on storage.

The utilitarian, no-nonsense design is like a navy submarine. That is, there is the sense that once submerged in work, the sub/woodshop is isolated and requires total self-sufficiency. This woodshop, like the submarine, requires incredible nook-and-cranny storage for all the things that might be needed. The artistic woodshop, while having the necessary tools plus a bit of the frivolous, is more like a backpacker's pack in its simplicity: You might choose to leave some essentials behind, while making room in your pack for a favorite book.

After you have conceptualized your woodshop design, it's time to make a master plan. The master plan is a general plan of room size, potential features and tools. These are, in turn, filtered through your woodworking discipline and style. Create this plan with as much intensity and enthusiasm as possible. Plan as if designing a kitchen or master bedroom. Obviously, the master plan can be changed as you proceed with developing the woodshop. However, the master plan is the ideal starting point. It will be the first visualization of your future woodshop.

Choose Your Tooling and Storage

Make a list of all the machines, the tools and the storage areas that you ultimately will want.

FURNITURE OR CABINETRY SHOP If you want to build furniture, consider:

- workbench
- drill press
- table saw
- disc/belt sander
- band saw
- joinery machine
- router table or shaper
- dust collector
- jointer
- scroll saw
- planer
- air compressor

Also consider storage cabinets and shelves for:

- routers
- biscuit joiner
- drills
- clamps
- sanders
- hand tools
- spray equipment
- finishing supplies
- air tools
- lumber and plywood

WOODCARVING SHOP

- workbench
- dust collector
- band saw
- scroll saw
- grinder (powered sharpening device)
- drill press
- disc/belt sander

And storage cabinets and shelves for:

- rotary carving tools
- clamps
- sanders
- drills
- burrs and bits for rotary tool
- finishing supplies
- assorted hand tools (carving chisels and mallets)
- lumber and small pieces of wood

WOODTURNING SHOP

- lathe
- drill press
- workbench
- dust collector
- band saw
- grinder (or a powered sharpening device)

And storage cabinets and shelves for:

- lathe tools
- lathe accessories
- drills
- hand tools
- sanders
- finishing supplies
- sanding supplies and sandpaper
- lumber, blocks, logs and small pieces of wood

MISCELLANEOUS NEEDS List all other important features that are useful for any woodshop:

- electrical service panel
- electrical outlets (110V and 220V)
- plumbing (sinks, toilets and so on)
- secondary lighting (spotlights)
- windows
- doors
- containers for scrap wood

Design the Woodshop on Paper

Use $1/4$" grid paper and use a scale of $1/4$" = 1'. First, draw the shape of the woodshop. Include all permanent elements of the room, such as support beams, steps, water heaters. On another sheet of paper, draw representational shapes of all machines, shelves and storage units and cut them out with scissors (or copy the images on page 31 and use those). Now, try the cutouts in different locations on the floor-plan drawing. Note the way that open space or machine positions differ from your preconceptions of an idealized layout. It may seem that particular machines, which should be easy to place, become difficult to locate because of windows or doors. Storage units may have to be modified from original designs because of machine placement or electrical outlets.

Designing With a Paper Grid and Paper Tools

Obviously, it's easier to move pieces of paper than machines and cabinets, and the benefits of this technique are far-reaching. Generally, the problem with home woodshops is too little space, not too much space. Placing items becomes a struggle toward efficiency. When arranging the paper cutouts, it might become apparent that the floor plan and machinery don't match. There may not be enough space for your needs. It may be impossible to have a comfortable blend of machines, cabinets, safe areas around machines and open work areas. The paper cutouts will aid in this discovery, which is part of the reason that you should include every possible item on the master plan list. Don't leave out machines and shop furniture that will be acquired in the future. Even if the purchase of something is several years off, include it in the master plan. All too often the owner of a cramped woodshop will spend too much time attempting to overcome the problem of space limitations. Storage becomes convoluted, machines are too close together and, instead of working on projects, time is spent either moving things around or finding, or hiding, objects. Be prepared for future acquisitions.

Planning for the Future

Here's an issue that's complicated and somewhat vexing: How do you know how to start out compared to where you will end up? Perhaps you've seen beautiful handmade furniture, bowls and carvings at a craft fair, and this has inspired you to take up woodworking. But you've had no woodworking lessons or experiences with other woodworkers. What do you do to get started? Let's assume that you read woodworking books and magazines, watch do-it-yourself videos and visit tool stores. All of these are very inspirationally produced by experts. But do these sources really help you to find a starting place? The ques-

(left) This is the exterior of Steve Balter's shop.

(above) Steve Balter has a display room in the front of his workshop.

tion is, will you make furniture, turn bowls or carve? What if you set up a woodshop for carving and later find that lathe-turned bowls are your real interest?

Relax. When you create the master plan, realize that most machines are for general-purpose applications. Table saws and band saws aren't designed for single-purpose use. However, carving chisels and lathe tools are single-purpose tools. Fortunately, you can start out with a half dozen of these tools and not spend a large sum of money. And if you decide that carving isn't for you, it's easy to sell them. If you aren't certain of the type of woodworking you want to pursue, initially stay as general as possible, realizing that some tools are worth purchasing, if for no other reason than for experimentation.

BUDGETING FOR SHOP SETUP

If you are setting up a woodshop for the first time and have never pur-

chased machinery, tools and supplies, don't get discouraged. I have talked with hundreds of beginning woodworkers and heard many very similar questions. Usually beginning woodworkers have specific budget amounts and space limitations as their first priorities. These conditions are quickly followed by questions about what type of machinery and hand tools should be purchased. After these issues, questions follow about specific brands, where to purchase machinery and tools, what books and magazines are recommended and where one can find how-to and hands-on instruction. The response to these questions is like the solution to a complicated mathematics problem: Start at the beginning, do your step-by-step work on paper, and progress through every step until the solution is found.

Translating that type of formula into designing a woodshop is straightforward. Suppose that your budget is $3,000 for machinery and tools,

the potential woodshop area has 200 square feet, and you are planning on generalized woodworking for yourself and your family. First, what will $3,000 purchase? Make a list of possible selections. Also factor into this list whether you are planning to purchase locally or through mail-order catalogs and whether you prefer machines made in the U.S.A. or those made in foreign countries.

Prioritize Your Purchases

Obviously both lists are over budget, and neither list includes hand tools, sharpening supplies, sandpaper and so on. The next step is to prioritize the tool list and purchase the most important items first. For general-purpose woodworking, the scroll saw and lathe may not be necessary. However, design the woodshop location as if all the listed machines and tool items were available. It's much easier to create the layout requirements in the planning stage than to

Potential Machines and Costs

LIST A		LIST B	
Cabinetmaker's table saw	$1,600	Contractor's table saw	$800
15" stationary planer	1,000	12" portable planer	400
6" stationary jointer	1,300	6" portable jointer	300
12" band saw	900	10" band saw	350
Heavy-duty lathe	2,000	Benchtop lathe	450
16½" floor drill press	400	Benchtop drill press	100
Scroll saw	500	Scroll saw	200
Cyclone dust collector with duct	1,000	2-bag dust collector on rollers	400
3-hp plunge router	280	1½-hp standard router	200
Router table w/additional router	400	Router table only	100
Plate jointer	200	Plate jointer	200
14V cordless drill	210	12V cordless drill	185
Finish sander	80	Finish sander	80
4" x 24" belt sander	225	3" x 21" belt sander	170
Total	$10,095	Total	$3,935

retrodesign a woodshop when space is unavailable or wasn't factored into construction plans.

If you plan on cutting large amounts of plywood and can't decide between a cabinetmaker's table saw (e.g., Delta's Unisaw), because you think it would be more advantageous for this procedure, and a contractor's table saw, because it better fits your space, consider the following alternative. Size plywood into smaller sections with a circular saw or jigsaw by cutting approximately ⅛" wider than the measured layout lines and cleaning the rough-cut plywood edges using a router, a straight bit and a clamped straightedge. Or construct auxiliary tables on both sides and outfeed areas of the table saw so that the plywood is manageable during cutting.

When I started woodworking, I had only a vague concept of what tools to purchase. At that time, there were no magazines devoted to woodworking and the hardware stores were primarily devoted to the trade (i.e., contractors and builders). And 20-some years ago, the main articles in the mechanic-type magazines were either "Table Saws Versus Radial-Arm Saws" or "How To Build a Plywood Dingy." It was difficult to find information or sources for antique tools, specialty tools, foreign-made tools or high-quality tools. Over the years, I have purchased a variety of table saws, routers, drills and assorted gadgets. Most of my earlier purchases have been replaced with upgraded versions, and the original tools were sold through the newspaper classified section. The point is, your skills, pocketbook and interests change with time. If you know what you want now, that's great. But don't worry if you aren't sure — you will know in time. So if you can't afford a particular machine at the moment, purchase something that is affordable and upgrade later on. If you want to try something different, go ahead and try it. If it isn't right for you, it's easy to resell most tools; there's always eBay.

PLANNING STORAGE

The storage in most woodshops that have evolved over years of use is generally haphazard. It's common to see cabinets built in odd locations because the space was unused or was too awkward for other uses. When a woodshop is properly planned and designed, cabinets and shelves fit the room and present an orderliness that makes work easier. If possible, construct storage cabinets in modular units. A set of smaller cabinets is easier to build and easier to move within the room. For example, a 9'-long wall is available for cabinets. It's conceivable that one 9' cabinet could be installed. However, it's difficult to build something that large and then install it. It would be much better to build a set of three cabinets, each 3' long. In fact, build one as a start, and then build the others as the need for more storage arises.

Make paper cutouts of generic rectangular shapes to represent potential storage units. If the storage is wall-mounted above another unit or apparatus, color the elements different colors so that they are visually separated.

Storage Options:
- floor to ceiling
- wall-mounted above machines or benches
- under stairs
- under machines
- flush fit between wall studs
- overhead in rafters

PLANNING MACHINE LOCATION

Two general rules apply to the locations of the major machines — table saw, radial-arm saw, jointer, planer and band saw, in the shop. First, certain machines, like the jointer and radial arm saw, are only used from one side. Second, there has to be enough room around other machines, such as the table saw and planer, for wood to enter and exit the machine. When using the paper cutouts, a logical starting point is to place the one-side-only machines against walls. Optionally, certain machines can be grouped together, such as placing the jointer and planer side by side. But make sure to allow enough space for long boards to safely clear a machine without bumping into other wood-

Tom Dailey's woodshop is located in a ground-level basement. Plywood is brought in through the back door, then cut with a panel saw.

shop items. For example, if a heavy board 2" × 8" × 80" is processed on a jointer, the operator not only has to maintain the board on the machine, but he also has to be able to take the board from the outfeed table and not ram it against other woodshop items. In other words, the entry and exit areas around certain machines must be clear: This space is as important as the space the machine occupies.

Table Saw

If full sheets of plywood are routinely cut, place the saw centrally in the woodshop and build secondary support tables. Keep the pathway to and from the table saw unobstructed so that the plywood can be safely handled and moved. For small woodshops, panel saws are an alternative to the table saw. These are wall-mounted units that support the plywood, with a track-mounted circular saw for making the cuts.

Radial-Arm Saw

If long boards are routinely cut with a radial saw, the saw should be placed against a wall, with long secondary support tables on either side. Many woodworkers with basement woodshops set up a radial-arm saw in the garage and perform rough cuts there, and then move the shorter pieces to the woodshop. Note: If the radial-arm saw is in the garage and away from the main woodshop, it should be equipped with a lock for the on/off switch. This prevents children or other curious types from turning on the saw when the owner isn't present.

Band Saw

If the band saw is used primarily for ripping and resawing long boards, it too can be located against a wall. The work is moved parallel to the wall, providing a clear pathway for board entry and exit from the blade. However, if the band saw is used to make curved cuts, the board is moved in a radial manner, much like a clock hand, with the blade at the center point. For this type of use, the band saw should be more centered in the woodshop, away from walls.

Dust Collector

The dust collector, although very useful, has to be one of the most difficult machines to place in the woodshop. It has an awkward shape, and certain models radiate fine dust and noise. Ductwork, gates and connectors are also potential complications. If you don't want multiple ducts or hoses, there are portable collectors with short lengths of hose, that can be placed near a machine. This method only works if you're doing limited work with the floor free of obstructions. The best method is placing the dust collector somewhere away from the work area and using ducts to the machines.

To control the dust that settles around a collector, and to reduce the noise level, the dust collector can be located in a closet-type of room. If you choose to do this, be certain that there is air flow into the room. Cut a square hole in the door and cover it with a furnace filter. The filter keeps dust from exiting the room, and the hole will reduce air pressure within the room. I've seen a dust collector room that, when the collector was running, created so much air pressure that the door couldn't be opened. That isn't wise.

Miscellaneous Tools and Machines

A number of machines are used to primarily process shorter lengths of wood. This allows for some freedom in floor plan use. The drill press, router table, shaper, scroll saw and joinery machines can be located in less open areas. Occasionally, the router table or shaper is used for longer pieces; the machines can then be moved for these specific operations.

PLAN FOR ELECTRICAL AND PLUMBING NEEDS

When a new building is under construction, there is a sequence to the order of events. That is, electricians and plumbers complete their work before drywallers and painters. While this sequence should apply when converting a basement or garage into

HIRING A CONTRACTOR

Some tasks may be too complicated or require specific expertise. There are many advantages to hiring a contractor or other specialist when remodeling or building a new woodshop. The problem is how do you know who to hire?

Never underestimate the complexities of building or remodeling a woodshop. Just as with a house, the fundamentals of framing, electrical, plumbing, concrete, trenching and all the other construction techniques are required.

While there are many who are skilled enough or have enough time to do their own work, often it is better and faster to have someone else do the work.

If you've done your design work and choose to hire a contractor, you must be comfortable with your choice. After all, this person is going to turn your drawings into your ideal woodshop.

Selecting a contractor isn't that simple. The building process is complex and expensive so you must be certain that it will go according to your stated objectives and budgetary limits.

- If you don't know of a reliable contractor, ask friends and colleagues for their recommendations.
- Watch for any remodeling work being done in your own area. Pay attention to any signage on trucks or yard signs. Ask the homeowner if they are satisfied with the work being done.
- Inquire at local lumber yards, building supply centers and hardware stores for recommendations.
- Check with local builders or trade associations.
- Ask all potential contractors for references and photographs of their work. Note: It's easy to have photos of any attractive project. Check photos for images of the contractor, the company's sign, some sort of indication the work was actually done by the person showing the photos.
- Once you have selected a contractor, talk with him concerning recommendations for subcontractors.
- Indirect recommendations often occur after several unrelated sources recommend the same person.
- A personal note: I don't like contractors' advertisements with only a telephone number listed. I want to see a street address or at least a city name.

a woodshop, the electrical wiring and plumbing are often undervalued. It is not uncommon to see that the one or two existing outlets in the garage or basement are overused with extension cords and extension bars. If there is a laundry sink or toilet already in the garage or basement, it is usually left as is. Wouldn't it seem to be much smarter to upgrade both the electrical systems and plumbing while designing the woodshop?

Wiring the Shop

The importance of having a proper electrical service cannot be overstated. First, I advise against using very long

extension cords. Not only do they create more floor clutter, but long extension cords can lead to unnecessary electrical motor wear. A representative from an air compressor company once told me that the majority of compressors returned for motor repairs were those that were used with extension cords. Apparently, owners forgot that longer air hoses were a better way to work at a distance from the compressor. I have one retractable ceiling-mounted extension cord in my woodshop. It's 30'-long 14/3 SJT wire and rated at 13A, 125V, 1,625 watts. I only use it with hand drills, finish sanders and similar tools. I would never use it for band saws and other stationary machines.

The placement of machines relative to the proper outlet is fundamental. If you want to use the table saw at a particular location, then having an isolated 110V or 220V outlet at that location is mandatory. Since this section is about guidelines for designing the woodshop, the key factors are: wiring from an existing service panel (interior or exterior to the wall), installing a subpanel, outlet locations and location of lights.

Interior wiring is difficult when the wall studs and ceiling rafters are already covered. The standard technique is to cut holes in the wall or ceiling and "fish" the new wires in place using a fish tape tool. New wiring that is not within walls should be run through metal conduits that are firmly attached to the walls. If the room framework is still exposed, it's straightforward to run wiring through the studs, around windows and door frames to the service. Subpanels are a very good choice when upgrading the woodshop. They are easily mounted near the main service panel, and conduit can then be routed anywhere in the woodshop.

The design of the outlets should accommodate both the placement of machines and the use of electrical tools at various locations. There should be outlets near both ends and at the center of the workbench, as well as outlets near the open areas in the woodshop that can be used for assembly and detail work. For example, you have constructed a 3'-wide by 7'-high bookcase and want to use a router for detail work on its sides. If the bookcase is set on the workbench, it may be too high for safe and easy work. If the bookcase is on the floor in an assembly area, the work height is correct. An overhead outlet or outlet about three feet from the floor will facilitate the router's use.

Shop Plumbing Concerns

The same generalities apply to plumbing. Is plumbing necessary in a woodshop? From a design viewpoint, if form and function are considered, the question is, "What value does plumbing serve?" What I value in a woodshop sink, besides washing my hands, is that it permits me to maintain waterstones for sharpening, mix dyes and water-soluble finishes, clean the HVLP spray gun and nozzle, clean restoration projects and use the new polyurethane glues. All of which are necessities. Warning: If there is a sink in the woodshop, don't use it to dispose of toxic solvents, flammable liquids and other hazardous wastes. Water, soap, dirt and grime are the only things that should go down the drain.

Garage and basement woodshops are often near laundry rooms. This proximity permits the addition of new water pipes to the woodshop area. Copper and PVC pipes are fairly easy to work with and it shouldn't be too complicated to route pipes several feet to the woodshop. If you aren't sure about cutting into water pipes, call a plumbing contractor for assistance. Undoubtedly, he can do the work faster than a woodworker!

Once the electrical system and plumbing needs have been determined, add these elements to the master plan and draw them onto the planning grid. Hopefully, the proposed design will accommodate all of these elements.

A SUMMARY OF THE WOODSHOP DESIGN PROCESS

1. Create a master plan of all the key woodshop elements: machines, tools, workbench, open areas, lumber racks, storage, electrical and plumbing.
2. Be realistic, as much as possible, and know your own personal interests.
3. Be somewhat hypothetical in choosing the woodshop elements. At this point you haven't spent any money.
4. Make paper mock-ups of different woodshop layouts.
5. Be reasonable. Understand that a woodshop takes time and money to create and that you can proceed at your own pace of acquisition.
6. Always consider alternatives. Buy inexpensive, resell and buy more expensive. Consider multipurpose machines. Consider hand tools instead of power tools.

CHAPTER 7

CHOOSING THE RIGHT SHOP LOCATION

The ideal woodshop location is the location that you already have. If I could make a wish, like most woodworkers, I would have a separate building with 2,000 square feet, high ceilings, skylights,

one or two windows with views of rivers and mountains, an oversize door (maybe even a garage door), wood flooring, heating and air conditioning, plumbing with sinks and a toilet, sound-insulated walls and a smaller secondary room for office needs and for displaying the things I've made.

Setting wishes aside, I know that I do have a woodshop for woodworking. And that is perhaps the the most important reality. In fact, this realization should always be the main consideration in the quest for the ideal woodshop. If you have a location or space that is usable, ask yourself which is more important — the woodshop or the things that you make? It's easy to be distracted by pinup pictures of fancy or well-appointed woodshops. What is more difficult to see in the coffee-table woodshop book pictures is that the ideal woodshop is really nothing more than the woodshop that is your own, where you can happily practice your woodworking. You can always improve on fixtures, storage and so on, but those things can evolve as you do your woodworking.

Most of us use the garage or basement for our woodshops. Sometimes,

if we are doing less messy work, we might be able to use a second bedroom or part of the laundry room, but the rooms with the most space for a shop are garages and basements. However, organizing a garage or basement is not necessarily a simple task. Garages are storage tunnels, and basements are storage holes. Room proportions and construction materials differ, and

the use of either room means displacing specific home utility functions.

THE GARAGE SHOP

Typically, garages are for one or two cars; this translates into approximately 10' × 20' (200 square feet) for one car and about 20' × 20' (400 square feet) for two cars. Garages usually have a garage door, a door into the house and a window. They can also have wall-mounted cabinets, a water heater, a built-in vacuum system for the house, a laundry and overhead storage in attic or open rafters. Garages in newer houses are generally framed but can also be constructed of concrete blocks or brick.

This is the view from my woodshop. I am surrounded by a forest of Douglas fir, Western red cedar and hemlock trees.

Let me create a hypothetical garage for the sake of solving a space-utilization problem and designing a woodshop. Imagine a two-car garage in which cars are parked at night. In addition, the garage is also used to store bicycles, sports equipment and garden tools. It has one window on a side wall, a door into the house and a door to the outside. Other noteworthy features include open rafters, one 4' × 5' wall-hung cabinet, the house electrical service panel, one overhead light and AC outlets on three walls.

Because the car is destined to remain in the garage for a certain number of hours each day, only the walls and the overhead areas can be used for permanent storage. These storage areas will determine the actual design and composition of the woodshop. Remember, even though the car will be outside when machines are placed in the open central area, all equipment must be returned to the wall areas or ceiling when the car is parked inside.

Begin by making a list of all permanent storage: household items, sports equipment and so on. Next, make a list of woodworking machines, tools and supplies that you own and also a list of things you plan on acquiring. Now, using ¼" graph paper, draw a floor plan of the garage, including doors, windows and steps (use ¼" = 1'). On a separate sheet of graph paper, using the same scale, draw all machines, cabinets and storage containers that you want in the woodshop (or use the icons found on the next page). Cut these drawings out, and place them on the graphed drawing of your garage floor plan to experiment with spatial arrangement, as shown on page 32.

The results of your graphing might look something like what you see above. Use the chart on this page as a quick reference for typical dimensions and areas of woodshop tools and other items.

Now, if you were to place all the items listed in the chart at left, you

Jon Magill converted his garage into a woodshop, and two of the car bays are used for woodworking. When the cars are parked outside, mobile machines and portable workstations are moved into their locations. There is ample open area for most construction projects.

This woodshop is permanently set up in a garage. Note the skylights, indirect lights, air filtration box and the location of the workbench relative to the permanent wall with the storage/countertop area.

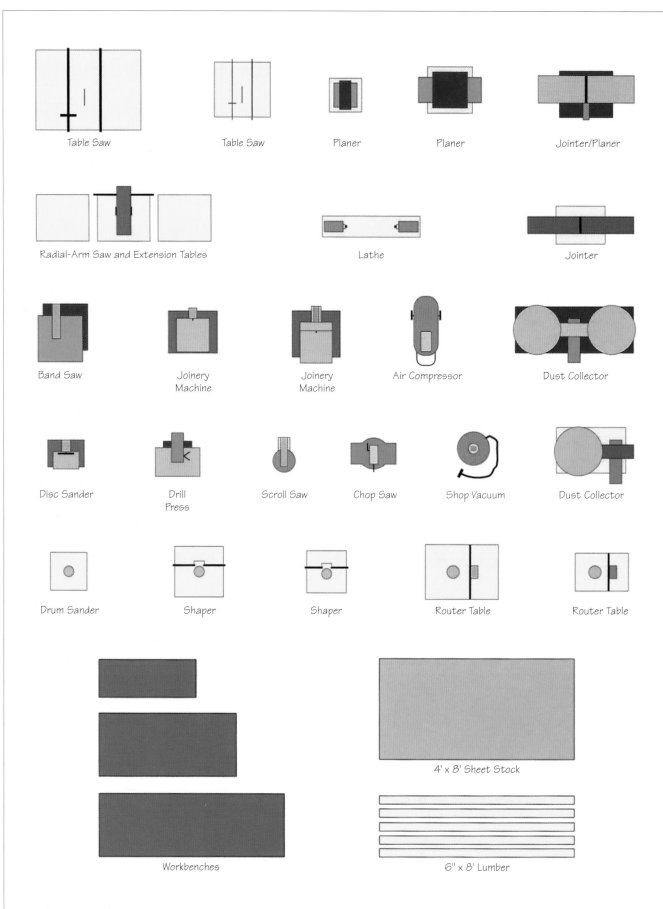

Table Saw Table Saw Planer Planer Jointer/Planer

Radial-Arm Saw and Extension Tables Lathe Jointer

Band Saw Joinery Machine Joinery Machine Air Compressor Dust Collector

Disc Sander Drill Press Scroll Saw Chop Saw Shop Vacuum Dust Collector

Drum Sander Shaper Shaper Router Table Router Table

4' x 8' Sheet Stock

Workbenches 6" x 8' Lumber

Scale ¼" = 1'. Use ¼" grid paper and copies of these icons to create woodshop layout arrangements.

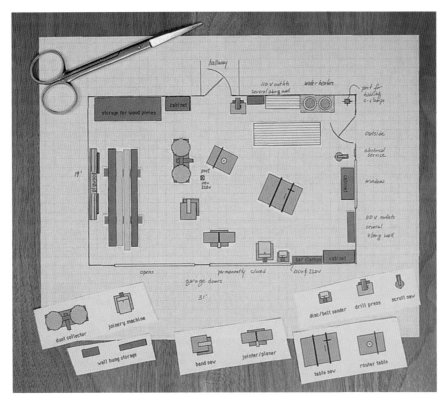

Use the icons on page 31 and lay out your shop on ¼" grid paper.

Typical Dimensions and Areas

ITEM	DIMENSION	AREA (SQ. FT.)
Car	6'×15'	90
Household storage	2'×5'	10
Sports equipment	2'×6'	12
Garden tools	1'×4'	4
Tool cabinet #1	2'×4'	8
Tool cabinet #2	2'×5'	10
Workbench	3'×6'	18
Table saw	4'×4'	16
Band saw	3'×3'	9
Drill press	2'×2'	4
Jointer	1'×4'	4
Planer	2'×2'	4
Dust collector	2'×3'	6
Lumber storage	2'×8'	16

would have 211 sq. ft. of tools and other objects. But the garage has only 200 sq. ft. of space. Obviously, there is less area available than the floor area required when the car is inside. Judicious wall and overhead storage is necessary to open up the woodshop area. So begin by rethinking the common ideas of storage. Consider ripping out the garage cabinet furnished by the house builders. Don't anticipate using secondhand bookcases, old kitchen cabinets, inexpensive metal shelvings or any other combination of odds and ends, and resist the urge to build new cabinets and storage units until you are reasonably certain of your needs and requirements. Sacrifice all of these things in the name of efficiency. In fact, the best approach might be to develop an overall plan that unifies the entire room using a design that incorporates both house and woodshop items. This plan might include floor-to-ceiling storage units near the garage door consisting of broom-type cabinets for storing rakes and shovels, with compartments for flower pots, located beside cabinets for storing skis and tennis rackets with drawers for storing camping supplies. Similar built-in units could be used for tools and supplies. Specialized features would allow for a lumber rack, a workbench and a clamp rack. Add mobile bases to your machines so they can be stored against the walls and easily moved to the center area when the car is parked outside. This unified design might even create enough open space so that some work (not machine work) can be done at the workbench even when the car is inside. Once there is a workable layout, the details of flooring, wall insulation, electrical service, lighting, ventilation and security can be addressed.

Flooring

If the garage floor is cracked, rough or oil-stained, it should be cleaned, repaired or reconditioned before any other remodeling. Cracked or rough concrete floors make it difficult to move machines and construction projects. Casters are generally too small to roll over wide cracks and mobile bases may not work well on rough or uneven floors. Engine-oil stains, besides being ugly, will contaminate wood and shoes.

There are several options for restoring, repairing or resurfacing concrete floors.

- Remove oil and grease stains with liquid degreaser or have the floor steam cleaned.
- Use concrete patching compounds to patch chips and holes. Cracks should be thoroughly cleaned and then filled with concrete repair caulk or patching compound.
- If the floor is too rough, consult with a floor finishing company that specializes in applying smooth surface coats.
- Consider alternative flooring materials: rubberized tile squares, wood tile squares, vinyl flooring, epoxy floor paint, solid wood tongue-and-groove strips or planks, and wood-composition tongue-and-groove strips.

Walls

Insulating a garage makes it more energy efficient and helps moderate ambient temperature. Insulation also acts as a sound barrier and reduces machine noise to the inside of the house or externally to the neighbor's house.

If the garage is already finished with wallboard, you will have to make a remodeling decision. One choice would be to remove the wallboard, install insulation between the studs and replace the wallboard. Alternatives to this approach include:

- Hiring an insulating company to drill holes in the wall for blowing insulation into the wall cavities.
- Attaching solid or rigid insulation board (sometimes referred to as *blueboard*) with a vapor barrier directly to the existing wallboard and then covering it with new wallboard (note: this extends the walls outward about 1½").
- Covering the existing walls with plywood or pegboard and painting them with fire-retardant paint.
- Weatherstripping both interior and exterior doors.
- Insulating the garage door. Be aware that this is not as easy as insulating walls. If the garage door is solid construction, solid insulation board might be attached to it. But don't make the door too heavy. Check with garage door companies

A SIMPLE FLOOR COVERING

Here's a rather crafty and simple floor covering: First tear large, irregular pieces of kraft paper. Lay those pieces on the bare concrete and brush on several coats of polyure-thane varnish. The result is a warm-colored floor that is also sealed and easy to clean.

regarding appropriate door weight and other methods of insulation.

Electrical Service and Wiring

Not having adequate electrical power in a woodshop is like having a sports car without gasoline. No matter how fine the woodworking machines or how sophisticated the lighting, unless the electrical service is specifically designed for the woodshop, you might as well whittle with a pocketknife. Not only do machines require adequate power for operation, but it is unsafe to use any electrical tool with an inadequate power supply. Underpowered electrical tools will wear out faster, as well as being potential fire hazards.

Typically, the electrical service panel for a house is located in the garage. This makes it easy to check the panel for service voltage to the house and determine whether there are unused circuits. If circuits are available, they can be dedicated to the garage woodshop. For example, if there are three 20-amp breaker circuits not in use, one could be used for lighting, another for the table saw and the third for outlets for hand power tools. An alternative option is to install a second electrical panel that is separate from the house electrical service, often referred to as a subpanel. The subpanel consists of circuit breakers dedicated to the woodshop. Subpanels are relatively easy to install; however, call a licensed electrician if you have any reservations about your ability to handle the installation.

Almost as important as adequate electrical power is the location of the electrical outlets. There is consensus among woodworkers that outlets should be everywhere in the room, including the ceiling. My suggestion is to first design the location of cabinets, the workbench and machines, and then determine the location of outlets. There should be outlets at either end of the workbench and approximately 5' apart around the open walls. And don't forget to place several outlets at overhead locations near the work-

INSULATION R-VALUES

All insulation types are rated with numbers called an R-value, which have been established by the U. S. Department of Energy for walls, floors and ceilings in different climate zones in the United States. Some manufacturers of insulation recommend R-values higher than the Department of Energy's recommendations. These higher R-value recommendations are usually based on the concept that more insulation is more energy efficient. Obviously, woodshops in Santa Monica, California, require less insulation than woodshops in Milwaukee, Wisconsin. Check with your local insulation suppliers to determine the correct R-values for your specific climate zone.

If you don't want machine sounds blasting through the garage door, drape sound insulation (and fireproof) curtains in front of the garage door. Or use manufactured garage doors made with insulation materials.

bench. Some woodworkers prefer having all outlets approximately 4' from the floor, others prefer lower outlets so that the cords aren't suspended in the air.

Why so many outlets? It's simple: so you can avoid potentially annoying electrical tool scenarios. If there are too few outlets in the woodshop area, you will either be constantly plugging and unplugging AC cords while you work, or you will be tempted to use extension cords with multiple sockets which could potentially damage your tools because the correct voltage is not being supplied.

It's better to have outlets at the ends of a workbench so that power cords are near you and away from the work area. Electrical cords positioned over a workbench can easily smear wet glue and scatter glue bottles, screws and smaller tools as you work with a tool and drag the cord back and forth. AC cords on a workbench also can be accidentally cut or damaged by belt sanders, routers and jigsaws. Finally, an adequate number of outlets means less opportunity for cords to become tangled or to be a problem for foot travel.

Electrical wiring in unfinished basements is simplified if the joists are exposed and there is no ceiling. Finished basements will require remodeling to locate and place new wiring. The type of wiring and conduit used will vary with different building codes. Generally, wiring is routed through the joists and installed in conduit when the wires are routed down the wall surfaces. I would suggest that you select conduit that, while meeting code requirements, is also tough enough to resist being bumped by lumber and other heavy objects. I had electrical contractors install wiring and lights in my woodshop in Syracuse, New York. They drilled holes in the joists and installed Romex cables from the subpanel to both the lights and the 110V and 220V outlet locations. Rigid conduit was used from the top of the basement wall to the outlet location.

Installing Adequate Lighting

Very often lighting is set up haphazardly; that is, the local hardware store will have a sale on 4'-long fluorescent lights and so these become the woodshop lights. Attached to rafters, they are turned on via a pull string. While this does produce light, there are better approaches.

The lighting possibilities for garage woodshops are more numerous than those for basements because of the ease of access to natural light through walls, the ceiling and the garage door. If the garage window is too small, it can be removed and replaced with a larger one.

The simplest replacement types are manufactured windows which are available in many sizes and types. If the garage has open rafters, it's easy to install skylights. Skylights offer wonderful lighting with a quality unlike any artificial lighting. Natural light makes the color of finishing products easier to identify and use, both on and off wood. And during the winter months, the psychological lift of working in sunlight is extremely positive.

Adding windows to garage doors is fairly straightforward. If the garage door is articulated, with frame and panel construction, some of the panels can be removed and replaced with either safety glass, acrylic or Plexiglas. I advise against using standard window glass because garage doors are easily bumped and the opening and closing process usually includes some sort of impact.

House contractors usually install little more than a single bulb with

GARAGE WOODSHOP SECURITY

Fear and worry are two different human conditions. Fear is a natural reaction to a terrible and immediate situation. Worry is self-manufactured nervousness. Secure your garage woodshop with common sense. There are a number of devices and procedures to keep everything safe: installing door locks and dead bolts; closing doors and windows; installing machine on/off switch locks; shutting off the circuit breakers to the woodshop; maintaining a low profile and minimizing noise (unwanted advertising); knowing your neighbors; not loaning tools; keeping fire extinguishers and first aid kits handy; and keeping a list of emergency telephone numbers near the telephone.

an on/off pull string in basements. Which, of course, is totally wrong for a woodshop. If the basement ceiling is finished, it's tempting to retrofit lights onto the ceiling surface. Although this is easy to accomplish, the effect is a lowered ceiling, which hinders your efforts to move long or tall objects. Consider recessed lights in finished ceilings; if the basement ceiling is unfinished, install 4' or 8' fluorescent lights between ceiling joists.

Garage Shop Ventilation

Fresh air is of paramount importance in a woodshop. Not only do you require clean air for breathing, but air that is too wet, dry, dusty or stale affects the quality of the woodworking project. Poor air causes finishes not to adhere or set up properly. Wet air causes wood to expand (and later shrink when moved to a drier area), as well as rust and stain tools and machines. Stale air contains assorted pollutants that affect wood, tools, finishes — and woodworkers.

The simplest ventilation system is windows and doors. However, some caution is in order. Open windows and doors lead to a degree of interaction with the outside world. Noise and dust will leave the shop and visit the neighborhood. Bugs seem to quickly find open shop doors and may bite you, leave tracks on freshly varnished surfaces or burrow into stacks of wood and lay millions of eggs. Open windows and doors also broadcast the fact that you are a woodworker. While this may be a good form of advertising, you may not want to tell the world that you have expensive tools and machines.

If a ventilation system is deemed a worthy investment for both woodworking and health reasons, it's prudent to consult with ventilation specialists. A system should be designed to bring a continuous flow of fresh air into the shop and to filter the exhausted air. This type of ventilation system is usually designed for specific shops — there are no off-the-shelf sys-

To heat this woodshop, a small gas furnace has been placed in the corner.

tems available. A basic unit will cost between $1,000 and $2,000.

If you decide to install a ventilation fan unit, the type found in most home improvement centers, there are a few cautions. Be certain that the fan motor is explosion-proof and dust-proof. Solvents such as lacquer thinner, alcohol, acetone and paint thinner are very flammable. When these solvents become fumes and are airborne, they are still flammable. It is very dangerous to vent fumes through a fan motor that could spark or that is not made for venting flammable solvents. Fine dust is also highly flammable and potentially explosive, so enclosed motors that are designed for use around dust should be used.

Also consider that when cold outside air is brought into the shop, the warm inside air is exhausted. If the woodshop is heated, that means higher heating bills due to the constant loss of warm air as it is vented from the shop.

In this day and age, you simply cannot vent fumes and dust into the outside environment without some

repercussions. Even home woodshops must — or should — abide by community air quality directives and laws. Furthermore, neighbors generally are not tolerant of noise, dust and clouds of fumes invading their space.

Heating the Garage Woodshop

Heating the woodshop is a difficult issue. Working in a warm room is often thought of as a luxury because heating units are potentially dangerous around woodworking solvents and materials and because a separate heating unit or system is thought of as too expensive. If you live in a warm climate, heating the woodshop might not be necessary. However, a warm, dry woodshop will stabilize humidity, thus keeping lumber at a constant moisture content; the warm air will also help prevent rust. Always check local building codes and with your local fire department regarding the installation of heating units in the woodshop.

THE BASEMENT SHOP

For many years I had basement woodshops, and I can say that although there were many good things about the location, there were also many disadvantages. However, the basement is a reasonable woodshop location, especially when cars, boats and motorcycles are parked in the garage.

There are many benefits to the basement shop. First, the basement woodshop that is accessed through the house is generally more secure and less apparent to the outside world than a garage. Noise isn't as likely to bother the neighbors. Basement woodshops are warmer during the winter months, and it is both easy and comfortable to work in a basement woodshop at any time of day. For example, on especially hot summer days, basements offer a wonderful escape from the heat. Since there are no large windows and doors, there can be generous amounts of wall storage. Unlike a garage, which is constantly used for storage and foot

travel, the basement is somewhat out of the main pathways and can usually be sealed off by closing a single door.

The main problems with basement woodshops are access, stairs, overhead height, ventilation, noise and dust. Moving lumber, heavy machines and finished constructions in and out of basements can be difficult because of basement stairs, hallways, corners, doors and less-than-straight-line pathways to the basement. Moving heavy objects can be further complicated by floor-to-ceiling heights, especially in stairways and around heating ducts, pipes, lights and other overhead projections.

Basement Shop Access

A typical basement might be accessed from the kitchen, often via a hallway and several doors from the garage. If you plan on using lumber, the transportation of that lumber to the basement may well cause serious family discussions! Carrying a single 10' board can easily damage doors and door frames, floor mouldings, walls, shelving, cabinets, picture frames, carpets, windows, lamps, lights and kitchen counters (along with everything on them). It's no wonder that some woodworkers have a radial arm saw in the garage for cutting boards into shorter lengths before moving them to the basement.

Installing Doors

One option for basement access is to install an exterior bulkhead hatch or cellar door. If your basement already has a cellar door, then you are set. However, if you are considering the installation of one, several factors must be considered. The cellar door requires its own foundation, normally to the same depth as the basement. That means that a hole approximately 8' × 8' × 10' will need to be dug, which may compromise existing drainage systems. The cellar door area should not interfere with plumbing pipes and electrical cables, and it should be placed where the grade is the lowest and slopes away from the foundation of the house.

Bulkheads are easier to install if your basement is constructed of cinder block, brick or stone. I considered having a bulkhead installed in our basement. Because the basement walls were solid concrete, I consulted a cellar door specialist. He said the job would not be a problem, but as we proceeded to discuss details a few red flags appeared. It would be necessary to use diamond saws to score the concrete, and both the sawing and the subsequent sledgehammer work would produce volumes of fine dust that would travel throughout the house. We decided that the work area could be isolated with plastic sheeting, but I wasn't thrilled with the idea of concrete dust floating around my stationary machines (downstairs) or my wife's kitchen (upstairs). However, what finally killed the project was that the contractor told me to remove all hanging lamps and wall-hung items from the entire house. When I asked why, he replied that the basement walls were about 12 years old and well-hardened and that the sledgehammer work would not only rattle the entire house but also pop out drywall nails throughout it. That did it. Since I wasn't willing to renail, replaster and repaint all the upstairs rooms, I decided that I could do without an outside entrance to the basement.

Reducing Irritants in the Basement Shop

It takes a very tolerant family to live with machinery noise just below their feet. The constant sound of dust collectors, the screaming sound of routers and the high-pitched whine of table saws all will travel throughout the house. Another invasive woodshop material is dust. Even when using dust collectors, dust seems to migrate to the furthest areas of the house. Fumes and odors from finishes also can permeate an entire house. Noise, dust and fumes are not the sorts of things most people want to have in their home.

Basement Shop Ventilation

Air in a basement woodshop can be damp, dry or stale. Humidity, dust, finishing fumes, mold, mildew, air circulation and ventilation all are related problems in the basement woodshop. The typical basement is more humid during the spring and summer months when the furnace isn't used; when the furnace is used, the basement dries. This alternating cycle of humidity and dryness will affect lumber and joinery by either swelling or shrinking the wood. The only effective method of moderating this cycle is to adequately moderate the air quality. Typically, the things that can be done are to cover sump pump holes, seal basement walls with sealers and basement paints, provide good air ventilation from the outside (windows and fans) and operate dehumidifiers all year long.

TIRED OF WORKING IN A GRAY BASEMENT?

Do you have a basement woodshop with bare concrete walls and are you tired of the drab bomb shelter look? First brush and clean the concrete or masonry walls. If there is efflorescence, that is, a powdery substance, it is likely that moisture is seeping through the wall. Wire brush the efflorescence. It may be further necessary to clean the walls with muriatic acid (carefully follow the product's instructions) or an etching compound, which is usually safer than muriatic acid. If water is seeping through cracks or seams, seal them with a hydraulic cement. After the walls are cleaned and sealed, apply a waterproofer, such as UGL Drylok Waterproofer. This type of waterproofer is a thick paint-like material which is brushed on. It is usually available in white, but it is also available in a limited number of other colors.

One other note, if there is basement moisture and water seepage, check the outside foundation areas for how the water is percolating into the basement. Look at the condition of rain gutters, the grade angle of the soil next to the house, and poorly functioning drainage pipes. Repair the problem.

CHAPTER 8

EXAMINING REAL WOODSHOPS

It's impossible to find representative woodshops that reveal all the mysteries of setting up a woodshop. Each of the shops that I have visited is unique and represents the owner's personality

and woodworking style. The quest for the perfect woodshop really begins and ends with each person's own effort. And while it's enjoyable to peek into another woodshop, often the only transferable items are bits and pieces of problem-solving. We seem to have a collective desire to construct "model cities," "dream houses" and "ideal workshops," but the reality is that these places are curiosities. Anyone remember the futuristic cities of the 1939 New York World's Fair, Disneyland's House of the Future or General Electric's 1960s All-Electric House? The point is, while we idealize a perfect woodshop, your perfect woodshop is right in front of you — it's in the garage, the basement, the extra room, the attic or a closet. All you need to do is get started.

The following perspective is from Alan Boardman, a highly regarded, very talented woodworker and authentic expert on tools, joinery and wood. I attended his lectures on joinery and tuning up hand tools about 20 years ago and he showed me the fantastic adventure of woodworking. I now prize the small (marble-size) wooden puzzles he makes.

"Regarding the ideal woodshop, if one exists, I'll bet it is owned by someone who does no woodworking whatsoever," says Boardman. "My shop is a total disgrace and I love it. Every minute I spend wondering how to make it closer to ideal is a minute I am not enjoying working in it. My wife calls it my hellhole. It is a jumble of offcuts and boxes that I have long ago stopped wondering

what's in them. I can hardly move about in the place or swing a board or find a precious piece of rare wood I have been saving for decades for that worthy project, yet I am always happy there and never think of food or aging pains. If others think like I do, maybe the ideal shop is better described in human terms than where every machine should be placed and how to store odd nuts and bolts. Incidentally, I haven't always felt this way. I used to dream of a perfect shop. But now that I am retired and theoretically have the time to redo it, I find that I don't want to. I like it the way it is."

The woodshops shown in this chapter can be classified into three types: the garage and basement woodshop, the separate-building woodshop on the home property and the rental-space woodshop. These example woodshops have been in existence for some time, and each of them definitely reflects the personality and style of the owner.

GARAGE AND BASEMENT WOODSHOP #1
MARK KULSETH'S WOODSHOP

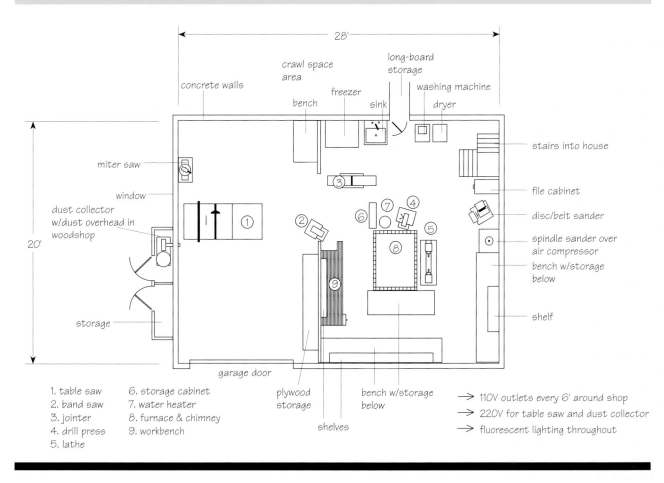

28'

concrete walls

crawl space area

long-board storage

bench

freezer

sink

washing machine

dryer

miter saw

stairs into house

window

file cabinet

dust collector w/dust overhead in woodshop

disc/belt sander

20'

spindle sander over air compressor

bench w/storage below

shelf

storage

garage door

plywood storage

shelves

bench w/storage below

1. table saw
2. band saw
3. jointer
4. drill press
5. lathe

6. storage cabinet
7. water heater
8. furnace & chimney
9. workbench

→ 110V outlets every 6' around shop
→ 220V for table saw and dust collector
→ fluorescent lighting throughout

Mark Kulseth has been using his woodshop for about five years. His woodshop is in a single-car garage and the adjacent laundry and storage areas in a 64-year-old house. His woodshop measures 20' × 28' (560 square feet). It is wired from the main house electrical service for both 110V and 220V use. Additionally, some areas of the woodshop have a floor-to-ceiling height of 6' 5". Mark is a part-time professional whose main woodworking interests are making custom furniture and some repairs and restorations. He also collects antique tools.

While there is little free space in Mark's woodshop, he has maximized the existing floor and wall areas so well that he can build standard-size cabinets and furniture.

His principal machinery (in order of importance) includes:

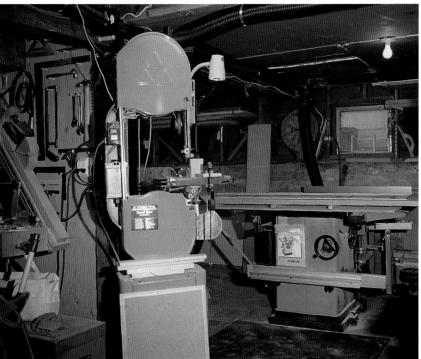

Mark Kulseth has an older home with a single-car garage attached to the laundry room and storage area. The table saw is located near the back wall of garage.

- 10" Delta Unisaw with 52" fence and outfeed table
- 14" Delta band saw with riser block
- 20" Jet drill press
- Delta 6" × 48" belt sander
- 12"-disc sanding machine
- Jet 1200 CFM dust collector
- Walker-Turner lathe
- traditionally designed workbench

If Mark had more floor space he would add a wide-belt sanding machine, a downdraft sanding table and a 5' square work surface that is accessible from all four sides.

There are several nifty features to Mark's woodshop: He has grouped benches and tools around the furnace and chimney, has displayed plumb bobs from under the stairs, has a hidden storage area for lumber and has combined built-in bench tops/cabinet storage and shelves for antique tools. When I first visited his woodshop I was taken with how Mark has stored tools and stuff in every conceivable location — between rafters, behind walls and suspended in corners. My thought was that if he ever moved to another woodshop, he would need significant cabinet storage to handle all of the tucked-away items hidden in his woodshop. He should also use a metal detector to be certain that nothing is left behind!

Safety is important in Mark's work. He says that he has learned from the mistakes of others and he always wears eye and hearing protection. There is a first aid box and three fire extinguishers in the woodshop. Also, flammable and combustible materials are kept in a metal locker. Rags are rinsed in water, air-dried and then placed in a small metal garbage can inside the woodshop.

I believe that woodworkers who work in confined areas, as Mark does, often develop a keen sense of what situations are best for ideal working conditions. Mark said that if he could design his ideal woodshop, he would have "a woodshop with ample space, wood floors, tall ceilings and maybe

Kulseth's woodshop with countertop area and shelf storage. Mark plans to install cabinet doors in the near future. Note that the spindle sander sits on the box that houses the air compressor.

Kulseth's woodshop and more countertop and shelving for antique tools.

a separate finishing room and office, free of dust. But more than anything, I would love a shop built in a natural setting, away from the city, with mountain views, trees, a river and so on. To do this, I must have the business demands for my products."

Mark sees a relationship between himself, his woodshop and his woodworking skills: "I try to make my shop reflect my personality and skills as a craftsman. If I'm making a tool rack, I make it with care and pride to show my skills. It makes it much more enjoyable to view my tools. I also collect antique tools and many are displayed in my work area. I often reflect on the craftsmen of old while trying to solve my building problems. This reflection seems to inspire a higher quality in my craft."

Mark Kulseth uses the underside of his staircase to display his plumb bob collection.

Mark Kulseth stores his antique plane collection above his workbench. An angled hold-down device is in the foreground.

A crawl space (hidden behind the chart in the photograph) is actually a large area for storing lumber.

GARAGE AND BASEMENT WOODSHOP #2
DAVID BEYL'S WOODSHOP

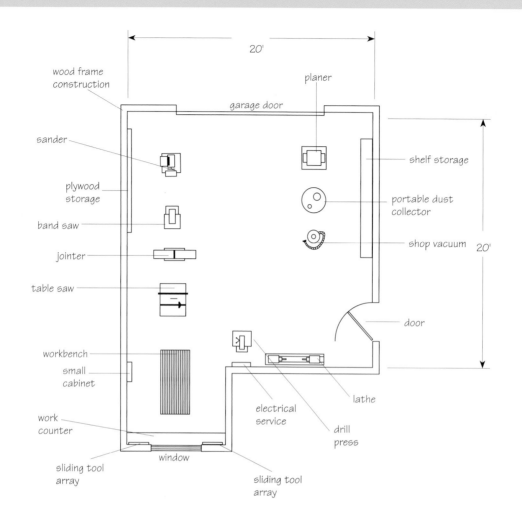

20'

wood frame construction

planer

garage door

sander

shelf storage

plywood storage

portable dust collector

band saw

shop vacuum

20'

jointer

table saw

door

workbench

small cabinet

work counter

lathe

electrical service

drill press

window

sliding tool array

sliding tool array

David Beyl's woodshop was a two-car garage. The house is 27 years old and David has had the woodshop for 13 years. It measures 20' × 20', with an 8' ceiling. It has a subpanel with both 110V and 220V wiring. David is a part-time professional who specializes in building furniture, repairing antiques and teaching woodworking. He spends about 20 hours a week in the woodshop. His principal machinery (in order of importance) includes:

- 10" Delta cabinetmaker's saw
- 6" Jet jointer
- 14" Delta band saw
- 12" disc, 6" × 48" belt sander
- 16" Delta radial drill press
- 12" Shopsmith planer

David Beyl has a two-car garage woodshop. To maximize space, there are numerous sliding panels mounted in front of the windows.

- Shopsmith dust collector
- 14" Delta scroll saw
- Campbell-Hausfeld air compressor
- 12" Delta lathe

David's woodshop is 20' × 20' feet, that is, a square floor pattern with almost no nooks or crannies. Interestingly, David's concept of woodworking seems to match the straightforward woodshop layout. He's somewhat of a minimalist and only has tools and machines that he uses. Nothing more, nothing less. The simplicity of the woodshop also lends itself to teaching woodworking. Students aren't working in clutter, and they are learning to use the basic machinery in a clean and straightforward woodshop environment.

Just because David has identified his woodworking style and woodshop arrangement doesn't mean that he wouldn't improve his woodshop. If he remodeled the woodshop he would include a built-in dust collection system, recessed lighting (fluorescent and incandescent), a sink with hot water, a gas heating system, a separate office area, convenient storage and a modern-design workbench.

A feature I particularly admired was David's use of sliding tool storage partitions. These partitions are four panels that slide like sliding closet doors, except the units are wall-mounted and slide back and forth in front of a window. Slender tools such as chisels, screwdrivers, pliers and files are stored on the racks.

David Beyl's workbench, shown here, features many small drawers.

David Beyl has small cabinets which have page-like sections for holding small tools.

The David Beyl woodshop has a wood storage unit that is hinged at one end and then rolls out at the other end. This storage unit is used primarily for plywood and cut-off pieces of plywood.

GARAGE AND BASEMENT WOODSHOP #3
GEORGE LEVIN'S WOODSHOP

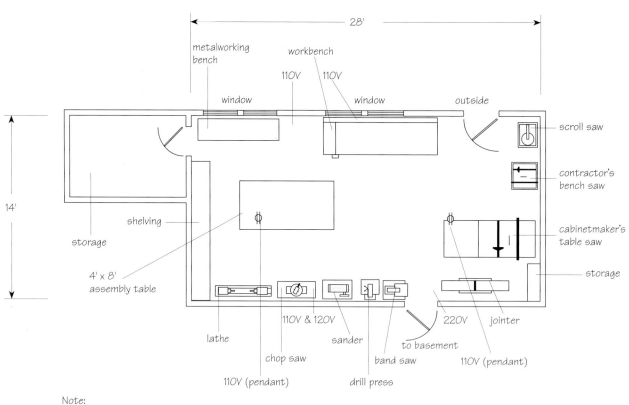

Note:
All stationary machines
(except lathe) are on casters.

George Levin's woodshop is about the size of a one-car garage. He has a beautifully designed workbench mounted against a wall.

(above left) George Levin's table saw is mounted on a shop-made mobile base.

(above right) A heavy belt sander is mounted on a shop-made mobile base. Note the customized sander fence.

George Levin's workbench and window view.

The George Levin woodshop is located at basement level with a window view and door access to the outside. The woodshop is approximately 14' × 29', it has standard-height ceiling and is equipped with 110V and 220V electrical wiring. The house is 71 years old, and George has been using the woodshop for 22 years. He considers himself to be a part-time professional and builds Federal and Deco style furniture and other built-ins. He spends about 20 hours a week in the woodshop.

His principal machinery (in order of importance) includes
- 10" Delta Unisaw
- 10" Inca Model 510 jointer/planer
- 8" Grizzly jointer
- 14" Powermatic band saw
- 10" disc, 6" Delta belt sander
- 24" Delta scroll saw
- 6" × 32" Delta (Homecraft) lathe

If there was space in the woodshop, George would have a panel saw. Also, if he could design an ideal woodshop, he would include a spray booth, large doors, plenty of windows, level access to the outside, wood

flooring, sink, toilet, dust collection system, room for wood and sheet goods storage.

George's woodshop is an elongated rectangle, and he has optimized working conditions within the space by making mobile bases for the machines. These bases are made of wood, have locking wheels, and they are both sturdy and easy to use. It is easy to roll the table saw into a more open position, use it and then return it. Another principal feature is a 4' × 8' assembly table. This table is about 24" high, and the top is a sheet of ³/₄" melamine particleboard. The table is used for stacking rough-cut pieces, for assembly and gluing of workpieces

and for finishing work. When the top surface is no longer workable, it is flipped over to access the other side. And when both sides are worn out, a new piece is installed and the old top is disposed of.

George has a spectacular workbench. Its wonderfully unique construction is a fine example of craftsmanship and represents an impressive comprehension of design. The workbench measures about 3' × 12' and it is mounted against a wall. Looking at the front, the right-side half is composed of two rows of drawers that have customized pockets for hand tools; the left side is an open area, usually filled with large sleeping dogs. There is only one metal vise, mounted on the left-front edge and it has an adjustable companion holder (workpiece support) that can be located on any of the four vertical bench supports. Instead of the typical bench dogs, the bench top has a metal track perpendicular to the vise. An adjustable stop slides in the track so that various width boards can be easily secured. Other details include a narrow tool tray located along the entire back edge, and the top surface material is hardboard. When the hardboard wears out, it is unscrewed, removed and then replaced with new hardboard.

George has a sense of humor and his woodshop reflects his personal view of things. In a way, his woodshop is a collage of bits and pieces of personal history, world events, successes of children and just fun stuff. A plain storage cabinet is totally covered with tiny pictures of dogs, and although the cabinet contains nuts and bolts, it's referred to as the "dog cabinet." George once was an avid aviator, and so it stands to reason that the ceiling is covered with pictures of airplanes and an upside-down remote control airplane! Where most of us have machines with the manufacturer's name prominently displayed, George has covered his band saw with vacation pictures, quotes and other less commercial concepts. There are numerous calendars from the 1960s, posters of long-ago lectures, old clocks and assorted keepsakes — enough interesting things to keep a smile on anyone's face. Judging by the woodshop, George Levin is a happy man. His comments about his woodshop: "This room is an extension of myself, so it contains pictures and memorabilia reflecting some of my other interests so that I really feel 'at home' when I am working there."

George Levin designed his workbench holding system which features a slot perpendicular to the vise. The slot contains a movable and lockable bench dog.

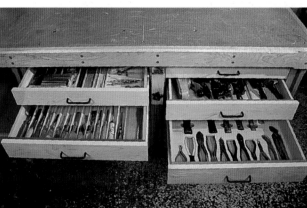

The Levin bench has drawers with custom locations for all tools.

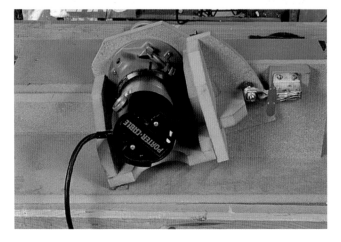

Because the Levin woodshop is small, George has many jigs and fixtures that he uses at his workbench. Shown is his mortising jig.

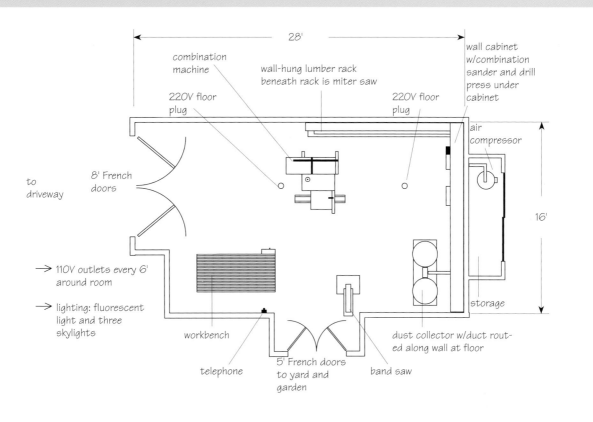

After years of working in other people's woodshops, Charles decided to build his ideal woodshop. His goal was to design a woodshop that would be on his own property and separate from the house. His house property's shape is that of a typical city lot, that is, a long and narrow rectangle. The house is an older style with the garage as a separate structure set back from the house and next to the property line. Charles removed the old garage and then designed the woodshop to look like a new garage. The exterior is reminiscent of the bungalow style, with door overhangs and clapboard siding. The major exterior feature that reveals something of the nature of the building is that Charles installed French doors instead of a garage door. Charles also built the walls with sound insulation so that the neighbors wouldn't be hearing machinery noise. From my own experiences visiting the woodshop, I had to be fairly

Here's the exterior of Caswell's shop. Note that double French doors are located where a garage door would be located.

close to it to hear the muffled sounds of a dust collector and planer being used. His soundproofing consisted of standard wall insulation between wall studs and then covering that with $1/2$" sound board. Drywall board was installed in the normal fashion and the wall was finished and painted.

Charles is a full-time professional woodworker and spends over 50 hours a week in the woodshop building furniture. His woodshop is 2 years old and has 450 square feet, 110V and 220V wiring. There are electrical outlets at convenient wall locations and 220V floor plugs near the table saw. His principal machinery (in order of importance) includes:

- 10" Robland X31 table saw with sliding table
- Robland X31 jointer/planer combination machine
- 18" Laguna band saw
- Ryobi miter saw
- AMC radial-head drill press
- Robland X31 shaper
- Robland X31 horizontal mortiser
- Grizzly belt/disc combination sander

Charles Caswell built a two-car-garage-size woodshop at the end of his driveway on a typical city lot. This interior view shows the open ceiling, skylights, lighting, main storage cabinets and machinery. Not seen, to the right side, is a traditional workbench. This woodshop is noteworthy for its straightforward layout and comfortable and uncluttered work conditions.

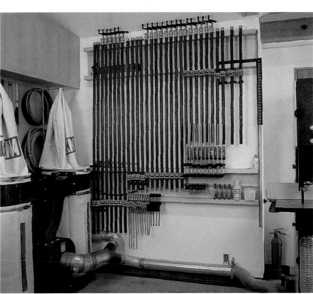

You can see here how clamps are stored in Caswell's woodshop.

Charles had a four-bag dust collector in the woodshop but he felt that the hookup at the machines was inadequate; that is, the factory-constructed fittings were ineffective at the source of dust. He also wanted a larger, more power unit, including a chip separator located in a separate space. After the first photographs of his woodshop were taken, he replaced the upper filter bags with filter bags that trap dust to the 5-micron level. This considerably reduced dust blow-back into the work area, but he still wasn't satisfied. Subsequently, he sold the four bag dust collector and all the 4" ductwork and installed a cyclone collector with 5" ductwork and a Delta ceiling hung air filtration unit. The cyclone was an immediate improvement; it is much quieter and there is now minimal dust in the shop.

Charles also has a 6-hp, 80-gallon air compressor located in a shed

behind the back wall. He doesn't consider it to be a principal tool because he uses it mostly for cleanup work. He bought the large compressor partly because of value and partly because it's quieter than the smaller "oil-less" compressors. Under normal usage it cycles on a few times a week.

The woodshop features a very comfortable bright and airy working area with an open ceiling, skylights and one 5'-wide and one 8'-wide French door. For storage, Charles built a single row of cabinets across the back wall. These cabinets are located at approximately head height and are the main storage in the woodshop. There is also a wall section with pegboard, used for oversize tools and accessories. There is lumber storage, positioned above the miter saw area, which is used for planed boards and material being prepared for the next work project.

When he first set up his woodshop, Charles made a beautiful, traditionally designed workbench. At the time, the workbench seemed like a good idea. Now that he is busy making furniture, the workbench is not used and is taking up floor space — space that he needs for other purposes. Currently, the workbench is supporting a vacuum press, and he is debating on what to do with the workbench — to sell it or put it in storage.

The woodshop reflects Charles's attitude about woodworking: It is thoughtful, organized and well crafted. He has enough tools and machinery for any work, and the room is clean and open so there's no inefficiency due to clutter and congestion. He is very content with his woodshop and would only add a warehouse area for curing and storing lumber.

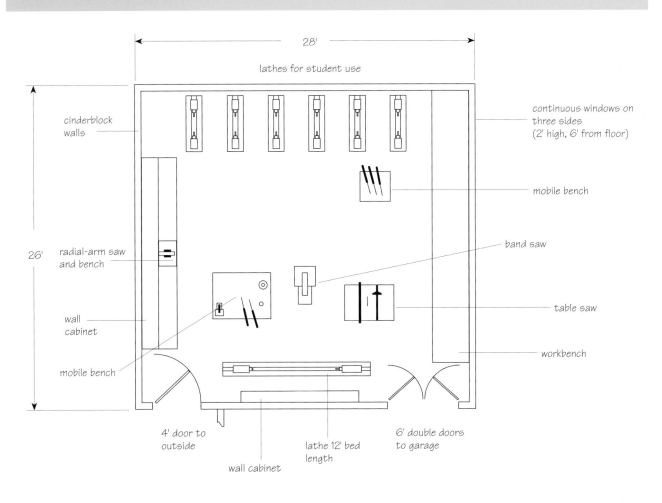

The Ted Bartholomew woodshop is one of the most unusual woodshops that I've visited. Ted's woodshop measures 26' × 28' (728 square feet) with a 9' ceiling. There is both 110V and 220V wiring. The room, built as a woodshop 20 years ago, is located next to a garage. The most noticeable feature of the room is that there are windows located 6' from the floor, continuous on three walls. These windows are 2' high, and the lighting is similar to that of skylighting. What makes the woodshop unique is that Ted is a "serious amateur" who specializes in woodturning: He manufactured his own wood lathe and likes turning large bowls. He also teaches woodturning.

There are large and small movable tables and carts for storing lathe tools

Ted Bartholomew's woodshop is attached to a two-car garage. Windows are continuous on three sides of the shop.

Ted Bartholomew's custom lathe is designed for working on either side of the machine. The portable tool storage cart is easily moved throughout the woodshop.

and accessories. His lathe features a pneumatic forward and reversing system so turning work can be done on either side of the lathe. In order to make it easy to access lathe tools, the tools are simply laid on a cart and the cart is moved to the area of work. These movable tables and carts also make it easier to work when there are several students working at the lathes. Ted is very happy with his woodshop but he would like to install a dust collecting system.

His principal machinery (in order of importance) includes:

- several Bartholomew lathes (the number varies)
- antique lathe — 4 hp, capacity of 22" overbed, 7' outboard, 12' overall
- various lathes for student work
- Walker-Turner 16" band saw
- Craftsman 10" radial-arm saw
- 10" Delta Unisaw
- drill press
- 1" belt sander

RENTAL-SPACE WOODSHOPS #1
DEAN BERSHAW'S WOODSHOP

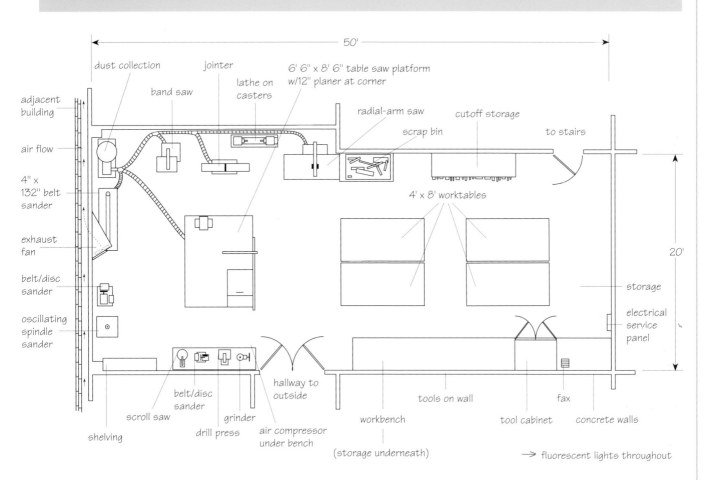

- dust collection
- jointer
- lathe on casters
- 6' 6" × 8' 6" table saw platform w/12" planer at corner
- band saw
- radial-arm saw
- cutoff storage
- scrap bin
- to stairs
- adjacent building
- air flow
- 4" × 132" belt sander
- exhaust fan
- belt/disc sander
- oscillating spindle sander
- 4' × 8' worktables
- storage
- electrical service panel
- tools on wall
- fax
- concrete walls
- hallway to outside
- scroll saw
- belt/disc sander
- grinder
- drill press
- air compressor under bench
- workbench
- tool cabinet
- shelving
- (storage underneath)
- → fluorescent lights throughout

50'
20'

Dean Bershaw is a full-time professional woodworker specializing in contemporary furniture. He has been in his current woodshop 3½ years and spends 30 to 50 hours a week there. He rents part of the basement in a commercial building that was built in the 1950s. His woodshop measures 50' × 20' (1000 square feet) with a ceiling height of 7' 8" under ceiling beams and 9' between beams. There is both 110V and 220V wiring. His principal machinery (in order of importance):

- 10" Jet 3-hp table saw
- 6" Grizzly jointer
- 12" Delta planer
- 10" Delta radial-arm saw
- 9" Grizzly disc sander
- Mark 1 drill press
- Grizzly 2-hp dust collector

Dean Bershaw's woodshop is located in the basement of a commercial building. This area is used for smaller work projects and tool storage.

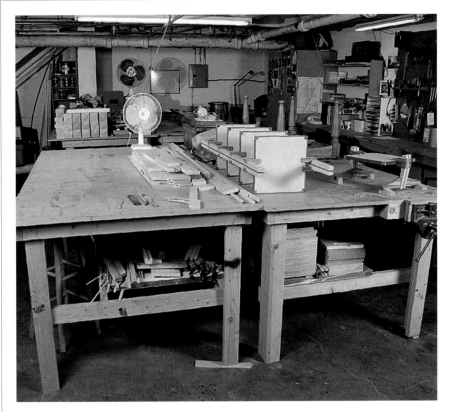

Dean Bershaw has four workstations with surfaces of 4' × 8' sheets of particleboard.

Air circulation and ventilation are critical in Dean Bershaw's basement woodshop. The only direct access to the outside is an opening to a 5" space between building walls. He built a diagonally mounted fan housing so that air could be exhausted into the narrow space between buildings.

- router table with Porter-Cable router, Incra jig fence
- 24" Windmaster fan
- Campbell-Hausfeld 6-hp, 30-gallon air compressor
- 4" × 132" Delta belt sander
- 12" Delta lathe
- Star oscillating spindle sander
- Delta sharpening center

Having a commercial operation in a concrete basement offers several challenges worth noting. Basements in industrial/commercial areas aren't necessarily the easiest locations to find. Both vendors and customers require clear instructions in order to find Dean's woodshop. Although Dean doesn't expect walk-in business, he does invite designers and buyers to visit him while projects are under construction. Other basement complications include no direct access to the outside, risk of water damage (broken/leaking pipes) and ventilation.

Dean's woodshop is in the back section of the building's basement; consequently there are no windows, doors or other vents to the outside.

However, at one time there was an opening in a wall which was later bricked in when another building was built next to that wall. Dean removed the bricks and discovered that there is a 5"-wide space between the buildings. He built an angled exhaust fan housing and installed it in front of the opening. This clever arrangement exhausts stale woodshop air into the 5" space. This fan, although it does remove residual dust particles, is not meant to be a dust collector — it is used to refresh and circulate air in the woodshop. And there are no windows on either of the walls at higher locations (i.e., no one will be bothered by exhausted woodshop air).

Although water leakage is always a worry, it has yet to happen. Preparing for such a problem, Dean has made all storage units, tables and workstations as modular units so that they are easy to move.

If Dean remodeled his woodshop, he would add a spray booth, office space and living quarters. He would include space for multiuse capabilities, such as automotive work and metalwork, and he would also add windows, higher ceilings and openings at opposite ends of the woodshop for through-circulation.

The principal factor that makes this location attractive is the rental rate. The rent is affordable, allowing him to keep his operating costs low. He is willing to compromise with ceiling height and no windows in order to be competitive. Dean realizes that time is of the essence when doing custom work. Any woodshop improvements have to serve a purpose and must not require significant amounts of time to accomplish. Dean also states: "I have bought tools for a specific job but they all have subsequent value for general-usage applications. In my view, the less specific the application, the better."

James Leary, a successful professional woodworker, does mostly house remodeling and refurbishing — without a woodshop building. Instead, he takes his woodshop with him to the job site. His large van holds all that he needs; he simply drives up and begins to work. He says that he made a design choice: He could have built custom storage within the van but decided not to. Instead, he decided to use tool cases that are specific for each power tool. His reasoning was that fixed storage is somewhat limiting. For example, if a job requires drills and reciprocating saws, but not routers and power washers, he can leave the unnecessary equipment at home. Also, the tool cases all have shapes and sizes that are easily identified for quick selection while working. And modern tool cases are easy to carry, are reasonably dustproof and water resistant and hold extra bits, blades and accessories. There is one other bonus: Customers enjoy and appreciate his readiness and thoroughness.

James Leary doesn't have the typical woodshop — his woodshop is his van. He does remodeling and general woodworking and drives his woodshop to the worksite.

Here is almost everything out of James' van.

APPLY TO YOUR OWN WOODSHOP

I have visited dozens of woodshops and they all have the basic assortment of tools, storage and such. Does having a particular brand of tools make the woodshop better? No. Does having a large space make woodworking better? Perhaps. Does personal problem-solving help make an ideal woodshop? Yes.

Although a woodcarver or someone working on small-scale projects doesn't necessarily require large areas for work, the general-purpose woodworker does benefit from having adequate space. Unfortunately, if you have 100 square feet of woodshop, you can't simply wish up another 50 square feet to make the room better. What you can do is:

- Wisely plan out the space.
- Buy appropriately sized machines.
- Have only the machines and tools that you need.
- Build storage units to fit space.
- Be happy and build things.

Even if you have more space than necessary (which hardly ever occurs), the same basic steps apply. Each of the woodshops I have featured is a

FROM THOSE THAT HAVE BUILT WOODSHOPS

"If I had only known ..." is often the start of conversations with those that have built their own woodshops. While there is universal satisfaction with the completed shops, everyone has tales of how complex or expensive the project was. I have listened to stories about wearing out too many tools, underestimating the volume of building materials and the hardships of doing heavy work without assistance. Some wished that they had planned for larger woodshops and others wished they had been less elaborate. And just like those that have woodshops in home garages or basements, these woodworkers also have wish lists — after the woodshop has been completed. "I need more space, I want to add a room for wood storage, I wish I had a sink and toilet, I should have added skylights, I didn't have enough money to ... ."

consequence of these basic steps. All of the woodworkers have adapted to the room configuration, organized the machinery and storage around their needs, and then proceeded to make furniture, turn bowls, repair antiques, collect old tools, remodel houses and lose themselves in the enjoyment, wonder and mystery of woodworking.

CHAPTER 9

BASEMENT TO SHOP CONVERSIONS

Conversions of existing space in basements are sometimes be the only way to create a practical workshop for shaping wood of any real size. Framing of basement partition walls can isolate regular basement and home spaces from sawdust and sanding dust. Entry may create some problems and may cause a

woodworker to examine project selections with great care, as changing some basement features to allow enough space for entry and exit of large projects may be totally uneconomical.

Certain tool advantages exist today, so that a wide array of individual tools, such as stationary belt sanders, table saws, band saws, radial arm saws, planers, and jointers may be easily fitted into a relatively small workspace.

Of course, the multi-tools also fit into small areas, and provide many now-classic solutions to limited shop space. With benchtop tools, there's less of a differential in price for the basic tools than there was some years ago, but overall, multi-tool advantages for small shop and limited budget needs still exist, though today the emphasis has to be more on the small shop area than before.

On a personal basis, if I had to work in a small shop area, I would select one of the 10" job-site table saws, and then select two of the benchtop tools I consider to be the most useful. For the basic shop, I'd probably stack a Palmgren 6" benchtop jointer with a 13" DeWalt 735 planer. This way, you can end up with a decent or better table saw, and three of the most useful tools you will find for a workshop. If you have the space, a small drill press completes the array. The basic three power tools, though, have a current cost of about $1,200 for a power woodworking shop of great capability, in a small space.

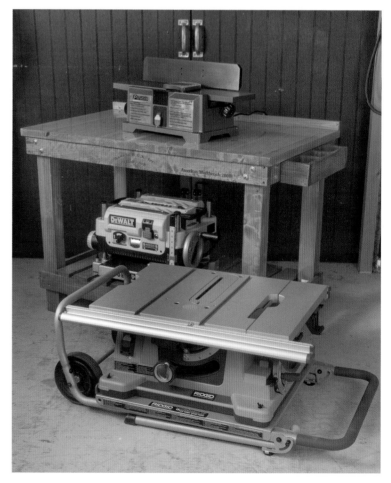

Pictured at left, the American Workbench, Palmgren 6" jointer, DeWalt 13" planer and Ridgid 10" table saw make my point about small shops. Tool selection is critical, but is easier than ever today.

Ryobi's easily-stored job-site saw is a type that has replaced junky benchtop saws for the most part. COURTESY OF RYOBI

With space conservation in mind, you begin working on your basement. Start with graph paper — or a drawing board or a drawing program on a computer — and measure the basement carefully, taking note of doglegs, lally columns, windows, current lighting, outlets, etc.

Make a rough drawing with rough dimensions and determine the basic area that you can allow for your woodworking space.

For greatest efficiency in living, as well as in working, close off the woodworking shop from the rest of the house as well as possible. That may mean installing a partition with a door or simply installing a door. If you keep noise and dust from filtering through the house, the shop stays a welcome addition.

Partition walls in such spaces are not installed in quite the same manner as they are in other areas. For a regular wall, partition or otherwise, in an area that has no present ceiling, you build the wall on the floor, and tip it into place. In a basement, you first make take note of any pipes and

wires running along under the joists. You next construct the wall without its sole plate (there are other ways to do this, but I prefer this one), place the sole plate and then set the constructed wall in place on the sole plate, setting each stud on its mark. The entire job is eased if you run a slightly diagonal 1×4 brace across the wall to keep studs from spreading too much (nail at each stud, with a 10d nail driven in most of the way, but leaving at least $1/2$" sticking out so it can be pulled easily to remove the brace when the wall is up).

Use a double top plate on partitions, and a single sole plate. If the basement floor is concrete you can use cut masonry nails or other concrete anchors to hold the sole plate. Mark for each stud, placing studs on 24" centers (these are not bearing walls). The simplest way to do this is to measure from the edge of the sole plate (or the top plate), and mark a straight line down, using a combination square set at $3^1/_2$" depth. At $25^1/_2$", mark to the edge side of that line and you have a 24" center for your second stud. At the edges, mark in $1^1/_2$" and use the combination

Stairs may be totally enclosed in this manner to help prevent dust infiltration. COURTESY OF GEORGIA-PACIFIC CORPORATION

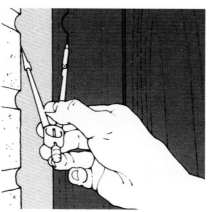

Use a compass to trace irregular surfaces onto wall board and cut with coping or scroll saw. COURTESY OF GEORGIA-PACIFIC CORPORATION

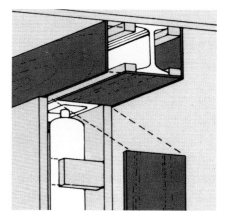

Lally columns may be enclosed, as may metal beams. COURTESY OF GEORGIA-PACIFIC CORPORATION

Cut out for electrical boxes. Coat the lips of the box with paint or chalk and tilt the already cut wall panel against the box. That marks the back of the panel, so you can drill all four corners and mark to cut on the front. COURTESY OF GEORGIA-PACIFIC CORPORATION

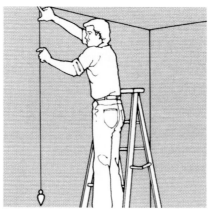

Use plumb bob or level to assure plumb of the all-important first panel. COURTESY OF GEORGIA-PACIFIC CORPORATION

A vapor barrier helps control basement moisture. COURTESY OF GEORGIA-PACIFIC CORPORATION

square to draw a line at that point. Place an X, in pencil, to the edge side of the line in both cases, marking where the stud end will go. Continue pacing down, measuring 24" on center and marking the penciled X where every stud end will fall. Match the top plate to the sole plate: This is most easily done by continuing the sole plate mark up ¼" or so onto the edge of the 2×4, and then placing the top plate on the sole plate. Mark the top plate. Use the combination square to draw the line and mark the required X. This sounds like a lot of extra work, but saves mistakes and the problems mistakes bring. Do this with each and every sole plate and lower top plate. Studs are measured and cut and nailed through the top plate and into the stud end. Once that's done, nail on the second top plate, place the brace, and tip the assembled wall into place. You may toe nail the studs to the sole plate, or you may use framing anchors (if you don't have a lot of experience toenailing, then the second method is much easier: You can get around your lack of toenailing experience by

starting the toe nails before tipping the wall into place, and then finishing nailing after the wall is in place. Jam your foot against the stud on the side opposite the nails to keep the angle nailing from causing it to skitter away from its proper place. (We'll hope you've gotten the nails in at a near correct angles — about 45° — because too shallow an angle has two results here, one of which is painful as one or more nails is driven into your instep. The other result is a weak wall). These days, most everyone uses pneumatic nailers. They cost more than hammers, but can save a tremendous amount of time and effort.

For concrete basement walls — block or poured — you have a couple of choices. Simply paint the walls with a good grade of concrete paint, or furr them out, insulate and cover with paneling or other drywall, including pegboard. Pegboard sheets may be hung directly on concrete and concrete block walls, too.

Furring strips go on easily, usually with cut masonry nails and a touch of construction adhesive. Place them on

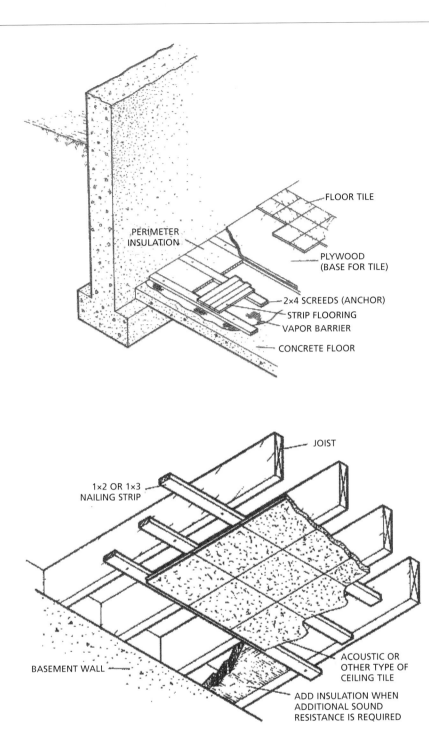

FLOOR TILE

PERIMETER INSULATION

PLYWOOD (BASE FOR TILE)

2×4 SCREEDS (ANCHOR)
STRIP FLOORING
VAPOR BARRIER
CONCRETE FLOOR

JOIST

1×2 OR 1×3 NAILING STRIP

BASEMENT WALL

ACOUSTIC OR OTHER TYPE OF CEILING TILE

ADD INSULATION WHEN ADDITIONAL SOUND RESISTANCE IS REQUIRED

Lay out sole and top plates together for accurate fit. COURTESY OF GEORGIA-PACIFIC CORPORATION

Make any basement partition wall 1" shorter than floor to ceiling distance, tip into place, plumb and wedge tightly. Then nail.
COURTESY OF GEORGIA-PACIFIC CORPORATION

24" centers. Insulate between furring strips on exterior walls if you wish, using a foam board insulation the same thickness as the furring strips. You may also add a vapor barrier to the warm side of the installation (always install vapor barriers on the heated side of insulation).

After that, install paneling or other drywall as you would in any installation, nailing according to manufacturers directions.

For an optional furring method, used primarily when a vertical installation of narrower planks, instead of large sheets of material, is nailed up, apply furring strips horizontally on 16" or 24" centers.

To properly place furring strips (plumb), use a chalk line with plumb bob attached (the case on most chalk lines can be used as a plumb bob). Mark the 24" centers high on the wall and drop a line from that point.

Keep a careful check on plumb as you shim out rough walls.

COURTESY OF GEORGIA-PACIFIC CORPORATION

Continue to check on plumb.

COURTESY OF GEORGIA-PACIFIC CORPORATION

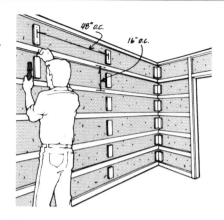

Furr walls and shim to plumb on 16" horizontal centers, with nailer blocks on 48" centers. Use 1" × 2" ($^3/_4$" × $1^1/_2$" $^1/_2$") furring strips or $^1/_2$" × $1^1/_2$" CDX plywood strips.

COURTESY OF GEORGIA-PACIFIC CORPORATION

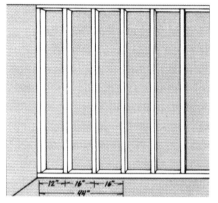

Vertical studs or furring may be used.

COURTESY OF GEORGIA-PACIFIC CORPORATION

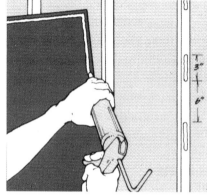

Install wallboard as shown.

COURTESY OF GEORGIA-PACIFIC CORPORATION

Make allowances for all electrical wiring as you place furring strips. When furring strips cross over, or are cut out around cable, you must protect that cable with inexpensive steel plates carried at most building supply stores. Surface wiring on concrete walls must be protected with conduit, either plastic or metal.

Ceiling installations in basements vary from none to fairly fancy fiberglass insulated drop ceilings. I'm not sure of my own preference here, as my current basement ceiling is fairly fancy, with a short drop (at my height, any drop is too much, though), and looks great until I move a board too fast and gouge a chunk of the vinyl overlay off the stuff. As far as insulation goes, something under an inch of fiberglass does keep heat from rising to the upstairs — but so what. It's already warmer up there than down here. Where the insulation shines a bit is in preventing extremes of sound from rising — the floor thumps come through pretty well down here, but the reverse isn't true. Certainly you can hear a router or table saw, but the piercing edge does seem to have been peeled off. Check out the ceiling tile types at a local supplier, and follow the manufacturer's directions for installations. There are so many systems and methods of installation, it serves no purpose beyond padding

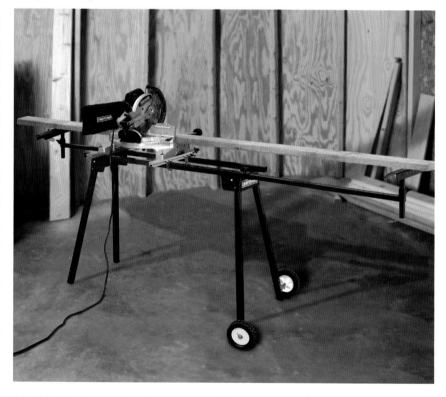

A good quality miter saw stand is a great help during framing and furring operations, supporting longer pieces of material with ease.

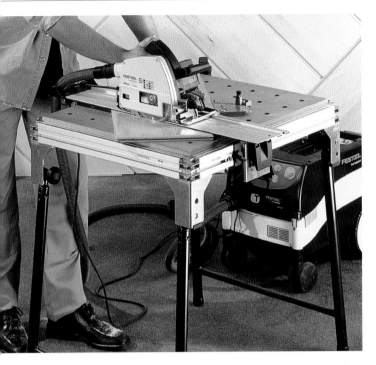

Festool produces what is close to a shop in a pack with their tools. The circular saw is using one of their guides, on one of their worktables with its own Festool dust collection system.

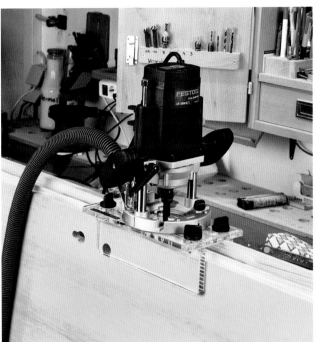

The Festool router offers a wide variety of jigs, plus a dust collection system.

for me to cover them in this book. Most are fairly simple, including drop ceiling installation, requiring little more than care in measuring and installation of the original support strips.

Floor problems in basements are created by concrete. Most basement floors are concrete (regardless of what the finished floor appears to be, if you have any kind of a finished floor in a basement, nine chances out of ten the subfloor is concrete). Concrete floors, as I've noted earlier, are not the greatest for woodworking shops because they're hard on feet and legs, hard on dropped tools, and not at all nice to projects that get dropped during assembly or at other times. Still, concrete beats pounded dirt, and can be covered with vinyl tiles, vinyl sheet, sleepers and wood, paint and many other substances. Too, if your feet really ache, you can get one of the industrial-type mats and place that in front of your most occupied work space. Check out local farm stores for prices on rubber sheet called cow or horse mats. These are usually considerably cheaper than floor mats from a woodworking tool supplier. Currently, a 5' × 8' horse stall mat is going for about $60 at a farm supply chain called Tractor Supply. Local farm stores may or may not do better than that.

The easiest flooring job is laying sheet vinyl or tile, and is best done by following the manufacturer's directions. A test is needed before you get started: If your floor doesn't pass moisture through, place any good, below-grade rated vinyl tile or sheet with the appropriate adhesive (some are self-adhesive and much sheet material doesn't use adhesive). Do a good, tight job and the floor will last for de-

Internally or externally, this plunge router is a major tool, useful and clean operating.

cades. Before you start out to buy tile, place a piece of vinyl tile, or a similar sized piece of plastic, down on the floor and leave it there overnight, and, if the weather is exceptionally dry, leave it a full week. Lift the plastic and check for moisture. If moisture is present, you must lay sleepers of pressure treated wood, then lay a wood subfloor over a vapor barrier, and come back with tile or vinyl sheet if you still want that. Personally, if this happened to my basement, I'd either paint the floor and forget it, or I'd come back with sleepers, put down a double, 10 mil vapor barrier, and use tongue-and-groove, $^5/_8$" plywood as a finished floor and coated with satin polyurethane.

Sleepers in this context are nothing more than 2×4s laid with the wide side flat on the concrete and nailed in place with cut masonry nails. You must use pressure treated wood for this part of the job — it only costs about $5-$10 extra and saves repeating the work a few years down the road.

Urban settings create problems with most forms of power woodworking and my experience in woodworking in an apartment setting is limited to small buildings — a couple of brownstones many years ago, and, in both instances, the neighbors were either not home or totally undisturbed by noise of any kind.

The basic requirement is the smallest, most readily stored tools possible, along with versatile workbenches and storage. Black & Decker is still selling its WorkMate series of folding workbenches, a series that offers some help in urban settings, but unless you own a building or an immense apartment, actual urban woodworking may be one of those times when a rented shop space makes sense — because of the noise. For basement or urban use power woodworking, probably Festool's line of varied hand power tools and accessories make the greatest sense.

Their vacuums are among the quietest I have ever heard, while the tools themselves are precisely made on wonderful and innovative designs (I separate those two because excellence and innovation do not often go hand-in-hand these days).

Both Veritas planes pictured are useful in basement and apartment shops — and in any shop. The little router plane is a particular delight, an improvement on the old, and barely available, Stanley pattern.

Greg Rambo uses his specially designed basement (actually, an extended, above ground part of the house and garage, so it qualifies in several directions) shop with great frequency.

Festool's circular saws offer plunge blades that make for easier plunge cut starts and easier storage.

Greg Rambo's shop is wonderfully airy and light, with recessed ceiling lighting powerful enough to take care of dim days and dark nights, but with enough windows and doors to allow almost light-free daytime use.

There are a number of plane makers still out there, but, in my opinion, the best of them for the average woodworker has to be Lee Valley, with its Veritas line of wood planes. This bench plane is superbly well made, but still reasonably priced. I am not knocking Lie-Nielsen here; L-N planes are also superb, but are usually copies of older Stanley planes. Veritas copies, but also improves, and is far less costly than the Lie-Nielsen planes.

CHAPTER 10

CONVERTING GARAGES TO SHOPS

In a garage, materials access is seldom a problem, and space itself becomes less of one, so the shop may, if desired, take on a more open-handed design for those people who do not garage their vehicles. Other options for those

who do garage their vehicles include the use of tilt-up workbenches and roll-away combination tools (such as the Shopsmith). Tool selection and placement has a considerable effect on ease of use of any space that is constructed for other than shop uses. In garages, a woodworker may not have the option of selecting door and window placement, ceiling height and flooring materials. Wood flooring is better than concrete. It's more resilient under foot, thus easier

on the leg muscles; it's also easier on dropped items and tools. I feel clumsy dropping a $25 chisel onto a wood floor and victimized dropping that chisel onto a concrete floor.

All of this can be worked around, usually at low cost, if appropriate planning is carried out when selecting tools, workbenches and other needs. The lessons of the early chapters need careful application to the specific opportunities and problems created by converting a garage into a

woodworking shop. In general, the fact that you've got an enclosed, wired and lighted space, with doors, and sometimes with windows, is a great place to start and saves 95% of the work involved in setting up a woodworking shop. The wiring and lighting are marginal for a woodshop, but those are reasonably simple to change.

GARAGES

A well built garage solves a lot of workshop space and construction problems. Most are simple frameworks with roof and siding, but there may also be a window or two, some electrical power and a light or two or more. Too, the modern garage door is close to an ideal material and equipment portal. If the garage is attached to the house, there may be enough heat bleeding off to reduce or eliminate any need for a separate heating system. Bob Grisso's shop (below left) qualifies as both freestanding and a garage, though it hasn't served as car parking space for years. There may also be circuits enough for a modest shop, but the odds are good you'll eventually need to install at least a 60-ampere subpanel. Some of the greatest shops in this book started life as car barns. Doug Johnson's shop is an example, possibly the most extreme. He had to add a second story to his garage to make space on his lot for the woodshop he wanted. His tale is more

Doug Johnson uses a winch and pulley to bring supplies up to his second floor shop. COURTESY OF DOUG JOHNSON

fully told in the display section, but some special arrangements were necessary to handle getting supplies into the shop. Brian Grella's shop is a garage in more traditional form, and is shown in the display section, as is Pete Bade's freestanding garage and shop. A large number of garages

Doug's second floor shop windows offer a wonderful view while working. COURTESY OF DOUG JOHNSON

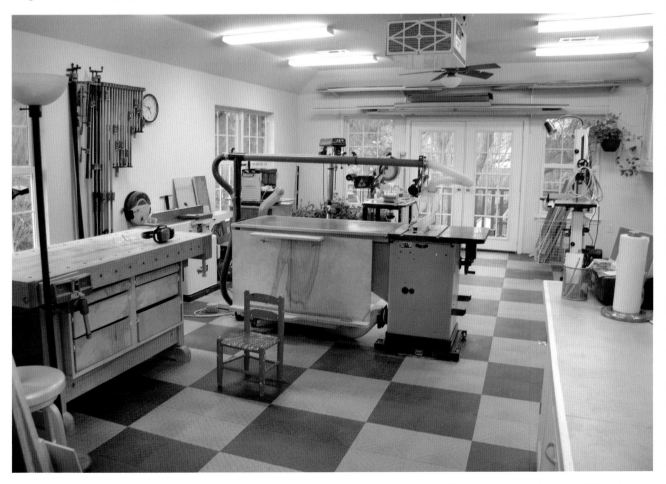

Garage door entries to woodshops are useful.

utility building, reminiscent of World War II (and later) Quonset huts (newer versions of the Nissen hut from the War To End All Wars, World War I).

Again, drawing the outline of the building's interior is a help, locating doors and windows. Decide whether or not the garage will ever be used for vehicular storage. As far as I am concerned, our vehicles could sit in the weather, if we even had a garage. With current paints, that doesn't seem to harm anything in a mild climate, but it has also been a lot of years since my All-American car bug has bitten me. Like most kids of my generation, I was a hot rod freak, let that bleed over into motorcycles, and lost interest in anything other than transportation by the time my reflexes slowed enough to make bikes less fun. So, now, cars and trucks are to be kept available and in good running shape, but otherwise are low key, and don't come close to being family members, as was the case in the "good old days". Now that age is really setting in, I appreciate more and more the cars of the 1930s, 1940s and even up to the 1960s, but for the most part, I couldn't afford them anyway, at today's prices. As one guy I know, who has a 1972 Plymouth Road Runner 340, has said, "If I hadn't bought it new, I couldn't afford it now."

appear to end up doing duty as woodshops. Sizes are right — though I have worked my wood in a single car garage built around 1915 and found that a very tight fit. Prices are reasonable. Contracted building is a very simple matter in most localities. Bobby Weaver's shop interior is reached by the garage door shown on the top of page 100, and another about 55' away. There are also two small access doors. This end is a contracted metal garage. The other end is a steel

Two-car garage shops offer terrific space for woodworking. In a pinch, you can actually park a car in one, sometimes.
COURTESY OF FRED PRESTON

Decide what tools will fit where and what kind of outlets you need. See if there's room and power for all. Go ahead and set up for the ones for which you're not ready. Install the electricity, pegboard and other accessories you need to complete the moderately large shop that even a single car garage provides. If you're fortunate enough to have a two car, or larger, garage, you're in woodworker's heaven — at least on a lower level. Most garages offer about 450 to 600 square feet of space, sufficient for all but the largest hobby shops. Fred Preston's shop is a garage and he says it's also his first "real" shop. He turns out some good work there, too. (Fred's shop was once a double garage, but now serves a better purpose.)

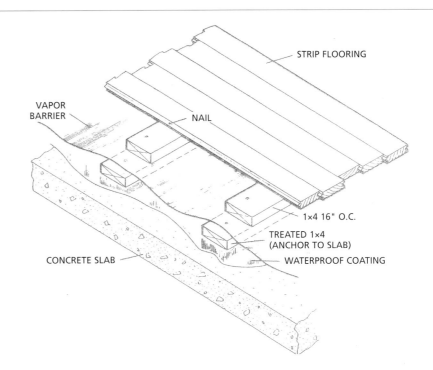

Drawing of sleeper installation and subfloor (use ³/₄" tongue and groove plywood for the shop floor and call it finished).

Most garages, as already stated, have open studs, probably open rafters, collar beams and maybe even ceiling joists. It's up to you as to how much finishing you do. There is sometimes a benefit in leaving joists open as they become storage helpers — don't store much overhead if you have trusses, though.

The floor is almost sure to be concrete and may demand some extreme clean-up before it takes a decent coat of paint. Check with the floor-paint makers to see what they recommend for cleaning up greasy floors. Or you may go the sleeper route, which is probably preferable if the floor is really nasty. Get enough grease in concrete over enough years and it cannot be properly cleaned well enough for paint to adhere. By the same token, the adhesive for various tiles also won't work. Sleepers become the

This garage shop ceiling offers a grid system that allows for insulation, storage and easy access to lighting.

only option, outside of actually just allowing the grease to be there on the floor until sawdust gets pounded into the existing mess.

You need to make up your mind whether or not you'll place a ceiling in the garage. In one sense, a ceiling is desirable, in another, it's not. Open rafters, or lower members of trusses, make decent storage spots for light items (very light in trusses) long enough to span at least two of the members. There are a lot of those in every woodworker's life. The ceiling is desirable because it tends to reduce heating and cooling needs while also providing a reflective surface (if light colored, which any ceiling should be) for light. Your storage needs may have to be balanced against the excessive heat loss and gain you face, plus the dust and general clutter accumulation that is always the case with open rafters over a woodworking shop.

You also must decide whether or not to add drywall to the studs. Certain areas are best left open, as the studs become a source of superb storage opportunities. Many woodshops end up with walls as shown at the right (jammed with storage) so covering them, rather than leaving open studs is usually the smart thing to do.

COURTESY OF RYOBI

COURTESY OF CRAFTSMAN

Workbenches may be built into garages, against stud walls, with only front legs for support.

The extent of the remodeling is up to you, as always, but make sure you've got sufficient circuits and as much wall space that can be taken up with pegboard and/or shelving. If you're lucky, you have expanded the vehicles right out into the driveway.

Today's garages are built with studs on 24" centers, which makes for easy installation of most kinds of drywall paneling, though I'd avoid getting involved with gypsum wallboard, which needs to be taped, have nail depressions filled and then needs priming and painting. My own shop has walls covered with OSB (oriented-strand board). That might not be legal (according to code) in some areas if you're working in an attached garage, because of the flammability. Plywood also works well, as shown in the photo below.

In most instances, attached garages with a wall next to a relaxing area of the home makes everyone happier if filled with insulation and covered with at least $\frac{1}{2}$" solid drywall (drywall in this instance means any non-plaster panel. Gypsum wallboard is too much work for the little extra sound deadening it adds in such a situation). If you want pegboard on such walls, come back and place it over the solid wall. The more substantial wall will reduce the passage of sound. None of these techniques prevent the passage of sound. That needs a second wall placed about 1" in front of the first, with no solid contact between the two, and with insulation woven in to help reduce sound travel. It is worth the expense and effort in only a very few cases.

Each garage is different, and unless built specifically as a shop (as might be the case if you pick up a garage package at a mega-lumberyard), each has a different history of use.

Evaluate the location of windows, doors and the condition of such things as overhead doors and automatic

openers when getting set to do your planning. Doors may be easily added — especially standard entry doors, up to 36" wide — but you are probably better off not adding any windows. Windows give glaring light and seem to do so always at the wrong time. They're also easily broken if too low, and most residential windows, including those in a garage, are too low for workshop use. Leave those that exist in place, but don't add more unless the sills are at least 54" from the floor.

For light, install overhead fluorescent lights. You want to evaluate the electrical system and work as in Chapter Nine. Make sure you have plenty of outlets in both 120 volts and 240 volts. Also make sure you have a properly grounded electrical system. Install a ground fault circuit interrupter at the first outlet to protect all the outlets from problems, following it in sequence. You can also add circuit breakers of the ground fault circuit interrupter type, though they tend to be more expensive than standard breakers.

Evaluate the floor. Many garages with poured concrete floors have a central drain, and the floor is sloped towards that drain. If there is too much slope, you'll want to install a wood floor over sleepers. It's not the hardest job in the world, but does take time and cost money. Ideally, you won't have to do a thing except wash and paint the floor, or lay tile, but in many cases, bet on working out some method of leveling the floor. The only effective way to do so is to install a leveled floor on sleepers. Shim the sleepers level as you install them, starting from the sides of the room and

The ability to open up an entire wall of your shop brings in wonderful sunlight, fresh air during the proper seasons and makes moving items (especially sheet goods and large equipment) significantly easier. COURTESY OF JELD-WEN

working towards the center (or towards the drain, or multiple drain). Level all succeeding sleepers with the high ones along the walls. Install sleepers with construction adhesive and cut masonry nails, using pressure treated pine. For problem areas that are apt to stay wet, use wood treated for ground contact. Use a good vapor barrier laid directly on the concrete (vapor barriers are made from polyethylene sheeting no less than 6 mils thick —10 mils is better).

Install the sleepers so centers are either 16" (for ⅝" plywood floor, no subfloor) or 24" (for ¾" floor, or ⅝" over board subfloor). If it's a normal installation, using a ¾" (1" nominal) sheathing lumber for subfloor, or rough-cut 1" lumber, with ⅝", tongue-and-groove, sanded B-C plywood finish floor works well. You can then either lay vinyl tile, or vinyl sheet on the plywood or you can simply coat it with a good brand of polyurethane (at least two coats, preferably three) and go about your business.

Heat installation in a garage may require the installation of a flue or wall vent, depending on the heat type selected — if any is needed at all. Connected garages typically have little need for extra heating, unless the house is under heated, but you may wish to add a couple of baseboard electric units or a small wood stove. If you do add a wood stove, you need to install a chimney with a solid fuel liner and have it and the rest of the installation inspected to make sure it conforms to regulations.

Connected garages also tend to offer easy access to any necessary circuitry upgrades by the simple process of adding a subpanel to a couple of unused circuit breaker spaces in the main service entry panel. You can, depending on the present load on the main panel, take off enough for six to ten circuits with very little problem. The six-circuit box doesn't need its own circuit breaker, but will use the breakers on the main panel. For a larger subpanel, you will need a separate breaker, either 60 or 100 amperes.

Windows in a garage will be like windows in most other buildings, too low for the most efficient shop use. The simplest solution with double-hung windows is to cover much of the bottom with a piece of plywood, raising the wall space 12" or more and reducing use of the window (opening) to the top sash unit. The plywood across the bottom should be at least ⅜" thick, to eliminate broken panes from swung lumber, kickbacks and other knocks from woodworking fate. Before actually stopping up any window spaces permanently check local codes. If codes forbid such stoppage, use two small butt hinges on one side, and a slide latch on the other. In most residences, rooms are required to have a window large enough for exit of a person if on the ground floor. Do *not* make a change without checking this first, because you may end up with a disapproved installation.

Permanent closing up of the bottom of a window allows you to run benches along the wall that are higher than otherwise. Certainly, if a garage has windows at the level of some of those in residences, you are going to be badly limited in placing anything against them. If such is the case, and

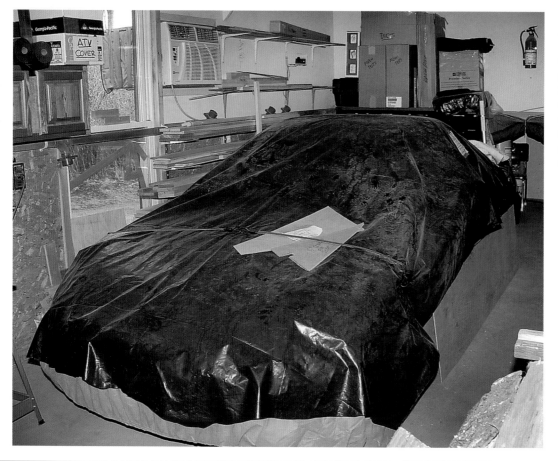

As I mentioned earlier, some garage shops still do duty as garages. It's a good idea to protect the vehicle during woodworking activities. Saw dust is only one of the concerns.
COURTESY OF PETE BADE

Never underestimate the value of a mouser (or two) in the shop. Keep them happy and they'll keep your shop rodent-free. COURTESY OF PETE BADE

you can't make a change buy stopping up the lower half of the window, placing a tool such as a band saw or drill press in front of the window makes good use of the space. Lathes also fit, but are a bit lengthy for most windows. Drill presses and band saws don't create a length problems.

That big garage door is a help. If you do not have an automatic garage door opener, install one. The installation isn't particularly difficult, and the bend-over time it saves is great, especially if there's no other exterior door in the garage. (Garage doors are fantastic materials-handling assets — and make getting larger finished projects out less of a chore.)

If the overhead door is all you have, install another exterior door, at least a 32" wide exterior model, with consideration given to a 36"- or 42"-wide unit.

In a normally-framed garage, that means removing a single stud and framing in to take the door. Build a header of 2×8 stock, with $1/2$" plywood used as a center spacer to get the $1\frac{1}{2}$" thick stock, doubled, to $3\frac{1}{2}$" to match the rest of the framing. If the framing is of rough-cut lumber, use double pieces of $1/2$" plywood as spacers. Use at least one jack stud under each side of the header and one cripple stud in its center to the top plate, if the space is large enough to allow it. Make sure the sill (floor) is level and the rough framing is plumb and insert the door unit. For a solid installation, nail through door jamb sides into the framing after shimming at the lock area and elsewhere as needed. Install moulding and the job is done.

If you decide to place a ceiling and/or use drywall construction to cover the wall studs, first insulate as local dictates make sensible. At a minimum, that's $3\frac{1}{2}$" in the walls and 6" over the ceiling (with a probable preference for at least 12" above).

Next, using either $7/16$" waferboard or oriented strand board (OSB) to cover the walls and ceiling. To decorate, you may use lath strips on the joints and maybe at 24" centers. Currently, my office is done in waferboard with

lath at 4' intervals (except where I had to cut and lay a seam closer), and the whole works painted off white. It looks fine, and is bright and cheery and cost very little. A shop will do as well. Mine does. I've used waferboard in shops before and find it an easy to use, sturdy, a low cost way to cover gaping spaces in walls and to cover old, deteriorating plaster walls without going to huge expense.

You can use another type of paneling, but I know of nothing else that works as well at low a cost (even in today's current high-priced sheet wood market, OSB in $7/16$" thickness is well under $7 per panel).

The panels go up quickly and are nailed, as is most manufactured wood paneling, at 8" intervals on internal seams and 6" intervals along the outside edges. Use a few dabs of construction adhesive to make for a surer bond, but be advised you are never going to be able to remove the panels that are glued down without taking some serious chunks out of the studs underneath.

Beyond that, setting a garage up as a workshop needs little extra work, unless you plan to leave one or more vehicles inside. Then it's more a matter of tool choice and the ability to move those tools into place easily when you have a job to do.

My old friend, Peter Bade, stores his Honda 2000 inside during the winter, as you can see from the tarp coverings. You don't drive that kind of car in upstate New York winters if you expect it to stay in good shape. He also worked out a solution for his shop cats in winter, keeping them comfy while they keep the mouse population under control.

Doug Johnson's garage shop shows a different approach: He built a second story to take the shop, because there wasn't enough room on his lot to get code approval for another building large enough to work, and his cars needed a home, so the elevated shop came into being. He then moved his tools in and has been working wood ever since, in a shop many of us would envy. He has a bathroom, and every tool he needs, all within the space of a large garage. A lift makes hauling lumber and other supplies easy, while the deck gives a great view of his neighborhood.

Thus, choose benchtop tools — assuming the garage is deep enough to allow at least a 22" deep bench against the back wall — or tools with wheels. The Shopsmith Mark V and variations make good selections, as does Ridgid's job-site table saw. Check the items in your local tool suppliers' showrooms, in the catalogs available from most tool manufacturers and on-line.

CHAPTER 11

WORKBENCHES

I can barely even begin to discuss the full range of benches available you can build from plans, such as the below reproduction of a bench by 18th century French woodworker Andre Roubo, built by author Christopher Schwarz

(*Workbenches*, Popular Woodworking Books, 2007), or that some company at some time or another has built. On my own, I figure I've used at least 100 types of benches over the years. Bobby Weaver has used all those, and some more, and once had five types in his shop. And the sizes varied all over the place, as noted in our earlier chapter. Pick what suits you and then place it as suits you.

Currently, I've got three WorkMates, plus two 8'-long benches of my own construction, and along-the-wall workbenches over cabinets that are very handy.

A look at the well-constructed bench-with-trough from Lee Valley, with wood base (top left) or cast iron legs (top right). Directly above is the excellent, chain-driven, twin-screw vise, also from Lee Valley/Veritas. COURTESY OF LEE VALLEY

Placement needs to feed into your work habits. I like at least one bench placed in the center of the floor, so that all four sides are easily accessible. That means, with a 24" wide bench, a space of at least 8' wide × 14' long (my shop-built workbenches tend to run long, with the shortest at 8'). My second bench goes up against the wall, and is 22" wide. WorkMates go anywhere and get shoved and stacked and hung out of the way when not in use. Bobby Weaver prefers to use wider benches when all four sides are accessible. One of his was a full 48" wide. Bobby also garnered a lot of school-lab cabinetry rejects and placed them around much of three walls of his shop, giving him a huge amount of flat space. There's still never enough horizontal space, but that's the case in any workshop. Whatever there is gets occupied quickly.

Try to leave yourself 3' of working space around sides of any benches that are intended to be accessible. You can often get away with 30", but more is better in this case.

LEE VALLEY WORKBENCH

This bench comes in two distinct models, one with heavy-duty cast iron legs and the other with heavy-duty wood legs. I'm assembling the model with the wood legs — I had hoped to have it done in time to photograph here but that won't happen. The slab tops are in two parts, each about 12" wide × 6' long. They are made of laminated maple and are drilled for Lee Valley's round bench dogs. The design accepts a center trough and your selection of vises: I've got an old Jorgenson standard woodworker's vise for a side vise and a new Lee Valley twin handle for an end vise. Eventually, I will build cabinets to go underneath, which is the primary reason for getting the wood base. The entire unit, including a front vise, is available, with either type of legs and the twin screw Veritas end vise. The end vise is chain driven and easily allows cocking of the vise plates around any item it is holding, but returns quickly to parallel when that's desired. This is close to an ultimate bench. Check it out at www.leevalley.com.

An American Workbench that I own, makes a great stand for a variety of benchtop machines.

AMERICAN WORKBENCHES

A few years ago, John Zirpola decided that a low-cost workbench styled to general, American woodworking, needed a solid place in the market. So, he designed and started building a couple of models, one of which I now have. This is an excellent workbench for power-tool woodworking, less so for hand-tool woodworking, but, then, John designed it for the modern woodworker. It fits. According to John, my American Workbench model is a new

John Zirpola's American Workbench can be bought with extensions and other add-ons. This bench is in John's shop.
COURTESY OF AMERICAN WORKBENCH/JOHN ZIRPOLA

design called "The Common Man". It is a suitable name for a workbench that is 50" × 30" × 1$\frac{7}{8}$". Legs are 3$\frac{1}{2}$" × 3$\frac{1}{2}$". It comes in three packages, with 16 lag bolts to hold it together and a neat little three-pocket assembly that attaches to hold smaller tools and supplies. This model is one up from my model.

Suitably enough, it is nearly ideal as a base for bench-top woodworking tools, such as planers and jointers. It also is handy as a site to do sanding, drilling or other woodworking operations. Price is low (as this is written, it is under $270, plus shipping). You supply our own vise, or John may have one that you like. He offers a large, reasonably priced vise, installed and ready to go.

As stated above, the Common Man workbench can serve as a base for benchtop tools, which makes it a great base for the small workshop, one that has to be stored in little room, and used in not much more. Stack a Palmgren 6" benchtop jointer on top, slip a DeWalt or other benchtop planer on the shelf, and stand a Ridgid job-site table saw next to this unit, and you're ready for most reasonably sized woodworking projects. As you work, start with the jointer, go to the planer, and then size your materials on the table saw.

Space for storage is about 6' long × 4' wide. Space for use depends on the materials being worked..

You can find this workbench in Charleston, SC, but to save driving, check out www.americanworkbench.com and see what you think. For the price, and the amount of handwork that goes into the bench, I have to wonder if John Zirpola is making much money on his benches. It is a worthwhile investment.

PLAN BUILT

Tom Watson is a cabinet and furniture maker from Gulph Mills, Pennsylvania (right outside Philadelphia). Something over 20 years ago, he needed a bench, saw a set of plans in the Garrett Wade catalog that he felt made sense for him and ordered them.

Tom says, "I built this bench in about 1985 from a set of plans from Garrett Wade. That plan was for a 6' bench and because of the kind of work that I was doing, I scaled it up so the top is 102" with the end vise closed and 113" with it open. It is 25" wide."

According to Tom, that length was nearly essential, because he was often working on ceiling-height cabinets,

Tom Watson's workbench has seen a lot of wood move across its surface in something over two decades of professional woodworking use. COURTESY OF TOM WATSON

Tom is using the bench as a sharpening station. COURTESY OF TOM WATSON

which in most homes are 96" tall. He says, "The bench dog arrangement lets me hold the side of an 8'-high cabinet without protruding above the working face."

Even after more than two decades of use, the rock maple bench is still solid as Gibraltar, with almost all of its original beauty shining through the patina of work and age.

Tom no longer recalls whether the vises are Record or Marples, but, he says, "I still have the catalog and could look it up." At this point, it doesn't matter since neither is available any longer so I didn't take him up on the offer. He does offer the following, "The vises are quick opening so that you give a sharp turn to the left and you can open them close to what you need, then turn right and tighten." Look for easy open screws on whatever vises you buy.

He states, "The hold-down is Marples and the bench dogs have no name on them."

For additional utility, Tom says, "I built two carriers for wheels that the bench just sits on, no screws. When I do carving I usually lift the bench off of the wheels."

He followed what is a good, standard procedure for smoothing tops when you don't wish to spend the time and effort hand planing them: "After I glued the top up I took it to a larger shop that had a Timesaver wide-belt sander and gave them fifty bucks to run it through a few times."

Tom Watson feels strongly that a good bench is essential and he very much likes this one. He says, "I'd build this same bench again. I've been offered a thousand bucks for it and wouldn't sell."

Bench dog, saw sharpening vise and Marples hold down. COURTESY OF TOM WATSON

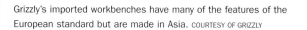

Grizzly's imported workbenches have many of the features of the European standard but are made in Asia. COURTESY OF GRIZZLY

IMPORTS

Grizzly has begun importing European-pattern workbenches in several styles. Tops are as much as 4" thick and both major models feature end and front vises; with the end vises being shoulder style. They are holed to accept square based dogs. The are priced well under European imports, with 84" long tops made of laminated birch. Tops are 24" wide. The unit (shown above) with nine drawers weighs over 360 pounds as shipped.

Several European bench manufacturers seem to be wobbling, on the market on year, not there the next, back again, gone again. Prices are well up there. Deifenbach (www.diefenbachworkbenches.com/ModernAmerican.htm) seems well sustained, though very costly. The benches are gorgeous and so is their construction. There are photos and information on the web site.

Sjoberg has become the popular version of the European workbench these days, primarily because they make ver-

Drawer slides of good quality and felt drawer linings add to the usefulness of the Grizzly bench.

sions priced in a range similar to the range American Workbench is in. Sjoberg's more expensive workbenches, though, are in the price range of the Diefenbach benches. I had one small Sjoberg for several years and liked it well enough. In fact, at times I miss it and its leg supports for material being jointed with a hand plane, even though it was far too light for such use. Those are typically European features, but a brace and bit can add them to almost any workbench that has wood legs. Drill ³/₄" holes at least 3" deep. Use dowels about 6" long to serve as material supports.

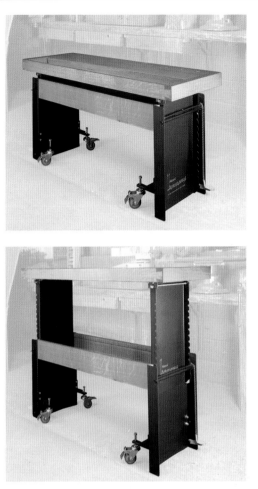

A unique design, and a great addition to any shop, the Noden Adjust-A-Bench can be used in it's low position (around 28" with top) or extended through a range of stops to a height of around 45". If you need an angled bench, it works that way as well. The legs are sold separately, so the size of the bench is determined by your needs. COURTESY OF ADJUST-A-BENCH

NOT AN IMPORT

For anyone who needs more than a single workbench height, the only real solutions I've seen involve two benches, or the Noden Adjust-A-Bench. The Noden uses two steel trays with a ratcheting mechanism to move its top up and down to suit the job at hand. The heavy ($1/8$") sheet metal is stable, so the bench can work with heavy loads. Standard vises attach in standard ways. Overall, this American-made bench qualifies as unusual and exceptionally useful.

The Noden inner tray slides over a range from $26^1/4$" to a height of $42^3/4$", with 12 ratchet locking steps along the way. A foot pedal releases the locking stops for security and easy adjustability. It thus becomes useful for fine detail work where you want to essentially be eyeball-to-eyeball with your work (as in carving). It is also heavy duty enough to be useful when doing some work as hand planing, a notoriously demanding chore for workbenches.

It's also touted as a workbench that can be readily shared with another woodworker who is either taller or shorter, or who is doing a different kind of work. For full details, visit www.adjustabench.com.

Another workbench concept that I like is one that appeared in *Popular Woodworking* magazine. Published originally in 2001, the workbench, built by editor Christopher Schwarz, added as much bang for the buck as possible. The result was a bench that originally priced at $175. In 2005, Chris redid the bench, adding some features and kicking the price up to $235. Still a great bench for the money, and with the magazine's blessing I've included the plans and steps for the bench here.

Chris is an admitted workbench enthusiast, and you'll find more plans for a variety of workbench styles on the magazine's website at www.popularwoodworking.com.

$230 WORKBENCH

by Christopher Schwarz

When I built this bench in 2000 my mission was to construct the best bench I could for just $175. When I completed the project, my plan was to take it to my shop at home to replace my grandfather's workbench. Plans, however, change. The bench turned out to be so useful that I left it at work and built a similar one for my shop at home.

Like anything in an active woodshop, the workbench evolved during the following four years. My work habits changed—I use hand tools even more now. And my knowledge of what makes a good workbench has deepened.

As a result, what you see here is the product of more than four years of tinkering and experimenting. I cannot say this is the ultimate workbench, but I can say it is a flexible design that can be easily altered as your work evolves.

THE BENCH'S FEATURES

The following is going to sound like a description from a woodworking catalog, but keep in mind that the price is about one-fourth of the sticker price of a commercial bench. It's a good deal. This bench features a simple—and yet versatile—system for clamping large or odd-shaped pieces. You can secure an entryway door in this bench. You can clamp a round dining room tabletop on the benchtop

with ease. A planing stop on the end of the bench allows you to plane material that is monstrously thick or even $\frac{1}{4}$" thin. The stop is an easy modification.

The bench is 34" high, so it can be parked as an outfeed table behind most brands of contractor saws and cabinet saws—and 34" is an ideal height for most planing and power-tool operations.

The bench is stout, heavy and designed for the long haul. The base is built like a bed with a system of bolts and nuts so you can tighten it up if it ever wobbles (I've had to do this once in four years).

And it is a tremendous value. When I first built the bench it was $175 in materials. With inflation, the price has risen to $184. However, a few years ago I replaced the original wooden face vise with the metal one shown here. I am so glad I did; this vise is much more stout. If you build the bench in this configuration (which I recommend), the price is $230. And that's still a good deal.

LET'S GO SHOPPING

First a word about the wood. I priced my lumber from a local Lowe's. It was tagged as Southern yellow pine, appearance-grade. Unlike a lot of dimensional stock, this stuff is pretty dry and knot-free. Even so, take your time

When you glue up your top, you want to make sure all the boards line up. Lay down your glue and then clamp up one end with the boards perfectly flush. Then get a friend to clamp a handscrew on the seam and twist until the boards are flush. Continue clamping up towards your friend, having your friend adjust the handscrews as needed after each clamp is cinched down.

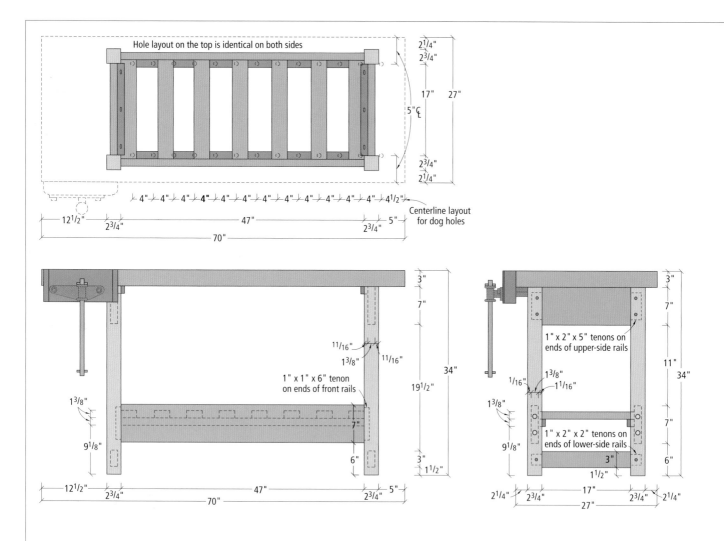

Hole layout on the top is identical on both sides

2 1/4"
2 3/4"
17"
27"
5" ℄
2 3/4"
2 1/4"

4" 4" 4" **4"** 4" 4" 4" 4" 4" 4" 4" 4" 4 1/2"

Centerline layout for dog holes

12 1/2"
2 3/4"
47"
2 3/4"
5"
70"

3"
7"
11/16"
1 3/8"
11/16"

1" x 1" x 6" tenon on ends of front rails

1 3/8"
9 1/8"
34"
19 1/2"
7"
6"
3"
1 1/2"

12 1/2"
2 3/4"
47"
2 3/4"
5"
70"

3"
7"
1" x 2" x 5" tenons on ends of upper-side rails

1 3/8"
1/16"
11/16"
11"
34"

1 3/8"
9 1/8"
1" x 2" x 2" tenons on ends of lower-side rails
3"
1 1/2"
7"
6"

2 1/4"
2 3/4"
17"
2 3/4"
2 1/4"
27"

SHOPPING LIST

8	2 × 8 × 12' Southern yellow pine boards @ $9.57 each	76.56
8	$3/8$" × 16 × 6" hex bolts @ $.51 each	4.08
8	$3/8$" × 16 hex nuts @ $.07 each	.56
16	$5/16$" washers @ $.03 each	.48
1	Veritas Bench Pup (#05G04.03)	7.95
1	Veritas Wonder Dog (#05G10.01)	24.50
1	Veritas Front Vise (#70G08.02)	69.50
	Total Cost	$183.63
1	Quick-release steel vise (#10G04.13)	$115.00
	Total cost with steel-jawed vise:	$229.13

SUPPLIES

Lee Valley Tools
800-871-8158 or leevalley.com

Prices as of publication date.

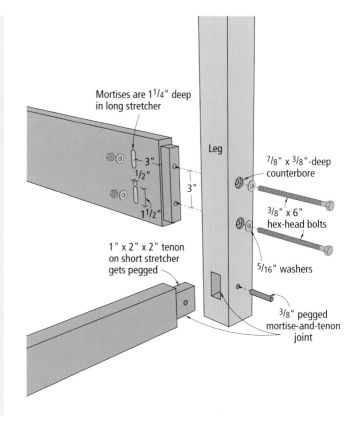

Mortises are 1 1/4" deep in long stretcher

Leg

3"
1/2"
3"
1 1/2"

1" x 2" x 2" tenon on short stretcher gets pegged

7/8" x 3/8"-deep counterbore

3/8" x 6" hex-head bolts

5/16" washers

3/8" pegged mortise-and-tenon joint

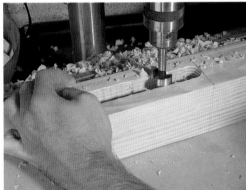

After you cut your tenons, lay them directly on your work and use the edges like a ruler to mark where the mortise should start and end (above). Use a 1" Forstner bit in your drill press to cut overlapping holes to make your mortise (left). Now square up the edges of the mortise using a mortise chisel and a mallet (right).

and pick through the store's pile of 12-foot-long 2 × 8s. Tip: Don't be tempted to use 2 × 4 stock for the legs and top. The 2 × 4s generally have more knots and twists.

To find Southern yellow pine in your area, visit southernpine.com. Fir and poplar also will work.

Here's the story on the hardware: The bolts, nuts and washers are used to connect the front rails to the two ends of the bench. Using this hardware, we'll borrow a technique used by bed makers to build a joint that is stronger than any mortise and tenon. The Bench Pup and Wonder Dog will keep you from having to buy an expensive tail vise. Using these two simple pieces of hardware, you can clamp almost anything to your bench for planing, sanding and chopping. The face vise goes on the front of your bench and is useful for clamping and holding with the assistance of the sliding deadman accessory.

PREPARING YOUR LUMBER
Rip and crosscut your lumber. You've probably noticed that your wood has rounded corners and the faces are not glass-smooth. Your first task is to use your jointer and planer to remove those rounded edges and get all your lumber to 1⅜" thick.

Once your lumber is thicknessed, start work on the top. The top is made from 1⅜" × 3⅜" × 70" boards turned on

edge and glued face-to-face. It will take five of your 2 × 8s to make the top. Build the top in stages to make the task more manageable. Glue up a few boards, then run the assembly through the jointer and planer to get them flat. Make a few more assemblies like this, then glue all the assemblies together into one big top.

When you finally glue up the whole top, you want to make sure you keep all the boards in line. This will save you hours of flattening the top later with a hand plane. See the photo below for a tip when you get to this point. After the glue is dry, square the ends of your assembled top. If you don't have a huge sliding table on your table saw, try cutting the ends square using a circular saw (the top is so thick you'll have to make a cut from both sides). Or you can use a handsaw and a piece of scrap wood clamped across the end as a guide.

BUILD THE BASE
The base is constructed using mortise-and-tenon joinery. Essentially, the base has two end assemblies that are joined by two rails. The end assemblies are built using 1"-thick × 2"-long tenons. Then the front rails are attached to the ends using 1" × 1" mortise-and-tenon joints and the 6"-long bolts.

Begin working on the base by cutting all your pieces to size. The 2¾"-square legs are made from two pieces of

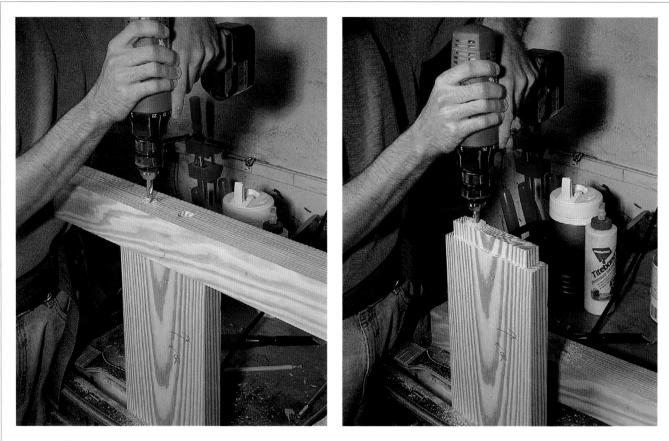

Drilling the $^3/_8$" holes for the bolts is easier if you do it in this order. First drill the holes in the legs using your drill press. Now assemble the leg and front rail. Drill into the rail using the hole in the leg as a guide (left). Remove the leg from the rail and continue drilling the hole in the rail. The hole you drilled before will once more act as a guide. You still need to be careful and guide your drill straight and true (right).

pine face-glued together. Glue and clamp the legs and set them aside. Now turn your attention to cutting the tenons on the rails. It's a good idea to first make a "test" mortise in a piece of scrap so you can fit your tenons as they are made. I like to make my tenons on the table saw using a dado stack. Place your rails face down on your table saw and use a miter gauge to nibble away at the rails until the tenons are the right size. Because pine is soft, make the edge shoulders on the upper side rails 1" wide. These deeper shoulders will prevent your tenons from blowing out the end grain at the top of your legs during assembly.

Now use your tenons to lay out the locations of your mortises. See the photo at right for how this works. Clamp a piece of scrap to your drill press to act as a fence and chain-drill the mortises in the legs. Make your mortises about $^1/_{16}$" deeper than your tenons are long. This will give you a little space for any excess glue.

Once you've got your mortises drilled, use a mortise chisel to square the round corners. Make sure your tenons fit, then dry-fit your base. Label each joint so you can reassemble the bench later.

BED BOLTS

There's a bit of a trick to joining the front rails to the legs. Workbenches are subject to a lot of racking back and forth.

A plain old mortise-and-tenon joint won't hack it. So we bolt it. First study the diagram at left to see how these joints work. Now here's the best way to make them.

First chuck a 1" Forstner bit in your drill press to cut the counterbore in the legs for the bolt head. Drill the counterbore, then chuck a $^3/_8$"-brad-point bit in your drill press and drill in the center of the counterbore through the leg and into the floor of your previously cut mortise.

Now fit the front rails into the leg mortises. Chuck that $^3/_8$" bit into a hand drill and drill as deeply as you can through the leg and into the rail. The hole in the leg will guide the bit as it cuts into the rail. Then remove the leg and drill the $^3/_8$" hole even deeper. You probably will have to use an extra-long drill bit for this.

OK, here's the critical part. Now you need to cut two small mortises on each rail. These mortises will hold a nut and a washer, and must intersect the $^3/_8$" holes you just drilled. With the leg and rail assembled, carefully figure out where the mortises need to go. Drill the mortises in the rails as shown in the photo at far right. Now test your assembly. Thread the joint with the bolt, two washers and a nut. Use a ratchet and wrench to pull everything tight. If you're having trouble getting the bolt to thread in the nut, try chasing your $^3/_8$" holes with a $^7/_{16}$" bit. That will give you some wiggle room without compromising the strength of the joint.

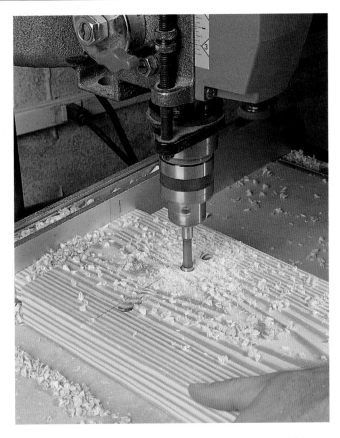

The mortises in the front rails are also made on the drill press. Make them 1¼" deep to make sure you can get a washer in there. If you can't, try clipping an edge off of the washer.

Drilling your dog holes may seem like hard work using a brace and bit. It is. However, you get an amazing amount of torque this way – far more than you can get with a cordless drill. Sadly, I had cooked my corded drill, so this was my only option.

BASE ASSEMBLY

This bench has a good-sized shelf between the front rails. Cut the ledgers and slats from your scrap. Also cut the two cleats that attach the top to the base. Now plane or sand everything before assembly – up to #150 grit should be fine.

Begin assembly by gluing up the two end assemblies. Put glue in the mortises and clamp up the ends until dry. Then, for extra strength, peg the tenons using ⅜"-thick dowel.

Screw the ledgers to the front rails. Make sure they don't cover the mortises for the bed bolts, or you are going to be in trouble. Now bolt the front rails to the two ends (no glue necessary). Rub a little Vaseline or grease on the threads first because after your bench is together you want to seal up those mortises with hot-melt glue. The Vaseline will ensure your bolts will turn for years to come.

Screw the cleats to the top of the upper side rails. Then drill oval-shaped holes in the cleats that will allow you to screw the top to the base. Now screw the seven slats to the ledgers.

FINISHING THE TOP

Before you attach your top, it's best to drill your dog holes and attach the vise. Lay out the location of the two rows of dog holes using the diagram. I made a simple jig to guide a ¾" auger bit in a brace and bit. The jig is shown in action in the photo at right.

Now position your vise on the underside of the top and attach it according to the directions from the manufacturer. I added a wooden jaw to my metal vise, which extends its clamping abilities and is easy on my workpieces.

Now you are almost done, but first you must flatten the top. Use "winding sticks" to divine the problem areas in your bench top.

Winding sticks are simply identical, straight lengths of hardwood. Put one on one end of the top and the other on the far end. Now crouch down so your eye is even with the sticks. If your top is flat, the sticks will line up perfectly. If not, you'll quickly see where you need work. Use a jack plane to flatten the high spots. Then work the top diagonally with a jointer plane. Finally, work the top along the grain. Rag on a couple coats of an oil/varnish blend on the base and top.

With the bench complete, I was pleased with the price and the time it took, which was about 30 hours. When you complete your bench, don't be afraid to modify it. I'm sure that my bench still has some changes in its future.

CHAPTER 12

THE PRACTICAL WORKBENCH

I'm sure there are one hundred ways to build a workbench, and all of them are correct if they meet your needs. Here's a workbench that fills all my requirements and one that will hopefully be useful in your workshop.

A bench doesn't have to be pretty. A good hardwood that's straight and flat, with a few blemishes, is just fine. After all, we're going to be pounding, clamping, dragging

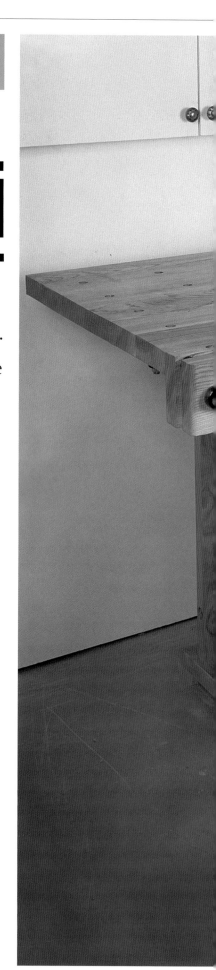

and abusing the top in the years to come. The bench should be strong and heavy enough to withstand a bit of pushing and pulling when we are working wood.

I used ash for my bench and tried to keep the best faces for my top surface. Even though I selected the wood carefully, I did have a few little checks and knots to fill. This wood wasn't a select grade, so I didn't expect perfection. Carefully sort through the lesser grades of lumber and pick the best pieces for your bench. It may not win a beauty contest, but the price will be a lot less than select-grade lumber.

A bench needs one or two good vises and, since a bench has a great deal of space below, a storage cabinet for frequently used tools. This bench has five drawers for tools and a shelf for tucking those tools aside when you are working on a project, keeping them within easy reach.

I installed two Veritas vises on my bench. The twin-screw model is a well-machined and very useful tool. The single-screw model mounted on the right side of the bench is perfect for my work. Both vises are available at Lee Valley Tools. The bench can be mounted on wheels, the vise styles and positions can be changed and the size can be altered for your shop. It's well worth your time and money to build a good workbench because it will be an important part of your shop for many years.

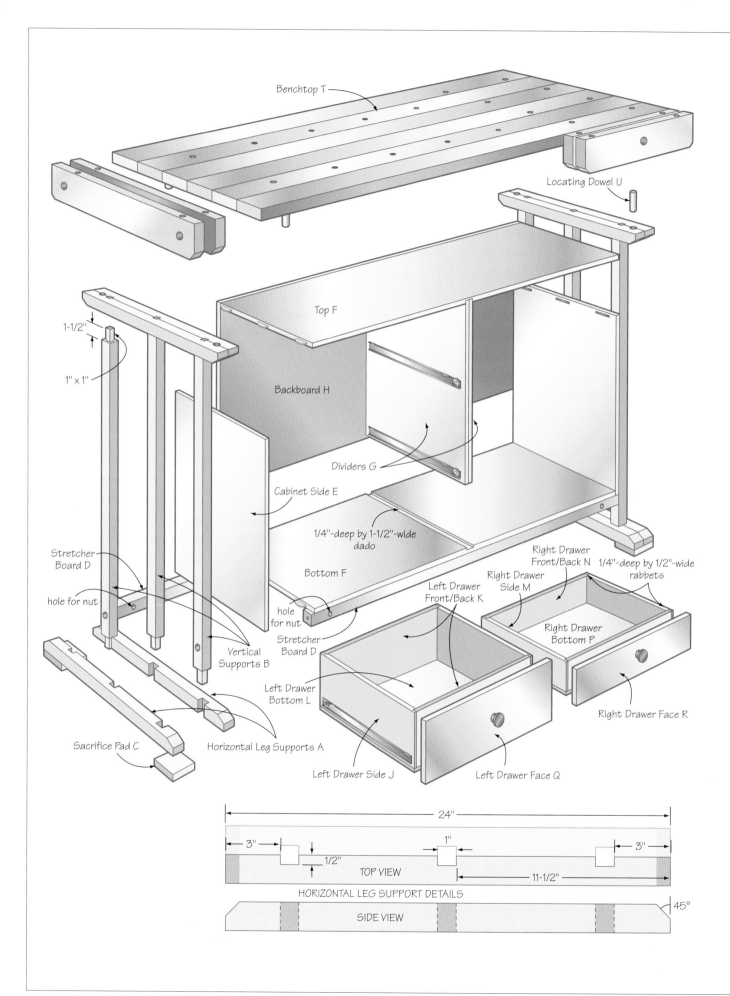

Benchtop T

Locating Dowel U

1-1/2"

1" x 1"

Top F

Backboard H

Dividers G

Cabinet Side E

1/4"-deep by 1-1/2"-wide dado

Bottom F

Right Drawer Front/Back N

Right Drawer Side M

1/4"-deep by 1/2"-wide rabbets

Stretcher Board D

hole for nut

hole for nut

Right Drawer Bottom P

Stretcher Board D

Left Drawer Front/Back K

Vertical Supports B

Left Drawer Bottom L

Right Drawer Face R

Sacrifice Pad C

Horizontal Leg Supports A

Left Drawer Side J

Left Drawer Face Q

24"

3"

1/2"

1"

3"

TOP VIEW

11-1/2"

HORIZONTAL LEG SUPPORT DETAILS

SIDE VIEW

45°

MATERIALS LIST ▪ INCHES

REFERENCE	QUANTITY	PART	STOCK	THICKNESS	WIDTH	LENGTH
A	8	horizontal supports	solid hardwood	1½	1½	24
B	6	vertical supports	solid hardwood	1½	1½	33½
C	4	sacrifice pads	solid hardwood	1	3	3
D	2	stretcher boards	solid hardwood	1½	2½	44
E	2	cabinet sides	veneer plywood	¾	16¾	20
F	2	bottom & top boards	veneer plywood	¾	16¾	42½
G	2	dividers	veneer plywood	¾	16¾	19
H	1	backboard	veneer plywood	¾	20	44

TWO LEFT-SIDE DRAWER BOXES

J	4	sides	birch plywood	½	6¾	16
K	4	fronts & backs	birch plywood	½	6¾	19
L	2	bottoms	birch plywood	½	16	19½

THREE RIGHT-SIDE DRAWER BOXES

M	6	sides	birch plywood	½	3⅝	16
N	6	fronts & backs	birch plywood	½	3⅝	19
P	3	bottoms	birch plywood	½	16	19½

DRAWER FACES

Q	2	faces	veneer plywood	¾	9¾	21½
R	2	faces	veneer plywood	¾	6¾	21½
S	1	faces	veneer plywood	¾	6	21½

BENCHTOP

T	1	benchtop	solid hardwood	1½	30	72
U	4	locating dowels	solid hardwood			
		(1" diameter by 2½" long)				

HARDWARE

5 Sets of 18"-long, ¾-extension glides (use full-extension glides if desired)

Drawer handles or knobs

PB screws

Bolts, nuts and washers as detailed

Plate joinery biscuits (#20)

Glue

4" x ⅜"-Diameter bolts with washers and nuts

Wood edge tape

1½" PB screws

1" Brad nails

½" Screws

1" Screws

OPTIONAL

1 Front vise (Veritas Tools by Lee Valley Tools #70G08.02)

1 Twin-screw vise (Veritas Tools by Lee Valley Tools #05G12.22)

4 Bench dogs (Veritas Tools by Lee Valley Tools #05G04.04)

MATERIALS LIST ▪ MILLIMETERS

REFERENCE	QUANTITY	PART	STOCK	THICKNESS	WIDTH	LENGTH
A	8	horizontal supports	solid hardwood	38	38	610
B	6	vertical supports	solid hardwood	38	38	851
C	4	sacrifice pads	solid hardwood	25	76	76
D	2	stretcher boards	solid hardwood	38	64	1118
E	2	cabinet sides	veneer plywood	19	425	508
F	2	bottom & top boards	veneer plywood	19	425	1080
G	2	dividers	veneer plywood	19	425	483
H	1	backboard	veneer plywood	1938	20	44

TWO LEFT-SIDE DRAWER BOXES

J	4	sides	birch plywood	13	171	406
K	4	fronts & backs	birch plywood	13	171	483
L	2	bottoms	birch plywood	13	406	496

THREE RIGHT-SIDE DRAWER BOXES

M	6	sides	birch plywood	13	92	406
N	6	fronts & backs	birch plywood	13	92	483
P	3	bottoms	birch plywood	13	406	496

DRAWER FACES

Q	2	faces	veneer plywood	19	248	546
R	2	faces	veneer plywood	19	171	546
S	1	faces	veneer plywood	19	152	546

BENCHTOP

T	1	benchtop	solid hardwood	38	762	1829
U	4	locating dowels	solid hardwood			
		(1" diameter by 2½" long)				

HARDWARE

5 Sets of 457mm-long, ¾-extension glides (use full-extension glides if desired)

Drawer handles or knobs

PB screws

Bolts, nuts and washers as detailed

Plate joinery biscuits (#20)

Glue

102mm x 10mm-Diameter bolts with washers and nuts

Wood edge tape

38mm PB screws

25mm Brad nails

13mm Screws

25mm Screws

OPTIONAL

1 Front vise (Veritas Tools by Lee Valley Tools #70G08.02)

1 Twin-screw vise (Veritas Tools by Lee Valley Tools #05G12.22)

4 Bench dogs (Veritas Tools by Lee Valley Tools #05G04.04)

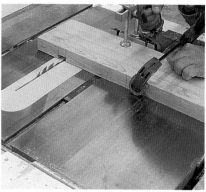

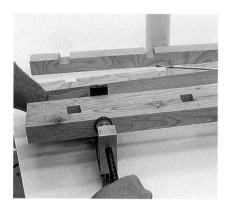

STEP 1 ▪ Rip and crosscut the eight horizontal supports A at 1¹/₂"-square by 24"-long, and the six vertical supports B at 1¹/₂"-square by 33¹/₂"-long. A good crosscut blade on a table saw will be required to cut the 1¹/₂"-thick material. A sliding table on your table saw, a radial-arm saw or power miter box can be used to crosscut the parts.

STEP 2 ▪ The eight horizontal supports A each require three dadoes that are 1"-wide by ¹/₂"-deep. Two of the dadoes are located 3" from each end, and the third is located directly in the center. Dadoes can be cut on a table saw. If possible, gang four pieces together at one time and mark the pairs; this will ensure that sets are matched for joining.

STEP 3 ▪ Glue two horizontal supports A together, forming a board with three 1"-square through-mortises. The eight supports will make four horizontal support members. Use dowels, biscuits or simply edge-glue the pieces to each other.

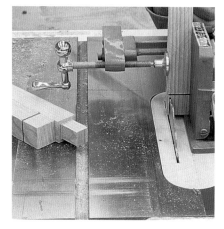

STEP 5 ▪ Cut a 45° corner on the end of all four horizontal supports A. Use a ¹/₄" roundover bit in your router to ease all the corners on the vertical supports B, and the top edges of the bottom two horizontal supports A. Don't round over the bottom of the lower horizontal supports that touch the floor or the two top horizontal supports.

STEP 4 ▪ The six vertical supports B require a 1"-square by 1¹/₂"-long tenon centered on each end. These tenons can be cut on a table saw with a miter slide or, if you have one, a tenoning jig.

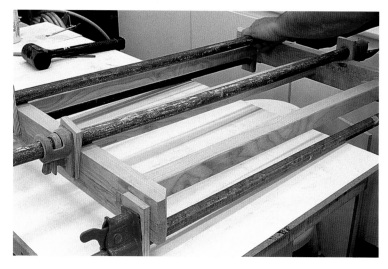

STEP 6 ▪ Build both leg assemblies using glue and clamps. The tenons should fit snugly into the mortises. Set aside both leg units until the adhesive cures.

STEP 7 ■ To save wear and tear on the lower horizontal supports, install sacrifice pads. These are 3"-square by 1"-thick and are attached with screws only. When the pads wear because the bench is moved a great deal or become damaged by moisture or liquids on the floor, simply replace the pads.

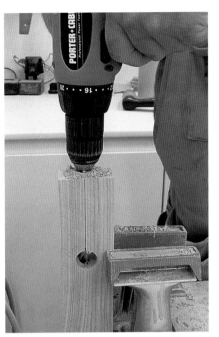

STEP 8 ■ Cut the two stretcher boards D to the size indicated in the materials list. Drill a 1"-diameter through-hole, centered 4" from each end on both stretchers. Then drill the ends of both boards using a $^3/_8$"-diameter bit. The holes are located on the center of each end and are drilled 4" deep to meet the 1"-diameter through-holes.

STEP 9 ■ Drill a $^1/_2$"-deep by 1"-diameter hole 4" above the bottom of each vertical support B. Center the hole on the four vertical uprights, making sure your measurements are from the bottom of the vertical supports and not the lower edge of the horizontal supports. Next, drill a $^3/_8$"-diameter through-hole in the center of each 1"-diameter hole for the assembly bolts. Attach both leg assemblies together using the two stretchers. Use 4"-long by $^3/_8$"-diameter bolts and washers to secure the base. The 1" hole on the outside of each vertical support will allow you to recess the bolt head, and the 1"-diameter through-hole in the stretcher board D will be used to attach the nuts to the bolts.

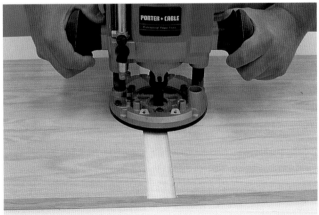

STEP 10 ■ Cut the drawer carcass parts as detailed in the materials list. I am using $^3/_4$"-thick oak veneer plywood to contrast the solid ash.

Apply wood edge tape to all front and top edges of the side boards E. The backboard H requires edge tape on the top and both side edges, as do the front edges of boards F.

Use a router to cut a $^1/_4$"-deep by $1^1/_2$"-wide dado in the center inside face of both top and bottom boards for the dividers.

STEP 11 ■ I used three #20 biscuits and glue to attach the carcass sides E to the bottom and top boards F. Dowels or screws and glue can also be used.

STEP 12 ▪ Apply glue to both dadoes and place the dividers G into those dadoes. Use a heavy weight on top of the carcass until the adhesive sets and the dividers are fixed solidly n place.

I'm using two dividers for strength because I don't want the dividers to flex, which may interfere with the drawer runners if a lot of weight is added to the top board of the carcass. It's possibly overbuilt at this point, but I'd rather have more support than needed instead of just enough.

STEP 13 ▪ The backboard H is attached with #20 biscuits and glue. Clamp it in place until the adhesive sets up.

STEP 14 ▪ Put the drawer carcass in the bench frame. Rest the bottom board on both stretchers, aligning the backboard with the outside face of the back stretcher. Use $1^1/2$" PB screws to secure the carcass to the bench frame. Do not use glue, so it can be removed if the bench must be moved.

STEP 15 ▪ I'm installing drawers on both sides of the carcass. One side will have three drawers and the other two.

Calculating drawer sizes means subtracting 1" from the interior carcass width for most drawer glides. However, it's well worth purchasing your glides at this point to verify the installation instructions.

In a frameless-style cabinet, such as this one, drawer height is found by following a few simple rules. Each drawer box should have 1" clearance above and below. That required space means there will be a 2" space between drawer boxes. The interior space is $18^1/2$" high, meaning on a two-drawer bank we must subtract 4" from that height (1" above and below each drawer box for purposes of calculating drawer height), and divide the result by two. The drawer height for the two-drawer bank will be $18^1/2$" minus 4" divided by 2, or $7^1/4$" high.

The same calculations apply to the three-drawer bank. The drawer boxes will be $18^1/2$" minus 6" divided by 3, or approximately $4^1/8$" high, to provide the correct clearance.

Cut all the drawer parts to size as detailed in the materials list. These boxes will be constructed using $1/2$" baltic birch plywood.

STEP 16 ▪ Each drawer box side J and M will need a rabbet cut $1/2$" wide by $1/4$" deep on each inside face at both ends. The back and front boards will fit into these rabbets. Use a router table or table saw to make the cuts.

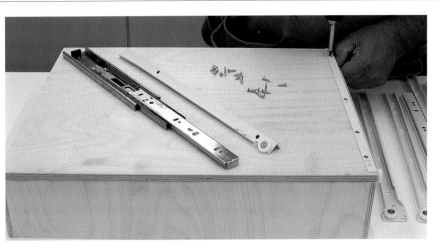

STEP 17 ■ Join the drawer box sides to the back and front boards using glue and 1" brad nails. The nails will hold the joint until the glue dries. Glue and nail the bottom boards to the drawer box frames.

STEP 18 ■ Attach drawer runners to each box. I am using $^3/_4$-extension glides, but full-extension glides (silver in the photo) can also be used if you require full access to the drawer. The full-extension models are two to three times more expensive than the $^3/_4$-extension type, but worth the extra cost if you need to fully access the drawer box.

Attach the runners using $^1/_2$" screws and follow the manufacturer's instructions.

STEP 19 ■ Mount the cabinet runners using a level line as a guide, or with a drawer glide-mounting jig.

Install one glide at the bottom of each cabinet section, and one 8" above the bottom board in the two-drawer cabinet. The three-drawer section has one set of runners at the bottom, one at 7" above the bottom board, and the top runner set 14" above the bottom.

STEP 20 ■ The drawer faces Q, R and S are made using $^3/_4$"-thick veneer plywood. All four edges of each drawer face have wood veneer tape applied.

STEP 21 ■ Here's an easy way to accurately locate drawer faces. First, drill the handle hole (or holes) in the drawer face, not through the drawer box at this point. Position the drawer face against the cabinet with the drawer box in place. Once located, drive a wood screw through the handle hole and into the drawer box until the face is secure. Next, open the drawer and drive 1" screws through the back of the drawer box front board, into the drawer face. Finally, remove the screws from the handle holes, drill holes completely through the box and install the handles or knobs.

STEP 22 ■ My benchtop T is constructed using six $5^1/_2$"-wide boards that are $1^1/_2$" thick. The boards are left longer than 72" and will be trimmed to size once the top is sanded. Thick boards can be joined with a double-biscuit technique that's shown in the photo.

STEP 23 ◾ To prepare rough boards for join-ing, flatten one face on a jointer.

STEP 24 ◾ Next, press the flat face against the jointer fence and mill one edge at 90° to the prepared face.

STEP 25 ◾ Cut the remaining rough edge parallel to the jointed edge, and at 90° to the prepared face, on a table saw. Hold the jointed edge of the board tight to the saw fence and the prepared face flat on the saw table.

STEP 26 ◾ Use a planer to dress the rough face parallel to the prepared face. The board is now ready to be joined to other boards.

STEP 27 ◾ Join the boards with clamps on the top and bottom face as shown. This over-and-under technique will help to ensure that your top will set up flat. Tighten the clamps until you see just a little of the glue squeeze out. Clamps set too tight will squeeze out a lot of glue, starving the joint and possibly making it fail.

STEP 28 ◾ Complete the top by scraping off the excess glue and sand-ing smooth. Trim to the required 30"-wide by 72"-long size. Turn the top facedown on the floor. Set the leg and carcass assembly upside down on the bottom face of the top so it's equally spaced side to side and front to back. Drill small pilot holes through the upper horizontal support and into the top. One hole at the end of each support is required.

STEP 29 ▪ Drill 1"-diameter holes, 1" deep, in the bottom face of the top using the small drill holes from the previous step as a guide. Cut and install four 2½"-long by 1"-diameter dowels in the holes using glue.

Drill 1"-diameter holes completely through the upper horizontal supports using the pilot holes as a guide. Once the adhesive sets, put the top on the base assembly with the dowels set into the four holes. You may need to widen the diameter of the horizontal support holes with sandpaper to install the top.

STEP 30 ▪ My front vise is a single-screw model made by Veritas Tools, available from Lee Valley Tools. I followed the installation instructions and added two 1½"-thick wood jaws.

STEP 31 ▪ The end vise I used is also made by Veritas and is a twin-screw model. When using large end vises on this bench, be sure the moving mechanics of the vise clear the bench supports. I used 7¼"-high wood jaws, centering the screws 3" up from the bottom edge of the boards, so both screws would clear the upper horizontal supports.

CONSTRUCTION
NOTES

I drilled ¾"-diameter holes in my benchtop to accommodate round bench dogs. Both vise jaws also had ¾"-diameter holes drilled for the round dogs. These bench dogs can be used with either vise to clamp flat boards that need to be sanded or planed.

The size of this bench, the number of drawers in the storage carcass, the height and the accessory equipment can all be modified to suit your requirements. My bench is 36" high, but that may not be suitable for everyone. If this plan isn't right for you, change the dimensions.

Hardwood is an excellent choice for any workbench. A bench will be around for many years, and may be passed to future generations of woodworkers, so use the best quality hardwood you can afford.

I finished my bench with three coats of oil-based polyurethane that is commonly used on hardwood floors. I gave the top a good coat of hard paste wax to further protect the surface from liquids and adhesive spills.

This is a great project. I hope you'll enjoy your new workbench as much as I enjoy mine.

CHAPTER 13

POWER MITER SAW STATION

I wanted to meet a number of requirements when I designed my ultimate power miter saw station.

First, the station tower had to be wide enough so I could tuck a large garbage pail inside. It also had to have easy access so I could clear and throw away scraps of wood. I sometimes get lazy and forget to remove the small scraps of wood after cutting. These pieces can contact the blade on the next cut and shoot out of the saw like a wild bullet. I have seen too many close calls using this saw, so this design feature was high on my list.

I also wanted the station fences or "wings" on my station to be high enough so I could use the floor space; I will be storing rolling workstations under the saw fences. My table height is 42" off the ground and the fences are about 2½" higher.

The station tower has a drawer to store wrenches, instruction books and any other saw accessories. I usually spend time searching the shop for these items, so I promised myself they would have a place in the station.

I was tired of using poorly designed stop blocks that could be used only for material cuts starting at 6" or more. Why couldn't a zero stop be made? I think that need was met with my stop-block system.

Finally, the "wings" had to be strong because they would be 4' to 8' long without a center support. I used hardwood and steel to edge the sheet material and make the stop-block system. The fences are extremely strong and will not deflect under heavy loads.

I used melamine particleboard (PB) for my sheet material and hardwood trim to absorb the bumps and hits during heavy use. I decided to install adjustable plastic cabinet legs so I could level the fences.

This power miter saw station is perfect for my work. It has met all my needs and is a pleasure to use. I'm sure it will be a useful addition to your shop, as well.

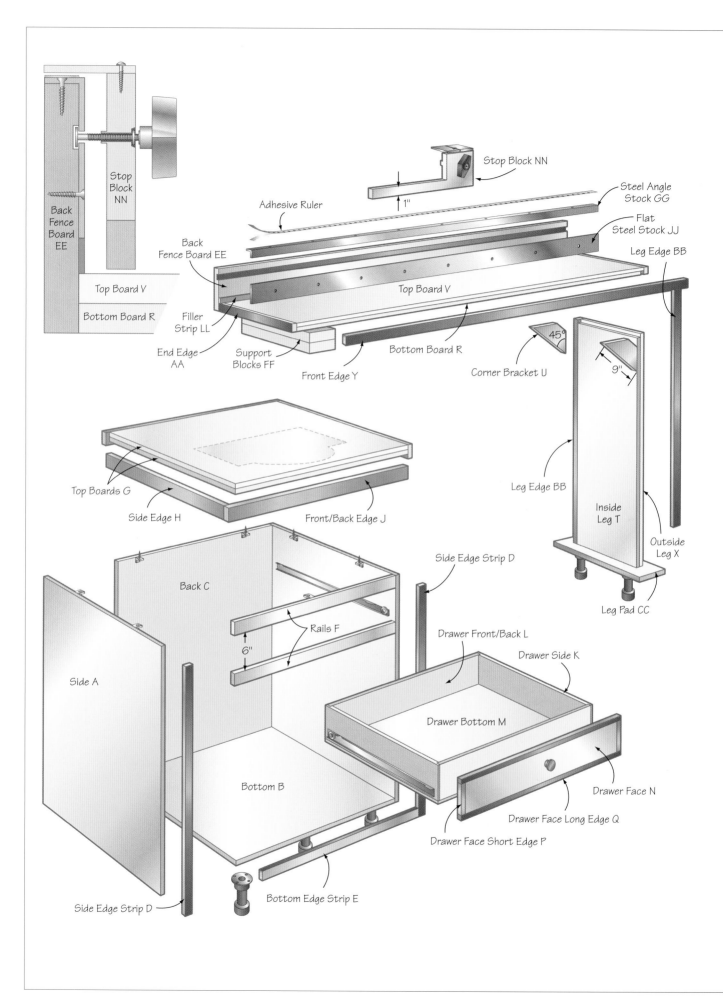

MATERIALS LIST ■ INCHES

TOWER

REFERENCE	QUANTITY	PART	STOCK	THICKNESS	WIDTH	LENGTH
A	2	sides	melamine PB	$5/8$	24	36
B	1	bottom	melamine PB	$5/8$	26	24
C	1	back	melamine PB	$5/8$	26	$35^3/8$
D	2	side edge strips	solid hardwood	$1/4$	$5/8$	36
E	1	bottom edge strip	solid hardwood	$1/4$	$5/8$	26
F	2	rails	solid hardwood	$1/4$	$1^1/2$	26
G	2	top boards	melamine PB	$5/8$	$25^1/4$	$30^1/2$
H	2	side edges	solid hardwood	$1/4$	$1^1/2$	$25^1/4$
J	2	front & back edges	solid hardwood	$1/4$	$1^1/2$	32
K	2	drawer sides	melamine PB	$5/8$	$4^3/8$	22
L	2	drawer front & back	melamine PB	$5/8$	$4^3/8$	$23^3/4$
M	1	drawer bottom	melamine PB	$5/8$	22	25
N	1	drawer face	melamine PB	$5/8$	$6^1/2$	$26^1/2$
P	2	drawer face edges	solid hardwood	$1/4$	$5/8$	$6^1/2$
Q	2	drawer face edges	solid hardwood	$1/4$	$5/8$	27

FENCE WINGS

REFERENCE	QUANTITY	PART	STOCK	THICKNESS	WIDTH	LENGTH
R	1	bottom board	melamine PB	$5/8$	7	$71^3/8$
S	1	bottom board	melamine PB	$5/8$	7	$47^3/8$
T	2	inside legs	melamine PB	$5/8$	7	$38^7/8$
U	4	corner brackets	solid hardwood	$3/4$	$3^1/2$	9
V	1	top board	melamine PB	$5/8$	7	72
W	1	top board	melamine PB	$5/8$	7	48
X	2	outside legs	melamine PB	$5/8$	7	$39^1/2$
Y	1	front edge	solid hardwood	$3/4$	$1^1/4$	$73^1/2$
Z	1	front edge	solid hardwood	$3/4$	$1^1/4$	$49^1/2$
AA	4	end edges	solid hardwood	$3/4$	$1^1/4$	7
BB	4	leg edges	solid hardwood	$3/4$	$1^1/4$	$38^7/8$
CC	2	leg pads	solid hardwood	$3/4$	$3^1/2$	$8^1/2$
DD	1	back fence board	solid hardwood	$3/4$	$5^1/4$	$49^1/2$
EE	1	back fence board	solid hardwood	$3/4$	$5^1/4$	$73^1/2$
FF	2	support blocks	solid hardwood	$1^1/2$	$2^{11}/16$	6
GG	1	angle stock	steel	$1/8$	1×1	72
HH	1	angle stock	steel	$1/8$	1×1	48
JJ	1	flat stock	steel	$1/8$	2	72
KK	1	flat stock	steel	$1/8$	2	48
LL	1	filler strip	solid hardwood	$1/8$	$3/4$	72
MM	1	filler strip	solid hardwood	$1/8$	$3/4$	48
NN	2	stop blocks	solid hardwood	$3/4$	$3^7/8$	14

HARDWARE

10 Adjustable plastic cabinet legs

1 – 22" Drawer glide set

7 Metal right-angle brackets

2 Metal self-sticking measuring tapes

1 – $5/16$"-Diameter closet bolt set

2 Stop-block handles

1 Drawer handle

2 – 2" x 3" Plastic or Plexiglass

Metal washers

White iron-on edge tape

Screw cover caps

Screws as detailed

Glue

Wood plugs

2" PB screws

Biscuits or confirmat screws

$5/8$" Screws

Brad nails

Wood putty

1" Screws

3" Screws

Pan head screws and washers

MATERIALS LIST ■ MILLIMETERS

TOWER

REFERENCE	QUANTITY	PART	STOCK	THICKNESS	WIDTH	LENGTH
A	2	sides	melamine PB	16	610	914
B	1	bottom	melamine PB	16	660	610
C	1	back	melamine PB	16	660	899
D	2	side edge strips	solid hardwood	6	16	914
E	1	bottom edge strip	solid hardwood	6	16	660
F	2	rails	solid hardwood	6	38	660
G	2	top boards	melamine PB	16	641	775
H	2	side edges	solid hardwood	6	38	641
J	2	front & back edges	solid hardwood	6	38	813
K	2	drawer sides	melamine PB	16	112	559
L	2	drawer front & back	melamine PB	16	112	603
M	1	drawer bottom	melamine PB	16	559	635
N	1	drawer face	melamine PB	16	165	673
P	2	drawer face edges	solid hardwood	6	16	165
Q	2	drawer face edges	solid hardwood	6	16	686

FENCE WINGS

REFERENCE	QUANTITY	PART	STOCK	THICKNESS	WIDTH	LENGTH
R	1	bottom board	melamine PB	16	178	1813
S	1	bottom board	melamine PB	16	178	1204
T	2	inside legs	melamine PB	16	178	987
U	4	corner brackets	solid hardwood	19	89	229
V	1	top board	melamine PB	16	178	1829
W	1	top board	melamine PB	16	178	1219
X	2	outside legs	melamine PB	16	178	1004
Y	1	front edge	solid hardwood	19	31	1867
Z	1	front edge	solid hardwood	19	31	1258
AA	4	end edges	solid hardwood	19	31	178
BB	4	leg edges	solid hardwood	19	31	987
CC	2	leg pads	solid hardwood	19	89	216
DD	1	back fence board	solid hardwood	19	133	1258
EE	1	back fence board	solid hardwood	19	133	1867
FF	2	support blocks	solid hardwood	38	69	152
GG	1	angle stock	steel	3	25 x 25	1829
HH	1	angle stock	steel	3	25 x 25	1219
JJ	1	flat stock	steel	3	51	1829
KK	1	flat stock	steel	3	51	1219
LL	1	filler strip	solid hardwood	3	19	1829
MM	1	filler strip	solid hardwood	3	19	1219
NN	2	stop blocks	solid hardwood	19	98	356

HARDWARE

10 Adjustable plastic cabinet legs

1 – 559mm Drawer glide set

7 Metal right-angle brackets

2 Metal self-sticking measuring tapes

1 – 8mm-Diameter closet bolt set

2 Stop-block handles

1 Drawer handle

2 – 51mm x 76mm Plastic or Plexiglass

Metal washers

White iron-on edge tape

Screw cover caps

Screws as detailed

Glue

Wood plugs

51mm PB screws

Biscuits or confirmat screws

16mm Screws

Brad nails

Wood putty

25mm Screws

76mm Screws

Pan head screws and washers

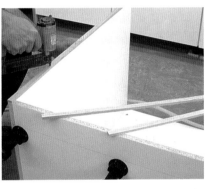

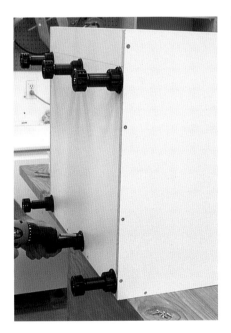

STEP 1 ■ Cut the two sides A and bottom board B as detailed in the materials list. The joinery can be PB screws (on the right in the photo), biscuits (center) or confirmat screws (left). The confirmat screws are European-designed fasteners that are used to assemble melamine PB cabinetry. They a re high-quality fasteners, but they do require a special step drill and accurate placement. The drill bits are expensive and brittle. The PB screws are de-signed to join this material, and the heads can be hidden with plastic cover caps.

I am using 2" PB screws placed 6" apart along the joint. Small white caps or white adhesive covers are available at woodworking and home stores.

STEP 2 ■ The inset backboard C is joined to the sides and bottom board with 2" PB screws. The back face of the backboard is flush with the back edges of the side and bottom boards.

STEP 4 ■ The cabinet edges could suffer a few knocks and bumps, so I installed hardwood edge strips D and E on the bottom and two side panels. Use glue and brad nails to secure the strips of wood. Fill the nail holes with wood putty and sand the strips smooth.

STEP 3 ■ I'm installing six adjustable plastic legs on my tower cabinet. The front legs are set back 3" and secured with four ⅝" screws. Position the flanges of the front and rear out-side legs under the edges of the side boards. The load will be transferred directly to the sides, through the legs and onto the floor.

You can build and install a 4"-high base frame made with solid lumber or sheet material if there isn't a danger of liquid spills or water leaks on your shop floor. If water is an issue, or your shop floor isn't level, adjustable cabinet legs are the perfect solution.

SHOP TIP

You can avoid splitting panels by keeping screws 1" away from any board end when joining sheet goods. Always drill a pilot hole for the screws to ensure maxi-mum hold.

STEP 5 ■ Install the two hardwood rails F, one at the top of the cabinet and the other below it, leaving a 6" space between the rails for a drawer. Secure the rails with right-angle brackets and ⅝" screws, or use pocket holes if you have a jig. Apply a little glue on the front edges to secure the rails to the side wood strips. Clamp until the adhesive cures.

STEP 6 ■ Install seven right-angle brackets using ⅝" screws. One is located in the middle of the top rail and two on each of the back and side boards. These brackets will be used to secure the cabinet top.

STEP 7 ■ The cabinet top G is 32" wide by 26¾" deep overall. It is made with two layers of ⅝"-thick melamine PB, and joined with 1" screws from the underside. A ¾"-thick by 1½"-wide hardwood band, H and J, is applied to all four edges. Use glue and 2" screws in a ⅜" counterbored hole and fill the holes with wood plugs. You can also use biscuits (plate joinery) if you prefer that method.

STEP 8 ■ Attach the banded top to the cabinet using 1" screws through the right-angle brackets previously installed. The top overhangs the back by ¾" and by 2⅜" on each side.

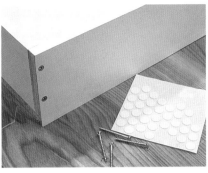

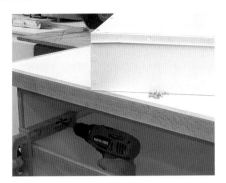

STEP 9 ■ Drawer boxes are commonly 1" less in height and width when using most ³/₄-extension drawer glide sets. This rule is also applied to most full-extension drawer glide sets. However, read the installation instructions with your hardware before cutting the drawer box parts.

Cut the drawer box parts K through M and apply iron-on edge tape to the upper edges of the side, back and front boards. The side edges of the bottom board also require edge tape.

STEP 10 ■ Join the sides to the back and front boards using 2" PB screws. The bottom board is also installed using 2" screws about 8" apart. Cut the bottom board square and it will ensure that your drawer box is square. The box should be 5" high by 25" wide by 22" deep. The screw heads can be covered with plastic caps or white stick-on covers. Refer to chapter one for more details.

STEP 11 ■ Mount the drawer glide runners on the cabinet sides, attach the two drawer runners to the box using ⁵/₈" screws and test fit your drawer. The cabinet runners can be installed using a straight line made with a carpenter's square, or a drawer glide-mounting jig.

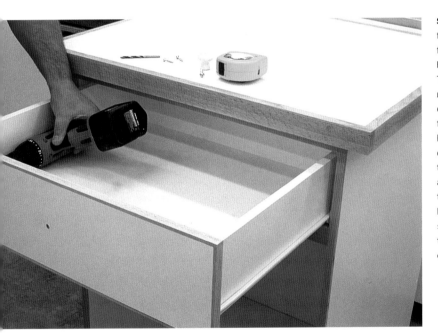

STEP 12 ■ The finished size of the drawer face is 7" high by 27" wide. I made my drawer face with ⁵/₈"-thick melamine PB and ¹/₄"-thick by ⁵/₈"-wide hardwood strips on all four edges. The strips were installed with glue and brad nails. To ensure perfect drawer-face alignment, drill the handle or knob holes in the drawer face only. Put the drawer box in the cabinet, hold the drawer face in its correct position, and drive screws through the holes securing it to the drawer box. Then carefully open the drawer and secure the face by driving 1" screws through the drawer box front board into the back of the drawer face. Remove the screw (or screws) in the handle holes and drill through the drawer box. Finally, install the handle to complete the installation.

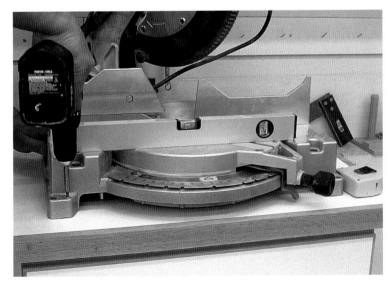

STEP 13 ■ Place the tower section where it will be used in your shop and level the cabinet front to back and side to side. Center the miter saw on the top and secure it with screws or bolts. It's difficult to generalize on methods to secure your saw because so many models are available. However, once you have it installed trace an outline on the top with a permanent marker. If the saw has to be removed from the station, it can easily be returned to the same position using the trace lines.

STEP 14 ▪ The right-side fence platform on my station will be 6' long, and the left side will be 4' long. Both will be built with 7"-wide melamine PB and edged with $\frac{3}{4}$" hardwood that's $1\frac{1}{4}$" wide so it will cover the double-thickness melamine PB pieces. The lengths of these fence platforms are determined by the amount of space you have available and the type of cutting you do in your shop. Change the lengths of the horizontal boards to suit your shop.

Cut the inside legs T and bottom boards R and S to size. Attach the horizontal bottom shelves to the inside leg top ends using 2" PB screws. Cut the four brackets U and attach two at each corner using 2" screws.

STEP 15 ▪ Cut the two top boards V and W, as well as the two outside legs X, to size. Attach the boards as shown in the drawing, using 1" screws from the underside of the bottom top board and back side of the inside leg board. The photo shows proper placement of the boards with the fence assembly's top board resting upside down on the workbench. Two screws, 8" apart and placed in 1" from the edges, will create a solid melamine "sandwich." Hide the screw heads on the legs with plastic caps or stickers.

STEP 16 ▪ All the exposed edges, with the exception of the two back edges on the horizontal platforms, are banded with $\frac{3}{4}$"-thick by $1\frac{1}{4}$"-wide hardwood. Use glue and screws, in counterbored holes, to attach the hardwood to the front and ends of both platforms, as well as the back and front edges of the legs. Fill the screw head holes with wood plugs.

STEP 17 ▪ The size of the leg pad CC will depend on the style of leg you install. My legs require a wide base so I attached a $3\frac{1}{2}$"-wide pad with screws and glue. The legs are secured with four $\frac{5}{8}$" screws.

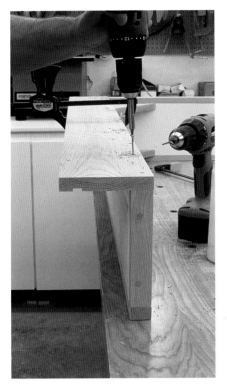

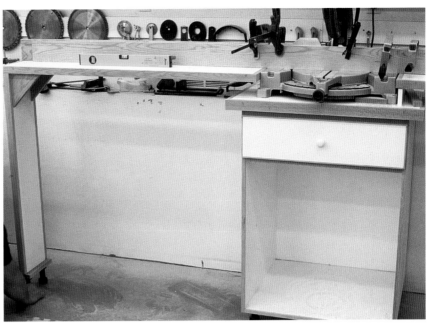

STEP 18 ■ The back fence boards must be cut and grooved before being attached. The groove is $1/2$" wide by $1/8$" deep and is located $3/4$" down from the top edge of each fence board. Attach the fence boards DD and EE with glue and 2" screws. The boards are installed with the groove at the top and facing inward toward the platform. The bottom of each fence board is flush with the bottom face of the lower melamine fence platform boards R and S.

STEP 19 ■ Clamp a long straightedge across the saw bed. Level each fence platform by blocking the end that rests on the tower tabletop and adjusting the legs at the ends. The fence platforms must be flush with the saw platform. Set the face of the platform fences $1/8$" behind the saw fence because we will be installing $1/8$"-thick steel on the fence.

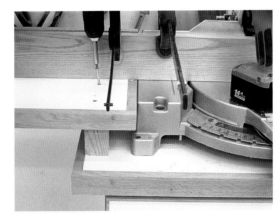

STEP 20 ■ Cut two support blocks FF (the block thickness I needed to match my saw's platform was $2^{11}/16$") and attach them to the tower tabletop with screws driven from the underside of that top. Use 3" screws to secure the platforms to each block, making certain the fence platforms are level with the saw's platform.

STEP 21 ■ The next step is to build a stop-block system. First, drill and attach $1/8$"-thick steel angle stock parts GG and HH on the top of each platform fence board. Steel angle and flat stock is available at most hardware and home stores. The steel angle stock is $7/8$" wide on the inside face and will rest $1/8$" lower than the top of the fence groove. Be sure to countersink the screw heads so the adhesive steel ruler will lay flat on top of the angle stock.

SHOP TIP

Construct or buy a wall bracket if you are concerned about bumping the platforms with heavy lumber. The platforms are solid and stable, but you may want extra support, so attach a bracket between the legs and a wall. The miter station tower can also be anchored to the wall for extra stability, however, the tower and fence platforms are rigid and will remain aligned under normal usage.

STEP 22 ■ Drill and countersink the $\frac{1}{8}$"-thick by 2"-wide steel flat stock pieces JJ and KK. The holes should be about 6" apart and countersunk so the screw heads are below the stock's surface. Attach the flat steel to the back fence boards using $\frac{5}{8}$" screws.

The bolts that will be used for the stop assemblies are a toilet or closet bolt set; they are $\frac{5}{16}$"-diameter bolts with large, flat oval heads. Clamp the flat steel below the angle stock with a bolt in the groove. The bolts should move freely, but you shouldn't be able to pull them out.

STEP 23 ■ Once the steel pieces have been installed and the bolts are moving freely along the length of each track, cut and install filler strips LL and MM. These strips will make the fence flush from top to bottom. Use glue and brad nails to secure the strips.

STEP 24 ■ Install self-sticking measuring tapes on top of each angle iron. You'll need left-to-right and right-to-left reading tapes. The zero mark on each ruler should align with the end of each angle iron closest to the miter saw.

SHOP TIP

You can use aluminum stock, but steel is about one-half the cost and is much stronger. The same fence system can also be built using an aluminum T-track set into a groove in the back fence board. I've opted for steel in this case because it strengthens the fence platforms.

STEP 25 ■ Cut stop-block boards NN as shown in the materials list. They will be trimmed to size on the miter station. Set the table saw fence for a $\frac{5}{8}$"-thick cut with the blade 1" high. Run both boards through the saw, on edge. Reset the blade $2\frac{1}{2}$" high and run both boards through the saw once again after flipping them. The result will be a $\frac{1}{8}$"-thick by $\frac{1}{4}$"-wide tenon on the back face of each board. The tenon will slide in the space between both pieces of steel and stabilize the stop block.

STEP 26 ■ Cut the stop-block boards on a band saw or with a jigsaw, as shown. The first 3" of the board should be full height and the remainder 1" high. Remember that you'll need a right and left stop-block assembly, so pay close attention to how the cut lines are laid out on each board.

STEP 27 ■ Drill a ³⁄₈"-diameter hole through the middle of each tenon on both stop blocks. The holes should be centered on the width of the full-height portion of each block. Use a closet bolt and washer with a suitable knob to attach each block. I found the knobs at my local hardware store with a thread pattern that matched the closet bolt set. Most woodworking stores also carry these knobs in many styles.

CONSTRUCTION
NOTES

I decided to use steel for these long fence platforms because I didn't want any deflection, and the result was impressive. Both fence systems are stable and rigid.

The fence platforms are high enough so I can store other workstations underneath, which is a real bonus in any shop. I used melamine PB for the field and oak hardwood for the edges; however, any sheet material and wood banding can be used. The smooth surface of the melamine makes it easy to slide the boards being cut, but materials such as medium-density fiberboard will serve the same purpose.

The dimensions of the tower can be changed if you find the height unsuitable. My tower interior width was designed to hold a large plastic pail for scraps, but it can be narrower if you don't need a scrap pail. My platform is wide because my 12" miter saw has a large bed. Smaller saws are common, so design your tower top to hold the saw you own. I don't think there are much wider miter saws on the market, but it's well worth taking the time to measure your saw before building the tower.

You can include many other features in your design. For example, a rack could be attached to the outside face of the side boards to hold saw blades. Or the drawer could be divided with partitions for various tools and documents that are needed for your saw. I also considered adding another cabinet beside the tower with adjustable shelves for storing small cutoffs that can be used for other projects.

If you don't have access to adjustable legs, or prefer a solid base, you can construct one with 2x4 material or plywood. The steel, closet bolts and knobs are common hardware items and should be readily available at your local hardware store.

STEP 28 ■ The stop-block position is determined by a clear plastic indicator screwed to the top of each stop block. Clear plastic or Plexiglass is available at craft and plastic supply stores.

Cut two pieces each 2" wide by 3" long. Scribe a fine line in the plastic with an awl or other sharp tool. Use a permanent marker to fill the scratch with ink. Attach the indicator to the stop block with pan head screws and washers in oval-shaped holes that will allow side-to-side adjustment. Align the mark on the plastic indicator to zero on the tape measure and trim the tongue on the stop block with your miter saw. That's your zero measurement for each block, and if you need to fine-tune the adjustment, loosen the screws and move the plastic indicator.

CHAPTER 14

MULTIFUNCTION POWER-TOOL CABINET

A power tool stand is a great addition to any workshop; however, if you have limited space, need to move the tools out of the way for your car or don't use certain tools on a regular basis, a dedicated power tool station is not much use. I think you'll find this tool cabinet answers all those needs.

This versatile tool cabinet has a removable platform that locks securely into place in less than a minute. It can be used with dozens of power tools that are secured to individual mounting boards. The cabinet has four locking wheels, an open shelf for accessories, and a drawer to store all the documentation and extra parts that come with your tools.

The cabinet is built with tough, inexpensive ⅝" melamine particleboard (PB) and hardwood edging so it will last for years. It can be tucked away in a corner or stored under the miter saw station wings described in chapter three.

The top and tool platforms are constructed using ¾"-thick medium-density fiberboard (MDF), which is another inexpensive sheet material. The drawer is ⅝" melamine PB and mounted on ¾-extension, bottom-mount drawer glides. The cabinet also has enough room to store a second power tool on its mounting platform, in the bottom section.

This has been one of the most valuable cabinets I've built for my shop. Moving the power tools to my work area, with all the accessories on board where I can quickly locate them, is a real benefit, and I'm enjoying my work even more. I was so pleased with this mobile tool cabinet that I built two and may build another in the near future. I hope you'll find it just as useful and build one or two for your shop.

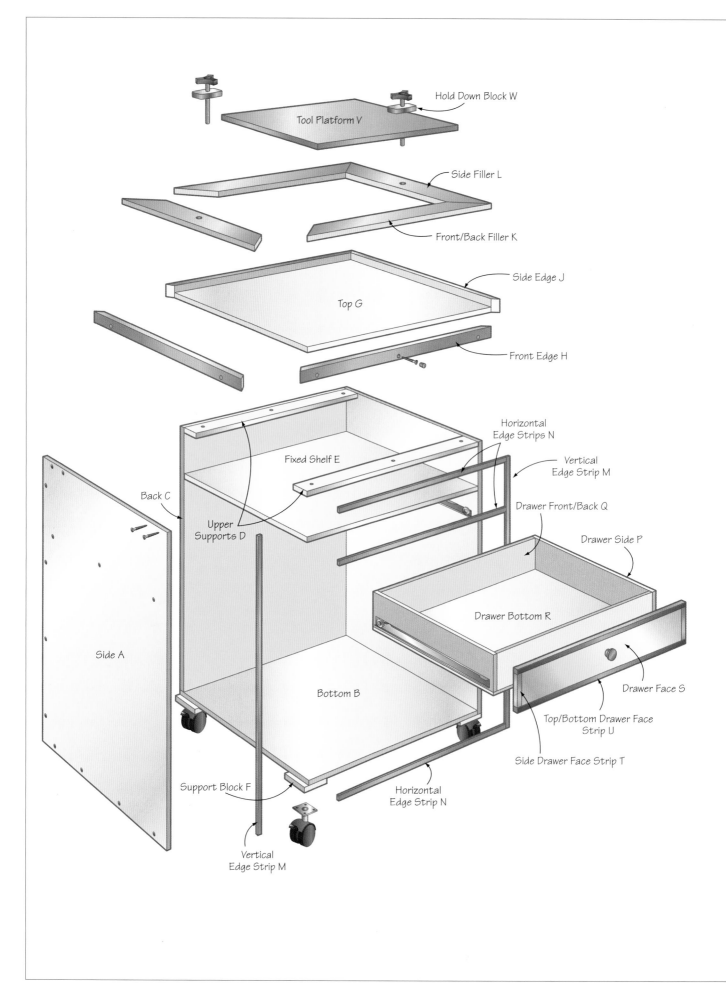

Tool Platform V

Hold Down Block W

Side Filler L

Front/Back Filler K

Side Edge J

Top G

Front Edge H

Horizontal Edge Strips N

Vertical Edge Strip M

Drawer Front/Back Q

Drawer Side P

Fixed Shelf E

Back C

Upper Supports D

Drawer Bottom R

Side A

Bottom B

Drawer Face S

Top/Bottom Drawer Face Strip U

Side Drawer Face Strip T

Support Block F

Horizontal Edge Strip N

Vertical Edge Strip M

MATERIALS LIST ■ INCHES

REFERENCE	QUANTITY	PART	STOCK	THICKNESS	WIDTH	LENGTH	COMMENTS
A	2	sides	melamine PB	⁵⁄₈	20	32	
B	1	bottom	melamine PB	⁵⁄₈	20	26	
C	1	back	melamine PB	⁵⁄₈	26	31³⁄₈	
D	2	upper supports	melamine PB	⁵⁄₈	4	26	
E	1	fixed shelf	melamine PB	⁵⁄₈	19³⁄₈	26	
F	4	support blocks	hardwood	³⁄₄	3¹⁄₂	3¹⁄₂	
G	1	top	melamine PB	⁵⁄₈	21	30	
H	2	front & back edges	hardwood	³⁄₄	1³⁄₈	31¹⁄₂	angle-cut
J	2	side edges	hardwood	³⁄₄	1³⁄₈	22¹⁄₂	angle-cut
K	2	front & back top fillers	MDF	³⁄₄	2¹⁄₄	30	angle-cut
L	2	side fillers	MDF	³⁄₄	2¹⁄₄	21	angle-cut
M	2	vertical edge strips	hardwood	¹⁄₄	⁵⁄₈	32	
N	3	horizontal edge strips	hardwood	¹⁄₄	⁵⁄₈	26	
P	2	drawer sides	melamine PB	⁵⁄₈	4³⁄₈	18	
Q	2	drawer front & back	melamine PB	⁵⁄₈	4³⁄₈	23³⁄₄	
R	1	drawer bottom	melamine PB	⁵⁄₈	18	25	
S	1	drawer face	melamine PB	⁵⁄₈	6¹⁄₂	26¹⁄₂	
T	2	side drawer face strips	hardwood	¹⁄₄	⁵⁄₈	6¹⁄₂	
U	2	top/bottom drawer face strips	hardwood	¹⁄₄	⁵⁄₈	27	
V	3	tool platforms	MDF	³⁄₄	16¹⁄₂	25¹⁄₂	
W	2	hold-down blocks	hardwood	³⁄₄	1¹⁄₂	3	

HARDWARE

4 Locking wheel casters
1 – 18" Drawer glide set
2 Knobs, ¹⁄₄"-diameter thread
2 Hanger bolts, 2¹⁄₂"-long x ¹⁄₄"-diameter thread
2 – ¹⁄₄" Metal washers
White iron-on edge tape
Screw cover caps
Screws as detailed
Glue
Wood plugs
2" Screws
Biscuits
Dowels
1¹⁄₄" Screws
1" Screws
Brad nails
Wood putty
⁵⁄₈" Screws

MATERIALS LIST ■ MILLIMETERS

REFERENCE	QUANTITY	PART	STOCK	THICKNESS	WIDTH	LENGTH	COMMENTS
A	2	sides	melamine PB	16	508	813	
B	1	bottom	melamine PB	16	508	660	
C	1	back	melamine PB	16	660	797	
D	2	upper supports	melamine PB	16	102	660	
E	1	fixed shelf	melamine PB	16	493	660	
F	4	support blocks	hardwood	19	89	89	
G	1	top	melamine PB	16	533	762	
H	2	front & back edges	hardwood	19	35	800	angle-cut
J	2	side edges	hardwood	19	35	572	angle-cut
K	2	front & back top fillers	MDF	19	57	762	angle-cut
L	2	side fillers	MDF	19	57	533	angle-cut
M	2	vertical edge strips	hardwood	6	16	813	
N	3	horizontal edge strips	hardwood	6	16	660	
P	2	drawer sides	melamine PB	16	112	457	
Q	2	drawer front & back	melamine PB	16	112	603	
R	1	drawer bottom	melamine PB	16	457	635	
S	1	drawer face	melamine PB	16	165	673	
T	2	side drawer face strips	hardwood	6	16	165	
U	2	top/bottom drawer face strips	hardwood	6	16	686	
V	3	tool platforms	MDF	19	419	648	
W	2	hold-down blocks	hardwood	19	38	76	

HARDWARE

4 Locking wheel casters
1 – 457mm Drawer glide set
2 Knobs, 6mm-diameter thread
2 Hanger bolts, 64mm-long x 6mm-diameter thread
2 – 6mm Metal washers
White iron-on edge tape
Screw cover caps
Screws as detailed
Glue
Wood plugs
51mm Screws
Biscuits
Dowels
32mm Screws
25mm Screws
Brad nails
Wood putty
16mm Screws

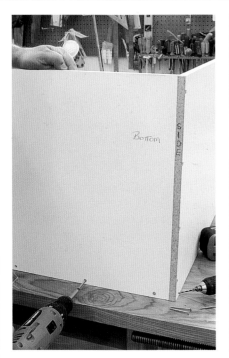

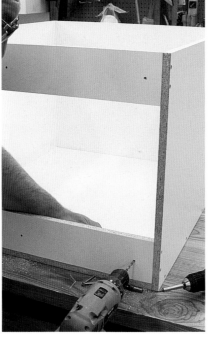

STEP 1 ■ Cut the sides A, bottom B and back C to the sizes listed in the materials list using ⁵⁄₈" melamine PB. Attach the sides to the bottom board using 2" PB screws in pilot holes spaced 6" apart. The inset backboard is also attached with screws through the side and bottom boards.

The joinery can be done with PB screws, biscuits or dowels and glue. The screw heads can be covered with plastic or self-adhesive cover caps.

STEP 2 ■ The two upper supports D are added so the cabinet sides remain parallel at the top. They will also be used to secure the top board. Cut the two supports to length, installing the front board flush with the edges of the side panels. Secure the boards with 2" PB screws, placed 1" in from each edge to avoid splitting the boards. Drill through-holes for the screws, which will be used to secure the top.

STEP 3 ■ The middle fixed shelf E is installed 6" below the bottom surface of the upper supports. Holding a shelf accurately in place is difficult, so I've cut two 24¹⁄₈"-high temporary spacers to properly locate the shelf. Use a square to mark the screw position in the center of the fixed shelf's edge on the side and back panels. Drive 2" screws, in pilot holes, through the panels to secure the shelf. Cover the screw heads with caps.

SHOP TIP

Many woodworkers have a sliding table for crosscutting panels; however, it isn't safe to use the fence and another guide device when crosscutting because there's a possibility that the board will bind in the blade and be thrown backwards. Instead you can use the measuring feature on your saw fence by adding a stop block. The panel being cut on a sliding table will leave the block before it completes the cut, making the operation safe. Remember to add 1" (with a 1"-thick block) to the fence distance to account for the stop-block thickness.

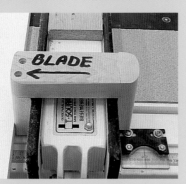

STEP 4 ■ Attach four caster support blocks F on the corners of the cabinet. Position the blocks so the outside edges are flush with the outside edges of the cabinet. Use 2" screws on the outside edges through the blocks and into the back or side boards. The inner edges are secured with 1¹⁄₄" screws into the bottom board.

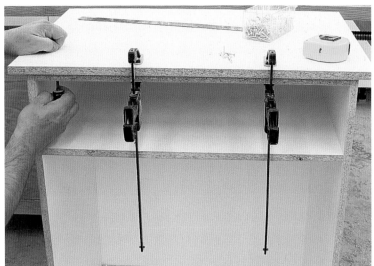

STEP 5 ▪ Mount four locking casters on the blocks using 1¼" screws or lag bolts.

STEP 6 ▪ Attach the cabinet top G with an overhang of ½" on the front and back. The sides will have an overhang of 1⅜". Use 1" screws through the upper supports D to secure the top board.

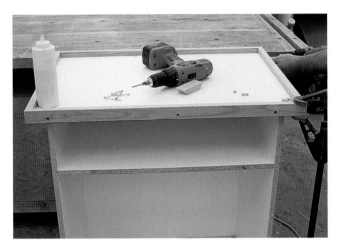

STEP 7 ▪ The top board G is banded with ¾"-thick by 1⅜"-high hardwood. The hardwood edge is flush with the bottom face of the top board and ¾" above the top's surface. Cut the corners of the hardwood banding at 45° and secure them with biscuits and glue or, as I'm using, screws and glue. Fill the counterbored holes with wood plugs and sand smooth.

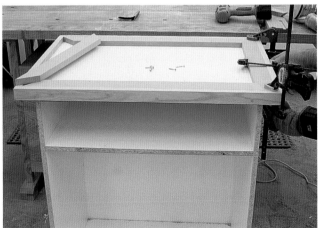

STEP 8 ▪ The tabletop fillers K and L are ¾" MDF. One sheet of 4x8 MDF has enough material for six tool platforms as well as the 2¼"-wide filler boards. The corners are joined at 45°, and the fillers are held in place with 1¼" screws from the underside of the tabletop.

STEP 9 ▪ Lay the cabinet on its back and trim the edges with ¼"-thick by ⅝"-wide hardwood strips M and N. Attach the strips with glue and brad nails. Fill the nail holes with wood putty and sand smooth.

STEP 10 ■ The next step is to build an accessory drawer under the fixed shelf. The drawer box is 5" high by 18" deep and 1" narrower than the inside cabinet width, or 25". It will be installed with bottom-mounted $^3/_4$-extension drawer glides. The drawer box is constructed using $^5/_8$"-thick melamine PB.

Cut the drawer sides P, front and back Q and drawer bottom R. Use iron-on edge tape to cover the top edges of the sides, back and front boards, as well as the side edges of the bottom board.

STEP 11 ■ Attach the drawer box sides to the back and front boards using 2" PB screws in pilot holes. Attach the bottom using 2" PB screws.

STEP 13 ■ The drawer face S is 2" wider and 2" higher than the drawer box, or 27" wide by 7" high. The drawer face is trimmed with $^1/_4$"-thick by $^5/_8$"-wide hardwood strips. To arrive at the final height, cut the melamine PB center $^1/_2$" less in width and height.

Attach the edge strips T and U with glue and brad nails. Fill the holes with wood putty and sand the edges smooth.

STEP 12 ■ Install the drawer glide hardware following the manufacturer's instructions. The cabinet runners are installed with the bottom track 6" below the fixed storage shelf E. Use a carpenter's square to draw a screw-hole reference line or a drawer glide-mounting jig to install the runners with $^5/_8$" screws.

STEP 14 ■ Attach the face to the drawer box using 1" screws through the back side of the drawer box front board. I drill the handle hole (or holes) in my drawer face and drive a screw through that hole to temporarily secure the face board in the proper position. Then I gently open the drawer and install the 1" screws through the back. Once the face is secure, I remove the screw from the handle hole and drill completely through the drawer box to install a knob or handle.

146

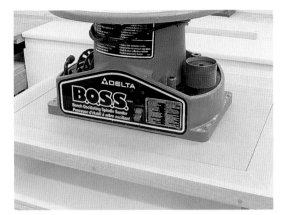

STEP 15 ■ The tool platforms V are ³/₄"-thick MDF. I cut three platforms for each of my two mobile tool stations. However, you can make as many as you need to mount your power tools. A platform without a tool can be used as a mobile worktable when needed.

CONSTRUCTION
NOTES

Most of the benchtop power tools in my shop will fit on the 16¹/₂"-deep by 25¹/₂"-wide platforms; however, the cabinet size should meet your needs. Build it to the dimensions shown in this chapter or change the width, height or depth as needed. If you do alter the platform size, be sure it will fit in the lower section of the cabinet to take advantage of all the storage space.

I used melamine particleboard and medium-density fiberboard, but any sheet material you feel comfortable with will work just as well. I like these materials because they are inexpensive and, in the case of melamine PB, already finished with a tough coating. Both materials can be securely joined using PB screws.

These power tool stations are mobile but can be made stationary by replacing the wheels with a fixed base. They'll work just as well against a wall if you have the space available. I opted for mobile units because they can be tucked away under the wings of my power miter saw station, built in chapter three.

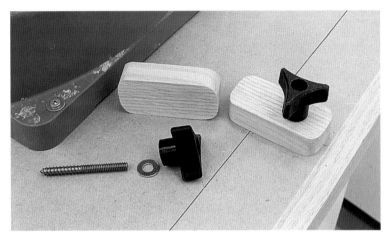

STEP 16 ■ The tool platforms are held in place with a simple lock assembly. Screw a 2¹/₂"-long by ¹/₄"-diameter hanger bolt into the side fillers, 1" back from the inside edge. Cut and round over the corners of a ³/₄"-thick by 3"-long piece of hardwood. Drill a ⁵/₁₆"-diameter hole in this hold-down block W, 1" from an end, and slip it over the hanger bolt. Place a metal washer on the bolt and attach a ¹/₄"-diameter threaded knob. One block on each side will secure the tool platform when the knobs are tightened.

STEP 17 ■ Benchtop power tools, like the planer shown in this photograph, require infeed and outfeed tables. If they were fixed in place, the tool would be larger than the platform's footprint, making storage difficult. You can easily build removable platforms using hanger bolts, spacer cleats and knobs. In this example my feed tables are longer than the factory-supplied models and will provide more support for the material being machined.

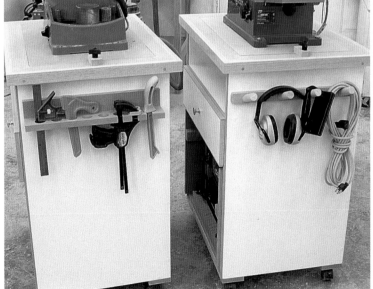

STEP 18 ■ Dozens of different tool holders can be attached to the sides of your mobile power tool cabinets. Extension cords, safety equipment and other accessories required when working with different benchtop power tools can be installed.

CHAPTER 15

POWER-TOOL STORAGE STATION

The multifunction power tool cabinets I built in chapter four are great. So great, in fact, that I've mounted a number of my benchtop tools on the interchangeable table inserts. However, I discovered that I needed more storage space for these tools on platforms.

I didn't want a cabinet that took up a lot of valuable space in my shop, so I designed this tall storage station. It uses less than 3' square of shop floor to store a number of power tools. This storage station is the perfect companion to the tool cabinet in chapter four.

The station is built with 5/8"-thick melamine particleboard (PB) and has holes drilled 2" apart for plastic-covered steel shelf pins. The pins can be placed in any of the vertical holes, allowing you to design your own storage arrangement.

You don't have to remove the benchtop tools from their drop-in platforms; they slide right into the storage station on the steel pins. Each platform rests on six shelf pins, so they are well supported.

The tool station can be made with less than two sheets of material, which means it's not expensive to build. The tools mounted to the platforms drop into the multifunction cabinet and you're ready to work. Fast access to tools, compact storage and a reasonable construction cost make this storage station well worth building. It can also be used with shelf boards for other shop tools, even if you don't build the multifunction cabinet in chapter four. Simply cut shelf boards to fit and locate the pins to suit your storage requirements.

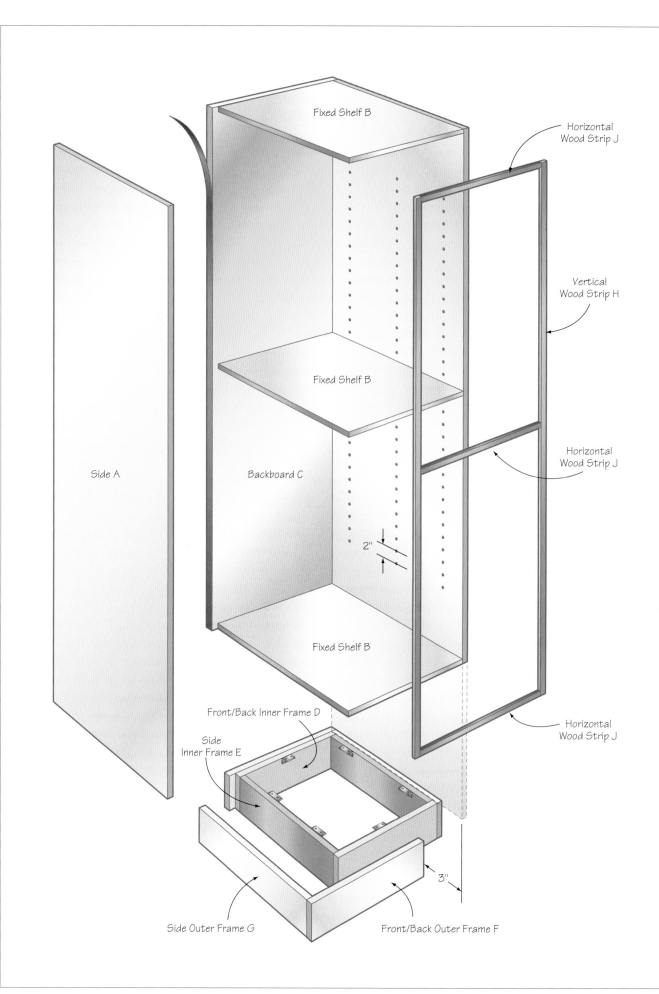

Fixed Shelf B

Horizontal Wood Strip J

Vertical Wood Strip H

Horizontal Wood Strip J

Fixed Shelf B

Side A

Backboard C

2"

Horizontal Wood Strip J

Fixed Shelf B

Front/Back Inner Frame D

Side Inner Frame E

3"

Side Outer Frame G

Front/Back Outer Frame F

MATERIALS LIST ■ INCHES

REFERENCE	QUANTITY	PART	STOCK	THICKNESS	WIDTH	LENGTH	COMMENTS
A	2	sides	melamine PB	$5/8$	$25^1/2$	84	
B	3	fixed shelves	melamine PB	$5/8$	$16^9/16$	$25^1/2$	
C	1	backboard	melamine PB	$5/8$	$17^{13}/16$	84	
D	2	front & back inner frame	melamine PB	$5/8$	3	$16^9/16$	
E	2	side inner frame	melamine PB	$5/8$	3	20	
F	2	front & back outer frame	melamine PB	$5/8$	3	$17^{13}/16$	
G	2	sides outer frame	melamine PB	$5/8$	3	$21^1/4$	
H	2	vertical wood strips	solid wood	$1/4$	$5/8$	84	
J	3	horizontal wood strips	solid wood	$1/4$	$5/8$	$16^9/16$	

HARDWARE

6 Metal right-angle brackets
Steel shelf pins as required
2" PB screws
Brad nails
Glue
White screw head cover caps
Iron-on edge tape
1" PB screws
$5/8$" Screws
Wood putty

MATERIALS LIST ■ MILLIMETERS

REFERENCE	QUANTITY	PART	STOCK	THICKNESS	WIDTH	LENGTH	COMMENTS
A	2	sides	melamine PB	16	648	2134	
B	3	fixed shelves	melamine PB	16	420	648	
C	1	backboard	melamine PB	16	453	2134	
D	2	front & back inner frame	melamine PB	16	76	420	
E	2	sides inner frame	melamine PB	16	76	508	
F	2	front & back outer frame	melamine PB	16	76	453	
G	2	sides outer frame	melamine PB	16	76	539	
H	2	vertical wood strips	solid hardwood	6	16	2134	
J	3	horizontal wood strips	solid hardwood	6	16	420	

HARDWARE

6 Metal right-angle brackets
Steel shelf pins as required
51mm PB screws
Brad nails
Glue
White screw head cover caps
Iron-on edge tape
25mm PB screws
16mm Screws
Wood putty

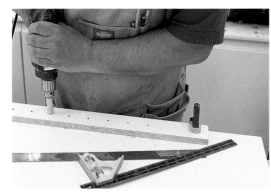

STEP 1 ■ Cut the two sides A and drill holes for the steel shelf pins. The hole diameter should match the shelf pin you decide to use. There are three vertical rows of holes in each side; one is in the center of the panel and the other two are located $1\frac{1}{2}$" in from the front and back edges. Space the holes 2" apart and begin drilling the columns 12" from the top and bottom.

I am using a shop jig made of $\frac{5}{8}$"-thick melamine and a wood dowel as a drill depth limiter. The dowel stop is set $1\frac{1}{8}$" above the drill end for a $\frac{1}{2}$"-deep hole in the cabinet sides.

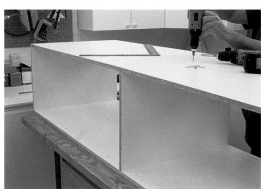

STEP 2 ■ The three fixed shelves B are located at the bottom, top and middle of each side panel. Use 2" PB screws in pilot holes to attach the two sides to the shelves. The screw heads can be covered with white cover caps, or you could use biscuits and glue if you don't want fasteners showing. The position of the middle shelf isn't critical as long as it's near the midpoint of the cabinet for side panel support.

STEP 3 ■ Cover both long edges of the backboard C with melamine iron-on edge tape. Attach the back to the cabinet carcass using 2" PB screws spaced about 8" apart. The carcass will be square if the backboard is cut square. You can ensure a proper fit by aligning one corner of the back with the carcass and securing it with a screw. Next, attach each of the following three corners in order, aligning and fastening each with a screw, then install the remaining screws between the corners.

STEP 4 ■ The base frame is built with $\frac{5}{8}$"-thick melamine PB. I normally build solid base platforms using two thicknesses of material. The 3"-high pieces of PB are often the waste or cutoffs after the carcass parts are cut, so doubling the base frame thickness is inexpensive insurance.

The inside frame is $16\frac{9}{16}$" wide by $21\frac{1}{4}$" deep, and the outside frame is $17\frac{13}{16}$" wide by $22\frac{1}{2}$" deep because the frame is set 3" back from the front edge of the cabinet. The base frame will support the cabinet sides and transfer the load to the floor. Apply white edge tape to the outside edges of the back and front boards as these cut ends will be visible.

STEP 5 ■ Build the inner frame using 2" PB screws. The outer frame parts are secured to the inner frame with 1" PB screws through the back faces of the inner frame.

STEP 6 ■ Attach the base frame to the cabinet using metal right-angle brackets and ⁵/₈" screws.

STEP 8 ■ Use steel or plastic-covered steel shelf pins to properly support the tool platforms.

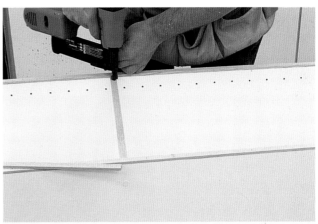

STEP 7 ■ Glue and nail the wood strips H and J to the front edges of the cabinet sides and fixed shelves. Fill the nail holes with wood putty and sand smooth.

CONSTRUCTION
NOTES

This project is simple to build and has become a valuable space saver in my shop. I've used melamine PB, but the storage cabinet can be built with any sheet material, such as MDF or plywood.

Plastic adjustable cabinet legs can be used in place of the solid base frame. The legs are often installed when moisture is an issue in the shop. If your shop floor is uneven, plastic adjustable legs may be the obvious choice for your base.

As discussed, the position of the middle shelf isn't critical; however, take note of the benchtop tools you plan to store and secure the shelf close to the middle to maximize tool storage. Three of your benchtop tools on platforms may fit below the fixed shelf if it is positioned at a certain height. Measure the spaces required for your tools and position the shelf accordingly to maximize storage.

If dust is a serious problem in your shop, you might consider installing a door on the cabinet. The door width equals the cabinet's interior width plus 1" when using hidden hinges. The door height is the same as the cabinet side board's height. Using those calculations, you'll need a door that's 17⁹/₁₆" wide by 84" high. Drill 35mm-diameter holes, ¹/₈" from the edge of the door, and install the hinges as detailed in chapter one. Standard-opening hinges, in the 100° to 120° range, cannot be used because the door edge opens into the cabinet's interior space. Use the wide 170° hinges for this application to permit easy installation and removal of the tool platforms.

CHAPTER 16

MOBILE TABLE SAW CENTER

The first and most important issue you should deal with before starting construction on this Mobile Table Saw Center is the determination of the final table saw height. My

saw table is 34" above the floor, which may not be suitable for everyone. The total height is the sum of the wheels, cabinet and benchtop saw heights.

Support your saw at different heights to find one that suits you, then, to determine the cabinet dimensions, subtract the height of the saw and wheels from the total height you've chosen.

Building a mobile table saw center for your benchtop table saw will improve the ease and accuracy of your work. It's well accepted that a good fence and sliding table or crosscut sled are valuable add-ons to any saw. Drawers for storage, a good dust collection system, quick access to accessories as well as the mobility feature combine to make using the saw fun and easy.

This cabinet top should accommodate any benchtop saw, but it's worth measuring yours before you start building the center. The cabinet length addresses a couple of issues. First, it allows you to store tools such as push sticks, hearing protection, miter slides and other often-used accessories in a place where they can be seen and easily accessed. Second, the top supports extended fence tables and protects the guide rail extensions. Finally, the cabinet is long enough for a dust chamber, two large drawers and a storage section with adjustable shelves.

My center will be used in a shop that needs access to a good saw once or twice a month. When the saw isn't needed, simply roll it against a wall or tuck it into an unused corner. If you have a small shop, use a table saw for your woodwork only on an occasional basis or share your garage shop with the family car, this project is for you.

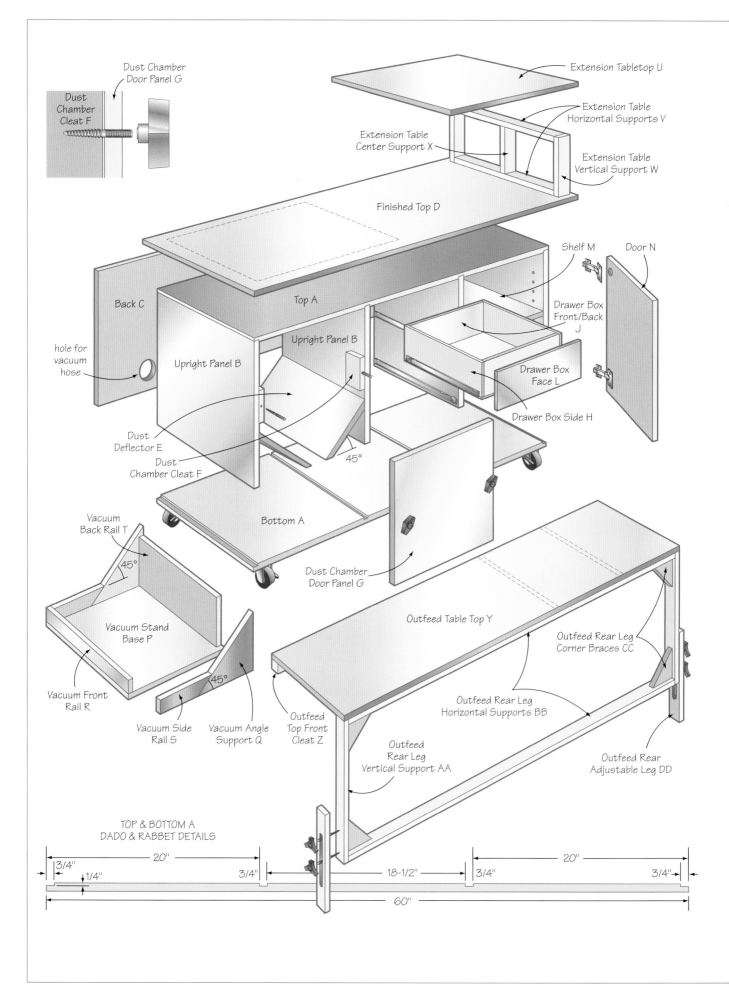

Dust Chamber Door Panel G

Dust Chamber Cleat F

Extension Tabletop U

Extension Table Horizontal Supports V

Extension Table Center Support X

Extension Table Vertical Support W

Finished Top D

Shelf M

Door N

Back C

Top A

Upright Panel B

Upright Panel B

hole for vacuum hose

Drawer Box Front/Back J

Drawer Box Face L

Dust Deflector E

Drawer Box Side H

Dust Chamber Cleat F

45°

Vacuum Back Rail T

45°

Bottom A

Dust Chamber Door Panel G

Vacuum Stand Base P

Outfeed Table Top Y

Outfeed Rear Leg Corner Braces CC

Vacuum Front Rail R

Outfeed Rear Leg Horizontal Supports BB

Vacuum Side Rail S

45°

Vacuum Angle Support Q

Outfeed Top Front Cleat Z

Outfeed Rear Leg Vertical Support AA

Outfeed Rear Adjustable Leg DD

TOP & BOTTOM A
DADO & RABBET DETAILS

3/4"   20"   3/4"   18-1/2"   3/4"   20"   3/4"

1/4"

60"

MATERIALS LIST ■ INCHES

REFERENCE	QUANTITY	PART	STOCK	THICKNESS	WIDTH	LENGTH	COMMENTS
A	2	top & bottom	MDF	3/4	22 1/2	60	
B	4	upright panels	MDF	3/4	22 1/2	16	
C	1	back	MDF	3/4	17	60	
D	1	finished top	MDF	3/4	25	62	
E	2	dust deflectors	MDF	3/4	10	22 1/2	angle-cut
F	2	dust chamber cleats	MDF	3/4	2	4	
G	1	dust chamber door panel	MDF	3/4	20	16 1/2	
H	4	drawer box sides	MDF	3/4	5 1/4	22	
J	4	drawer box fronts & backs	MDF	3/4	5 1/4	16	
K	2	drawer box bottoms	MDF	3/4	17 1/2	22	
L	2	drawer box faces	MDF	3/4	8 3/16	19	
M	1	shelf	MDF	3/4	19 3/16	22 3/8	
N	1	door	MDF	3/4	20	16 1/2	
P	1	vacuum stand base	MDF	3/4	18	23 1/4	
Q	2	vacuum angle supports	MDF	3/4	11 1/4	11 1/4	cut at 45°
R	1	vacuum front rail	MDF	3/4	3	23 1/4	
S	2	vacuum side rails	MDF	3/4	3	8 3/4	angle-cut
T	1	vacuum back rail	MDF	3/4	10	21 3/4	
U	1	extension tabletop	MDF	3/4	27	33	
V	2	ext. horizontal supports	hardwood	3/4	1 1/2	24	
W	2	ext. vertical supports	hardwood	3/4	1 1/2	12	
X	1	ext. center support	hardwood	3/4	1 1/2	10 1/2	
Y	1	outfeed tabletop	MDF	3/4	27	64	
Z	1	outfeed top front cleat	hardwood	3/4	1 1/4	64	
AA	2	rear leg vertical supports	hardwood	3/4	1 1/2	28	
BB	2	rear leg horizontal supports	hardwood	3/4	1 1/2	62 1/2	
CC	4	rear leg corner braces	hardwood	3/4	5 1/4	5 1/4	angle-cut
DD	2	rear adjustable legs	hardwood	3/4	1 1/2	16	

HARDWARE

8 Locking wheel casters

2 - 22" Drawer glide sets

Adjustable shelf pins as detailed

2 - 107° Hidden hinges

8 Knobs

8 Hanger bolts, 2"-long x 1/4"-diameter thread

Door and drawer handles as detailed

Electrical switch, plug and junction boxes

Screws as detailed

Glue

2" PB screws

Biscuits

1 1/4" Screws

Brad nails

5/8" Screws

1 1/2" Screws

1 1/2"-Long by 1/4"-diameter carriage bolts with washers & nuts

T-square fence system

2" Wood screws

MATERIALS LIST ■ MILLIMETERS

REFERENCE	QUANTITY	PART	STOCK	THICKNESS	WIDTH	LENGTH	COMMENTS
A	2	top & bottom	MDF	19	572	1524	
B	4	upright panels	MDF	19	572	406	
C	1	back	MDF	19	432	1524	
D	1	finished top	MDF	19	635	1575	
E	2	dust deflectors	MDF	19	254	572	angle-cut
F	2	dust chamber cleats	MDF	19	51	102	
G	1	dust chamber door panel	MDF	19	508	419	
H	4	drawer box sides	MDF	19	133	559	
J	4	drawer box fronts & backs	MDF	19	133	406	
K	2	drawer box bottoms	MDF	19	445	559	
L	2	drawer box faces	MDF	19	208	483	
M	1	shelf	MDF	19	488	569	
N	1	door	MDF	19	508	419	
P	1	vacuum stand base	MDF	19	457	590	
Q	2	vacuum angle supports	MDF	19	285	285	cut at 45°
R	1	vacuum front rail	MDF	19	76	590	
S	2	vacuum side rails	MDF	19	76	222	angle-cut
T	1	vacuum back rail	MDF	19	254	552	
U	1	extension tabletop	MDF	19	686	838	
V	2	ext. horizontal supports	hardwood	19	38	610	
W	2	ext. vertical supports	hardwood	19	38	305	
X	1	ext. center supports	hardwood	19	38	267	
Y	1	outfeed tabletop	MDF	19	686	1626	
Z	1	outfeed top front cleat	hardwood	19	32	1626	
AA	2	rear leg vertical supports	hardwood	19	38	711	
BB	2	rear leg horizontal supports	hardwood	19	38	1588	
CC	4	rear leg corner braces	hardwood	19	133	133	angle-cut
DD	2	rear adjustable legs	hardwood	19	38	406	

HARDWARE

8 Locking wheel casters

2 - 559mm Drawer glide sets

Adjustable shelf pins as detailed

2 - 107° Hidden hinges

8 Knobs

8 Hanger bolts, 51mm-long x 6mm-diameter thread

Door and drawer handles as detailed

Electrical switch, plug and junction boxes

Screws as detailed

Glue

51mm PB screws

Biscuits

32mm Screws

Brad nails

16mm Screws

38mm Screws

38mm-Long by 6mm-diameter carriage bolts with washers & nuts

T-square fence system

51mm Wood screws

STEP 1 ■ Cut the top and bottom boards A to the size indicated in the materials list. Each panel requires two ³/₄"-wide dadoes and two ³/₄"-wide rabbets. All of the cuts are ¹/₄" deep. Refer to the illustration for positioning.

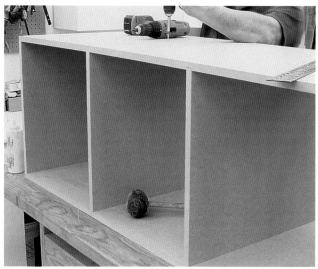

STEP 2 ■ The four upright panels B are attached to the top and bottom boards in the dadoes and rabbets. Use glue and four 2" PB screws per end, in pilot holes, to secure the panels.

STEP 3 ■ The back C is attached to the carcass using biscuits and glue. If you don't have a biscuit joiner, screws and glue will work just as well.

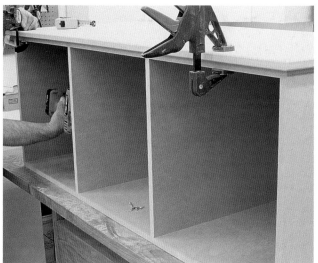

STEP 4 ■ The finished top D is a ³/₄"-thick piece of MDF with the upper and lower edges rounded over. Use a ¹/₄"-radius roundover bit in your router to ease these edges. The front and both sides overhang the cabinet carcass by 1". Use glue and 1¹/₄" screws, from the underside, to attach the top board. Four screws per section will be enough to secure the top.

STEP 5 ■ The left-end compartment will be used as a dust collection chamber. Install the two deflectors E by first cutting the edges at 45° and securing them to the cabinet bottom board and panels using glue and brad nails.

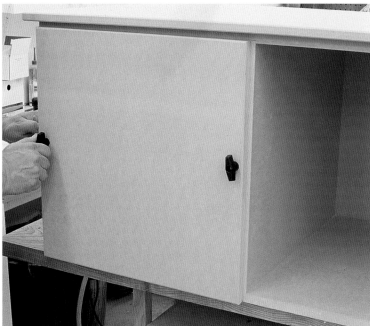

STEP 6 ▪ Two support cleats F are attached to the dust chamber side panels with glue and 1¼" screws. They are aligned flush with the front edges of the vertical panels. Drill pilot holes in the center edge of each cleat to accept the wood screw end of ¼"-diameter hanger bolts. Leave about 1" of the ¼"-diameter machine thread in front of the cleat's edge so a handle can be threaded onto the shaft.

STEP 7 ▪ Cut the dust chamber door panel G to the size indicated in the materials list and round over its front face edge with a ¼"-radius router bit. Hold the door so its bottom edge is flush with the bottom face of the bottom board and press it into the hanger bolts to mark their location. The door overlays each vertical partition by ³⁄₈". Drill ³⁄₈"-diameter holes in the panel and attach it to the cabinet with ¼" threaded knobs on the hanger bolts. The hanger bolts and knobs are available at many woodworking and home improvement stores.

STEP 8 ▪ Drill a hole as low as possible between the dust chamber deflectors through the backboard of the cabinet. This hole will be used to attach a vacuum hose. My vacuum, along with many others on the market, comes with a 2¼"-outside-diameter hose. This is a common hose size, but you should check the size of your hose before drilling the hole. The hole diameter can be as large as 4", with an appropriate fitting, if you plan on using a large dust collection system.

STEP 9 ▪ The center section is 18½" wide and will contain two drawers. My drawer boxes are 17½" wide. They are 22"-deep by 6"-high, made with ¾"-thick MDF.

Cut all the drawer parts H, J and K and assemble by attaching the sides H to the back and front boards J using glue and 2" PB screws. Keep the screws at least 1" away from any edge to avoid splitting the MDF.

Once the sides are secured to the back and front boards, install the bottom using glue and screws. If the bottom board has been cut square, your drawer box will be square.

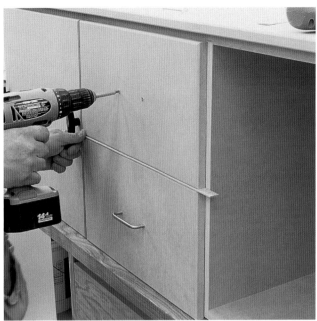

STEP 10 ▪ Install the drawer glides on the drawer boxes and inside the cabinet. Use ³⁄₄- or full-extension glides, installing them following the manufacturer's instructions. One set of glides is mounted at the bottom of the cabinet, and the other set is attached 8" above the bottom board.

STEP 11 ▪ The drawer faces L are secured to the drawer boxes using 1¹⁄₄" screws through the back face of each front drawer board. I made the total height of the two drawer faces the same as the dust chamber door. Leave a ¹⁄₈" gap between the faces so each one will measure 8³⁄₁₆" high. The drawer faces will overlay each vertical partition edge by ¹⁄₄" so the faces are 19" wide.

Use a ¹⁄₄" roundover router bit to ease the front face edges of each door panel, then install the handles of your choice.

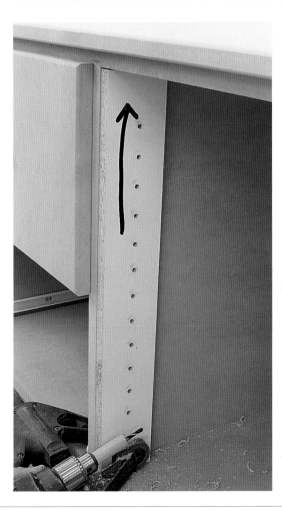

STEP 12 *(left)* ▪ You can add an adjustable shelf to the right-side compartment if required. For drilling the shelf-pin holes, you can make a jig with a 3"-wide by 15¹⁄₂"-high piece of ³⁄₄"-thick sheet material scrap. Drill a series of holes in the jig, spacing them about 1¹⁄₄" apart. Place a short piece of wood dowel on the drill bit, leaving about 1¹⁄₄" of drill bit exposed. Drill two columns of holes in each vertical partition in that section using the jig and drill stop. You'll get accurately aligned holes without drilling all the way through the cabinet sides.

STEP 13 *(above)* ▪ Cut the shelf board M to size. Install adjustable shelf pins in the holes and put the shelf in place.

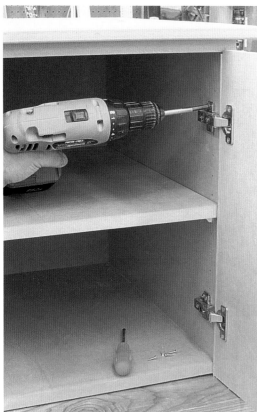

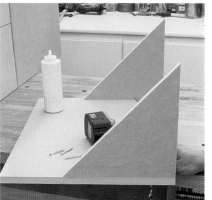

STEP 15 *(left)* ■ The left side of this saw cabinet has a platform that will hold my vacuum cleaner. Check the dimensions of your vacuum cleaner to verify it will fit before cutting the parts.

I have cut and attached two support boards Q, cut in the shape of a triangle, to help secure the platform. Use glue and 2" screws to attach the angle supports to the stand base.

STEP 16 *(below)* ■ The rails R, S and T are 3" high and attached to the base with screws and glue. The front and back rails are straight, while the side rails are angle-cut on one end at 45° to meet the angle supports.

STEP 14 ■ The right-end cabinet door N is made of ³⁄₄" MDF with the front face edges rounded over using a ¹⁄₄"-radius router bit. It's 16¹⁄₂" high to align with the tops of the drawer faces, and is mounted using 107° full-overlay hidden hinges. Normally, door width is determined by adding 1" to the interior dimension of the cabinet. However, I'm sharing a partition with the drawer faces, so I've added ³⁄₄" to the interior width so my door will be 20" wide. Drill two 35mm holes, 4" from the top and bottom edges, with the holes ¹⁄₈" from the door edge. Install the hinges with mounting plates attached.

Hold the door in the open position, 90° to the face of the cabinet, and put a ¹⁄₈" spacer between the door and cabinet edge. Drive ⁵⁄₈" screws through the plates to secure the hinges to the cabinet sides. Check the door fit and adjust.

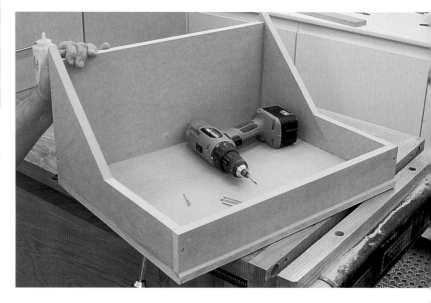

STEP 17 ■ Attach the vacuum stand to the cabinet carcass, aligning it flush with the underside of the bottom board. Use 1¹⁄₂" screws through the back rail into the cabinet side boards to secure the platform.

STEP 18 ▪ I used 4"-high, heavy-duty locking wheels on my saw station. They are attached with 1½"-long by ¼"-diameter carriage bolts through the cabinet base board. The wheels are located directly under the center panels and as close to the right end as possible. The left-end casters are positioned halfway under the cabinet, and the other half of the caster flange supports the vacuum stand. Push the carriage bolts through the holes in the base board and secure the casters with washers and nuts.

STEP 19 ▪ Locate your benchtop saw on top of the cabinet, above the dust chamber where it will be permanently attached. The table saw blade throws most of its dust ahead and directly below the blade. Mark the hold-down bolt locations as well as the leading edge position of the saw blade on the cabinet top. Cut a large hole in the tabletop through the two layers into the dust chamber. Most of the dust will be directed into the hole by the blade, and the vacuum cleaner will draw air through that hole to collect the dust. Test the dust collection and adjust the hole size if necessary.

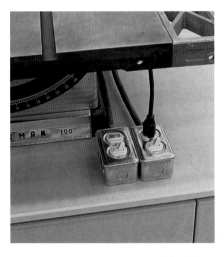

STEP 20 ▪ I wired my saw to a switch with a power-indicator light. Your saw may already have a switch, so this step won't be needed. However, if you do need one and are uncomfortable with electrical wiring, call a professional.

I also installed a switched plug to control my vacuum cleaner. Both electrical boxes are surface mounted to the cabinet top in front of the table saw.

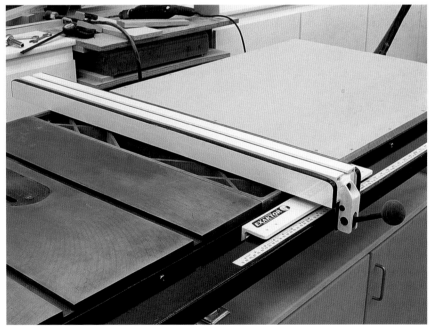

STEP 21 ▪ The best upgrade for your table saw is a high-quality T-square fence system. Older saws often had poorly designed fences that were sometimes hard to keep in adjustment and required constant maintenance. The new fences are accurate, well built and easy to align. Many of the new T-square fence systems, like this model from Exaktor Woodworking Tools, come with a rear angle bar that provides support for an extended table.

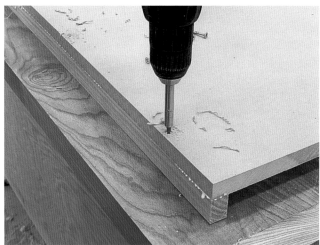

STEP 22 ■ The extension table material is ³/₄"-thick MDF with a hardwood frame. The length of panel U will depend on the model of T-square fence you purchase and the remaining distance on your cabinet after a table saw has been installed.

STEP 23 ■ The outfeed table is also made with ³/₄"-thick MDF. The front edge that rests on the table saw support bracket has a hardwood spacer, cleat Z, to level the outfeed tabletop's surface to the bench saw top surface. I will be supporting the front edge of my outfeed table on the angle bar that was supplied with the T-square fence I installed. If you don't have the fence upgrade, attach metal angle stock or a hardwood cleat to the back of your saw.

STEP 25 ■ Cut two adjustable legs DD about 16" long and rout a ¹/₄"-wide slot in the center of each one starting and stopping 2" from each end. Use ¹/₄"-diameter hanger bolts and knobs to attach the adjustable legs to the leg frame. Position the hanger bolts so they can be adjusted 2" above and below the correct table height, assuming the workstation is resting on a level floor.

STEP 24 ■ The rear leg assembly (AA and BB) is made with ³/₄"-thick by 1¹/₂"-wide hardwood. Use 2" wood screws and glue to build the assembly. I wanted to keep the weight to a minimum, so I used this light-duty leg system. Most of the support will be provided at the front edge of this table because it's attached to the saw. When not in use, lower the saw blade and move your fence to the far right end of the saw, then rest the table on top and wheel the workstation to its storage area.

The frame is about three-quarters of the distance between the floor and underside of the outfeed table, or 28" in my case. Attach the leg frame to the underside of the outfeed table with glue and 1¹/₄" screws.

STEP 26 ■ Install two ¹/₄"-diameter hanger bolts into the bottom edge of the front support cleat on the outfeed table. Align the table on the rear support of your saw and drill a ³/₈"-diameter hole at each end to match the position of the hanger bolts. Attach the outfeed table to the saw by placing the hanger bolt shafts in the holes and securing them with the proper-size knobs.

STEP 27 ■ Rout slots in the outfeed table in line with the table saw's miter slide slots.

CONSTRUCTION
NOTES

You will need about four sheets of ¾"-thick MDF and one 10' length of 1x6 hardwood for the cabinet construction, plus the hardware as noted.

I used MDF, but any sheet material is suitable, so pick one that meets your budget and preference. Melamine particleboard would be a good choice or, if you prefer, any plywood with a smooth surface.

This is the perfect saw cabinet if your workshop is located in a garage. At the end of each woodworking session the entire station can be quickly pushed against a wall. The cabinet can be used as a static saw station by replacing the wheels with a simple base frame.

Final table saw height is the most important issue to deal with before starting construction. There are many types of benchtop saws and all of them are different heights and widths. The cabinet tabletop should be suitable for most saws, if not all, but it would be wise to verify the depth of your equipment before cutting the sheet material to size. Wheel assemblies also come in different heights, so purchase the style you want before starting the project.

STEP 28 ■ If you plan on doing a lot of crosscutting on your saw workstation, consider buying one of the new sliding table systems. They increase the flexibility of the saw and let you cut wide panels easily and with increased safety. Some of the table systems, like this Exaktor EX26 table, have a release feature that will let you quickly install and remove the unit without disturbing any adjustments.

STEP 29 ■ The extended side table is a great place to install a router. The workstation can then be used for sawing and router work because the T-square fence system is used for both operations.

BUILDING A TABLE SAW CROSSCUTTING SLED

MATERIALS LIST ▪ INCHES

QUANTITY	PART	STOCK	THICKNESS	WIDTH	LENGTH	COMMENTS
1	platform	plywood	$^3/_4$	30	36	
2	runners	hardwood	$^3/_8$	$^3/_4$	30	
2	fences	2x4 stock	$1^1/_2$	$3^1/_2$	36	
1	blade guard	2x4 stock	$1^1/_2$	$3^1/_2$	10	

HARDWARE

1" Screws

Glue

MATERIALS LIST ▪ MILLIMETERS

QUANTITY	PART	STOCK	THICKNESS	WIDTH	LENGTH	COMMENTS
1	platform	plywood	19	762	914	
2	runners	hardwood	10	19	762	
2	fences	2x4 stock	38	89	914	
1	blade guard	2x4 stock	38	89	254	

HARDWARE

25mm Screws

Glue

A crosscutting sled is one of the handiest and safest table saw accessories you'll ever own. It is simple to build and a real pleasure to use when cutting wide panels.

STEP 1 ▪ Cut the platform, making sure it's accurately sized and square. Cut the two hardwood runners and test fit them in the table saw miter grooves. A proper fit will allow the runners to run freely with minimal side play. Attach the runners to the platform with 1" screws and glue. Make sure they're accurately spaced to match the table saw grooves.

STEP 2 ▪ Using your saw fence and a framing square, install the back rail with screws and glue and align it at 90° to the fence.

STEP 3 ▪ Install the front rail using the same procedures.

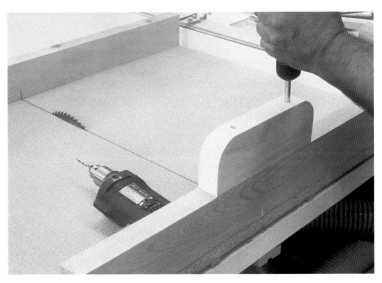

STEP 4 ▪ Attach the blade guard centered over the blade on the back rail. Round over each end of the guard board with a belt sander to eliminate the sharp corners.

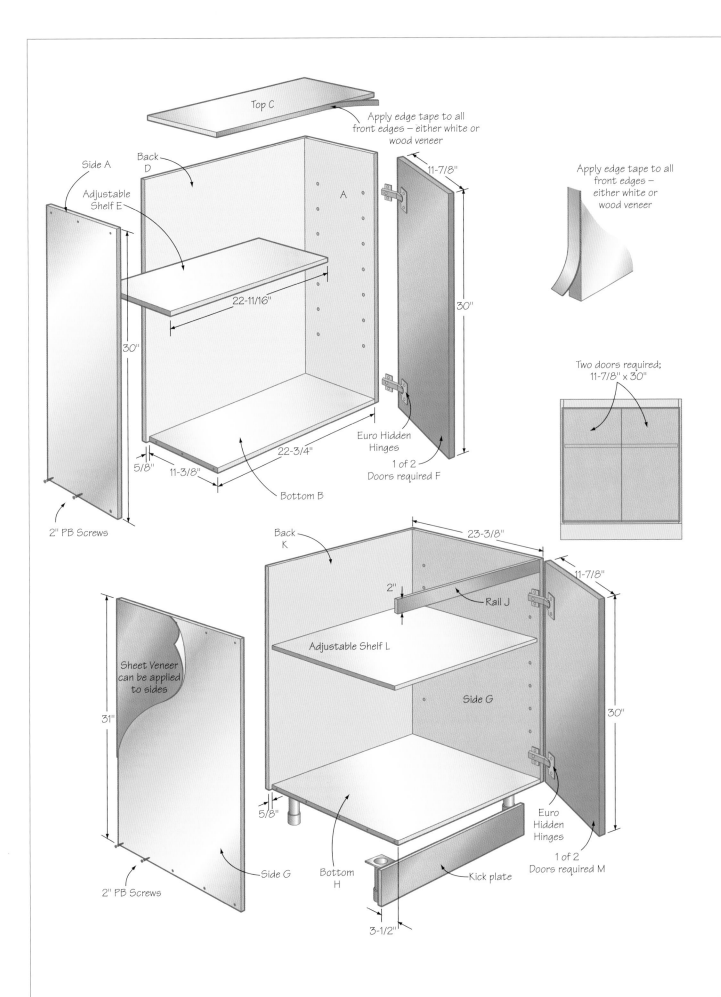

Top C

Apply edge tape to all
front edges – either white or
wood veneer

Side A

Back
D

Adjustable
Shelf E

A

11-7/8"

Apply edge tape to all
front edges –
either white or
wood veneer

22-11/16"

30"

30"

Euro Hidden
Hinges

Two doors required;
11-7/8" x 30"

1 of 2
Doors required F

5/8"

11-3/8"

22-3/4"

Bottom B

2" PB Screws

Back
K

23-3/8"

11-7/8"

2"

Rail J

Adjustable Shelf L

Sheet Veneer
can be applied
to sides

Side G

30"

31"

Side G

Bottom
H

5/8"

Euro
Hidden
Hinges

1 of 2
Doors required M

2" PB Screws

Kick plate

3-1/2"

MATERIALS LIST ▪ INCHES

REFERENCE	QUANTITY	PART	STOCK	THICKNESS	WIDTH	LENGTH	COMMENTS
24"-WIDE WALL CABINET							
A	2	sides	melamine PB	$5/8$	$11^3/8$	30	
B	1	bottom	melamine PB	$5/8$	$11^3/8$	$22^3/4$	
C	1	top	melamine PB	$5/8$	$11^3/8$	$22^3/4$	
D	1	back	melamine PB	$5/8$	24	30	
E	2	shelves	melamine PB	$5/8$	$11^3/8$	$22^{11}/16$	
F	2	doors	melamine PB	$5/8$	$11^7/8$	30	
24"-WIDE BASE CABINET							
G	2	sides	melamine PB	$5/8$	$23^3/8$	31	
H	1	bottom	melamine PB	$5/8$	$23^3/8$	$22^3/4$	
J	1	top rail	melamine PB	$5/8$	2	$22^3/4$	
K	1	back	melamine PB	$5/8$	24	31	
L	1	shelf	melamine PB	$5/8$	$23^3/8$	$22^{11}/16$	
M	2	doors	melamine PB	$5/8$	$11^7/8$	30	

HARDWARE

Edge tape
Shelf pins
2" PB screws
Hidden hinges
$5/8$" PB screws
3" Screws
1" Screws
Right-angle brackets
Adjustable cabinet legs
Plinth clip
Drawer glides
Drawer handles
Door handles

MATERIALS LIST ▪ MILLIMETERS

REFERENCE	QUANTITY	PART	STOCK	THICKNESS	WIDTH	LENGTH	COMMENTS
610MM-WIDE WALL CABINET							
A	2	sides	melamine PB	16	289	762	
B	1	bottom	melamine PB	16	289	578	
C	1	top	melamine PB	16	289	578	
D	1	back	melamine PB	16	610	762	
E	2	shelves	melamine PB	16	289	577	
F	2	doors	melamine PB	16	301	762	
610MM-WIDE BASE CABINET							
G	2	sides	melamine PB	16	594	787	
H	1	bottom	melamine PB	16	594	578	
J	1	top rail	melamine PB	16	51	578	
K	1	back	melamine PB	16	610	787	
L	1	shelf	melamine PB	16	594	577	
M	2	doors	melamine PB	16	301	762	

HARDWARE

Edge tape
Shelf pins
51mm PB screws
Hidden hinges
16mm PB screws
76mm Screws
25mm Screws
Right-angle brackets
Adjustable cabinet legs
Plinth clip
Drawer glides
Drawer handles
Door handles

SHOP TIP Both wall and base cabinet materials lists are based on using $5/8$"-thick melamine particleboard.

Wall cabinets are usually 12"-deep by 30"-high. Base cabinets are 24"-deep by $35^1/4$"-high. Adding a $3/4$"-thick top to the base cabinet means the top surface will be 36" from the floor. If you want a different height, alter the height of the back and side boards.

CALCULATING CABINET DOOR SIZES

The size of cabinet doors that will be mounted on hidden hinges (100°-opening, full-overlay hinges) can be easily calculated. First, measure the inside dimension of the cabinet to be fitted with doors.

A 24"-wide cabinet, built using the materials list shown for this project, has an inside dimension of 22¾" (24"-wide cabinet minus two ⅝" side thicknesses). Add 1" to this measurement and that's the required door width. In this example, the door width would be 23¾", which is a little too wide. Door widths should be less than 18" wide if possible.

I can install two doors that are 11⅞" wide in place of the 23¾" door. The width for each of the two doors is found by adding 1" to the inside cabinet dimension, then dividing by 2.

STEP 1 ▪ The exposed edges of all cabinet parts must be covered. I use a heat-activated edge tape and apply it with an old household iron. Run a small roller along the tape surface before the glue cools and dries to properly seat the tape. Excess edge tape can be trimmed with a sharp chisel or double-edged trimmer that is available at woodworking stores.

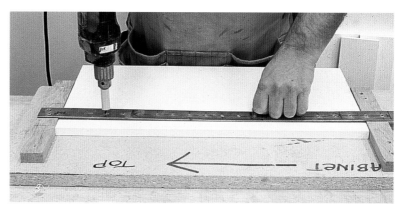

STEP 2 ▪ Holes for the adjustable shelves are drilled in the cabinet sides before assembly. I use a simple jig made with a flat steel bar and wooden blocks mounted to a small sheet of plywood. The drill bit's travel is limited by a piece of dowel on the drill bit. My shelf pins are 5mm (³⁄₁₆") in diameter. Holes in the steel bar on my jig are 5mm in diameter and spaced 1¼" apart. Drill as many holes as you require. The spacing isn't critical but be sure you know the diameter of your shelf-pin holes before drilling.

STEP 3 ▪ Attach the two side boards A to the bottom B and top C using 2" PB screws. Drill a pilot hole for each screw and align the bottom and top boards with the top and bottom edges of the sides.

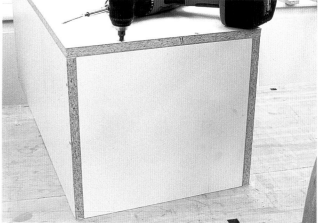

STEP 4 ▪ The full-thickness back D should be as wide and as high as the cabinet. It is attached using 2" PB screws in drilled holes spaced about 6" apart.

CABINET SIZES

The dimensions for a cabinet of any width from 10" to 36" can easily be calculated. Begin your calculations by deciding the final cabinet width. If a 33"-wide wall cabinet is needed, I subtract the two $\frac{5}{8}$" side thicknesses from the total width needed to find my bottom and top board dimensions. Thus, they would have to be $31\frac{3}{4}$" wide by the standard $11\frac{3}{8}$" deep. The backboard size equals the total width and height of the cabinet, or 33" wide by 30" high.

Determine the door sizes as previously detailed, install hinges and the cabinet is complete. Follow the construction steps for all cabinets, no matter how wide.

STEP 5 ■ As discussed, the inside dimension of a cabinet determines the door size when using full-overlay hidden hinges. Adding 1" to the interior width and dividing by 2 means I will need two $11\frac{7}{8}$"-wide doors F. Upper frameless cabinet doors normally cover the edges of the top and bottom board, and are the same height as the cabinet.

STEP 6 ■ Apply heat-activated edge tape to all four edges of each door. Using a flat-bottomed hinge-boring bit in a drill press, drill two 35mm-diameter holes into each door to accept the hidden-hinge assemblies. The holes are normally located 4" from each end and $\frac{1}{8}$" from the door's edge.

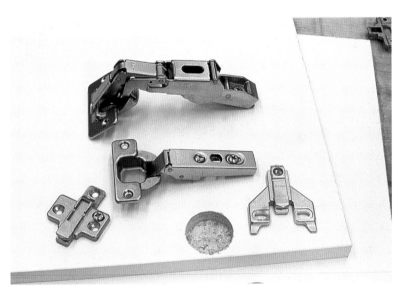

STEP 7 ■ The standard hidden hinge is a full-overlay 100°–120°-opening hinge. The term full-overlay refers to the door position when attached with this hinge. It will overlay or cover the side end edge by almost $\frac{5}{8}$". The mounting plate attaches to the cabinet side. The standard hinge is shown in the middle, and the mounting plate that is commonly used is shown on the left.

The top hinge is a 170°-opening model, and the mounting plate on the right is used to attach the hinge to a face frame.

BASIC
CONSTRUCTION PRINCIPLES OF FRAMELESS CABINETRY

Frameless cabinetry is strong and sturdy when properly constructed, however, you should use quality materials such as cabinet-grade melamine particleboard. To be designated cabinet-grade, the board must have a high-quality core material and a melamine layer. Inexpensive board isn't a low-pressure laminate type and often has a melamine layer that's painted or glued.

The cabinet parts are joined with special fasteners, like the ones used in this project, such as the particleboard screw. Drill pilot holes for all screws to achieve the maximum hold.

Melamine particleboard is available in different thicknesses. The $^5/_8$" and $^3/_4$" sizes are the most common, so use whichever size is readily available in your area. I will be using $^5/_8$"-thick material, but if you decide to use $^3/_4$", or that's all there is available in your area, follow the same process as previously described to determine cut sizes. The steps are the same no matter which thickness is used. The cabinet width, minus the side thicknesses in total, equals the bottom and top board width, and so on.

STEP 8 ■ Use $^5/_8$" particleboard screws to secure both hinges to the door. Align the hinge body with a square to ensure it's parallel to the door edge.

STEP 9 ■ Attach the hinge plate on the hinge body and align the door (in its normally open position) against the cabinet. Place a $^1/_8$"-thick spacer between the door edge and the cabinet edge. Next, drive $^5/_8$" PB screws through the holes in the hinge plate to secure the door.

This is a simple and accurate alignment procedure for mounting doors with hidden hinges without measuring or using jigs. The procedure will work only with 100° to 120° full-overlay hidden hinges. If you want to install the wider 170°-opening hinges, follow the procedures for using a 100° to 120° hinge. Once the hinge plate is secured, remove the standard hinge and install the wide-opening model on the door. The mounting plate is correctly located for all hinges but must be installed using the standard-opening model.

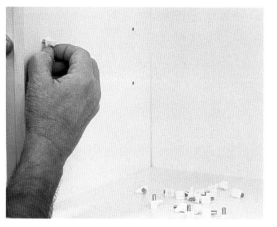

STEP 10 ■ Mount the cabinets to the wall using 3"-long screws driven into wall studs. If you have a series of cabinets, secure the front edges to each other with 1" screws. Complete the installation by installing the shelves E on shelf pins in the drilled holes.

STEP 11 ▪ Apply tape to all exposed panel edges as detailed in previous steps. If you plan on having adjustable shelves in your base cabinet, drill the holes at this point. Attach the cabinet sides G to the bottom board H using 2" PB screws.

STEP 12 ▪ A base cabinet does not require a top board because the cabinet will be covered with a counter or other work surface. Attach the backboard K making sure the bottom and sides are aligned flush to the outside edges. Drill pilot holes and attach the backboard with 2" PB screws 6" to 8" apart.

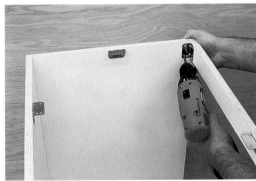

STEP 13 ▪ A 2"-high upper rail J must be installed on a frameless base cabinet. This will provide overhang clearance for the countertop and doors. The 30"-high doors are 1" below the top edge of this rail. Use one 2" PB screw per end. Drive the screw into a pilot hole that's located as close to the center of the rail as possible.

STEP 14 ▪ Install right-angle brackets to strengthen the upper rail. One bracket per end using ⅝" screws will support the rail. The other brackets installed on the base will be used to secure the countertop. The number of brackets required will vary with cabinet size; however, one every 12" apart will be adequate to secure the counter.

STEP 15 ▪ I use adjustable cabinet legs on most of my base cabinets. I don't have to build a base frame, and the legs are adjustable for easier cabinet installation. The legs are plastic, so water and other liquids that sometimes spill in the shop do not affect them. Cabinet legs are secured with ⅝" screws and are set 3" back from the front edge of the cabinet.

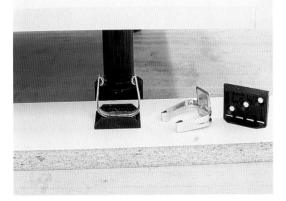

STEP 16 ▪ Kick plates aren't necessary with shop cabinets, but if you want to use them, they can be attached with a plinth clip. This piece of hardware is designed to secure kick plates to cabinet legs with spring clips.

Finally, complete the base by installing cabinet doors M. They are 30" high and are located 1" below the top edge of the cabinet rail. The space above both doors is used to provide clearance for a countertop. Follow the same procedures as detailed for building the wall cabinet.

STEP 17 ▪ Tip an upper cabinet on its back and you have a drawer box. The same construction procedures are used for both units. Drawer boxes don't need adjustable shelf holes or doors, but they are identical to upper cabinets in every other way.

STEP 18 ▪ Drawer boxes can be mounted with many glide systems. I use $^3/_4$-extension glides (a 22" drawer box pulls out about 15") and full-extension glides (the 22" drawer box comes all the way out). The full-extension (FX) glides mount on the drawer box side, and the $^3/_4$-type glides mount on the drawer bottom and side. Both styles require a $^1/_2$" clearance on each side of the box between the cabinet sides. The clearance dimensions required with most glide systems are critical, so accurate cutting of parts is important. The FX glides (chrome model in picture) are used when full access to the drawer box is needed, but they are about three times more expensive than the standard $^3/_4$-extension models.

STEP 19 ▪ Follow the manufacturer's instructions when installing drawer glides. Most of the drawer hardware on the market can be installed by drawing a guideline inside the cabinet using a carpenter's square. The square's tongue is held tight to the cabinet's face so the guideline will be at a perfect right angle to the side board's front edge.

Frameless cabinets do not have rails, so it can be tricky calculating drawer box sizes with a multiple bank of drawers. A good rule is to leave 1" of space below and above each drawer box. That means there will be a 2" space between drawer boxes because each one requires that 1" clearance above and below.

Each drawer box height can be found by dividing the number of boxes needed into the final space available. I will need three boxes approximately $7^1/_2$" high ($22^3/_8$" divided by 3). Or, I can have any combination of three box heights that equal $22^3/_8$" high. You may want two large bottom drawers at 9" each and a small top-drawer box that's $4^3/_8$" high. Any combination of sizes is fine as long as the 1" clearance above and below the drawer box is respected.

STEP 20 ■ The drawer face is similar to a door because all four edges must be covered with tape. The width of each drawer face is 1" greater than the inside dimension of the cabinet; the same calculation is used to find door widths. The height of drawer faces is determined by the position of the free space above each drawer box.

Here is an easy way to accurately locate drawer faces on the drawer box. First, determine which handles or pulls will be used and drill the mounting holes in the drawer face only. Install the drawer boxes. Position the drawer face on the cabinet and drive a screw through the handle holes into the drawer box. The face is located and secured properly, so you can pull out the drawer and install screws from the interior of the drawer box into the back of the drawer face. Now remove the screws from the front of the drawer face and finish drilling the handle holes. Finally, install the handles.

CONSTRUCTION
NOTES

These cabinets are a handy addition to any workshop. The wall cabinets are easily secured using 3" screws into the studs. Screws can be driven anywhere through the cabinet backboard because it's full thickness. It's an incredibly strong cabinet design that can stand alone without any added support.

The base cabinets stand on plastic legs and will accept a dozen different countertop or work-surface styles. You can use plywood with a coat of paint or a fancier laminate-covered top. Countertops or work surfaces for the base cabinets can be built in many ways. The design depends on your needs. I'll build different work surfaces throughout the book and you can select the style that's best for you.

You aren't limited to melamine particleboard when building these cabinets. Sheet goods such as medium-density fiberboard (MDF), plywood or plain particleboard are all fine. Low-cost sheet material can be protected with a coat of paint.

CHAPTER 18

ROUTER-TABLE CABINET

I've seen a lot of router table systems, tried many and had a number of different designs in my shop over the years. However, I always found something lacking in the designs and often promised myself that I would

build a router table cabinet to suit my needs one day. Well, that day has arrived, and I'm pleased with the results.

My list of design demands included an adjustable fence that had an opening range of at least 12". How many times have you wanted to run a groove in a wide board and couldn't because your router fence system opened only a couple of inches? My dream table had to have a miter slide track, be at least 35" high and have a large, solid-surface table to support boards properly. I was really tired of balancing large panels on small flimsy tables.

Accessory storage and proper dust collection rounded out my list of "wants" for the ideal router cabinet. I hesitate to say ultimate router station because there's always something missing that I'll discover later, but this cabinet is close to perfect for my work and it didn't cost a fortune to build.

I used ¾"-thick MDF sheet material. It's a great board for this application because the MDF is heavy, which will keep the cabinet stable, and it's easy to machine. I've detailed two leg options, one for a movable cabinet and the other for a cabinet that will be permanently located. The knobs and aluminum tracks are available at all woodworking outlets and are reasonably priced.

Have fun building of this router cabinet. You'll have easy access to the router and good dust collection. I'm sure you'll appreciate the bit storage slide-outs and great storage drawers for all your router accessories.

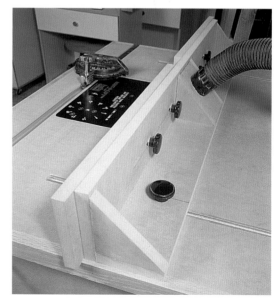

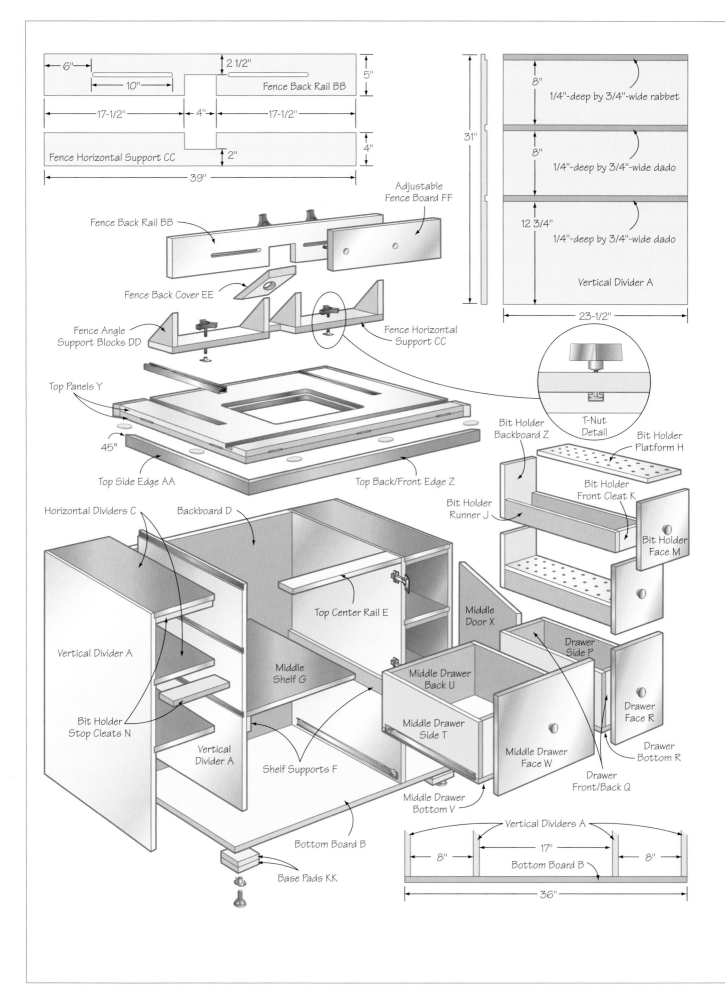

6"

10"

2 1/2"

5"

Fence Back Rail BB

17-1/2"   4"   17-1/2"

Fence Horizontal Support CC   2"   4"

39"

8"   1/4"-deep by 3/4"-wide rabbet

8"   1/4"-deep by 3/4"-wide dado

31"   12 3/4"   1/4"-deep by 3/4"-wide dado

Vertical Divider A

23-1/2"

Adjustable Fence Board FF

Fence Back Rail BB

Fence Back Cover EE

Fence Angle Support Blocks DD

Fence Horizontal Support CC

T-Nut Detail

Top Panels Y

Bit Holder Backboard Z

Bit Holder Platform H

45°

Bit Holder Runner J

Bit Holder Front Cleat K

Top Side Edge AA

Top Back/Front Edge Z

Bit Holder Face M

Horizontal Dividers C

Backboard D

Top Center Rail E

Middle Door X

Drawer Side P

Vertical Divider A

Middle Shelf G

Middle Drawer Back U

Bit Holder Stop Cleats N

Vertical Divider A

Shelf Supports F

Middle Drawer Side T

Middle Drawer Face W

Drawer Face R

Drawer Bottom R

Drawer Front/Back Q

Middle Drawer Bottom V

Bottom Board B

Base Pads KK

Vertical Dividers A

8"   17"   8"

Bottom Board B

36"

MATERIALS LIST ■ INCHES

REFERENCE	QUANTITY	PART	STOCK	THICKNESS	WIDTH	LENGTH	COMMENTS
A	4	vertical dividers	MDF	3/4	23 1/2	31	
B	1	bottom board	MDF	3/4	23 1/2	36	
C	6	horizontal dividers	MDF	3/4	8 1/2	23 1/2	
D	1	backboard	MDF	3/4	31 3/4	36	
E	1	top center rail	MDF	3/4	3	17	
F	2	shelf supports	MDF	3/4	3	23 1/2	
G	1	middle shelf	MDF	3/4	17	23 1/2	
H	4	bit holder platforms	MDF	3/4	7 15/16	22	
J	8	bit holder runners	MDF	3/4	2 1/2	22	
K	4	bit holder front cleats	MDF	3/4	2 1/2	6 7/16	
L	4	bit holder backboards	MDF	3/4	7 15/16	7 15/16	
M	4	bit holder front faces	MDF	3/4	9	8 1/2	
N	4	bit holder stop cleats	MDF	3/4	2	8	
P	4	drawer sides	MDF	3/4	9 1/4	22	
Q	4	drawer fronts & backs	MDF	3/4	9 1/4	5 1/2	
R	2	drawer bottoms	MDF	3/4	7	22	
S	2	drawer faces	MDF	3/4	9	13 7/8	
T	2	middle drawer sides	MDF	3/4	7 3/4	22	
U	2	drawer front & back	MDF	3/4	7 3/4	14 1/2	
V	1	drawer bottom	MDF	3/4	16	22	
W	1	middle drawer face	MDF	3/4	17 3/4	13 7/8	
X	1	middle door	MDF	3/4	17 3/4	17 1/4	
Y	2	top panels	MDF	3/4	37 3/4	27 3/4	
Z	2	top back & front edges	hardwood	3/4	1 1/2	39 1/4	
AA	2	top side edges	hardwood	3/4	1 1/2	29 1/4	
BB	1	fence back rail	MDF	3/4	5	39	
CC	1	fence horizontal support	MDF	3/4	4	39	
DD	4	fence angle support blocks	MDF	3/4	4	4	angle-cut
EE	1	fence back cover	MDF	3/4	4	5 1/4	angle-cut
FF	2	adjustable fence boards	MDF	3/4	5	19 1/2	

BASE OPTION #1

REFERENCE	QUANTITY	PART	STOCK	THICKNESS	WIDTH	LENGTH	COMMENTS
GG	2	sides	MDF	3/4	3	20	
HH	2	front & back boards	MDF	3/4	3	4 1/2	
JJ	1	top	MDF	3/4	6	20	
	2	heavy-duty wheels, 3 3/4" high					

BASE OPTION #2

REFERENCE	QUANTITY	PART	STOCK	THICKNESS	WIDTH	LENGTH	COMMENTS
KK	8	base pads	MDF	3/4	3	3	
	4	metal adjustable leveling feet					

HARDWARE

4 Drawer knobs or pulls

3 Sets of 22" drawer glides

2 - 107° Hidden hinges and plates

1 - 48"-Long aluminum miter slide track

1 - 48"-Long aluminum T-track

6 - 1" by 1/4"-Diameter threaded knobs

1 Power bar with switch

11/2" PB screws as detailed

5/8" PB screws as detailed

Glue

Pocket screws

Brad nails

2" Screws

T-nuts

MATERIALS LIST ▪ MILLIMETERS

REFERENCE	QUANTITY	PART	STOCK	THICKNESS	WIDTH	LENGTH	COMMENTS
A	4	vertical dividers	MDF	19	597	787	
B	1	bottom board	MDF	19	597	914	
C	6	horizontal dividers	MDF	19	216	597	
D	1	backboard	MDF	19	806	914	
E	1	top center rail	MDF	19	76	432	
F	2	shelf supports	MDF	19	76	597	
G	1	middle shelf	MDF	19	432	597	
H	4	bit holder platforms	MDF	19	202	559	
J	8	bit holder runners	MDF	19	64	559	
K	4	bit holder front cleats	MDF	19	64	163	
L	4	bit holder backboards	MDF	19	202	202	
M	4	bit holder front faces	MDF	19	229	216	
N	4	bit holder stop cleats	MDF	19	51	203	
P	4	drawer sides	MDF	19	235	559	
Q	4	drawer fronts & backs	MDF	19	235	140	
R	2	drawer bottoms	MDF	19	178	559	
S	2	drawer faces	MDF	19	229	352	
T	2	middle drawer sides	MDF	19	197	559	
U	2	drawer front & back	MDF	19	197	369	
V	1	drawer bottom	MDF	19	406	559	
W	1	middle drawer face	MDF	19	451	352	
X	1	middle door	MDF	19	451	438	
Y	2	top panels	MDF	19	959	705	
Z	2	top back & front edges	hardwood	19	38	997	
AA	2	top side edges	hardwood	19	38	743	
BB	1	fence back rail	MDF	19	127	991	
CC	1	fence horizontal support	MDF	19	102	991	
DD	4	fence angle support blocks	MDF	19	102	102	angle-cut
EE	1	fence back cover	MDF	19	102	133	angle-cut
FF	2	adjustable fence boards	MDF	19	127	496	

BASE OPTION #1

REFERENCE	QUANTITY	PART	STOCK	THICKNESS	WIDTH	LENGTH	COMMENTS
GG	2	sides	MDF	19	76	508	
HH	2	front & back boards	MDF	19	76	115	
JJ	1	top	MDF	19	152	508	
	2	heavy-duty wheels, 95mm high					

BASE OPTION #2

REFERENCE	QUANTITY	PART	STOCK	THICKNESS	WIDTH	LENGTH	COMMENTS
KK	8	base pads	MDF	19	76	76	
	4	metal adjustable leveling feet					

HARDWARE

4 Drawer knobs or pulls

3 Sets of 559mm drawer glides

2 - 107° Hidden hinges and plates

1 - 1219mm-Long aluminum miter slide track

1 - 1219mm-Long aluminum T-track

6 - 25mm by 6mm-Diameter threaded knobs

1 Power bar with switch

38mm PB screws as detailed

16mm PB screws as detailed

Glue

Pocket screws

Brad nails

51mm Screws

T-nuts

STEP 1 ■ Prepare the four vertical dividers A by cutting them to size and forming the dadoes and rabbets in each panel as shown. All the rabbets and dadoes are ³/₄" wide by ¹/₄" deep.

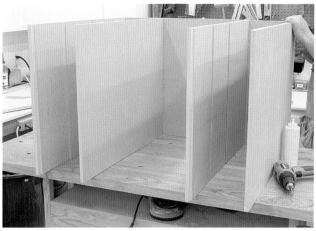

STEP 2 ■ The bottom board B is secured to the dividers with glue and 1¹/₂" screws in pilot holes. Align the two sets of dividers, spaced 8" apart, with the dadoes and rabbets facing each other. The middle section should be 17" wide between panels. Keep the screws 1" away from any panel end and use four screws per divider, driven through the bottom board.

STEP 3 ■ Install the six horizontal dividers C in the dadoes and rabbets. Use glue and clamps to secure the sections.

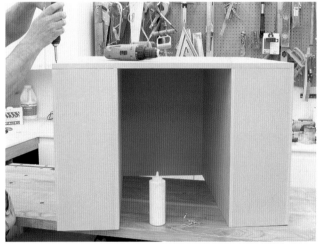

STEP 4 ■ Attach the backboard D to the cabinet using glue and 1¹/₂" screws. If you've carefully cut the back panel square, the cabinet will be properly aligned.

STEP 5 ■ The top center rail E is attached with one ³/₄"-thick edge facing forward. Secure it with biscuits, or pocket screws and glue if you don't have a biscuit joiner. This rail will be attached to the underside of the tabletop.

This cabinet is on its back with the top facing the camera.

STEP 6 ■ If you plan to use base option #1, attach two heavy-duty locking wheel assemblies to one side of the cabinet.

STEP 7 ■ The other half of base option #1 is a box made with ³/₄" MDF using the parts GG, HH and JJ. It's attached to the bottom of the cabinet with 1¹/₄" screws and glue. If the cabinet has to be moved often, you can lift the fixed base end and push it along the floor on the wheels.

The height of my fixed base portion is 3³/₄" to match the wheel height. If you do use this setup, purchase the wheels first so the correct height can be verified. After installing both options, I've decided to use base #2 on my cabinet, as described in step 29.

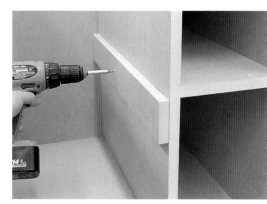

STEP 8 ■ Install the two shelf supports F in the middle section. They are secured with glue and 1¹/₄" screws. Their top edges are 12³/₄" above the bottom board. Cut the middle shelf G to the size indicated in the materials list and secure it to the cleats with glue and brad nails.

STEP 9 ■ The four bit holder slide-outs are made with ³/₄"-thick MDF. Each holder board has a series of holes for ¹/₄"- and ¹/₂"-diameter router bits. I spaced my holes 2" apart with the two outside rows 1¹/₂" in from each board's edge and the third row in the center.

The holder platforms H are attached to the runners J with glue and 1¹/₂" screws. The runners are flush with the outside long edges of the holder platforms. A front lower cleat K is also attached to the holder platform in the same way. The backboards L are attached to the rear of each assembly with glue and 1¹/₂" screws. Use a ¹/₄" roundover bit in your router to soften the front edges of the slide-out faces M. Once the face is aligned on the slide-out, attach each face with 1¹/₄" screws through the front lower cleat.

STEP 11 ▪ The two outside lower drawer boxes are 7" wide by 10" high by 22" deep and made with ³/₄"-thick MDF. Attach the drawer sides P to the back and front boards Q using glue and 1¹/₂" screws. The bottom boards R are also secured to the sides, front and bottom board edges with 1¹/₂" screws and glue to form the drawer boxes. Use 22" bottom-mount drawer glides, or full-extension glides if you prefer, to install the drawer boxes in the cabinet.

STEP 12 ▪ The lower outside drawer box faces S have their front edges rounded over using a ¹/₄" router bit. They are secured to the drawer boxes with 1¹/₄" screws through the inside of the box. Install the faces so they are aligned with the slide-out fronts, leaving a ¹/₈" gap between each front.

STEP 10 ▪ Cut and attach the four stop cleats N with glue and 1¹/₄"-long screws. These cleats will stop the slide-out when fully extended. When it's necessary to remove or install the slide-outs, simply tip them upward to move past the stop cleats.

STEP 13 ▪ The lower middle drawer box is 8¹/₂" high by 16" wide by 22" deep. Build the box using ³/₄" MDF with parts T, U and V following the same steps as the outside lower drawer boxes. Mount this box using 22" drawer glides.

STEP 14 ▪ Round over the front edges of drawer face W using a ¹/₄" router bit. Attach it to the drawer box with 1¹/₄" screws, being careful to leave equal spacing on both sides, with its top aligned to the two outside drawer faces.

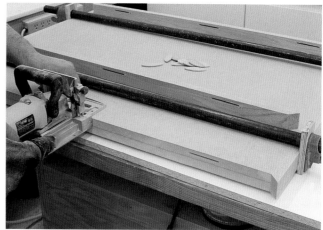

STEP 15 ▪ Cut the door X to size and round over the front face edges. I used full-overlay 107° hinges with standard mounting plates. Drill 35mm holes, ⅛" from the door edge, to secure the hinges. Hold the door in its normally open position, with a ⅛"-thick spacer between the door and cabinet edge, and secure the mounting plates with ⅝" screws.

STEP 16 ▪ The top is made by gluing two ¾"-thick MDF panels together. Cut both panels Y a little oversize so they can be trimmed to a finished size when the adhesive has cured. The top is banded with 1½"-high by ¾"-thick hardwood and is secured in place with biscuits. Cut the edges Z and AA to size with 45° miters on each end to join the corners.

STEP 17 ▪ Turn the top upside down on the router cabinet. It should overhang the front edge by 1½" and the sides by 1⅝". I will be using a Rout-R-Lift plate made by JessEm Tool Company, but any plate can be installed using the following method. Place the router plate on the center of the table and 5" back from the front edge of the top. Fasten strips of wood around the plate with screws. These strips will be used as a template to guide your router.

STEP 18 ▪ The router base should have a bushing guide installed to run against the strips of wood. The size of the bushing should equal the depth of cut for the wing or slot cutter bit that will be used to form a groove on the top side of the table to inset the router plate flush with the top face. My wing bit cuts ½" deep, so I want the hole to be smaller than the strip edges by ½" on all sides. Cut the hole using the guide bushing and router bit.

STEP 19 ▪ Flip the top right side up and use the wing cutter to groove the top. The router plate should be flush with the tabletop's surface. I hand-formed the corners to match my router plate. It may also be necessary in your case to use a sharp knife and chisel to carve the corners. Fasten the top to the cabinet using 2" screws through the horizontal supports and middle top rail.

STEP 20 ▪ I installed a ³/₄" miter slide track in my tabletop. Cut the groove for the slide track as close to the front edge of your router plate as possible. This track required a 1"-wide groove cut parallel to the router plate. I drilled the track and secured it to the top with ⁵/₈" screws. The track is available through most woodworking supply stores.

STEP 21 ▪ The T-track, which will be used to lock the adjustable fence, is also attached to the top in grooves. Rout the grooves on each side, parallel to the plate, and match the size of track you purchased, making sure they are flush with the tabletop surface. Once again, the tracks are secured with ⁵/₈" screws.

STEP 22 ▪ All of the fence parts are made with ³/₄"-thick MDF. The fence back rail BB has two ³/₈"-wide grooves routed into the center and through the board. The grooves start 6" from each end and stop 16" from each end. This rail also requires a 4"-wide by 2¹/₂"-high notch, centered on the length of the board. The horizontal support CC also has a notch that is 4" wide by 2" high in the center of the board. Both notches can be cut with a band saw or jigsaw.

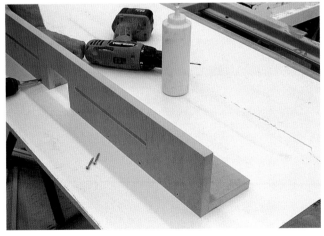

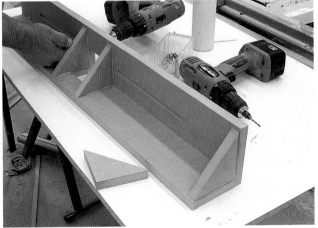

STEP 23 ▪ Attach the fence back rail BB to the horizontal support CC with 1¹/₂" screws and glue at about 4" on center.

STEP 24 ▪ The four right-angle fence supports DD are 4" x 4" blocks of ³/₄" MDF cut at 45°. Use glue and 1¹/₂" screws to attach the supports to the fence assembly. One support is installed at either end and the remaining two on each side of the cutout notch in the fence boards.

STEP 25 ▪ The back cover EE for the fence cutout has a 45° miter on both ends. Apply glue to all edges and secure the cover with a few brad nails on the top and bottom edge.

STEP 26 ▪ Drill a 2¼"-diameter hole in the center of the back cover. This will be used to friction-fit a vacuum hose.

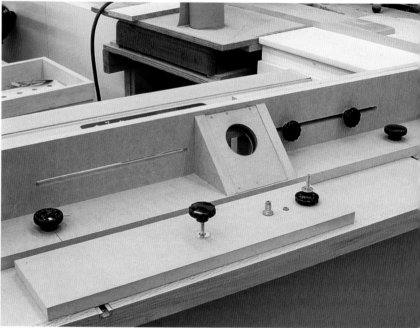

STEP 27 ▪ Center the fence assembly on the router table and drill two ⅜"-diameter holes in the horizontal support over the center of each T-track. Use a T-nut and knob with a 1"-long by ¼"-diameter threaded shaft screwed into the nut. Tighten the knobs and verify that the fence locks securely.

STEP 28 ▪ The adjustable fence boards FF have two T-nuts driven into the front faces. Counterbore the hole so the nuts are slightly below the fence face. Position the nuts so both fences can come together in the center and travel about 4" out from the center.

STEP 29 *(left)* ▪ I will be using base option #2, as illustrated. Two pads KK are glued together and attached to the bottom, 3" back from the front edge of the cabinet and on both back corners. Drill holes for 1/4"-diameter T-nuts and install a threaded metal foot in the center of each block as shown.

STEP 30 *(above)* ▪ My 2¼"-outside-diameter vacuum hose on my shop vacuum is a snug fit in the dust hole and provides good particle removal.

CONSTRUCTION
NOTES

You will need four sheets of ¾"-thick MDF to build this cabinet. I used about 13' of hardwood to edge the top, as well.

I used MDF, but any ¾" sheet material will be fine, and the same construction dimensions and procedures can be used. If you decide to use another material, look for a smooth surface so your router work will slide easily on the top.

Pay special attention to the final height of your cabinet. My cabinet, with the adjustable legs in base option #2, puts my top surface at about 35" above the floor. That's a comfortable height for me, but your re-quirements may be different. Adjust the vertical divider heights to meet your needs.

All of the aluminum track, knobs and related hard-ware are sold at most woodworking stores. Woodwork-ers tend to make jigs and shop-built tool accessories, so this line of hardware has become very popular.

I considered adding a dust collection port in the router compartment, but the dust doesn't seem to be that great a problem. My vacuum pulls most of the dust at the fence; however, routing a material that creates fine dust may cause a buildup in the compart-ment. If that's the case, drilling a dust port and mak-ing a Y-fitting so the vacuum could collect from the fence and router compartment would be an easy fix.

STEP 31 ▪ I purchased and attached a construction-grade power bar, made by Belkin Components, called a SurgeMaster HD. This device is designed to control electrical equipment such as saws, compressors and routers. The vacuum cleaner and router will be plugged into the power bar and controlled by a switch. I will also have spare plugs that are overload protected, which I can use in the shop for other electrical equipment.

CHAPTER 19

DRILL-PRESS CENTER

A drill press is a valuable asset in any woodworking shop. Drill presses are available as floor or bench models and have adjustable tables or heads. However, they all lack storage space and have tables that are difficult to adjust.

I built the storage cabinet portion of this project to be used with both floor and bench drill presses. The bench model can be bolted to the top, or the cabinet can be wheeled over the base on floor-model units. If you do own a floor-model press, measure the width and height of the base to be sure the cabinet can be rolled over the base. If the base is too large, change the cabinet dimensions to suit your drill press.

The full-extension top cabinet drawer can hold drill bits on an indexed board, while the remaining drawers can contain accessories, literature and other tools used with your drill press. If you need the drill press table on your floor-model unit lower than the cabinet height, simply roll it out of the way. Bench-model presses can be mounted on the top, and the station, both cabinet and drill press, can be rolled to any area of your shop.

Many woodworkers will appreciate the wide adjustable table. It can be tipped for angular drilling to the front or rear of your drill press. The adjustable fence is an important option that is missing on most drill units. Woodworkers use drill press fences a great deal and often have to clamp a straight-edged board to the press table. This fence is adjustable, easily locked in place and quick to move where needed.

The drill press center is easy to build, inexpensive and well worth the time invested. It's a great workstation to use, and I'm sure you'll quickly appreciate its value.

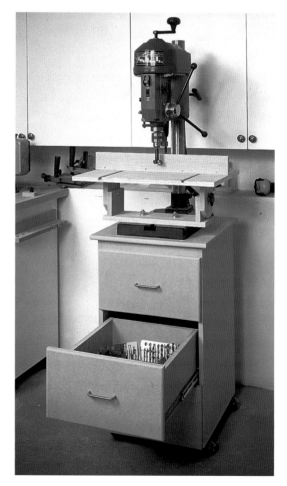

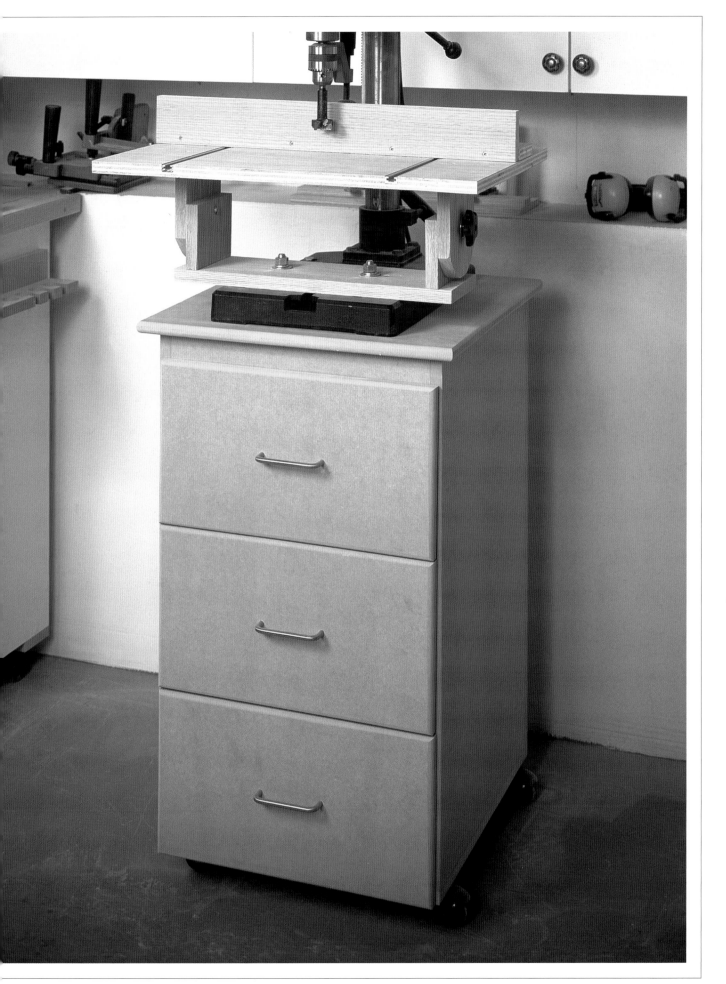

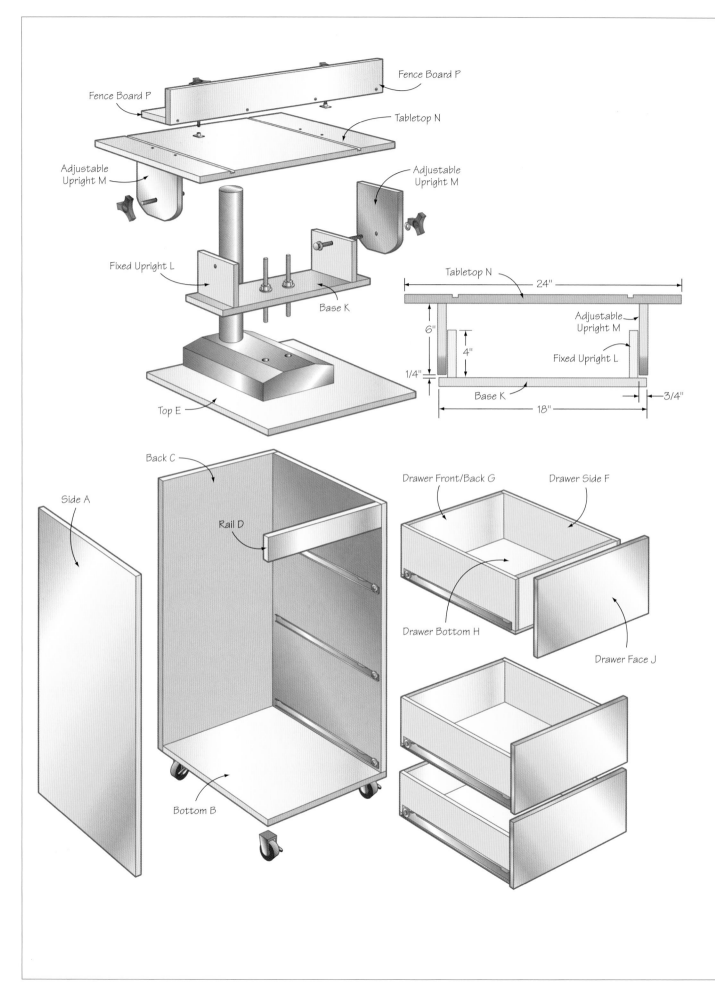

Fence Board P

Fence Board P

Tabletop N

Adjustable
Upright M

Adjustable
Upright M

Fixed Upright L

Base K

Top E

Tabletop N

24"

Adjustable
Upright M

6"

4"

Fixed Upright L

1/4"

Base K

3/4"

18"

Back C

Drawer Front/Back G

Drawer Side F

Side A

Rail D

Drawer Bottom H

Drawer Face J

Bottom B

MATERIALS LIST ■ INCHES

REFERENCE	QUANTITY	PART	STOCK	THICKNESS	WIDTH	LENGTH	COMMENTS
CABINET							
A	2	sides	MDF	³/₄	19	30	
B	1	bottom	MDF	³/₄	18	19	
C	1	back	MDF	³/₄	18	30³/₄	
D	1	rail	MDF	³/₄	2	16³/₄	
E	1	top	MDF	³/₄	20	21	
F	6	drawer sides	MDF	³/₄	6¹/₄	18	
G	6	drawer fronts & backs	MDF	³/₄	6¹/₄	14	
H	3	drawer bottoms	MDF	³/₄	15¹/₂	18	
J	3	drawer faces	MDF	³/₄	9⁵/₈	17¹/₂	
ADJUSTABLE DRILL TABLE							
K	1	base	hardwood	³/₄	5¹/₄	18	
L	2	fixed uprights	hardwood	³/₄	5¹/₄	4	
M	2	adjustable uprights	hardwood	³/₄	5¹/₄	6	
N	1	tabletop	veneer ply	³/₄	16	24	
P	2	fence boards	veneer ply	³/₄	3	24	
Q	2	drill platforms	MDF	³/₄	14	16³/₄	

HARDWARE

Screws as detailed

Glue

3 Drawer handles

3 Sets of full-extension drawer glides

Right-angle brackets

Bolts and nuts as detailed

T-track

T-nuts

Knobs

1¹/₂" Screws

⁵/₈" Screws

1¹/₄" Screws

4 Wheels

2" Screws

¹/₄" Carriage bolts with washer and knobs

¹/₂" Screws

¹/₄" x 20 Bolt and knob assembly with 1"-long shaft

MATERIALS LIST ■ MILLIMETERS

REFERENCE	QUANTITY	PART	STOCK	THICKNESS	WIDTH	LENGTH	COMMENTS
CABINET							
A	2	sides	MDF	³/₄	19	30	
B	1	bottom	MDF	³/₄	18	19	
C	1	back	MDF	³/₄	18	30³/₄	
D	1	rail	MDF	³/₄	2	16³/₄	
E	1	top	MDF	³/₄	20	21	
F	6	drawer sides	MDF	³/₄	6¹/₄	18	
G	6	drawer fronts & backs	MDF	³/₄	6¹/₄	14	
H	3	drawer bottoms	MDF	³/₄	15¹/₂	18	
J	3	drawer faces	MDF	³/₄	9⁵/₈	17¹/₂	
ADJUSTABLE DRILL TABLE							
K	1	base	hardwood	³/₄	5¹/₄	18	
L	2	fixed uprights	hardwood	³/₄	5¹/₄	4	
M	2	adjustable uprights	hardwood	³/₄	5¹/₄	6	
N	1	tabletop	veneer ply	³/₄	16	24	
P	2	fence boards	veneer ply	³/₄	3	24	
Q	2	drill platforms	MDF	³/₄	14	16³/₄	

HARDWARE

Screws as detailed

Glue

3 Drawer handles

3 Sets of full-extension drawer glides

Right-angle brackets

Bolts and nuts as detailed

T-track

T-nuts

Knobs

38mm Screws

16mm Screws

32mm Screws

4 Wheels

51mm Screws

6mm Carriage bolts with washer and knobs

13mm Screws

6mm x 20 Bolt and knob assembly with 25mm-long shaft

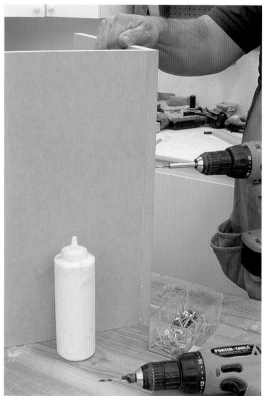

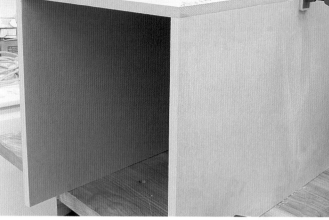

STEP 2 ■ The back C is attached to the cabinet sides and bottom board with $1^1/2$" screws and glue. A properly cut back will square the cabinet.

STEP 1 ■ Cut the two sides A and bottom board B to size as detailed in the materials list. Attach the bottom to the sides using $1^1/2$" screws, spaced 6" apart, and glue. Note that both sides rest on the bottom board, and the screws are installed on the underside of the bottom, into the edges of the side boards. Remember to drill pilot holes for the screws.

STEP 3 ■ Cut and attach the top rail D using right-angle brackets and $5/8$" screws. Apply glue to the rail ends and clamp securely when installing the brackets. The brackets are also installed on the sides, back and rail boards, and will be used to secure the cabinet top board.

STEP 4 ▪ Round over the two sides and front edges of the top board E using a ³⁄₈" roundover bit in a router. Use ⁵⁄₈" screws in the right-angle brackets to secure the top. There should be a 1" overhang on both sides and a 1¹⁄₄" overhang at the front edge. The top's back edge is aligned flush with the back face of the backboard.

STEP 5 ▪ The drawer boxes are 7" high by 15¹⁄₂" wide by 18" deep. I made my drawer boxes using the same ³⁄₄"-thick MDF as was used to build the cabinet carcass.

Cut the drawer box parts F, G and H to size. Begin the assembly by attaching the sides to the back and front boards using 1¹⁄₂" screws and glue. Two screws per joint, making sure the screws are kept 1" away from the tops and bottoms of the boards, will secure the joints.

STEP 6 ▪ The bottom boards are also attached to the side, back and front boards using 1¹⁄₂" screws and glue.

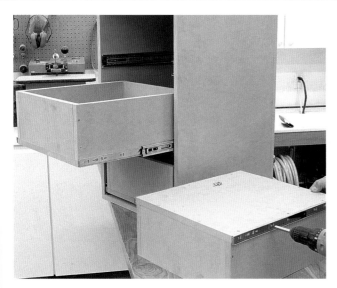

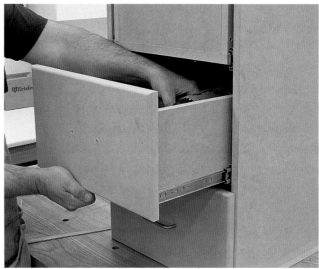

STEP 7 ■ I used 18" full-extension drawer glides to mount my drawer boxes. The bottom drawer is installed as close to the bottom board as possible. The remaining two drawer boxes are installed leaving a 2" space between them.

STEP 8 ■ The drawer faces J are $9^5/8$" high by $17^1/2$" wide using $^3/4$" MDF. The front edges are rounded over with a $^3/8$" bit in a router. The bottom drawer face is aligned flush with the bottom edge of the cabinet base board and spaced $^1/8$" apart. Secure the faces to the drawer boxes using $1^1/4$" screws from inside the drawer box. Attach handles or knobs of your choice.

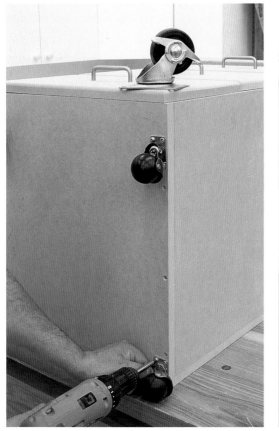

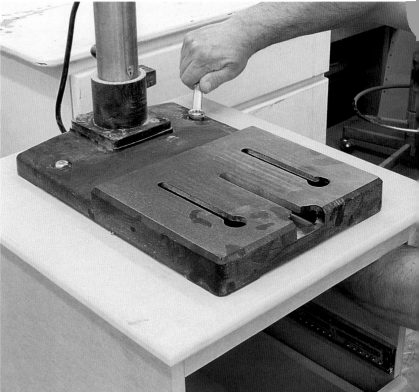

STEP 9 ■ Install four wheels on the base, setting back the front set by 2". Use medium- or heavy-duty wheels, making sure they are high enough to straddle the drill press base if you own a floor model.

STEP 10 ■ If you are using a benchtop drill press, mount it securely to the cabinet top with bolts or screws. If you own a floor-model press, you can skip this step.

STEP 11 ■ Using hardwood, cut the table base K and the two fixed uprights L to size. Secure both uprights to the base K with glue and 2" screws. The uprights are attached ¾" in from each end of the base K.

STEP 12 ■ Prepare the two adjustable uprights M by cutting them to the size indicated. Remove both lower corners on each board with a 45° cut that's 1½" from each end. Round over the corners with a belt sander, creating an arc on the bottom edge of each upright.

STEP 13 ■ Following the rough shaping with the belt sander, clamp the two uprights together and finish-sand so both have the same profile.

STEP 14 ■ Place the adjustable uprights M on the outside faces of each fixed upright L, aligning the edges of all boards. Use a ¼"-thick spacer under the adjustable uprights and drill a ¼"-diameter hole 3" down from their top edges through both boards. Center the hole on the width of each board and insert a ¼"-diameter carriage bolt, a large washer on the outside face and a knob to lock the uprights together.

STEP 15 ■ Bolt the assembly to the table on your drill press. Each model will have different bolt hole patterns, so choose a method that suits your drill press table. Align the drill chuck center to the center of the table base board and tighten securely.

STEP 16 ■ The tabletop N is a piece of ³⁄₄"-thick veneer plywood. Form two dadoes along the width of the board, 5" in from each edge. The T-track I'm using requires ³⁄₈"-deep dadoes, but your hardware may be different, so verify the track depth before cutting the dadoes. Cut the tracks to length and secure them in the dadoes using ¹⁄₂" screws in countersunk holes at the bottom of the tracks.

STEP 17 ■ Attach the top to the adjustable uprights using two 2" screws per upright. Align the top so it's equally spaced on both upright edges, side to side and back to front. Don't use glue in case the top has to be replaced in the future.

STEP 18 ■ The fence is made with ³⁄₄"-thick veneer plywood. The horizontal and vertical members P are 3" high by 24" long. Attach the vertical board to the horizontal member with glue and four 2" screws. This simple but strong fence can be easily replaced if necessary.

STEP 19 ■ Drill two ¹⁄₄"-diameter holes in the horizontal fence board over the center of each T-track slot. To lock the fence, use a ¹⁄₄" x 20 bolt and knob assembly with a 1"-long shaft screwed to T-nuts in the track.

STEP 20 ■ I'm using one of the drawers, on full-extension drawer glides, to store and index my drill bits. Cut a piece of ³⁄₄" MDF to size for a drill platform Q. Drill the appropriate holes to store your bits and loosely sit the platform in the drawer box. New holes can be drilled as your bit inventory increases.

CONSTRUCTION
NOTES

If you build the drill press center as detailed, you'll need about 1¹⁄₄ sheets of MDF, a 2' x 2' piece of veneer-covered plywood and a 40"-long piece of 1x6 hardwood. The hardware is available at most woodworking stores.

Many configurations are possible for the cabinet, and the final dimensions will depend on the size of your drill press. The sizes shown in this project should be suitable for the majority of floor and benchtop drill presses.

Any ³⁄₄" sheet material can be used. I decided to use MDF because it's inexpensive, can be easily worked with standard woodworking tools, doesn't require edge finishing and is a stable material. However, particleboard or plywood can be substituted if one of them is a personal favorite of yours.

An additional knob and bolt can be added to double-lock each set of uprights. If you do a lot of heavy work on the drill press, you might want some added insurance that the table will remain level, so add another ¹⁄₄" x 20 bolt and knob to each side. Remove the extra lock when adjustments to the table are needed. However, the one-knob-per-side setup securely locks the table, and it would take quite a bit of weight to move it.

You may want to drill a large round hole in the table to insert a sanding drum. The drum can be installed in the drill chuck and lowered through the hole. The large table and a drum will make a great power sanding accessory on your press. Dozens of drill press accessories are available, such as planers, plug cutters, hollow chisel mortise attachments and so on. The cabinet can be made with one drawer over a door with adjustable shelves or, as shown, three drawers on full-extension (FX) glides. The FX glides are the most expensive part of the project. To reduce costs, use an FX glide set on the drill bit drawer and bottom-mount glides on the remaining drawers.

CHAPTER 20

TOOL-SHARPENING AND TOOL-MAINTENANCE STATION

Sharpening equipment is a necessity in every woodworking shop. Dull tools are aggravating to work with and dangerous. Keeping chisels, turning tools, plane blades and carving tools in good condition is a fact of life in the woodshop.

Many woodworkers use water stones and waterwheel grinders. The stones have to be kept wet to work effectively, so that means a water bath. However, woodworking tools create dust, and when mixed with water, a brown sludge forms in the water bath. Those of you who use oil stones have the same problem with dust — a brown paste covering the stones and lapping plates. I'm sure I've spent more time cleaning the stones and water baths than on actual tool maintenance.

I decided to build a dedicated sharpening station for my 1" belt sander, wet and dry wheel grinder and water bath for my stones. But I vowed to solve the dust and water problems with this station. The flip-up cover is my answer for a dust-free center, and it works great!

This project may not look sleek and stylish, but it keeps my water baths and stones "paste free" and saves me a great deal of time previously wasted cleaning the equipment.

The power cords are routed through the top and plug into a power bar. Two large drawers provide all the space I need for sharpening accessories, extra blades for my tools and manuals related to my equipment. The section below the drawers is enclosed with doors for added dust-free storage. The station is mounted on locking wheels that allow me to bring it to any area in my shop.

If you want clean, almost dust-free sharpening equipment that's ready to use, then this project is for you. The cabinet won't win any beauty awards, but it's number one in the functional category.

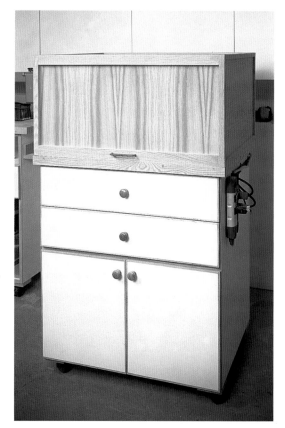

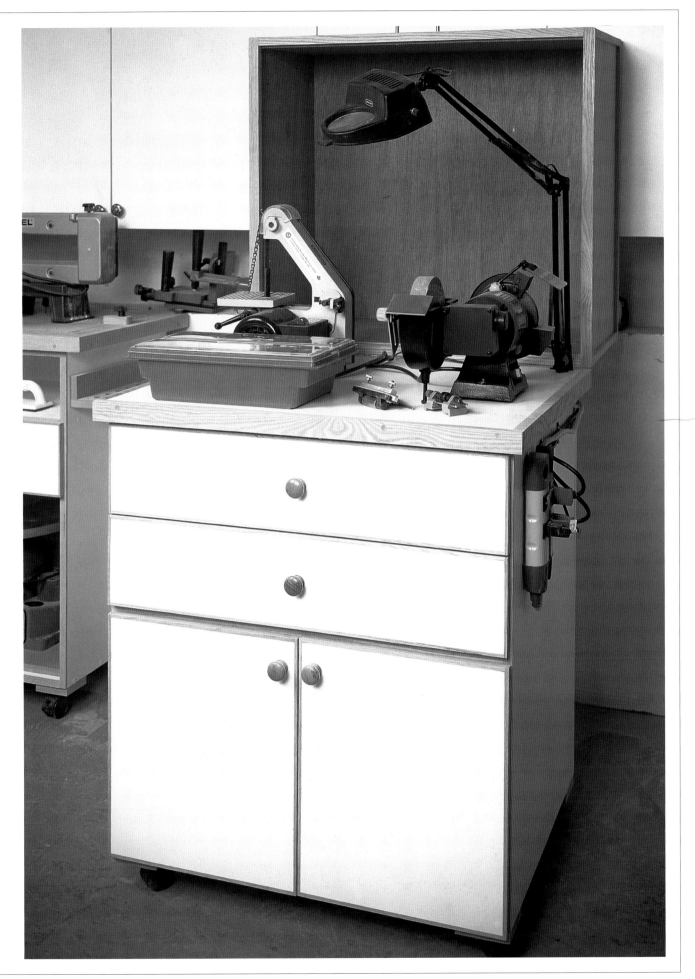

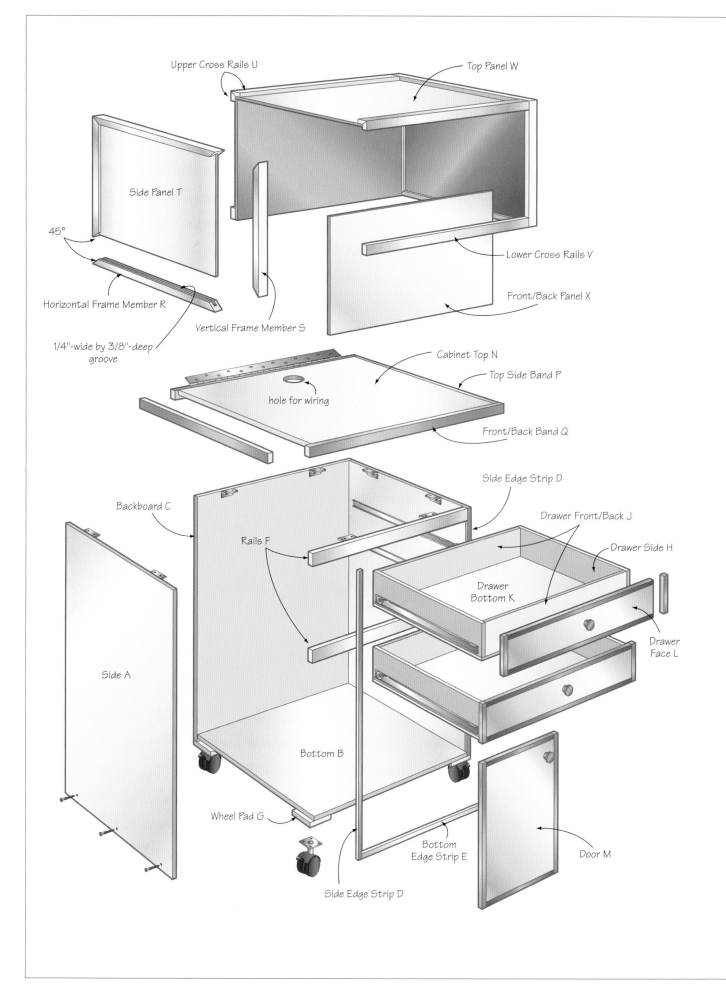

Upper Cross Rails U

Top Panel W

Side Panel T

45°

Horizontal Frame Member R

Vertical Frame Member S

1/4"-wide by 3/8"-deep groove

Lower Cross Rails V

Front/Back Panel X

Cabinet Top N

Top Side Band P

hole for wiring

Front/Back Band Q

Backboard C

Rails F

Side Edge Strip D

Drawer Front/Back J

Drawer Side H

Drawer Bottom K

Drawer Face L

Side A

Bottom B

Wheel Pad G

Bottom Edge Strip E

Side Edge Strip D

Door M

MATERIALS LIST ▪ INCHES

REFERENCE	QUANTITY	PART	STOCK	THICKNESS	WIDTH	LENGTH	COMMENTS
CABINET							
A	2	sides	melamine PB	5/8	23 3/8	32	
B	1	bottom	melamine PB	5/8	23 3/8	28 3/4	
C	1	backboard	melamine PB	5/8	30	32	
D	2	side edge strips	hardwood	1/4	5/8	32	
E	1	bottom edge strip	hardwood	1/4	5/8	28 3/4	
F	2	rails	hardwood	3/4	1 1/2	28 3/4	
G	4	wheel pads	hardwood	3/4	3 1/2	3 1/2	
H	4	drawer sides	melamine PB	5/8	4 3/8	22	
J	4	drawer fronts & backs	melamine PB	5/8	4 3/8	26 1/2	
K	2	drawer bottoms	melamine PB	5/8	22	27 3/4	
L	2	drawer faces	melamine PB	5/8	6 1/2	29 3/4	
M	2	doors	melamine PB	5/8	14 7/8	17 1/2	
N	1	cabinet top	melamine PB	5/8	30 1/4	26 1/2	
P	2	top side bands	hardwood	3/4	1 1/2	26 1/2	
Q	2	front & back bands	hardwood	3/4	1 1/2	31 3/4	
COVER							
R	4	horizontal frame members	hardwood	3/4	1	28	angle-cut
S	4	vertical frame members	hardwood	3/4	1	16	angle-cut
T	2	side panels	veneer ply	1/4	15 1/4	27 1/4	
U	4	upper cross rails	hardwood	3/4	1 1/2	29 3/4	angle-cut
V	2	lower cross rails	hardwood	3/4	1 1/2	29 3/4	
W	1	top panel	veneer ply	1/4	30 3/8	26 3/8	
X	2	front & back panels	veneer ply	1/4	30 3/8	14 1/4	

HARDWARE

8 Metal right-angle brackets

2" PB screws as detailed

Brad nails as detailed

Glue

White screw head cover caps as detailed

4 Locking wheels

Iron-on edge tape

2 – 22" Drawer glide sets

4 Knobs

4 – 107° Hidden hinges

1 – 28" Piano hinge

12" Length of small chain

1 Handle

1 Wire grommet

Metal angle brackets

Pocket screws

1 1/4" Screws

5/8" Screws

1" Screws

1/2" Screws

Biscuits

Wood plugs

Wire protector

MATERIALS LIST ▪ MILLIMETERS

REFERENCE	QUANTITY	PART	STOCK	THICKNESS	WIDTH	LENGTH	COMMENTS
CABINET							
A	2	sides	melamine PB	16	594	813	
B	1	bottom	melamine PB	16	594	730	
C	1	backboard	melamine PB	16	762	813	
D	2	side edge strips	hardwood	6	16	813	
E	1	bottom edge strip	hardwood	6	16	730	
F	2	rails	hardwood	19	38	730	
G	4	wheel pads	hardwood	19	89	89	
H	4	drawer sides	melamine PB	16	112	559	
J	4	drawer fronts & backs	melamine PB	16	112	673	
K	2	drawer bottoms	melamine PB	16	559	705	
L	2	drawer faces	melamine PB	16	165	756	
M	2	doors	melamine PB	16	378	445	
N	1	cabinet top	melamine PB	16	768	673	
P	2	top side bands	hardwood	19	38	673	
Q	2	front & back bands	hardwood	19	38	806	
COVER							
R	4	horizontal frame members	hardwood	19	25	711	angle-cut
S	4	vertical frame members	hardwood	19	25	406	angle-cut
T	2	side panels	veneer ply	6	387	692	
U	4	upper cross rails	hardwood	19	38	756	angle-cut
V	2	lower cross rails	hardwood	19	38	756	
W	1	top panel	veneer ply	6	772	670	
X	2	front & back panels	veneer ply	6	772	362	

HARDWARE

8 Metal right-angle brackets
51mm PB screws as detailed
Brad nails as detailed
Glue
White screw head cover caps as detailed
4 Locking wheels
Iron-on edge tape
2 – 559mm Drawer glide sets
4 Knobs
4 – 107° Hidden hinges
1 – 711mm Piano hinge
305mm Length of small chain
1 Handle
1 Wire grommet
Metal angle brackets
Pocket screws
32mm Screws
16mm Screws
25mm Screws
6mm Screws
Biscuits
Wood plugs
Wire protector

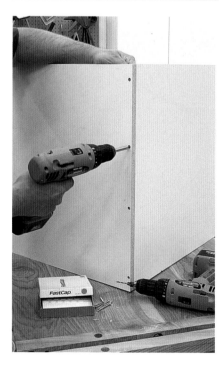

STEP 1 ▪ Join the sides A to the bottom board B by drilling 2" PB screws in pilot holes. Cover the screw heads with white stick-on caps or plastic covers.

STEP 2 ▪ Apply iron-on edge tape to both long vertical edges of backboard C. Attach the back to the sides and bottom board using 2"-long PB screws.

STEP 4 ■ Cut and install the two wood rails F. Secure them to the cabinet with metal angle brackets, screws through the cabinet's side or, as I'm using, pocket screws. The top rail is flush with the top edges of the cabinet sides, and the middle rail is 13½" below the top edges. There should be a 12"-high opening between the two rails for the drawers.

STEP 3 ■ Glue and nail the solid-wood edge strips D and E to the front edges of the side and bottom boards. Fill the nail holes and sand smooth. I'm using oak hardwood for all my edge trim, but any solid wood can be used.

STEP 5 ■ Install the eight right-angle brackets that will be used to secure the cabinet top board. The brackets are attached flush with the top edges of the side, backboard and upper rail. I installed two brackets on each panel and two on the rail.

STEP 6 ■ The four wood wheel pads G can be installed using 1" screws through the bottom board into the pads. They should be installed under the edges of the back and side boards so the load on those panels will shift through the pads and wheels to the floor. Four screws per pad will hold them securely to the cabinet bottom. The locking wheels are attached with 1¼" screws. The wheels I used are 2½" high, and including the pads, the cabinet is 3¼" off the floor.

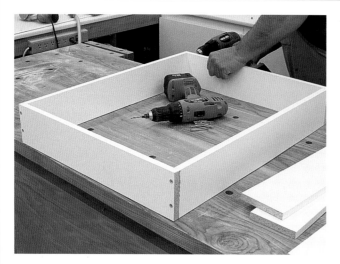

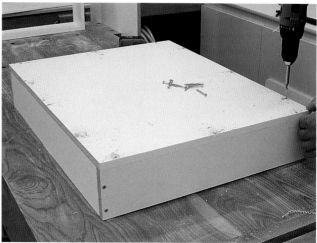

STEP 7 ■ The two drawer boxes are 5" high by 27¾" wide. Cut all drawer parts H, J and K to size. I used ⅝"-thick melamine and secured the butt joints with 2" PB screws. Before assembling the boxes use iron-on edge tape to cover the top edges of the back, front and side boards, as well as the side edges of the bottom board. Attach the sides to the back and front boards using two screws per joint. Keep the screws at least 1" away from the edges of all boards to avoid splitting.

STEP 8 ■ The drawer box bottom board is attached to the bottom edges of the side, back and front boards with 2" PB screws.

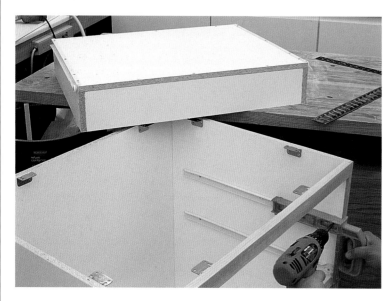

STEP 10 ■ The drawer faces L are secured to the boxes with four 1" screws. Leave a ¹⁄₁₆" space between the upper and lower drawer face. I used ⅝"-thick melamine PB trimmed with ¼"-thick oak hardwood for my faces. You can use any material to make the drawer faces and doors as long as the finished sizes are the same as the dimensions detailed in the materials list. The drawer faces will overlap the top and middle rail by approximately ½".

STEP 9 ■ Install the drawer boxes in the cabinet using 22" bottom-mount or, if you prefer, full-extension side-mount glides. The top glides are installed so the bottom of the top drawer box will be 5¾" below the lower edge of the top rail. Use ⅝" screws and follow the installation instructions that come with your hardware.

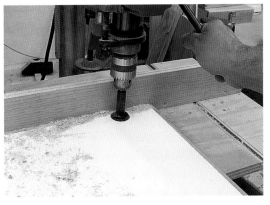

STEP 12 ■ Drill two 35mm holes in each door, 3" on center from each end. The flat-bottomed hinge holes are drilled $\frac{1}{8}$" in from the door's edge.

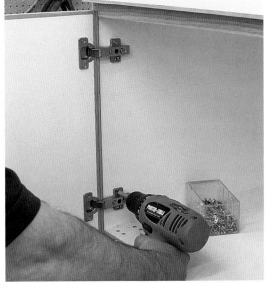

STEP 13 ■ Install two standard-opening hinges (between 100° and 120°) in each door and secure them with $\frac{1}{2}$"-long screws, making sure the hinges are 90° to the door's edge. Attach the hinge plates to the hinge body and hold the door against the cabinet in its normally open position with a $\frac{1}{8}$" spacer between the door and cabinet edge. Drive screws through the hinge-plate holes to secure the door. Remove the spacer and test the door alignment. Install handles or knobs on the drawers and doors.

STEP 11 ■ The door width is calculated by measuring the cabinet's inside width and adding 1". Since I want two doors on my cabinet, I will divide that number by two, (28$\frac{3}{4}$" plus 1" divided by 2), which means I'll need both doors to be 14$\frac{7}{8}$" wide. The doors are installed flush with the lower edge of the bottom board and overlay the middle rail by about $\frac{3}{8}$". I trimmed my door edges with oak, but as mentioned earlier, any material can be used as long as the overall dimensions of the doors are as stated in the materials list.

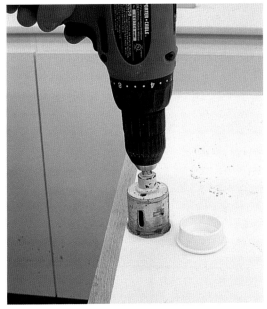

STEP 14 ■ The cabinet top N is a sheet of $\frac{5}{8}$"-thick melamine PB with hardwood edge-banding. Attach the edge-banding P and Q with glue and biscuits or screws with wood plugs. Install the top with $\frac{5}{8}$" screws through the metal brackets previously installed. There should be a $\frac{7}{8}$" overhang on each side, a 1$\frac{1}{4}$" overhang on the front edge and a 2$\frac{1}{2}$" overhang at the back edge. The larger overhang on the back will be used to install a wire hole and grommet.

STEP 15 ■ Drill a wire hole in the back of the top, 1" from the rear edge. Use a wire protector (commonly found at stores that sell electronic supplies). The power cords can pass through the hole and be attached to a power bar.

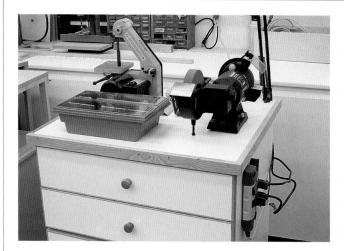

STEP 16 ■ Install your sharpening tools on the cabinet top, keeping them 1" from any edge. I have a 1" belt sander, wet and dry wheel grinder, a water stone bath and a magnifying lamp. I also attached a power bar made by Stanley Tools on the cabinet side. Your equipment will be different from mine, but it should be installed at this time to determine the minimum inside height of the cover.

STEP 17 ■ My cover is the full width and depth of the top, so I need 15" of inside clearance based on my equipment. The side frame will be made with hardwood that's 1" wide by ³⁄₄" thick. Both ends on frame members R and S are cut at 45° to create a mitered corner at each intersection. The side panels will be ¹⁄₄"-thick veneer plywood.

Cut a groove that's ¹⁄₄" wide on one 1" face of each horizontal and vertical ³⁄₈"-deep frame member. Miter the ends of each member so the long edge is the dimension stated in the materials list. The grooves are on the inside, short dimension of each mitered board. Assemble the two side frames with the panels T installed in the grooves. Use glue and brad nails, then clamp securely until the adhesive cures.

STEP 18 ■ Prepare the four upper cross rails U by ripping a 45° miter along one edge of each board. The face of these rails should be 1¹⁄₂" wide after ripping the angle. Create a back-and-front upper cross rail assembly by gluing the boards together in pairs at the miter. You should have two assemblies that form a right angle. The boards can be glued and brad nailed or clamped. If you use brads, keep them ³⁄₈" back from the corner intersection so the edges can be rounded with a router bit.

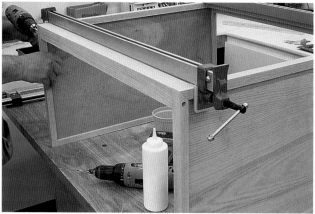

STEP 19 ■ Join the two sides with the upper cross rails using glue and 2" screws in counterbored holes. These holes can be filled with wood plugs. One 2" screw and glue at each joint will securely hold the rails to the sides.

STEP 20 ■ The two lower cross rails V are also secured with glue and one 2" screw at each end. Counterbore and fill the screw holes with wood plugs.

STEP 22 ■ The top panel W and front and back panels X are attached to the inside of the cover with glue and ⁵⁄₈" brad nails.

STEP 21 ■ Use a ¼" roundover bit to ease all the outside edges of the frame members. Do not round over the bottom edges of the cover, because it should sit tight and flat on the cabinet top.

STEP 23 ■ Clamp the cover in place on the cabinet so its edges are flush with the outside edges of the top. Use a 28" piano hinge on the back side to secure the cover to the cabinet.

STEP 24 ■ Use a small chain about 12" long to limit the travel of the cover. Then install a handle on the front lower cross rail of the cover so it can be easily raised and lowered.

CONSTRUCTION
NOTES

You need to deal with two important issues before beginning construction of this sharpening station. First, decide on a comfortable work-surface height and, if it is different from mine, change the height of the sides and backboard to suit your requirements.

Second, the type of equipment that will be mounted on this station will determine the size of the top and clearance requirements for the cover. The belt sander is normally the tallest piece of equipment and is the unit that determines the cover height.

I built my station using ⁵⁄₈"-thick particleboard and oak hardwood for the trim; however, any sheet material will work just as well. If you do use another sheet material such as MDF or plywood, consider installing a melamine PB or high-pressure laminate top. A smooth surface that's easy to clean is a real bonus.

You may also want to put a self-adhesive foam or rubber gasket on the bottom edge of the cover to further protect the equipment from dust. The cover can be built in another style, with other materials, but a ⁵⁄₈"-thick melamine PB prototype that I built was very heavy to lift. The frame and panel cover is light and easy to manage, which convinced me that it was the best design for this application.

Finally, change the drawer and door compartments if they don't meet your needs. Three or four small drawers may be more suitable, or for some of you, one drawer will be fine. This project should be designed and built to accommodate your sharpening requirements.

CHAPTER 21

MOBILE WORKBENCH AND TOOL CABINET

Does your woodworking shop share space with the family car? If you have a garage workshop, this project is perfect for you. The cabinet is mobile, has a large worktable and plenty of tool storage that can be secured with locks.

Many garage woodworkers spend half their time hauling out tools and setting up worktables. A mobile center reduces that lost time because all the tools are in one cabinet. The cabinet is also a worktable, so it can be wheeled to the center of your shop and you're ready to go with tools close at hand.

I used ¾" veneer plywood to build my cabinet, but the project can be built with plywood, MDF or any other ¾" sheet material that's reasonably priced. You'll need about three 4' × 8' sheets of material, locking wheels and drawer glide hardware, so calculate all the costs before you begin.

The storage space on the four pullouts should hold all of the tools you frequently use. The two large drawers can be used for smaller tools and documents. The mobile feature allows you to roll the cabinet to the side of your shop. Add a few locks as a safety feature, to stop curious youngsters from playing with potentially dangerous equipment.

I built my cabinet so it would do double duty as an outfeed table for a table saw and a handy table at my miter station. In fact, the cabinet can be moved beside any power tool where a table is required. If you want the saw outfeed table feature, verify the height needed before cutting the panels. You should purchase the locking wheel assemblies to determine their height before cutting. The top thickness, side panel height, wheel pads and wheel height will determine the final dimensions of the cabinet.

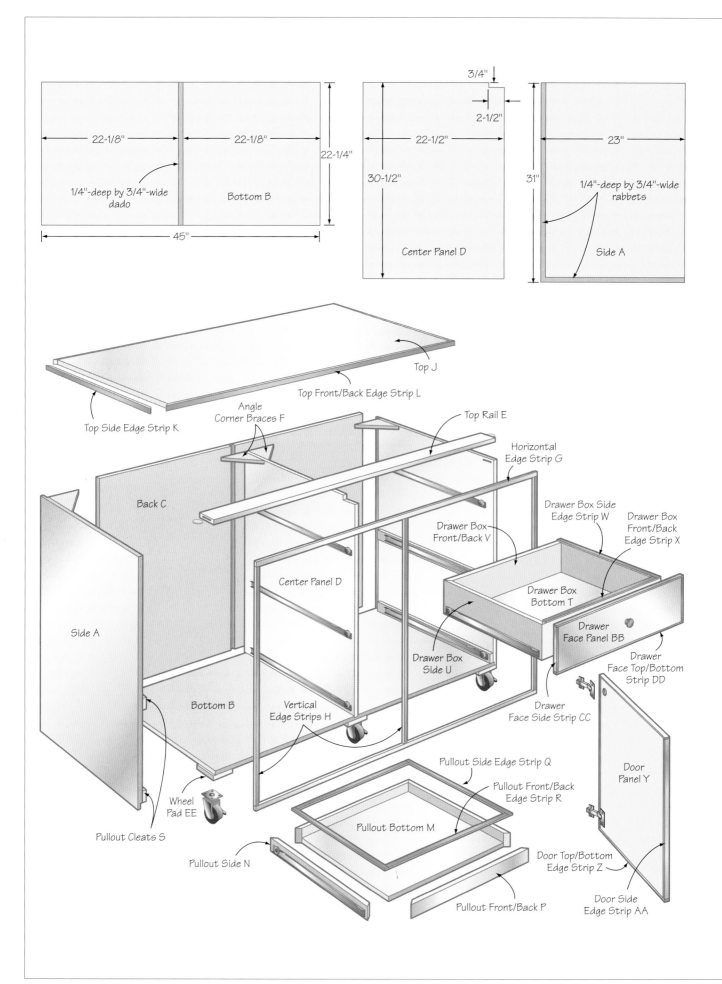

22-1/8"

22-1/8"

22-1/4"

1/4"-deep by 3/4"-wide dado

Bottom B

45"

3/4"

2-1/2"

22-1/2"

30-1/2"

Center Panel D

23"

31"

1/4"-deep by 3/4"-wide rabbets

Side A

Top J

Top Front/Back Edge Strip L

Top Side Edge Strip K

Angle Corner Braces F

Top Rail E

Horizontal Edge Strip G

Back C

Drawer Box Side Edge Strip W

Drawer Box Front/Back Edge Strip X

Drawer Box Front/Back V

Drawer Box Bottom T

Drawer Face Panel BB

Center Panel D

Side A

Drawer Box Side U

Drawer Face Top/Bottom Strip DD

Bottom B

Vertical Edge Strips H

Drawer Face Side Strip CC

Wheel Pad EE

Door Panel Y

Pullout Cleats S

Pullout Side Edge Strip Q

Pullout Front/Back Edge Strip R

Pullout Bottom M

Door Top/Bottom Edge Strip Z

Pullout Side N

Pullout Front/Back P

Door Side Edge Strip AA

MATERIALS LIST ▪ INCHES

REFERENCE	QUANTITY	PART	STOCK	THICKNESS	WIDTH	LENGTH	COMMENTS
A	2	sides	plywood	$3/4$	23	31	
B	1	bottom	plywood	$3/4$	$22^{1}/_{4}$	45	
C	1	back	plywood	$3/4$	31	45	
D	1	center panel	plywood	$3/4$	$22^{1}/_{2}$	$30^{1}/_{2}$	
E	1	top rail	plywood	$3/4$	$2^{1}/_{2}$	$44^{1}/_{2}$	
F	4	angle corner braces	hardwood	$3/4$	3	3	angle-cut
G	2	horizontal edge strips	hardwood	$1/4$	$3/4$	46	
H	3	vertical edge strips	hardwood	$1/4$	$3/4$	$29^{1}/_{2}$	
J	1	top	plywood	$3/4$	26	48	
K	2	top side edge strips	hardwood	$1/4$	$3/4$	26	
L	2	top front/back edge strips	hardwood	$1/4$	$3/4$	$48^{1}/_{2}$	
M	4	pullout bottoms	plywood	$3/4$	$18^{5}/_{8}$	$20^{1}/_{2}$	
N	8	pullout sides	plywood	$3/4$	2	22	angle-cut
P	8	pullout fronts & backs	plywood	$3/4$	2	$20^{1}/_{8}$	angle-cut
Q	8	pullout side edge strips	hardwood	$1/4$	$3/4$	22	
R	8	pullout front/back edge strips	hardwood	$1/4$	$3/4$	$18^{5}/_{8}$	
S	4	pullout cleats	plywood	$3/4$	2	22	
T	2	drawer box bottoms	plywood	$3/4$	$19^{3}/_{8}$	$20^{1}/_{2}$	
U	4	drawer box sides	plywood	$3/4$	5	22	angle-cut
V	4	drawer box fronts/backs	plywood	$3/4$	5	$20^{7}/_{8}$	angle-cut
W	4	drawer side edge strips	hardwood	$1/4$	$3/4$	22	
X	4	drawer front/back edge strips	hardwood	$1/4$	$3/4$	$19^{3}/_{8}$	
Y	2	door panels	plywood	$3/4$	$22^{1}/_{8}$	23	
Z	4	door top/bottom edge strips	hardwood	$1/4$	$3/4$	$22^{5}/_{8}$	
AA	4	door side edge strips	hardwood	$1/4$	$3/4$	23	
BB	2	drawer face panels	plywood	$3/4$	$6^{3}/_{4}$	$22^{1}/_{8}$	
CC	4	drawer face side strips	hardwood	$1/4$	$3/4$	$6^{3}/_{4}$	
DD	4	drawer face top/bottom strips	hardwood	$1/4$	$3/4$	$22^{5}/_{8}$	
EE	6	wheel pads	hardwood	$3/4$	5	5	

HARDWARE

2" PB screws

Brad nails as detailed

Glue

6 Locking wheels

4 - 22" Drawer glide sets

2 - 22" Full-extension drawer glide sets

4 Knobs

4 - 107° Hidden hinges

24 - $1^{1}/_{2}$"-Long x $5/_{16}$"-diameter lag bolts

Finishing nails

#10 Biscuits or dowels

Wood putty

$1^{1}/_{4}$" Screws

Iron-on edge tape

$5/_{8}$" Screws

MATERIALS LIST ▪ MILLIMETERS

REFERENCE	QUANTITY	PART	STOCK	THICKNESS	WIDTH	LENGTH	COMMENTS
A	2	sides	plywood	19	584	787	
B	1	bottom	plywood	19	565	1143	
C	1	back	plywood	19	787	1143	
D	1	center panel	plywood	19	572	775	
E	1	top rail	plywood	19	64	1131	
F	4	angle corner braces	hardwood	19	76	76	angle-cut
G	2	horizontal edge strips	hardwood	6	19	1168	
H	3	vertical edge strips	hardwood	6	19	750	
J	1	top	plywood	19	660	1219	
K	2	top side edge strips	hardwood	6	19	660	
L	2	top front/back edge strips	hardwood	6	19	1232	
M	4	pullout bottoms	plywood	19	473	521	
N	8	pullout sides	plywood	19	51	559	angle-cut
P	8	pullout fronts & backs	plywood	19	51	511	angle-cut
Q	8	pullout side edge strips	hardwood	6	19	559	
R	8	pullout front/back edge strips	hardwood	6	19	473	
S	4	pullout cleats	plywood	19	51	559	
T	2	drawer box bottoms	plywood	19	493	521	
U	4	drawer box sides	plywood	19	127	559	angle-cut
V	4	drawer box fronts/backs	plywood	19	127	530	angle-cut
W	4	drawer side edge strips	hardwood	6	19	559	
X	4	drawer front/back edge strips	hardwood	6	19	493	
Y	2	door panels	plywood	19	562	584	
Z	4	door top/bottom edge strips	hardwood	6	19	575	
AA	4	door side edge strips	hardwood	6	19	584	
BB	2	drawer face panels	plywood	19	171	562	
CC	4	drawer face side strips	hardwood	6	19	171	
DD	4	drawer face top/bottom strips	hardwood	6	19	575	
EE	6	wheel pads	hardwood	19	127	127	

HARDWARE

51mm PB screws

Brad nails as detailed

Glue

6 Locking wheels

4 - 559mm Drawer glide sets

2 - 559mm Full-extension drawer glide sets

4 Knobs

4 - 107° Hidden hinges

24 - 38mm-Long x 8mm-diameter lag bolts

Finishing nails

#10 Biscuits or dowels

Wood putty

32mm Screws

Iron-on edge tape

16mm Screws

STEP 1 ▪ Cut the two side panels A to the size shown in the materials list. Form a rabbet that's ¼" deep by ¾" wide on the inside bottom and back edge of each panel.

STEP 2 ▪ Before preparing the bottom B and back C, refer to the construction notes at the end of this chapter regarding cutting the sheets for maximum yield. In the middle of each panel, rout a dado that's ¼" deep by ¾" wide. See the exploded illustration earlier in this chapter for positioning details.

STEP 3 ▪ Attach the sides to the bottom and back panels, being careful to align the center dadoes. Use glue on all the joints and clamp tightly until secure. If you don't have long clamps for the case, use finishing nails to hold the joints until the glue sets.

STEP 4 ▪ The center panel D needs a ¾"-deep by 2½"-long notch at the top front edge to receive the top rail E. Secure the panel with glue and clamps or finishing nails.

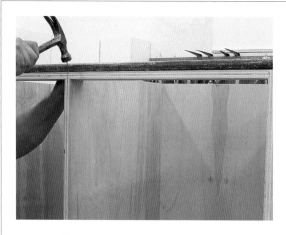

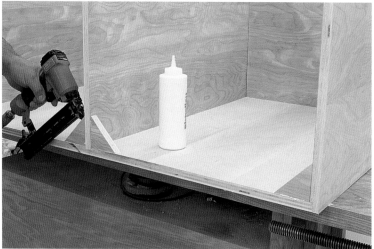

STEP 5 ■ The top rail E is secured to the center panel with glue and finishing nails. Carefully align the center panel so there is equal spacing in both sections of the cabinet. I secured both ends of the rail to the side panels using #10 biscuits; however, you can use dowels, pocket holes on the top side or screws and glue.

STEP 6 ■ The rear corners will have right-angle corner braces installed. These will be used to attach the top panel but will also add strength to the mobile case. Attach the four braces F with glue and brad nails.

STEP 7 *(above left)* ■ The exposed front edges of the sides, rail and bottom panel are covered with 1/4"-thick by 3/4"-wide hardwood strips. Use glue and brad nails to attach the strips G and H. Fill the nail holes with wood putty.

STEP 8 *(above right)* ■ The top panel J is attached with 1 1/4" screws through the front rail and four corner braces. Adjust the top so it extends 1 1/4" past each side and 1 1/2" on the front of the cabinet. Cover the four edges of the top panel with hardwood edge strips K and L using glue and brad nails.

SHOP TIP

Don't glue the top in place, so it can be replaced after a few years of use. You might also decide to cover the top panel with a 1/4" piece of hardboard that is tacked in place with a few screws. This inexpensive cover can be easily replaced if the top is damaged.

STEP 10 ■ Trim the top edges of the pullout trays using ¼"-thick by ¾"-wide hardwood strips Q and R. Attach the trim with glue and brad nails, then fill the nail holes with wood putty.

STEP 9 ■ The four pullouts are constructed using ¾" plywood veneer or other sheet material. The side, back and front boards are mitered at 45° on each corner. Cut the parts to the sizes detailed in the materials list and assemble each pullout using glue and brad nails. Notice that each pullout is 1¾" narrower than the cabinet space to allow for drawer glide clearance, and that a ¾"-thick spacing cleat is needed so the tray will clear the door.

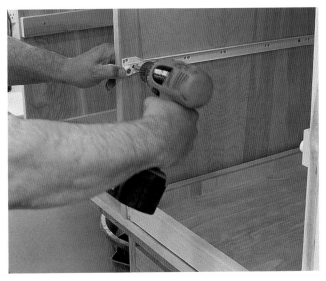

STEP 12 ■ The four pullout trays are installed using Blum 22" bottom-mount drawer glide hardware. Fit the slides and test for proper operation.

STEP 11 ■ Both cabinet sections require two spacing cleats S on the door hinge side. This will provide proper clearance for the pullouts. Attach the cleats with 1¼" screws. Cover the exposed edges of the plywood with iron-on edge tape or hardwood strips. The cleats are positioned to meet the needs of your storage requirements.

STEP 13 ■ The two drawer boxes are constructed following the same steps as the pullout trays; however, the sides are 5" high and the width is increased by $^3/_4$" to $20^7/_8$" because they don't have to clear door hinges. The box corners are mitered and assembled using glue and brad nails. The bottom board T is inset like the pullout tray bottoms. Trim the top edges with $^1/_4$"-thick hardwood strips W and X, or you can use iron-on edge tape.

STEP 14 ■ I mounted my drawers using Accuride 22" full-extension side-mounted drawer glides. Position the glide hardware so the bottom of each box is 6" below the underside of the top rail.

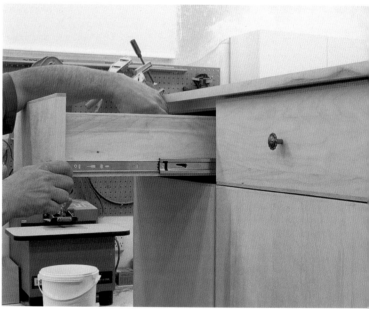

STEP 15 ■ The finished doors measure $22^5/_8$" wide by $23^1/_2$" high after the trim is attached to the panels. Cut the two panels Y and install the trim pieces Z and AA with glue and brad nails. Drill two 35mm holes, $^1/_8$" away from the door edge, centered 4" from the top and bottom edge of each door. Install the hinges on the doors with the hinge plates attached. Align each door flush with the bottom edge of the cabinet in its normally open position. Put a $^1/_8$"-thick strip of wood between the cabinet front edge and door. Drive $^5/_8$" screws in the plate holes to secure the hinges to the cabinet sides. Remove the $^1/_8$" spacing strip and test the operation of each door.

STEP 16 ■ Follow the same assembly steps when building the drawer fronts. The finished size of each front will be $7^1/_4$" high by $22^5/_8$" wide. Use $1^1/_4$" screws to attach the drawer faces to the boxes. Use a $^1/_8$"-thick spacer on top of the door to properly align the drawer faces.

STEP 17 ■ Use glue and two 1¼" screws to install the six wood wheel pads EE on the cabinet base. These pads should be placed at each corner and under the center vertical divider. The load on, and in, the cabinet will be transferred through the cabinet sides and center panel to the wheel pads and onto the wheels to the floor.

STEP 18 ■ Attach one heavy-duty swivel locking wheel on each pad. Use 1½"-long by 5⁄16"-diameter lag bolts in pilot holes to secure the wheels.

CONSTRUCTION
NOTES

Cost is a concern when building this cabinet. Making the best use of the sheet materials is important, so plan your cutting diagrams carefully. You should crosscut along the width of the 4' x 8' sheet for large back, bottom and top panels. The top is a full 4', and the other two panels are almost as wide. Use a circular saw to crosscut each panel to a manageable size, then finish the cuts on your table saw.

You can, as I mentioned in the introduction, use any ¾" sheet material. Some reasonably priced plywood can be painted. MDF is inexpensive and a good material to paint, or you may want to use melamine PB. If your shop isn't too damp, any of the mentioned materials would be fine. If the shop is damp and water leaks are possible, you should use plywood.

Align the pullouts in the cabinet to suit your storage requirements. Don't use glue to secure them, so they can be moved should your needs change. The pullout trays work well on the bottom-mount drawer glides, but full-extension hardware can be used. The drawers can also be fitted with regular bottom-mount glides in place of the more expensive full-extension hardware to lessen the cost.

Install the hardwood wheel pads and use six heavy-duty locking wheels that swivel. Four wheels wouldn't support the load properly and may cause the bottom board to sag. The center wheels support a large part of the load and guarantee proper cabinet alignment for the pullouts and drawers.

CHAPTER 22

TABLE-SAW
OUTFEED TABLE AND
STORAGE
CABINET

For years my table saw outfeed table was part of a sheet of melamine particleboard (PB) supported by a pair of those inexpensive folding legs you can buy at a home store. The table wasn't very stable and could, and often did, move

when I was cutting heavy sheet material on the saw. That safety issue alone made me look toward designing a better outfeed table.

Storage under the metal folding support legs was reduced because of their angle locking system. The legs weren't adjustable, so I was always leveling the table with small pieces of wood. It was a poor outfeed support system and something better, and safer, was needed.

This outfeed table and storage cabinet meets all of my needs. I built it using ¾"-thick MDF, so it's heavy and stable. It has an adjustable leg system, and the cabinet box provides a great deal of storage space. Adjustable shelves and doors allow me to customize the cabinet for my storage requirements.

The outfeed tabletop I need for my table saw is 3' wide by 6' long. Yours will most likely be different, so change the dimensions to suit your needs. The height will also be different for many of you, so adjust the vertical panel dimension. The cabinet top should be flush with your table saw top.

The cabinet height is a combination of top thickness, vertical panel length and adjustable leg height. If you plan on using an adjustable leg system, buy it before you start and note the height in the middle of the adjustment range. Then cut the side and center panels to the size required based on your table saw height.

The cabinet doesn't require doors if you plan on adding extra shelves to store short lengths of wood. You might want one section with doors for dust-free storage and the other without for small panel storage. There are many ways to configure the cabinet storage section based on your needs. No matter which storage setup you choose, you'll appreciate all the benefits of this solid outfeed table and storage center.

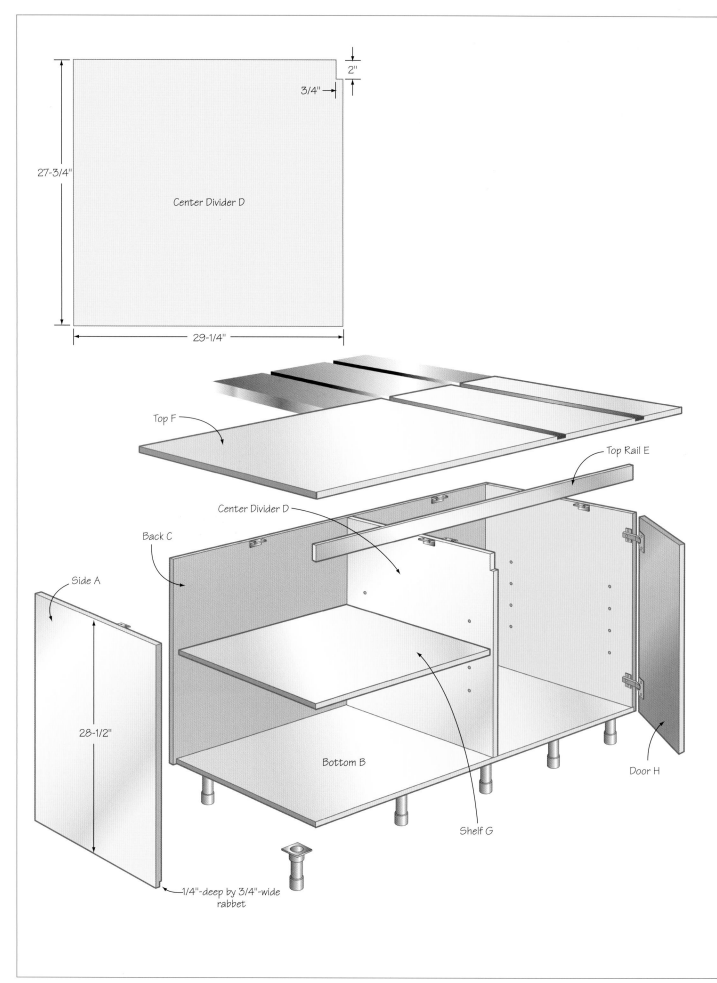

2"

3/4"

27-3/4"

Center Divider D

29-1/4"

Top F

Top Rail E

Center Divider D

Back C

Side A

28-1/2"

Bottom B

Shelf G

Door H

1/4"-deep by 3/4"-wide
rabbet

MATERIALS LIST ■ INCHES

REFERENCE	QUANTITY	PART	STOCK	THICKNESS	WIDTH	LENGTH	COMMENTS
A	2	sides	MDF	3/4	29 1/4	28 1/2	
B	1	bottom	MDF	3/4	29 1/4	66 1/2	
C	1	back	MDF	3/4	28 1/2	67 1/2	
D	1	center divider	MDF	3/4	29 1/4	27 3/4	
E	1	top rail	MDF	3/4	2	66	
F	1	top	MDF	3/4	36	72	
G	2	shelves	MDF	3/4	32 9/16	29	
H	4	doors	MDF	3/4	16 5/8	27 1/2	

HARDWARE

2" PB screws as detailed

5/8" Screws as detailed

Glue

11 Right-angle brackets

10 Adjustable legs

8 Shelf pins

4 – 107° Full-overlay hinges

4 – 107° Half-overlay hinges

8 Standard hinge plates

4 Door handles

5/8" Screws

MATERIALS LIST ■ MILLIMETERS

REFERENCE	QUANTITY	PART	STOCK	THICKNESS	WIDTH	LENGTH	COMMENTS
A	2	sides	MDF	19	743	724	
B	1	bottom	MDF	19	743	1689	
C	1	back	MDF	19	724	1715	
D	1	center divider	MDF	19	743	705	
E	1	top rail	MDF	19	51	1676	
F	1	top	MDF	19	914	1829	
G	2	shelves	MDF	19	827	737	
H	4	doors	MDF	19	422	699	

HARDWARE

51mm PB screws as detailed

16mm Screws as detailed

Glue

11 Right-angle brackets

10 Adjustable legs

8 Shelf pins

4 – 107° Full-overlay hinges

4 – 107° Half-overlay hinges

8 Standard hinge plates

4 Door handles

16mm Screws

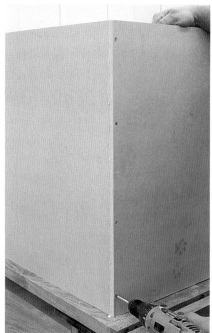

STEP 2 ▪ Both side panels require a rabbet that's ¼" deep by ¾" wide on their bottom inside edge. Next, cut the bottom board B to size and join the sides to the bottom board in the rabbets. The joints are secured with glue and four 2" screws on each panel. Remember to drill pilot holes for the screws.

STEP 1 ▪ Cut cabinet sides A to the dimensions listed in the materials list. Drill adjustable shelf-pin holes in the inside face of each side panel. Mark the top of each panel so the first hole distance is referenced from the top edge. This important step will ensure that the center divider's shelf-pin holes will be in alignment with the side panel holes.

SHOP TIP

Keep screws a minimum of 1" away from the end of MDF panels to avoid splitting the material.

STEP 3 ▪ The back C fully overlays or covers the back edges of the sides and bottom board. Use glue and 2" screws, about 6" apart, to secure the back.

STEP 4 ▪ Drill a series of shelf-pin holes on each side of center divider D, being sure to mark and reference the first hole from the top edge of the panel. This will align the side and center divider shelf-pin holes.

Offset the columns of holes on each side of the panel by 1" to avoid drilling through the divider. On the top front edge of the panel, cut a notch that's ¾" deep by 2" high to receive the top rail. Secure the divider in the center of the cabinet, creating two sections that are 32 ⅝" wide. Use glue and screws through the back and bottom board to secure the divider.

STEP 5 ■ The top rail E is attached to the sides and in the notch of the center panel. The rail is only 2" wide, so screws driven in the end will usually split the MDF. I secured the rail with glue and right-angle brackets using $^5/_8$" screws. Both ends of the rail are aligned with the side's top and face edges. The rail will be secured to the underside of the cabinet top with more right-angle brackets and screws.

STEP 6 ■ The base support for my table is its adjustable legs. You might opt for a solid base, made with $^3/_4$" MDF, but most shop floors are uneven and the adjustable leg is an ideal solution. These legs are available at most woodworking stores.

Attach 10 legs using the manufacturer's fastening recommendations. Two legs are placed under each cabinet side board and two under the center divider. The other four are attached in the middle of each section span.

A base or leg system placed directly under the cabinet's vertical panels will properly transfer the cabinet load to the floor. Set the legs 2" back from the front edge of the cabinet to provide space when someone is standing at the front of the cabinet.

STEP 7 ■ Attach eight right-angle brackets in the center of each panel and on the center of each rail span in every section. These brackets, which will be used to secure the cabinet top, should be flush with the top edge of each panel.

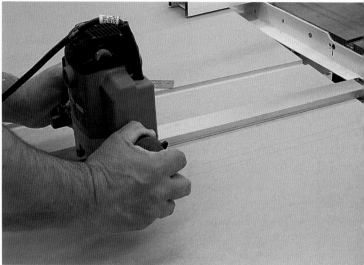

STEP 8 ■ The top board F is ³/₄"-thick MDF. Secure it to the cabinet using screws through the previously installed brackets.

The sides overhang the cabinet by 2¹/₄". The front overhang is 1", and the top extends past the back of the cabinet by 5". I've offset the front and back overhang so the cabinet won't interfere with my vacuum system behind the table saw. Adjust the top overhang to suit your shop setup.

STEP 9 ■ Place the cabinet in its permanent location and level the top to the table saw top. Use a router and straightedge to cut two dadoes in the cabinet top that are in line with the miter slide tracks of the saw. Adjust the dado depth to match the track depth on the saw.

STEP 10 ■ I installed two shelf boards G in my cabinet, but your storage needs may be different, so install as many as needed. The best shelf pin for this application has a full-metal shaft to support heavy loads. Install the pins in the drilled holes and test fit the shelves.

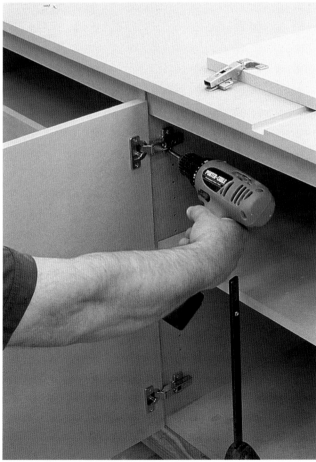

STEP 11 *(top left)* ▪ The cabinet can be left as an open shelving unit or have doors installed. The doors are attached using 100° to 120° hidden hinges. Cut the four doors H, then drill two 35mm-diameter holes in each that are 4" on center from each end and $1/8$" away from the door edge. Hinge holes are approximately $1/2$" deep, but test fit the hinges to ensure they are seated correctly.

STEP 12 *(bottom left)* ▪ The hinges on the two outside doors are full-overlay models, and the four on the inside doors are half-overlay. Install the hinges, with hinge plates attached, then mount the doors on the cabinets.

Hold the door in its normally open position, flush with the bottom edge of the base board. Place a $1/8$"-thick strip of wood between the door edge and cabinet front edge. This spacing is needed to properly set the door-to-cabinet gap. Drive screws through the hinge-plate holes into the cabinet to secure the doors. Adjust the doors if necessary so there's a $1/16$" gap in the center of each pair. Finally, install four handles of your choice.

CONSTRUCTION
NOTES

You can avoid using a combination of half- and full-overlay hinges by installing two center dividers. Follow the same installation steps for the second divider, being sure to leave equal spacing in both sections of the cabinet. You won't have to worry about offsetting shelf-pin hole columns with two dividers, and standard full-overlay hinges can be used on all the doors. Door width will change with the two-divider system, however. Measure the inside width of the cabinet, add 1" to that dimension and divide by 2; that's the required width of each door.

The cabinet interior is easily modified to suit your needs. Vertical dividers can be installed to create more than two sections, extra shelves can be added and doors can be installed on all or one section only. The cabinet can be easily customized for your shop.

If you plan on storing a lot of heavy items on the shelves, I suggest you use $3/4$"-thick plywood in place of the MDF. This two-section cabinet design requires wide shelves that can bend with heavy loads. If the shelves will be used to support heavy material or equipment, consider building the cabinet with three sections as a possible option.

As previously discussed, this cabinet design suits my table saw. Most saws are close in style and dimension, but you will have to make minor dimensional changes to suit your equipment. You might also consider mounting this cabinet on locking wheels if your table saw is mobile; however, you will need a level workshop floor for this option.

STEP 13 ■ The two drawer boxes are constructed following the same steps as the pullout trays; however, the sides are 5" high and the width is increased by $^3/_4$" to 20$^7/_8$" because they don't have to clear door hinges. The box corners are mitered and assembled using glue and brad nails. The bottom board T is inset like the pullout tray bottoms. Trim the top edges with $^1/_4$"-thick hardwood strips W and X, or you can use iron-on edge tape.

STEP 14 ■ I mounted my drawers using Accuride 22" full-extension side-mounted drawer glides. Position the glide hardware so the bottom of each box is 6" below the underside of the top rail.

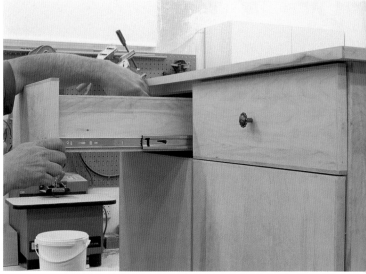

STEP 16 ■ Follow the same assembly steps when building the drawer fronts. The finished size of each front will be 7$^1/_4$" high by 22$^5/_8$" wide. Use 1$^1/_4$" screws to attach the drawer faces to the boxes. Use a $^1/_8$"-thick spacer on top of the door to properly align the drawer faces.

STEP 15 ■ The finished doors measure 22 $^5/_8$" wide by 23$^1/_2$" high after the trim is attached to the panels. Cut the two panels Y and install the trim pieces Z and AA with glue and brad nails. Drill two 35mm holes, $^1/_8$" away from the door edge, centered 4" from the top and bottom edge of each door. Install the hinges on the doors with the hinge plates attached. Align each door flush with the bottom edge of the cabinet in its normally open position. Put a $^1/_8$"-thick strip of wood between the cabinet front edge and door. Drive $^5/_8$" screws in the plate holes to secure the hinges to the cabinet sides. Remove the $^1/_8$" spacing strip and test the operation of each door.

STEP 17 ▪ Use glue and two 1¹/₄" screws to install the six wood wheel pads EE on the cabinet base. These pads should be placed at each corner and under the center vertical divider. The load on, and in, the cabinet will be transferred through the cabinet sides and center panel to the wheel pads and onto the wheels to the floor.

STEP 18 ▪ Attach one heavy-duty swivel locking wheel on each pad. Use 1¹/₂"-long by ⁵/₁₆"-diameter lag bolts in pilot holes to secure the wheels.

CONSTRUCTION
NOTES

Cost is a concern when building this cabinet. Making the best use of the sheet materials is important, so plan your cutting diagrams carefully. You should crosscut along the width of the 4' x 8' sheet for large back, bottom and top panels. The top is a full 4', and the other two panels are almost as wide. Use a circular saw to crosscut each panel to a manageable size, then finish the cuts on your table saw.

You can, as I mentioned in the introduction, use any ³/₄" sheet material. Some reasonably priced plywood can be painted. MDF is inexpensive and a good material to paint, or you may want to use melamine PB. If your shop isn't too damp, any of the mentioned materials would be fine. If the shop is damp and water leaks are possible, you should use plywood.

Align the pullouts in the cabinet to suit your storage requirements. Don't use glue to secure them, so they can be moved should your needs change. The pullout trays work well on the bottom-mount drawer glides, but full-extension hardware can be used. The drawers can also be fitted with regular bottom-mount glides in place of the more expensive full-extension hardware to lessen the cost.

Install the hardwood wheel pads and use six heavy-duty locking wheels that swivel. Four wheels wouldn't support the load properly and may cause the bottom board to sag. The center wheels support a large part of the load and guarantee proper cabinet alignment for the pullouts and drawers.

CHAPTER 23

SHOP-MADE DISC SANDER

This project is inexpensive and easy to build, providing you have an electric motor lying around your shop, or you plan on picking one up at the next neighborhood garage sale.

The cabinet, motor support and adjustable table system are built using ¾" MDF sheet material. A few pieces of hardware such as screws, hinges and a motor pulley are all that is needed to build this handy 12" disc sander.

I will be using the sander to round over small parts, sand flat edges and smooth band saw cuts. My wife wants this sander for her craftwork because it's a great tool for finish-sanding dozens of small parts. The disc runs quietly and quickly removes material with the proper paper grit.

The self-adhesive 12"-diameter sanding discs are available at woodworking stores. I use an 80-grit paper for general work and 150-grit paper for finer work. This disc sander is a safe tool, so woodworkers of all ages can use it. The platform is close to the disc and is an ideal support for your work, but it also serves as a safety guard should the disc loosen.

The woodworkers who have dropped into my shop while I was building this sander were impressed with the project, and a few more are being built. All my friends are hunting through old motors that they've been storing for years. Finally, a use for that electric motor you knew couldn't be thrown out!

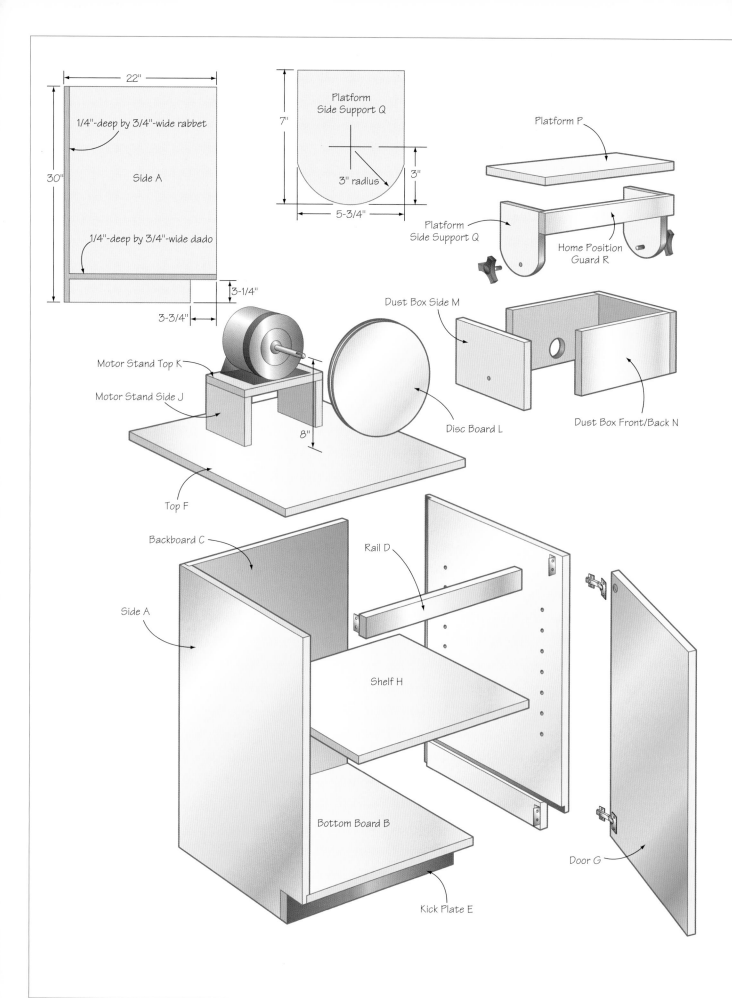

22"

1/4"-deep by 3/4"-wide rabbet

Side A

30"

1/4"-deep by 3/4"-wide dado

3-1/4"

3-3/4"

Platform
Side Support Q

7"

3" radius

3"

5-3/4"

Platform P

Platform
Side Support Q

Home Position
Guard R

Dust Box Side M

Motor Stand Top K

Motor Stand Side J

8"

Top F

Disc Board L

Dust Box Front/Back N

Backboard C

Rail D

Side A

Shelf H

Bottom Board B

Door G

Kick Plate E

MATERIALS LIST ■ INCHES

REFERENCE	QUANTITY	PART	STOCK	THICKNESS	WIDTH	LENGTH	COMMENTS
A	2	sides	MDF	3/4	22	30	
B	1	bottom board	MDF	3/4	16	22	
C	1	backboard	MDF	3/4	16	26	
D	1	rail	MDF	3/4	2	15 1/2	
E	1	kick plate	MDF	3/4	3 1/4	17	
F	1	top	MDF	3/4	19	23 1/2	
G	1	door	MDF	3/4	16 1/2	26	
H	2	shelves	MDF	3/4	15 7/16	21	
J	2	motor stand sides	MDF	3/4	4 1/4	7	
K	1	motor stand top	MDF	3/4	10	7	
L	1	disc board	plywood	3/4	12 1/2	12 1/2	
M	2	dust box sides	MDF	3/4	8	6	
N	2	dust box front & back	MDF	3/4	13	6	
P	1	platform	MDF	3/4	8	18	
Q	2	platform side supports	MDF	3/4	5 3/4	7	
R	1	home position guard	MDF	3/4	3	16 1/16	

HARDWARE

1 1/2" Screws as detailed

Glue

8 Right-angle brackets

8 Shelf pins

2 – 107° Full-overlay hinges

1 Motor

1 Motor pulley

2 Knobs with 1/4" x 20" threaded shafts

2 T-nuts 1/4" x 20"

1 Door handle or knob

5/8" Screws

1 1/2" Screws

MATERIALS LIST ■ MILLIMETERS

REFERENCE	QUANTITY	PART	STOCK	THICKNESS	WIDTH	LENGTH	COMMENTS
A	2	sides	MDF	19	559	762	
B	1	bottom board	MDF	19	406	559	
C	1	backboard	MDF	19	406	660	
D	1	rail	MDF	19	51	394	
E	1	kick plate	MDF	19	82	432	
F	1	top	MDF	19	483	597	
G	1	door	MDF	19	419	660	
H	2	shelves	MDF	19	392	533	
J	2	motor stand sides	MDF	19	108	178	
K	1	motor stand top	MDF	19	254	178	
L	1	disc board	plywood	19	318	318	
M	2	dust box sides	MDF	19	203	152	
N	2	dust box front & back	MDF	19	330	152	
P	1	platform	MDF	19	203	457	
Q	2	platform side supports	MDF	19	146	178	
R	1	home position guard	MDF	19	76	408	

HARDWARE

38mm Screws as detailed

Glue

8 Right-angle brackets

8 Shelf pins

2 – 107° Full-overlay hinges

1 Motor

1 Motor pulley

2 Knobs with 1/4" x 20" threaded shafts

2 T-nuts 6mm x 508mm

1 Door handle or knob

16mm Screws

38mm Screws

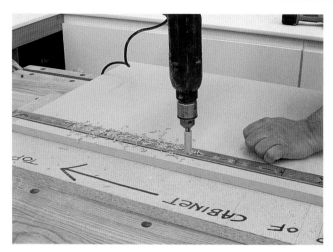

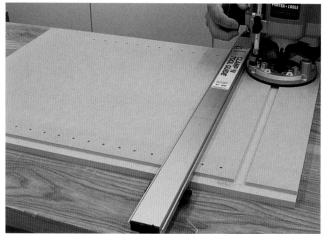

STEP 1 ▪ Cut the sides A to size and drill two columns of holes for adjustable shelves on the inside face of each panel. Start the columns 4" from the top and end them about 4" from the bottom edges. Each column should be 2" in from the panel edge.

STEP 2 ▪ Rout a ¼"-deep by ¾"-wide rabbet on the back inside face of each side panel A. They also need a ¼"-deep by ¾"-wide dado to accept the bottom board. The top edge of each dado should be 4" above the bottom edge of the side panel.

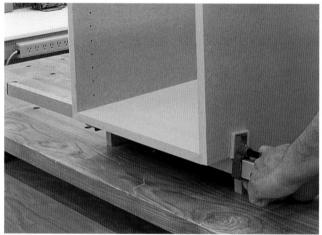

STEP 3 *(above left)* ▪ The side panels also require a 3¼"-high by 3¾"-deep notch on their bottom front edge for the kick plate. Use a jigsaw, scroll saw or band saw to cut the notches.

STEP 4 *(above right)* ▪ The bottom board B is attached to the side panels in the previously cut dadoes. Apply glue to the dadoes and clamp the sides to the bottom board until the adhesive sets.

STEP 5 *(left)* ▪ The backboard C is installed in the two rabbets with glue. The assembly is clamped and 1½" screws are driven through the bottom board into the lower edge of the backboard. Once again, wait until the glue sets before removing the clamps.

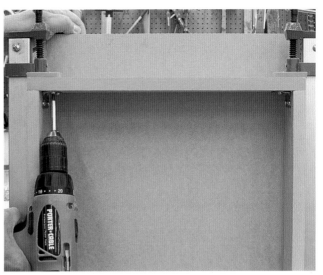

STEP 6 ▪ The upper rail D can be attached with small biscuits, dowels or brackets and glue as I'm using. The top edge of the rail is flush with the top edges of the side panels.

STEP 7 ▪ The kick plate E can also be secured with glue and right-angle brackets on the back side.

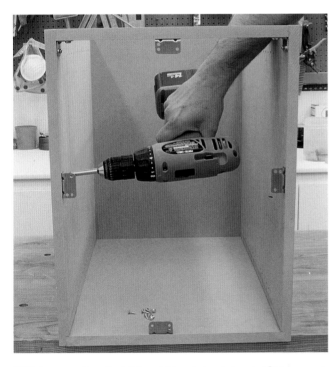

STEP 8 *(above left)* ▪ Install four right-angle brackets using ⅝" screws. The top of these brackets should be flush with the top edges of the sides, back and front rail. The brackets will be used to secure the cabinet top board.

STEP 9 *(above right)* ▪ Place the top board F on the cabinet with a 1" overhang on each side and a 1½" overhang on the front edge. The back edge is flush with the outside face of the backboard. Use ⅝" screws in the previously installed brackets to secure the top.

STEP 10 *(right)* ▪ Install the hinges, with their hinge plates attached, on the door. Hold the door G in its normally open position, flush with the bottom edge of the base board B. Place a ⅛"-thick strip of wood between the door edge and cabinet front edge. This spacing is needed to properly set the door-to-cabinet gap. Drive screws through the hinge-plate holes into the cabinet to secure the door. Install a knob or handle of your choice, then cut and install the two shelf boards H.

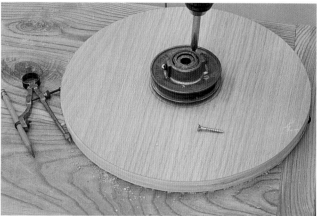

STEP 11 ■ Build a stand to raise the center of the motor shaft 8" above the cabinet top. Leave about 10" in front of the stand. Your motor will probably be different from mine, so exact measurements are not given. The suggested dimensions should suit most electric motor sizes. See the construction notes at the end of this chapter for information on selecting a motor.

Use glue and 1½" screws through the underside of the top board to secure the motor stand. Attach the motor to the stand. My motor came equipped with a bracket, so I bolted the assembly through the stand top K.

STEP 12 ■ For the disc board L, draw a 12⅛"-diameter circle on a ¾"-thick piece of plywood with a compass. Cut the circle as accurately as possible using a band saw, jigsaw or scroll saw. Measure the diameter of your pulley and draw a circle matching that size on the wood disc using the same center point.

Drill four holes through the pulley and attach it to the back face of the wood disc. Use screws that are long enough to anchor all the way into the thickness of the wood disc without puncturing the front face.

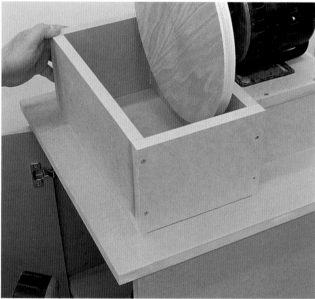

STEP 13 *(above left)* ■ Install the disc and pulley assembly on the motor shaft, then lock it securely using the fastening system on your pulley. Wire the motor to a switch box and attach the box on the motor stand with screws.

Start the motor and true the disc using sandpaper. The disc should be sanded to 12" in diameter. Install 12"-diameter self-adhesive sandpaper to the front face of the wood disc.

STEP 14 *(above right)* ■ Build a simple dust box with ¾"-thick MDF that's 14½"-wide by 8"-deep. The box should be 6" high and is assembled using glue and 1½" screws. Align the box on the cabinet top board with equal spacing on both sides. You will have to temporarily remove the disc to install the dust box. Secure the box to the cabinet with 1½" screws through the underside of the top.

STEP 15 *(left)* ■ Cut the platform P and place it on the dust box with equal spacing on each side and ⅛" away from the sanding disc face. Trace the outline of the dust box on the underside of the platform.

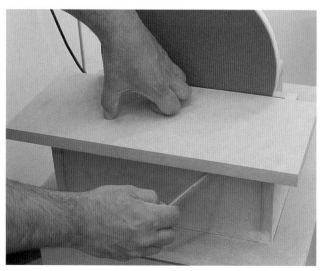

STEP 16 *(above left)* ▪ Cut platform side supports Q, and draw a 3"-radius arc on the bottom edge of each board. Use a belt sander to form the arc on each support by sanding to the compass lines. Use glue and three 1¹/₂" screws to attach the side supports to the platform Q, keeping ¹/₃₂" away from the lines.

The home position guard R is secured to the sides of the platform supports with glue and screws. This guard will keep most of the dust in the box and help align the platform at its home position.

STEP 17 *(above right)* ▪ Block the platform assembly so the top surface is aligned with the center of the sanding disc. Use a T-nut and knob with a threaded shaft on each side support to lock the platform in place. The home position guard will reference the platform at 90° to the sanding disc face, and the curved bottoms on the side supports will allow you to move the platform to any angle. The assembly can also be quickly tipped back to permit easy sandpaper removal and installation.

STEP 18 ▪ Tip the platform assembly back and remove the sanding disc. Drill a 2¹/₄"-diameter hole in the backboard of the dust box. You can easily access the backboard through the rear of the motor stand. A standard 2¹/₄"-diameter vacuum hose can now be attached to the dust box.

CONSTRUCTION
NOTES

The electric motor should be rated at ¹/₃ horsepower or more. These are common motors and should be available for a reasonable price at garage sales and flea markets.

The ¹/₃-horsepower motor I installed is powerful enough to handle my sanding requirements. However, you might be fortunate enough to find a good ¹/₂- or ³/₄-horsepower motor that will have the power to tackle any sanding job.

If you're not comfortable wiring the motor and switch unit, have someone who is familiar with electrical work complete this part of the project. Also, many motors have a reversible rotation feature so you might want to change the direction. My motor rotates counterclockwise as you face the disc, but it doesn't seem to matter which direction it rotates because the sander performs equally well in either rotation.

The cabinet can be built with any sheet material. I have one door and adjustable shelves for sandpaper storage, but drawers can be installed just as easily. The vacuum feature works well and does reduce the dust level that can be a serious concern with this tool. I think it's a worthwhile feature and suggest you have the vacuum on when using the sander.

MATERIAL STORAGE

BY SCOTT GIBSON

It takes more than a room full of tools to make a productive woodworking shop. Along with stationary power tools and a collection of hand planes and chisels comes a diverse list of materials that must be kept on hand and accessible when you need them.

Not surprisingly, most of us focus on storing lumber. In addition to being the basic raw material that woodshops must have to operate, lumber has its own intrinsic pleasure. We can always make room for it.

Lumber also varies tremendously in size, shape and potential use. Rough hardwood that needs jointing and thickness planing before it can be used is nothing like the finished pine we can buy at the local lumberyard. In addition to various kinds of solid lumber, most shops also will need at least a modest inventory of plywood and other panel goods.

And wood is only the beginning. Shops also need everything from stains and finish to boxes of wood screws, pencils and paper, nuts and bolts, glue, cleaning supplies and light bulbs.

It's not hard to find yourself awash in shop clutter. You know you're in trouble when you'd rather go to the hardware store and buy a tube of 5-minute epoxy rather than take the time to look for the tube you know you already have. It's just plain easier than pawing through the stuff you can't seem to keep organized.

Keeping all of these supplies straight is something like the process of organizing tools. By balancing work flow, convenience and safety, you can come up with a quartermaster's plan for your shop. All you have to do is stick with it.

Finished work, whether it's a turned bowl or an entertainment center, is at center stage in most woodworking shops. But material storage and handling, such as these racks of lumber in the background, play an important if not as obvious supporting role.

PHOTO BY AL PARRISH

Storing Lumber Outdoors Saves Space in the Shop

Many woodworkers keep a good deal of lumber on hand – not just enough for the current project but hundreds of board feet tucked away for future use. Maybe the wood was available at a great price, or the big cherry tree in a neighbor's front yard came down in a storm and you've paid to have it sawn into boards.

If you can spare the room, stocking lumber is an excellent approach. It's liberating to have a stack of rough lumber at the start of a project. Rest-

ing in those planks is a diversity of grain and range of color that opens many possibilities as a piece of furniture takes shape. You'll have an easier time matching figure in adjacent boards when it really counts or finding a board of exactly the right width when you need it.

A big stack of lumber represents not only opportunity but also responsibility. If properly cared for, those boards will be sound and straight years down the road. I still have some walnut that came from a tree my father cut on the family's

(left) Careful stacking will help preserve these walnut boards for *Popular Woodworking* Publisher Steve Shanesy. The wood pile should start on a flat base elevated off the ground.

(above) Layers of boards are separated from each other by narrow stickers that should be aligned with each other vertically. The ends of these freshly sawn cherry boards will be painted with a wax-based product to help prevent end checks.

southern Maryland farm in 1949. Among the planks is one that's 11' long, 18" wide and 2½" thick. I'm saving it for a table.

If, on the other hand, wood is improperly stored you'll have a king-sized headache but nothing you can make furniture with.

It's always better to keep lumber indoors where it's protected from harsh sunlight, rain, snow and insects, than outside. But lumber can successfully be stored outside, too, as long as you're careful about it.

Never store lumber on the ground. It will rot. Start with a sturdy, level foundation of 4×4s spaced 16" to 24" apart. Take the time not only to level each 4×4 individually but also to arrange them so they are all in the same plane. The idea is to create a stable platform that's as flat as you can get it.

The space beneath the bottom layer of lumber and the ground will promote air circulation. If the lumber is just coming from a mill, that will also help it dry. And moving air will reduce the risk of mold. It's also a good idea to put a layer of polyethyl-ene plastic or tar paper on the ground beneath the 4×4s to keep moisture from migrating upward into the bottom layer of lumber.

Next are the stickers, the narrow pieces of lumber that are used to separate each row of lumber. It's better to use dry material for stickers to minimize the risk of mold. Keep them narrow to get the most air circulation possible; material that's 1" wide and ¾" to 1" thick is more than adequate. Use a consistent thickness throughout each layer.

When you go to build the pile, the key is to align the stickers in the pile with one another, beginning with the first ones that are placed directly over the 4x4s at the very bottom of the heap. Here's the sequence: 4×4s, then a layer of boards separated by an inch or so of space between them. Then a layer of stickers placed exactly over the 4×4s, then another layer of lumber, then stickers. As long as the stack is stable and in no danger of toppling, you can make it as high as you like.

Stickers aren't arranged in that way to satisfy some pathological need for neatness and order. They help the lumber stay flat. If you locate stickers without regard to the layer below you run a good risk of getting lumber that dries into a series of delicate waves – like the pasta that goes into lasagna. The distortion may be too much to joint out of the wood, rendering it useless. If the 4×4 foundation is not flat, it's easy to create a twist in wood that will likewise make it useless for building furniture.

A piece of salvaged corrugated roofing, weighted down with scrap wood or rocks, will keep most of the rain and snow off the lumber. If you buy the lumber green, paint the ends of the boards or use a specialty sealer from a lumberyard supplier to keep the boards from drying at the ends first and splitting.

Just remember that wood that's been stored outside will need to shed some of its moisture before it can be used in furniture. Bring it into the shop and let it acclimate for a couple weeks. If you have a moisture meter, take advantage of it. Also, outside storage probably shouldn't be viewed as an indefinite solution for furniture woods.

Inside the Shop, Build Racks or Store Lumber Vertically

There are two basic strategies for storing lumber inside a shop: It can be organized in wall-mounted racks, or stood on end vertically and leaned against the wall. Both methods have their advantages and disadvantages.

Wall racks can be made from either wood or metal. They don't have to be fancy, just strong and mounted securely to wall framing with adequately sized lag bolts. One advantage of a rack is that lumber can be sorted by width or species or in some other way that makes it easy to find what you want. The closer that supports are to each other vertically, the greater number of shelves the rack will provide. Even when supports are separated only by 12" or so, they can provide lots of usable space.

Another plus is that a lumber rack can be mounted on a wall that otherwise would go to waste. In a shop with a high ceiling, a two- or three-shelf rack above window height is a great way of storing wood you don't need access to very often. When the time comes, get a stepladder and haul down what you need. For the rest of the time, you're saving a lot of floor space.

The downside of a rack is that you usually end up moving lumber to get the board you want. Unless you can slide the board from beneath the stack you'll end up removing a number of boards, retrieving the one you're after, and then re-stacking the entire pile. At the same time, you can't see everything in this sort of stack. Visibility is limited to the top board and then a series of edges along the side of the stack. For a really good look at what you have, count on taking the boards off the rack and examining them one at a time.

Another disadvantage is that the space in front of a rack should be kept relatively clear of clutter so getting to a piece of lumber is not akin to running an obstacle course – not only a pain in the neck but potentially hazardous. Avoiding this problem can be

A rack made of 2x4s and pipe lagged securely to the wall makes excellent wood storage. Here, it makes use of wall space that's not practical for other uses.

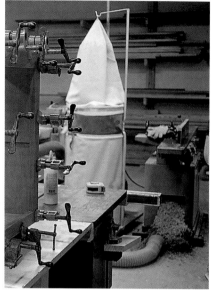

The lumber rack on the far wall of this shop doesn't take up much floor space. But one disadvantage is that the area in front of the rack must be kept relatively free of clutter to make the lumber accessible.

A lumber shed at the shop of Kelly Mehler provides lots of storage possibilities. This open-ended rack makes it easy to see what's available.

tough in many shops where space is at a premium.

The other school of thought is to store boards vertically on their ends and lean them against a wall. George Nakashima, the influential post-war furniture maker whose studio is still in family hands, used this approach to store some of his lumber.

He was a great collector of wood in many forms. Nakashima would buy whole trees and cart them to a mill where they were turned into boards. He had them stacked in exactly the same order in which they came off the saw and banded together so they could dry. That method of storing wood, is beyond most of us. But vertical storage is not.

In his book "The Soul of a Tree" (Kodansha), there is a wonderful photograph of Nakashima in his wood room, surrounded by a thicket of wide hardwood planks as if he were standing in a grove of trees. All of that beauty in anyone's shop is inspiring. You will be limited, of course, by the height of the room. And the more lumber you collect and store this way, the harder it will be to get to any particular board you're looking for.

But one advantage is that you can easily see all sides of a board once you've found it. By tilting a plank up on one of its lower corners and holding the board in a near-vertical position you can pivot the wood freely to

Woodcarver David Monhollen has ready access to lumber that's stored upright. He can easily leaf through what he has on hand.

see either the front face or back face.

For shorts and small offcuts – those boards that are left over when you cut a big plank – vertical storage is probably the best solution. They won't easily fit on a rack horizontally and a large number of pieces can be stored on a relatively small amount of floor space. The only caveat here is to remind yourself to sort through the pile periodically and get rid of anything that doesn't serve a genuine purpose. It's easy to hang on to every bit of scrap lumber you create ("I just know I'll use that for something someday") but the truth is that without periodic weeding every garden becomes overgrown.

Another approach for short scraps is to make a storage bin from short lengths of PVC pipe. In these makeshift bins, you can sort short pieces of moulding, lumber and dowel for easy retrieval when you need them.

Panel Products Need Their Own Kind of Storage

Panel goods are a mainstay of many cabinetmaking jobs and shops often gather a good assortment of them: MDF, veneer-core plywood, high-

strength Baltic-birch plywood, particleboard for countertops. A time will come for all of them. And because most panel goods come in 4' × 8' sheets, there is often a good deal of leftover when a job has been completed so you may find yourself the curator of many pieces in different thicknesses and materials.

Their size dictates that panels be stored on edge. Very few shops will have the kind of room you need to store panels flat. And besides, unless you have a lot of one kind of panel, this is probably the least practical of all storage solutions because you'll have to move a lot of material to get the one sheet you need (remember that a 4' × 8' sheet of MDF weighs nearly 100 pounds).

A practical solution is to build a narrow rack, a couple feet wide and 8' long, to hold panels on edge. Locate it so you can pull a full sheet of plywood straight out without running into anything else. The width can be divided into two or more individual bays to help you organize different types of panel goods – 3/4"-hardwood plywood can go in one, a mixed lot of sheet goods in the others. Make the

bottom of the rack smooth and flat so the sheets will slide easily and elevate it slightly from the rest of the floor (hardwood plywood is ideal for this). This works especially well if you have a shop with a concrete floor – it's hard work to drag plywood across rough concrete, and it's tough on the material as well.

Unless you have a very large shop with lots of wall space, try not to store plywood against a wall so you have to approach it from the side. Only the top sheet will be readily accessible (everything else will have to be moved to get to sheets on the inside) and it is virtually impossible not to lean offcuts and shorts against the pile. Before you know it, the sheet of plywood you need is buried beneath a pile of scrap lumber you don't want to handle.

Whenever sheet goods are stored on edge, take care to get them as vertical as possible and rotate unused sheets once in a while. If not, the sheet will take on a bow that will make it tough to build straight cabinets and shelves. One way to avoid this if you do store plywood against a

Jigs and patterns are another kind of material that most shops have plenty of. Furniture-maker Troy Sexton is in good company keeping them on a wall over a bench.

wall is to secure it flat against the wall with bungee cords, rope or by some other means so it can't sag.

Liquid Storage: Paints, Stains, Finishes and Glue

The many liquid materials that woodshops accumulate present their own storage and handling challenges. While the containers take up far less room than does lumber, what's inside all those bottles and cans can be a good deal more finicky. In some cases, liquids can present safety hazards if not handled carefully.

Finishes come in a wide variety, from water-based latex paints to lacquers and shellacs made with volatile solvents. In general, water-based finishes must be protected from freezing temperatures if they are to remain useful. If you work in an unheated shop in a cold climate, these materials will have to be stored inside when it gets cold.

Solvent-based finishes are not as temperature sensitive, but they are usually more flammable and the powerful solvents they contain can be a fire or explosive hazard in an enclosed space. Companies that specialize in safety equipment sell metal cabinets made specifically for hazardous liquids – it's a good investment if you have a lot of finish on hand and want to protect your shop from the possibility of fire.

Finishes also don't last forever. Polymerizing oils, varnishes and similar finishes have a way of turning into thick gunk over time. It's a good practice to mark the cans with the date of purchase, or the date on which they were mixed if you make your own brew, so that you know when they should be retired. (When the time comes, don't toss them out the back door or dump them down the drain. Contact your local municipal offices or state environmental office for advice on getting rid of expired finishes.)

Try to store finishes out of direct sunlight and away from sources of heat. They will last longer.

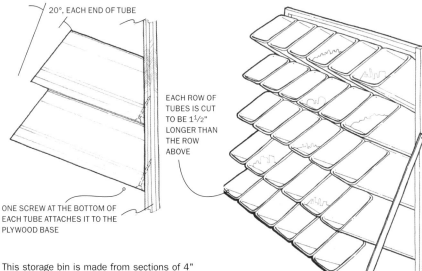

20°, EACH END OF TUBE

EACH ROW OF TUBES IS CUT TO BE 1¹/₂" LONGER THAN THE ROW ABOVE

ONE SCREW AT THE BOTTOM OF EACH TUBE ATTACHES IT TO THE PLYWOOD BASE

METAL STRAP KEEPS UNIT TOGETHER

This storage bin is made from sections of 4" PVC posts. Its graduated rows provide lots of inexpensive storage for just about anything a shop produces, including short scraps.

In Scott Phillips' large workshop, panel goods can be stored upright against a wall. Rotate the panels once in a while if they sit around so they don't develop a bow.

These metal racks, in the workshop of Tom Willenborg, hold a lot of plywood. Storing panel goods on edge, as Willenborg does in the rack in the foreground, saves floor space and makes access relatively easy.

Some materials common to woodworking shops are hazardous if not handled properly. Rags soaked in oil finish can ignite spontaneously if they are not spread out to dry or immersed in a pail of water.

Glue is another material that can be sensitive to time, sunlight and temperature. Yellow and white polyvinyl acetate glues (Titebond and Elmer's Carpenter's Glue, for example) as well as liquid hide glues are happier if they are not allowed to freeze. Even if still in a liquid state, these glues should not be used if they are too cold because the bond will not be reliable – check the label for the specifics. If you have a heated space for water-based finishes, store your glue in there as well.

Epoxy and other two-part adhesives that are not water-based don't need as much hand-holding although these adhesives do have a limited life span. The manufacturer of West Systems epoxy says this adhesive has a shelf life of about one year from the date of manufacture, although this is probably a conservative estimate.

Polyurethane glue and liquid hide glue also are given about a year's shelf life from the time of manufacture before they should be discarded. Glue that comes in powder form can pick up moisture from the air over time. As with finish, it's a good idea to keep an eye on glue containers and get rid of those that are no longer reliable. Glue is one of those things you should buy as you go and use when it's fresh – you're not accomplishing much when you buy a 10-year supply of an adhesive that only lasts a year.

Nuts, Bolts and All Those Other Loose Ends

Who hasn't been in a woodshop at least once and looked up to see a series of neatly labeled baby-food jars suspended from the ceiling for storing nuts, screws and washers?

(above) A locker specifically designed for flammable materials is a good investment. Its double-wall construction would help prevent the spread of fire.

(right) This easy-to-build cabinet holds a series of plastic trays – perfect for storing everything from ferrules to rivets.

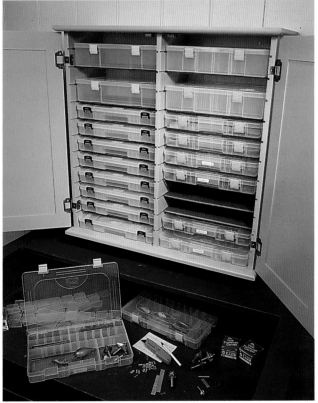

In theory, it's an ingenious approach to storage. All you have to do is nail the lid to the ceiling and screw on the jar. When you need what's inside, just reach up and remove the jar.

But in truth, most of have trouble staying that organized. Even with the best of intentions, nails, screws and everything else too small to bother with ends up in a couple coffee cans under the bench. In time, we have absolutely no idea what's in them. Like the missing tube of 5-minute epoxy, the fastener we need is easier to replace at the hardware store than to find under our haphazard storage system.

Open bins and trays for the fasteners used most frequently can help. With a few hours to spare and a bit of ½" plywood, you can make a stack of sturdy storage containers that will hold a dozen kinds of wood screws in plain view. These stackable containers can be parked on a shelf and pulled out when you need something.

Plastic storage bins – either those with flip-up tops or banks of small drawers – are an excellent way of organizing very small parts that you don't need many of and don't use all the time. Cotter pins, set screws, small lock-washers, machine screws and small electrical components may not be what we think of first when it comes time to build a highboy. But when your router is on the fritz you'll be glad to know where to find an extra switch.

Sandpaper is another commodity item that's easy to lose track of. A few pieces of leftover hardboard or plywood can be turned into a storage rack with multiple shelves in very little time. Even if your system is as simple as lumping "rough," "medium" and "fine" grits of paper with each other it will save you time in the long run.

For bulk storage, there are a variety of low-cost avenues to explore. Used kitchen cabinets are worth looking at (skip cheaply made cabinets because they won't last). Yard sales, used furniture stores and newspaper classified

Wire shelving helps turner Judy Ditmer stay organized. These shelves not only hold a lot of material, their design promotes air circulation.

ads all are good places to look.

If all this organization makes you nervous, try to remember that it really will make the shop safer, because it eliminates clutter, and more enjoyable, because it eliminates the frustra-

tion of never finding what you need. It's worth a try.

Ditmer's system includes a labeling system for material stored on shelves. It makes identification and retrieval much easier.

SMALL TOOL STORAGE

BY SCOTT GIBSON

Many of us plan our workshops around big things – workbenches, table saws, planers and jointers. It's a challenge to arrange these large tools so the shop is efficient and comfortable, especially when space is limited. But as we ponder the best layout for these giants it's the small tools that can catch us by surprise.

It begins innocently enough. We typically have so few tools at the start that it hardly seems to matter where we store them; many woodworkers dive in with only a few used hand tools and a couple basic power tools. They all seem to fit handily in a couple of cardboard boxes. But in time, shops and tool collections have a way of getting bigger and more complicated. Eventually we have to deal with a jumble of small tools that accumulated in our shops while we weren't paying attention.

Cardboard boxes won't work any longer. There are too many tools, and they are too valuable to dump together in a box or a drawer where they can bang against each other. Moreover, some of them are used all the time, some only rarely. And mixing layout tools with router bits, or chisels with sandpaper, will seem a lot less than helpful when you're in a hurry to find the right tool for the job.

Start by Identifying Tools You Need All the Time

For a lot of furniture makers, the workbench is the hub of the shop, like a traffic circle through which every major road must pass. Dozens of tasks take place here: joinery is laid out and cut, lumber planed and sanded and furniture parts glued

Most woodworking shops keep dozens of small tools on hand, many of them with sharp or delicate edges. Keeping track of them and protecting them from damage is an organizational challenge.

and assembled. We might even eat lunch here.

Given this central role for the workbench, one way to organize small tools is by gathering the ones you use most frequently and keeping them nearby. It's not hard to come up with a good list: chisels, planes, a square or

two, a hammer or mallet, a marking knife (or a handful of sharp pencils), rules or measuring tapes, scrapers and more than likely a few other odds and ends.

These tools should be the first ones that are housed at or near the bench, within arm's reach of where you will be using them. Although it may take a little experimentation, when the arrangement works you will know it. You should be able to reach for exactly the tool you need without spending any unnecessary time scouting for it and without moving your feet.

Tool collections can become more specialized as time goes on, forcing you to make decisions about which tools need a front-row seat and which can be relegated to more distant storage. For example, you may routinely need a block plane, a smoothing plane, a small rabbeting plane and a jointer. That's four planes you use frequently. But you use that old moulding plane you picked up at a flea market only once in a blue moon. Why clog up shelves or cabinets near the bench with tools you rarely need?

Virtually any tool category can use the same kind of attention. An adjustable square or try square is something you'll pick up a dozen times a day so keep it close at hand. But a framing square may not be used more than once a month so it can happily live on an overhead rafter or on a nail in the wall some distance away. A little common sense will go a long way in helping you identify what you need close at hand.

No one's list of "must haves" will be exactly the same. Every discipline has its own list of everyday tools, and those needs and habits will become evident with time in your shop as well.

A Tool Cabinet Keeps Important Tools Close

Thumb through any book about woodworking shops and you're likely to see all kinds of bins, shelves and cabinets that inventive woodworkers have devised to organize their tool collections. Browsing is an excellent way of getting ideas for your own shop. After all, few ideas are really brand-new.

But a common theme in many shops is a large, wall-mounted tool cabinet. Christian Becksvoort, a Maine artisan specializing in Shaker-style furniture, has just such a cabinet mount-

This traditional European workbench has more than a flat, sturdy top; drawers and cabinets provide abundant storage space for hand and portable power tools.

ed on the wall behind his workbench. It's a beautiful piece of furniture in its own right, made from cherry, the wood that Becksvoort uses for virtually all of the furniture he makes.

More important, it holds many if not all of the bench tools he needs to make a piece of furniture. Everything from files to chisels, augers to mallets, is stored neatly behind a pair of folding doors. Even the space on the inside of the doors is put to use.

Racking up frequently used tools near the workbench keeps them close to their point of use and cuts down on wasted steps to distant cabinets or drawers.

Neatly labeled drawers house drafting tools, bits, a first-aid kit and other small items. Carved into the drawer housing is "C.H. Becksvoort."

Becksvoort has been at it a long time and his collection of close-at-hand tools accurately reflects the sort of work he does. There's a heavy emphasis on hand tools – chisels, planes, scrapers – rather than portable power tools. This formula works for him but he'd be the last person to argue it's the right arrangement for everyone.

Building a first-rate cabinet to hold personal tools is a long-standing tradition for carpenters and furniture-makers. It's part of the curriculum for

Infrequently used tools may exist happily on a shelf in the corner of the shop, but their haphazard arrangement will make it tough to find the one you want to use and heaping tools together is an invitation to damage.

furniture-making students at Boston's North Bennet Street School. Building a tool chest gives students a chance to develop their furnituremaking and design skills and in the end they have something that will serve them for many years.

Tool cabinets can be infinitely variable, made to house only planes, a collection of chisels and carving tools or an entire suite of hand tools. What may be the most photographed American tool chest ever was made by a Massachusetts piano maker named Henry Studley over a 30-year career. It's a marvel of planning and design, deceptively small, only 39" high, 9" deep and 18" wide. Yet it holds 300 individual tools packed tightly together but still accessible. A more modern version of a grand cabinet is one built by Glen and Malcolm Huey to celebrate their move into a new workshop.

If you have the space, a wall cabinet can grow into more of a tool locker with space for small power tools as well as hand tools. A larger cabinet not only helps keep shop clutter to a minimum but it also can provide security if you live in an area where crime is a worry. With a cabinet bolted to the wall and doors equipped with sturdy locks, tools are a lot safer than they would be if left out in the open.

You might want to leave a tool cabinet of any size and complexity for the future, until individual preferences and

As cabinetmaking skills increase, so do the possibilities for building beautiful and unique tool chests. Glen and Malcolm Huey, a father/son team in Ohio, built this one when they moved into a new shop. It's designed for both hand and portable power tools.

Maine furnituremaker Christian Becksvoort built a large wall-hanging tool chest that's mounted behind his workbench. It neatly holds a variety of hand tools where they can be reached easily.

PHOTOS BY THE AUTHOR

This 10-drawer chest, 24" high and 15" wide, will hold a variety of small tools and isn't difficult to build. It's small enough to park on or near a workbench.

These very simple, stackable storage boxes are a good example of low-tech ways of organizing tools. Drop-down doors make it easy to find what you need, and the materials list won't break the bank.

Tool cabinets can be more than utilitarian cupboards. At their best, they are expressions of personal tastes and skill.

needs are a little clearer (to say nothing of developing the skills required to make one). Start with a more modest wall cabinet for tools. It's an excellent project that doesn't have to consume a lot of expensive materials or take a lot of time. Tool chests can be very simple and as your skills improve you can move on to more complex designs.

A machinist's tool chest includes a tool tray under a hinged top plus a number of drawers that can be protected by a fold-up front piece. Handles make it easy to move.

Don't Overlook
Ready-made Cabinets

Another possible route is to buy inexpensive storage cabinets at used office-supply or furniture stores. Older steel cabinets and open shelving units can handle a lot of weight. Even if they need a fresh coat of paint and have a dent or ding here and there, these cabinets will provide a lot of useful storage at a relatively low cost.

Be more cautious about buying used kitchen cabinets. Some of them will be fine as either wall-mounted or free-standing storage, but inexpensive stock cabinets are often made from thin particleboard or plywood and won't stand much abuse. It's worth checking the classified ads in your local newspaper but look the cabinets over carefully.

As libraries convert from paper to digital files they are getting rid of those classic wood card catalogues. If you can manage to get your hands on one, adopt it right away; the small drawers are ideal for storing everything from nails and screws to router bits and collet wrenches.

Tool Boards Keep
Everything in Sight

If your workbench is against a wall, you can arrange a surprising number of tools directly in front of you on nails or hooks. It doesn't take much

time to move a tool if you decide it's in the wrong spot. The down side is that you're not going to squeeze the volume of tools here that you would be able to put in a well-designed cabinet. But they are in plain sight and instantly accessible.

We've all probably been in a garage or two where one wall was devoted to $1/4$" perforated hardboard and the outlines of different tools neatly painted in red or white. A strict arrangement like that probably encourages the owner to put tools back where they came from, and being able to move hooks quickly from one spot to another is an advantage. But driving nails or screws right into the wall works just as well. If your workshop has been clad in drywall, you might want to add a layer of plywood so you can put a nail or screw in wherever you want. T1-11 plywood $3/8$" or $1/2$" thick is inexpensive and attractive.

For tools that won't hang (chisels, files, carving tools, screwdrivers and the like), you can make simple racks and attach them to the wall. One easy

Chairmaker David Fleming keeps part of his hand-tool arsenal hanging within easy reach on a wall. Tools are close at hand and sharp edges won't get dinged.

Hanging tools on the wall over a bench is a time-honored approach to keeping things straight. Homemade racks, hooks and magnetic strips all work.

Storing tools where they will be needed is usually a good start to staying organized. In simple racks over the lathe in the workshop of Sam Maloof are both turning tools and extra tool rests.

way to make a rack for chisels or files is to cut a series of slots in a board with a dado blade and then glue another board to it. The width and depth of the slots can be made to suit tools of different sizes. A series of holes in graduated sizes bored through the face of a board will handle chisels or screwdrivers. Magnetic strips will accomplish the same thing. Racks don't have to be fancy to be useful.

For the variety of odds and ends that almost always end up on a bench, drill holes in scrap blocks of wood and put them on a low shelf over the back of your bench. Blocks can store drill bits, nail sets, awls and similarly slender tools with points or sharp edges. You won't lose track of them and their delicate edges will be well protected. It's also a great way to preserve and make use of the especially beautiful offcuts of a prized piece of lumber you just can't seem to throw away.

Rolling Cabinets Keep Like Tools Together

There are two good approaches to making a tool cabinet mobile. One is, in effect, to take the cabinet off the wall and stick a pair of casters underneath it to create a rolling tool garage and workbench. The other is to make

one or more rolling workstations dedicated to a single power tool.

Mobile workbenches and tool caddies can be as elaborate or as simple as you want to make them. For example, a design by David Thiel, Popular Woodworking Books executive editor, is actually a modular bench consisting of two 21³⁄₄"-high rolling boxes and a 6'-long bench that spans them. Adjustable support assemblies attached to the sides of the boxes can be raised to support the benchtop at a variety of working heights or hold a tool, such as a drill press, router table or a hollow-chisel mortise machine, when it's needed.

It's a good design for a small shop (Thiel's is in a two-car garage) because the boxes can be used alone or together depending on the need, and parked out of the way when it's time to bring the cars in for the night. Another successful design from Thiel and Michael Rabkin incorporates foldout lids, roomy storage compartments and a series of shallow drawer for fasteners and tools.

In this or a similar work cart, drawers can be built to suit your interests and internally divided in whatever manner makes the most sense for the user. Use a power sander a

lot? Devote one of the drawers to your collection of random-orbit and block sanders with separate trays for different grades of sandpaper and other accessories. A heavy bottom shelf could be used for a belt sander. Repair a lot of chairs? Build a mobile tool station that houses just those supplies and

Versatile as well as mobile, this modular cabinet design not only houses a variety of tools but also can serve as workbench or portable workstation for a drill press or other benchtop power tool.

This rolling tool cabinet holds a lot of tools in bins and drawers. When folded up, the cabinet doesn't take up much room and it can be wheeled out of the way.

can be rolled to any part of the shop where it might be needed.

A rolling cabinet devoted to a single tool saves space in a small shop because it can be pushed into a corner when it's not needed. More than that, having one or more of these rolling workstations helps parcel tools and their many accessories into dedicated spaces where they won't get lost.

As an example, consider the router. Many woodworkers eventually will own several: A laminate trimmer, a mid-size router and a big plunge

router all might be found in a single shop. Each has a collet wrench (or wrenches), one or more bases, edge guides and a trammel for cutting circles and curves. Plus there are a lot of bits in one or more shank diameters. It all adds up to a lot of tooling. Building a rolling cart around a router table is a good way of keeping it all straight.

Devote a drawer to bits, divided for $1/4$" and $1/2$" shanks, and another for bases and edge guides. Routers themselves can go in a large enclosure at the base of the cabinet.

Tools that Travel: Totes & Rolls

In addition to working at a bench or around the shop, many furniture makers will also find it necessary to leave the shop once in a while with some of their tools. Maybe it's a repair around the house or construction of a shed or outbuilding or even a working stint a good distance from home. Tools that travel need to be organized and protected from damage just as much as those that never leave the shop.

Depending on how often you need them, carpentry tools can be kept in a separate, out-of-the-way cabinet or segregated on their own shelf. These tools are just as specialized as woodworking and cabinetmaking tools – just a little different. They aren't generally used for woodworking so there's no sense in mixing the two together.

One way of keeping them straight is to build a wooden tote with a handle and keep it in a corner of the shop where it won't get in the way. When

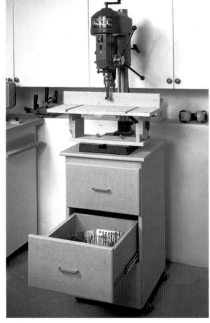

A storage cabinet dedicated to a single tool is one way of ensuring that tool accessories are always close at hand. Making the base mobile is an advantage, too.

A canvas or leather tool roll is a simple way of protecting and organizing tools whether you're in the shop or traveling.

Kentucky craftsman Don Weber with a sturdy traveling tool chest that he designed and built. Keeping tools organized on the road presents its own challenges.

you need to fix something in the house – trim a sticky door, for instance, or patch a hole in a drywall ceiling – the tools are ready and waiting.

Totes can be very simple and still very useful; even a box with rope handles made from scraps of plywood or rough lumber and nailed together at the corners will prove practical. Make it long enough to house at least a 2' level and a handsaw. Adding a row of

shallow drawers in the bottom of the tote is a good way of organizing small things – drill bits, a compass, drivers and the like – as well as protecting tools with sharp edges that would be dulled if they were thrown in with everything else. Or you can build internal trays and dividers to make it easier to find things as well as protect sharp edges.

Tool rolls are another way of keeping sharp-edged tools safe when you travel. These are simply pieces of leather or canvas with a series of pockets sewn into them. Tools are tucked into a protective sleeve and the whole thing rolled up and tied. They are equally as useful for housing tools

that aren't used all the time and must be stored in a drawer. For example, a set of augers isn't an everyday item in many shops but you may have an old set you use from time to time. Investing in an inexpensive canvas roll is a good way of protecting sharp edges when the bits have to share drawer space with other tools.

Power Tools Deserve A Space of Their Own

Portable power tools represent a different kind of organizational challenge; they are not as delicate and easily damaged as many hand tools, but they are generally heavier and bulkier and they often come with a number of accessories of which you have to keep track.

Although they can be kept in cabinets or drawers, heavy power tools will be easier to get if they are stored on a shelf about waist high or in a simple plywood cubby. An open-faced cabinet or set of shelves a couple of feet square and divided into individual compartments is a good way of housing power tools. They can be kept in the same general part of the shop but all given their own space.

The surprising number of accessories, ranging from wrenches for changing blades to replacement motor brushes, should be kept nearby. Devoting one drawer or part of one cabinet to repair and replacement parts for power tools helps to keep these important bits of hardware from getting lost.

Devoting a cabinet to power tools is a good way of making even a large collection easily accessible. This cabinet is at Cerritos College in Norwalk, Calif.

In the same general area, keep all parts lists and operating manuals for the tools in the shop. When you need to replace a part or adjust the tool the manual will be invaluable. An expanding plastic organizer, available at any office supply store, makes a good library for tool manuals. A separate organizer can be used for small replacement parts, such as O-rings, gaskets and drive belts.

Accessories for larger power tools are easy to find when they are kept as close to the tool as possible rather than in some distant cabinet across the shop. The space beneath a table saw extension is a good place to tuck a small cabinet that can house saw blades, dado blades, wrenches and other supplies. A separate drawer in the same cabinet can also be used for router bits or drill bits. Grouping tool parts in this way makes them a lot easier to find and will protect them from damage.

If you can, try housing cordless tools in the same general area and mount your chargers on a nearby wall. Having all of the tools and batteries in a single location is a plus.

Finding Room For All Those Clamps

Most of us apparently believe that old chestnut about woodworking: there is no such thing as too many clamps. We do, in fact, need a lot of clamps and they come in a variety of sizes and styles.

If you have a large collection of bar and pipe clamps (and assuming you have the space for it) consider making a rolling or stationary clamp rack. Building in a series of crossbars at different heights makes it convenient to hang clamps of different lengths. The rack should be tapered top to bottom, and in the shape of an "A" when viewed from the side, so the clamps are not easily jounced off as the cart is moved.

Racks can provide two separate sides for storage so they can hold a large number of clamps conveniently. A wall-mounted or freestanding stor-age rack also keeps long clamps available and out of the way, but when you need a lot of clamps for a big glue-up it's a lot easier to wheel a rack over than it is to make a half-dozen trips across the shop.

If you work in a basement shop, or in any shop with a low, unfinished ceiling, you'll find an ideal storage area for spring clamps and handscrews by looking up; the bottom edge of a joist or rafter will hold many clamps and keep them within easy reach. To store a row of spring clamps beneath a shelf, string a length of heavy wire between two eyescrews so it hangs an inch or two below the shelf. Compress the clamp, pop it over the wire and release it.

Keeping Up with the Clutter

Providing specialized storage cabinets, shelving and rolling racks is certainly a big part of winning the war against shop clutter and keeping small tools organized. These fixtures can represent a significant investment of time and materials, but you don't have to build a shop full of them right away. Let your ideas percolate for a while, take a look at what other woodworkers have done to solve the same problems you have and then set about to fix one storage problem at a time.

Many shops have sizeable numbers of clamps, although few will rival the collection of Sam Maloof. A tapered rack keeps them organized. Adding casters would make the rack portable, an advantage in any shop.

The other side of it, of course, is taking the time to keep tools organized once you've made room for everything. Few people return a tool to its proper place the instant they've finished using it. We're more likely to put it aside and get the next tool we need. In the end, though, shops with plans for managing that mountain of small tools will be more efficient, safer and happier places to work.

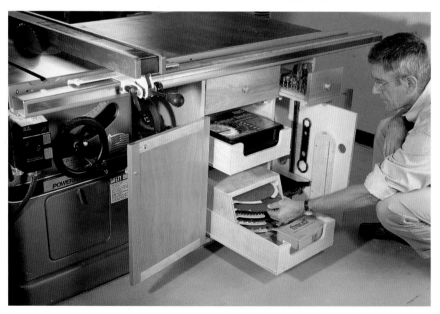

Don't overlook the space beneath a table saw extension table. This cabinet holds extra saw blades and other accessories.

WALL-MOUNTED CLAMP RACK

BY DAVID THIEL

You may never have enough clamps, but you need a place for them to call home.

We chose $1/2$" birch plywood for the top and back — it offers enough support and strength without looking clunky. The triangular braces are made from $3/4$" plywood rather than $1/2$" — primarily to make it easier to get screws into the brace.

Start by cutting a piece of $1/2$" plywood to $12^1/8$" × 36", then cut eight dadoes as shown in the diagram. If you change the length of the clamp rack, make sure there are no more than four clamp slots between braces to ensure adequate support. I used a dado stack in my table saw to make the dadoes. When complete, remove the dado stack, reset the saw's rip fence for 6" and rip the piece in half, forming the top and back pieces.

Next, mark the top piece for the slots as shown in the diagram. The $1/2$" × 4" slot holds the majority of clamps on the market today. Your clamp rack might perform better with a different-size slot, so check your clamps and adjust the dimensions if necessary.

The clipped corners at the slots guide the clamp bar into the slot. Use your band saw or jigsaw to cut the slots.

Cut 4 braces. The finished size is a triangle measuring $5^{11}/16$" × $6^3/16$" on the two legs. You can save material by interlocking the brackets.

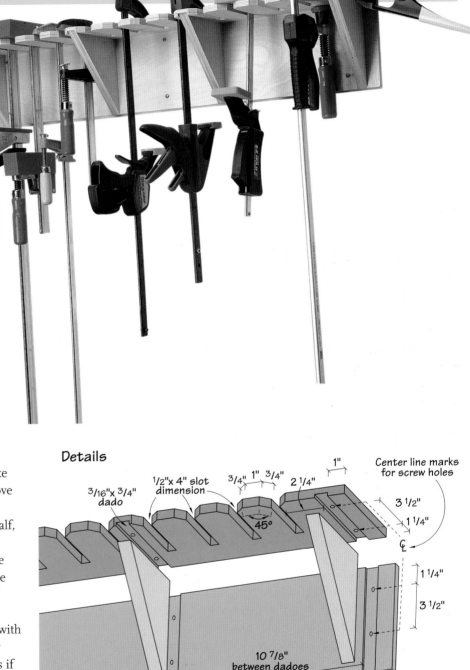

Details

3/16"x 3/4" dado

1/2"x 4" slot dimension

3/4" 1" 3/4"

2 1/4"

1"

45°

Center line marks for screw holes

3 1/2"

1 1/4"

1 1/4"

3 1/2"

10 7/8" between dadoes

9 1/4" between dadoes

Mark the top and back pieces for clearance holes used to screw the braces in place, drill the $3/16$" clearance holes and countersink for a flathead screw. I nailed the top onto the back to hold the rack's "corner" flush while drilling a pilot hole into the braces. Now glue and screw the entire rack together. Sand all the sharp edges and go find some studs to hang your rack.

A PRACTICAL SHOP CABINET

BY TROY SEXTON

Troy designs and builds custom furniture in Sunbury, Ohio, for his company, Sexton Classic American Furniture. He is a contributing editor to *Popular Woodworking*.

One of my favorite things to do when I have free time is to tinker around my shop, organizing my small stuff. I actually enjoy sorting through nails, bits and staples; and a pile of differently sized screws all thrown together drives me crazy. For this reason, I have become fond of Plano's plastic utility boxes. I have about 100 of them.

This might seem excessive, but I also use the boxes to organize and store fishing lures. In fact, these boxes often are advertised as miniature tackle boxes.

Any woodworker or angler knows that the amount of screws, nails, bits and lures one owns tends to grow exponentially, resulting in a lot of little stuff. (After sorting through my fishing lures recently I realized I own almost 1,000.) Plano's boxes have dividers to keep everything organized and they're easy to carry around the shop, to a job site or on a boat. However, 100 loose boxes is a bit like a pile of differently sized screws. I needed a box to organize my boxes. The cabinet you see here is the result.

This project is simple and quick to build – as a shop project should be. The plastic boxes merely slide in and out on pieces of Masonite that are slipped into dados cut on the inside of each side piece and both sides of the cabinet's center divider. The cope-and-stick doors are entirely optional.

While any miniature tackle box will work, this cabinet fits Plano's 3700-series utility boxes. For more information, see "About Plano Utility Boxes" below.

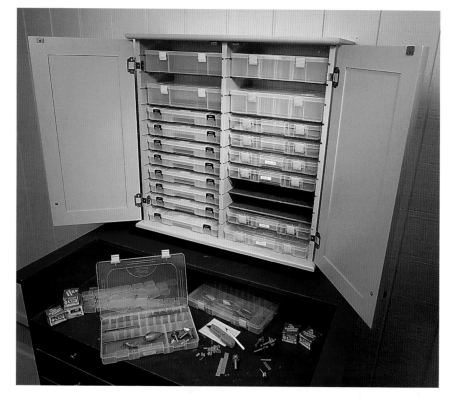

Rows of Dados

Cut the poplar top, bottom, sides, divider, plywood back and Masonite shelves to size, as stated in the cutting list. Now it's time to cut the dados. Install your dado stack in your table saw. The dados are 1/4" wide by 1/4" deep so you need only the outside cutters. There's no need to mess with chippers or shims.

I spaced my dados 2 1/4" apart. You need to cut each dado on the inside of each side piece and on both sides of the center divider. Cut the first dado in the four places required, adjust your fence and then cut the next one. You're cutting 11 dados on each piece, which amounts to 44 dados. This method ensures you move your fence as little as possible.

With the dados complete, cut a 1/4" × 1/4" rabbet on the rear edge of the side pieces that will hold the 1/4"-thick plywood back.

Cutting the dados is simple work with a dado set installed in your table saw. Cut four dados (one on each side piece and two on the divider), move the fence, then cut four more and so on.

Some heavy-duty screws will ensure this cabinet will stay put, even when fully stocked.

Two screw strips, one on the top and one on the bottom, allow you to screw your cabinet to your shop wall. Notice the notch cut into the divider to allow the screw strip to fit.

Assembling the Cabinet

Once the dados are cut, round over the edges of the top and bottom pieces using your router and a $\frac{1}{2}$"-radius roundover bit. Sand all the case pieces to #180 grit.

Lay out where the sides and divider will go on the top and bottom, as shown in the illustration at right. Use these layout lines to drill your clearance holes, then screw the sides, top and bottom (but not the divider) together with #8 × 2" screws.

You need two screw strips to hang the cabinet on the wall – one on the top and one on the bottom, as shown in the drawing. While the screw strips fit between each side piece, you must first notch the center divider to make

it work. Using your band saw, cut a $\frac{3}{4}$"-wide by $1\frac{1}{2}$"-long notch at the top and bottom of the back side of the divider. Screw the divider in place and then nail the screw strips in place as well, as shown above.

If you did everything correctly, the $\frac{1}{4}$"-thick plywood back should fit snugly between each side piece and flat against each screw strip. Basically, it fits into a $\frac{1}{4}$"-deep rabbet you created when assembling the cabinet. Cut your back to size, sand it smooth and, using your brad nailer, nail it in place.

Cope-and-stick Doors

The doors are optional. In a shop, they'll keep the boxes from getting dusty. Plus, they show off your craftsmanship. If and how you make them is up to you.

I made my two doors using stile-and-rail cutters on my router table. I used my table saw to raise the panel. First, cut all your door parts to size. Then, using your rail bit (sometimes called the cope-cutting bit), cut the tenon on the four rails. Then cut the beaded moulding profile and groove on your four stiles with the stile bit from your stile-and-rail bit set.

It's always a good idea to do test cuts when using stile-and-rail bits. If you want additional instruction on using stile-and-rail bits, check out my "Frame & Panel Dresser" story in the February 2005 issue.

To raise the panel, head to your table saw and bevel the blade to 7°. Adjust the rip fence to leave a shoulder on the panel at the top of the blade and a thin-enough edge to fit into the grooves you just cut in your stiles and rails. Again, cutting a test piece first is a good idea to ensure a snug fit.

Sand the panels to #180 grit before gluing them up in the frame-and-panel assemblies. Don't sand the inside edges of the rail-and-stile pieces at the point where they mate to form the joints. You could easily create an ugly gap.

Glue up the door assemblies. It's a loose-panel assembly, so don't glue the frames' grooves. As the seasons change, you want your panel to expand and contract.

ABOUT PLANO UTILITY BOXES

I built this cabinet to hold any of the plastic utility boxes in Plano's 3700 series. I've been using Plano utility boxes for years and they work great. The 3750 has a good, solid latch and the 3770 is perfect for storing a combination of woodworking and fishing accessories. Most cost less than $5 each and can be found at any large sporting-goods store. For more information about the boxes, call 800-226-9868 or visit planomolding.com.   – TS

SUPPLIES

Plano
800-226-9868 or
planomolding.com

• plastic utility boxes
  3700 series, price varies

Rockler
800-279-4441 or
rockler.com

4 • partial wrap-around hinges
  #31495, $6.39/pair

2 • narrow magnetic catches
  #26559, $1.49/each

2 • classic wooden knobs
  #15257, $3.39/pair

Prices correct at time of publication.

A PRACTICAL SHOP CABINET

	NO.	ITEM	DIMENSIONS (INCHES)			MATERIAL
			T	W	L	
❏	1	Top	3/4	11 1/2	32 1/2	Poplar
❏	1	Bottom	3/4	11 1/2	32 1/2	Poplar
❏	2	Sides	3/4	10	30	Poplar
❏	1	Divider	3/4	9 3/4	30	Poplar
❏	1	Back	1/4	30	30	Plywood
❏	22	Shelves	1/4	8	14 13/16	Masonite
❏	2	Screw strips	3/4	1 1/2	29 1/2	Poplar
❏	4	Door stiles	3/4	2 1/2	30	Poplar
❏	4	Door rails	3/4	2 1/2	11 1/4*	Poplar
❏	2	Door panels	3/4	11 1/8*	25 11/16*	Poplar

*Finished size will vary depending on your set of rail-and-stile bits.

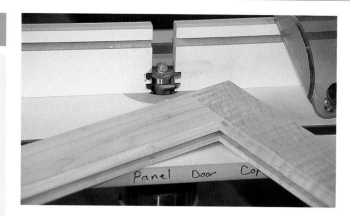

I built my cope-and-stick doors using a stile-and-rail bit set in my router. The doors are optional and can be made however you wish.

I used four Amerock partial wrap-around hinges to attach the doors to the cabinet and two magnetic catches to keep them shut. Don't forget the wooden knobs.

Initially I painted my cabinet yellow, which is the color shown here. But I decided I didn't like the yellow, so later I painted it black and then distressed the finish. There's no need to finish the Masonite shelves. Simply cut them to finished size and slide them into place.

This cabinet is the perfect solution for my woodworking and fishing storage needs. Whenever people visit my shop they comment on its ingenuity. It's so simple! There's only one problem: I didn't build this cabinet big enough. I'm currently working on a chimney cabinet design to resolve this issue.

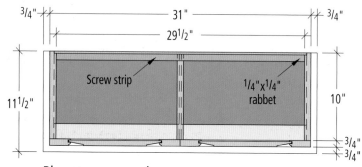

3/4"   31"   3/4"

29 1/2"

11 1/2"   Screw strip   1/4" x 1/4" rabbet   10"

3/4"
3/4"

Plan - top removed

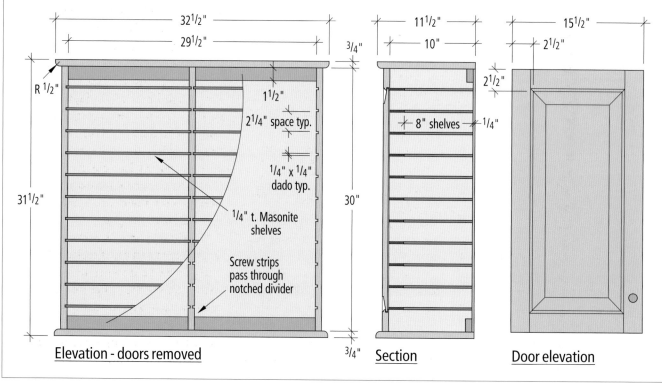

32 1/2"

29 1/2"

3/4"

R 1/2"

1 1/2"

2 1/4" space typ.

1/4" x 1/4" dado typ.

1/4" t. Masonite shelves

Screw strips pass through notched divider

31 1/2"

Elevation - doors removed

3/4"

11 1/2"

10"

8" shelves   1/4"

30"

Section

15 1/2"

2 1/2"

2 1/2"

Door elevation

256

ONE-WEEKEND ROUTER TABLE

BY DAVID THIEL

David is Executive Editor of Popular
Woodworking books

I think it might have been seeing a
$1,000 router table setup at a recent
woodworking show (it's very cool, but
$1,000?). Or maybe it was realizing
that our shop's router table's cabinet
mostly takes up space and fills with
dust. Either of these observations
was enough to get us rethinking our
router table needs.

Essentially you need a stable, flat
working surface that can support
most work. You need a fence that
guides, supports and moves easily for
adjustments (both the fence location
on the table and the faces themselves
toward the bit). You also need easy access to the router for bit changing and
height adjustment. Other than that,
it just needs to be up off the floor,
hence the cabinet.

So we decided that a lightweight,
easily stored router tabletop that
would still offer all these benefits
would be preferable. Oh, and we
wanted to be able to make it in a
weekend for less than $120. No
problem! The hardware came to $65
and change. You can purchase the
plywood locally or we've included a
source on page 73 that will provide
the necessary wood for less than $50.

An Ingenious Design

For a stable, lightweight top the solution that made sense was a torsion
box made of high-density plywood.
The size that seemed most functional
was a 20"-deep × 24"-wide platform
that only needed to be about 4" tall.
The box itself has an open center
section on the bottom to accommodate the router body. There are two
lengths of T-track installed front to

Allowing the proper clearance for your router
is critical. You can see that I've removed the
handles from the tool to allow as much space
as possible. Mark out the space and then assemble the frame to fit.

back on the tabletop to easily reposition the fence.

The fence itself is a variation of
one we've built half-a-dozen times.
The fence base is almost a torsion box

– more of a torsion corner – that provides stable support for the laterally
adjustable fence faces and allows for
dust hook-up.

For the router itself, we went shopping. After looking at a number of
router lifts and router table plates
we chose the Milwaukee 5625-29,
a 3$\frac{1}{2}$ horsepower router that offers
through-the-base height adjustment.
And, no, the price of the router is
not included in the $120 figure. You
don't have to use this router, but in
our opinion it has the horsepower you
want to swing large panel-raising bits
on your router table, and the through-
the-base adjustment means you don't
need to buy a router lift. The variable
speed is also a big plus.

We chose a circular router plate
from Veritas because it replaces the
sole plate on your router and allows
you to still use the router freehand
or in the table without changing the
base. The base also fits into the table
without the use of any tools, and slips
in and out from above in seconds.

Now the fun part: To bring the router table up to height, but still make it compact, we designed a brace that is mounted to the table and then the entire thing is simply clamped in your bench vise. Instant router table!

Torsion Top Construction

The top itself is very simple to make. A frame made of ¾" × 3" plywood pieces is sandwiched between two pieces of ¾" plywood. The bottom piece is notched to accommodate your router (you'll need to test fit your router to locate the center frame pieces and the notch). The top piece extends 1½" beyond the frame on all sides to allow for clamping featherboards or other guides to the top surface.

Start by cutting out the top, bottom and seven frame pieces. If you opt to use the Veritas plate, the instructions are very clear on how to cut the hole in the tabletop to fit the plate. Otherwise, follow the instructions for your individual router plate.

We chose to locate the router plate closer to the front of the table rather than in the center of the table. Most router table work happens within 6" of the fence and this location keeps you from having to lean across the table for operations. If you have a larger piece to run, the fence can be reversed on the table to give you a larger support surface.

With the router plate located in the top, suspend the router from the top and locate the two center frame members the necessary distance to clear the router. Make a note of that dimension, then lay out your frame accordingly.

I used glue and an 18-gauge brad nailer to assemble all the pieces for this project. While perhaps not the height of joinery, it's fast and reliable.

With the frame assembled, place the frame on the bottom, and mark and notch the center section to allow clearance space for the router body.

More marking: With the frame assembled and resting on the bottom piece, mark out the notch that will allow the router to extend through the top.

With the bottom notched, simply glue and nail it in place on the frame.

ONE-WEEKEND ROUTER TABLE

	NO.	LET.	ITEM	DIMENSIONS (INCHES)			MATERIAL
				T	W	L	
❏	1	T1	Top	¾	20	24	Plywood
❏	1	B1	Bottom	¾	17	21	Plywood
❏	2	B2	Frame F&B	¾	3	21	Plywood
❏	4	B3	Frame dividers	¾	3	15½	Plywood
❏	1	B4	Frame divider	¾	3	10½	Plywood
❏	2	B5	Support stems	¾	3	7	Plywood
❏	2	B6	Support braces	¾	3	21	Plywood
❏	2	F1	Fence faces	¾	4	14	Plywood
❏	1	F2	Fence sub-face	½	3½	28	Plywood
❏	1	F3	Fence base	½	3	28	Plywood
❏	4	F4	Fence braces	¾	3	3	Plywood
❏	1	F5	Hood top	½	5	3½	Plywood
❏	2	F6	Hood sides	½	2½	3	Plywood
❏	1	F7	Hood back	½	5	3	Plywood
❏	2	H1	Fence T-tracks	⅜	¾	14	Aluminum
❏	4	H2	Hex-head bolts	¼"-20	1½"		
❏	4	H3	Star knobs				
❏	2	H4	Cam clamps				
❏	2	H5	Table T-tracks	⅜	¾	20	Aluminum

After cutting the grooves for the T-track, tap it in place using a backing block. If you have to tap too hard with the hammer, your groove is too small. Attach the track with ½" x #4 flathead screws. Pre-drill and countersink each hole.

You could leave the center section open, but the extra strength along the back of the tabletop is worth the effort.

Attach the bottom the same way you assembled the frame.

Before fastening the top to the table, you need to install the aluminum T-track inserts for fence adjustment. I used a dado set on my table saw to run the grooves before attaching the top.

Next, attach the top, centering it on the frame assembly. Pay extra attention when attaching the top to keep the fasteners below the surface of the tabletop. This will keep you from scratching your work, or worse, allowing your wood to hang up on a brad head during an operation.

Down and Dirty Fence

The fence is also absurdly simple to make. Accuracy is important to make sure it sits square to the tabletop, but other than that, it's brads and glue.

Start construction on the fence by cutting out the base, sub-face, faces and braces. All but the braces are very straightforward. The braces are actually triangles. The best method is to

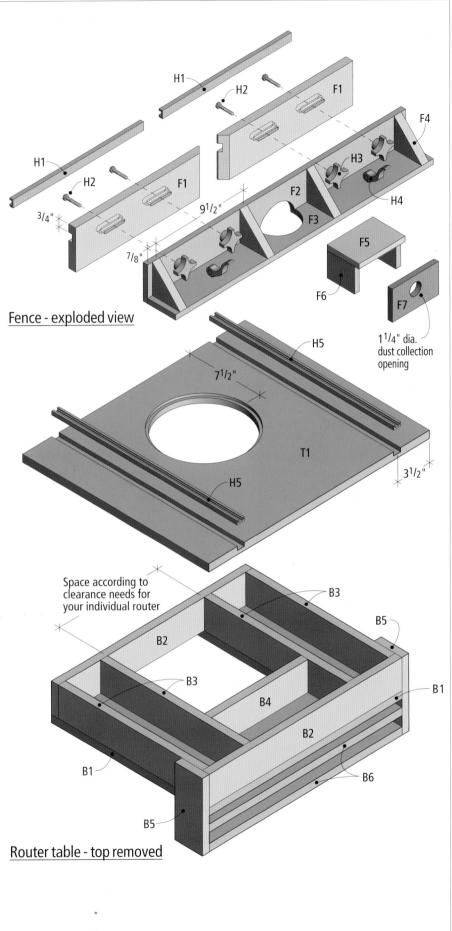

Fence - exploded view

Router table - top removed

SUPPLIES

Lee Valley Tools
800-871-8158 or
leevalley.com

4 • Four-arm knobs
#00M55.30, $1.50 each

1 • Veritas Router Base Plate
#05J25.01, $29.50

2 • 2' T-slot extrusions
#12K79.01, $6.50 each

1 • 3' T-slot extrusion
#12K79.03, $9.50 each

2 • Cam clamp mechanisms
#05J51.01, $3.50 each

The Wood & Shop Inc.
314-731-2761 or
woodshop.com

2 • ³⁄₄" x 30" x 30" Birch ply
#BBP ³⁄₄C30X30, $18 each

1 • ¹⁄₂" x "20" x 30" Birch ply
#BBP¹⁄₂ 20X30, $6.90 each

Available from any
hardware store:

4 • 1¹⁄₂" ¹⁄₄"-20 hex-head bolts

2 • 1 ¹⁄₄" ¹⁄₄"-20 hex-head bolts

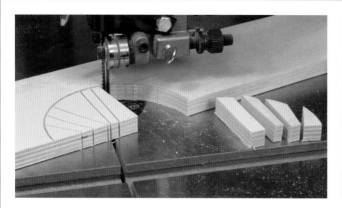

Cutting out the bit clearance hole on the band saw is made simple by first cutting "spokes" toward your line. These relief cuts allow the pieces to fall out in small chunks, rather than fighting with one bigger piece.

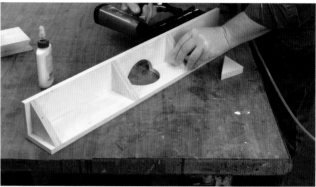

With the sub-face and base assembled, add the four triangular braces with glue and brads. Space them adequately to support the fence, but make sure you leave room for the knobs.

The dust collection hood completes the router table fence. It should seal tightly around the fence to provide the best dust collection, so don't skimp on the glue here.

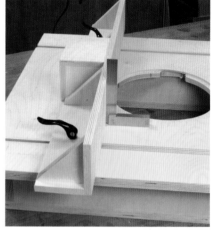

After installing the cam clamps, lock the fence in place on the top and check for square. If adjustment is necessary, you can do it by sanding the base or adding thin shims. You don't want to add shims behind the fence faces because they're moving parts. Adjust the base.

rip a piece of plywood to 3" wide, then head to the miter saw. First miter both ends of the strip at a 45° angle, then reset the miter saw for a 90° cut and cut the 3" triangles from the strip. Repeat this process and you've got four braces.

The sub-face and base need to have a 3"-wide half-circle cut at the center of each piece along one edge as shown on page 74. This space will be the opening for the router bits.

The sub-face is then glued and nailed to the base. Then glue the braces into the corner formed by the sub-face and base. Make sure to locate the braces as shown to avoid interference with any of the fence handles. I again used brad nails to hold the braces in place.

For the router table to be as useful as possible it needs dust collection.

This is achieved by building a simple hood to surround the bit opening in the fence. Drill a hole in the hood back piece. Adjust the hole size to fit your dust collection hose, usually 1 1/4" in diameter.

Then attach the hood sides to the hood back, holding the sides flush to the top edge of the back. Then add the top to the box.

The next step is to locate and drill the holes for the cam clamps that hold the fence to the table and for the knobs that hold the faces. Place the fence assembly over the table and orient the cam clamp holes so they fall in the center of the T-tracks in the top. There can be a little bit of play, but not too much.

Secure the fence to the table with the cam clamps so it seats tightly. Use an engineer's square to check the

fence against the top. If it's not square you need to adjust the base slightly, either by shimming or removing material from the underside of the fence base to make it square.

Next, drill the holes for the fence knobs, again avoiding the braces so the knobs can be easily turned. The holes should be 2" up from the tabletop.

The fence faces are next. To allow the best fence clearance near the bit, I beveled the inside lip of each of the faces at 45°. Next you need to rout two, 2 1/2"-wide stepped slots in the front of each fence face. These will allow the faces to be moved left-to-right to accommodate different bit sizes.

The easiest way to do this is on a router table, but if you're building

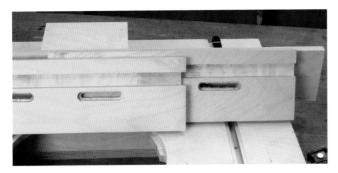

Seen from the front, the fence faces have been grooved for the T-tracks, and the clearance holes to attach and adjust the faces are drilled. Note that the face slot shows the rough edges from the overlapping holes made on the drill press. A few minutes with a file and some sandpaper will clean up the slots so the bolt will move smoothly.

After drilling clearance holes, you can locate the holes in the fence faces and add the knobs.

Here you can see the fences in place and the fence attached and ready to run. The T-tracks in the fence faces can be used for featherboards and you can use them to attach a simple guard to keep your hands a safe distance from the bit.

The support brace (customized for my bench vise) holds the router top firmly in place with plenty of clearance (and no wasted space).

your first, you can use a drill press with two different bits. Use a $1/2$"-diameter Forstner bit to first cut a $1/4$"-deep slot. Then change to a $5/16$"-diameter bit to drill through to the back of the fence face. This will create a slot that will let a $1/2$"-hex-head bolt drop into the slot, recessing the head, but capturing the sides of the bolt head to keep it from spinning.

I also added a T-slot fixture to the front of each face. This allows you to attach featherboards, a guard to protect your fingers and other guides. Again, you can use a router or your dado set in the table saw to make the slot (about 1" down from the top of the fence).

Attach the fence faces using the bolts, washers and knobs.

The Mounting Support

To make the whole thing work, you need to be able to secure the table in your bench vise, but still have access to the router motor. We used a U-shaped support screwed to the sides of the table. The actual size of the support will depend on your bench vise, but you want the tabletop to rest on the vise as much as possible. In fact, if you can also get the top to rest on the vise at the rear of the table, that's even better support. Our larger router forced us to move the support all the way to the rear of the table. This is something else that can be in-dividualized on your table.

You'll see in the photo that we used two support braces to catch the vise at

both the top and bottom of the jaws for more support. Your vise may require a different arrangement, so give it a test run to make sure it's held tight.

Finishing Touches

With the support mounted you can put your table to work. But you may want to add a step – finishing. While a bare plywood surface will perform reasonably well, a slicker surface will make things move easier. You can add a topcoat of spray-on lacquer (as we did), or a coat of oil or shellac.

Other additions for your table can include shop-made featherboards (that will fit nicely in the T-tracks on the fence face) and a couple of storage drawers to either side of the opening in the top.

BENCHTOP ROUTER TABLE STAND

BY TROY SEXTON

Troy designs and builds custom furniture in Sunbury, Ohio, for his company, Sexton Classic American Furniture. He is a contributing editor to *Popular Woodworking*.

At first it might seem a bit odd to build a cabinet base that will convert a benchtop router table into a floor model. But it really makes great sense for a couple of reasons.

This setup takes up less space than a commercial floor-model router table, yet it has just as much storage for accessories than the big boys; in fact, it probably has more. On the whole, this setup costs less than buying a floor-model router table, and it lets you easily remove the benchtop unit if you need to take it with you on a job or to the garage.

As you'll see, I've come up with an ingenious way to slip the router table into place without clamping. I also added an inexpensive power strip to the side to make turning on the router (and a shop vacuum) a convenient, single-switch operation.

How it's Built

While this stand is built using solid poplar, you easily could build this project from ³⁄₄" plywood.

The joinery is pretty simple, but I got a little fancy on the drawers. The case is held together with rabbets and dados. The bottom is held in place between the sides in ¹⁄₄" × ³⁄₄" through dados. At the back edge of each side is a ¹⁄₄" × ¹⁄₄" rabbet to hold the back.

For the drawers, I took advantage of a joint-cutting router bit I've been wanting to try for a while: the drawer-lock bit. This bit cuts an interlocking rabbet that adds extra strength against racking and separation to a drawer joint. Because there were going to be a lot of heavy router bits in the drawers, I figured the extra strength was a good idea.

Case Joinery

I used solid poplar for my stand, which means I started by jointing and planing the wood into straight and true ³⁄₄"-thick boards. Then I edge-glued some together to make up the panels for the sides, bottom and top. If you've opted for plywood, you've saved yourself a couple of steps, but you're still going to have to cut all the pieces to size according to the cutting list.

With everything cut to size, it's time to make some rabbets and dados. I prefer making these cuts on my table saw, but you can certainly opt for a router.

First, you should cut the through dado that holds the bottom in place between the side pieces. After installing a dado stack in my saw (and shimming it to a perfect ³⁄₄" thickness) I set the height of the dado to ¹⁄₄" and set my rip fence to 4¹⁄₄" up from the bottom edge of the side. Mark the bottom and inside surface of each cabinet side so you don't get confused, then cut each dado with the side's bottom edge against the fence and the inside surface of the side down on the saw table.

With that joint complete, it's time to cut the rabbets on the sides that will hold the back. Increase the height of the dado blades to ¹⁄₂" and add a sacrificial fence to your table saw's rip fence to allow only ¹⁄₄" of the stack to be exposed by the fence. Then cut the two inside back edges of each side to form the rabbets.

Glue and Nails

Except for the drawers, you've completed all the necessary carcase joinery. Sand the inside of the case and decide

A dado stack in my table saw makes quick work of the dado for the bottom in each side. The cut is made 4¼" up from the bottom edge.

After resetting the dado height and adding a sacrificial fence to my rip fence, I was able to cut the rabbets for the back on each side.

how you want to assemble it. I chose glue and a pneumatic nailer, but you could use screws, or hammer and nails.

Put one of the sides on your bench and glue the bottom piece into the dado. Add glue in the dado of the second side and then use one of the brace pieces between the two sides to temporarily prop the side piece up. Flush up all your joints and then nail the bottom in place.

Flip the assembled side and bottom over, and repeat the process for the second side. Then slide the brace to the upper back corner of the case, and glue and nail it in place (vertically) between the sides. Keep this brace flush with the rabbets in the sides.

The next step is to shape and attach the two lower braces. One brace goes in the front and the other one goes in the back.

By notching the lower braces and both sides of the stand, I formed sturdy "legs" for my cabinet. This makes it more likely that your stand will sit flat on an uneven floor. Mark the cutouts using the illustrations at right, then use a jigsaw to cut away the waste. Nail the braces in place.

Topping it Off
The next part of the cabinet is the top. Evenly space the top's overhang on the cabinet and start nailing it in place at the back of the cabinet.

Before nailing the top at the front, be sure to measure the drawer opening at the front of the cabinet to make sure it's the same at the top and at the bottom. Otherwise your drawers will be difficult to install because the case will not be square.

The last part to make is the back. Cut your back to fit in the rabbets, but don't nail it in place yet. It's a lot easier to put the drawer slides in with the back off.

A Bit of a Cavern
This cabinet has a remarkable amount of storage space; in fact, it gave me some room to grow my already extensive collection of router bits and accessories.

For shop furniture, I prefer drawers to shelves and doors because it's easier to organize small things in a drawer.

Making the drawers for this piece is pretty simple: I used a drawer-lock bit in my router table. To keep my setups to a minimum, I ran both the front and back at the same setting, then trimmed the back to length before assembling the drawer. For the drawer fronts and backs, I needed to inset the joinery ½" on each end to accommodate the mechanical drawer slides I was using. This meant taking off a pretty serious amount of wood on each end, so I quickly notched

each end on the table saw first (the dado stack was still set up).

Then, by working with the inside surface of the drawer backs and fronts down against the router table, I was able to make the compatible joinery parts on different thicknesses of wood.

With the front and backs of the drawers complete, I ran the drawer sides vertically to form the mating pieces.

Drawer Assembly
The last step before assembling the drawers was to cut a ¼" × ¼" groove along the inside face of the front and side pieces to capture the plywood bottom piece. I did this with a ¼"-diameter straight bit in my router table, but a couple of passes with a standard blade on the table saw also would work, if you prefer. I started the grooves ¼" up from the bottom edge of each piece.

The drawer backs are narrower than the other drawer pieces, allowing the bottom to slide into the groove after assembly.

Dry-fit the drawers to make sure everything fits tight. While the drawers are together, mark the extra length on the drawer backs with a pencil. Then take the drawer apart and cut the backs to finished length.

The drawers now are ready to assemble. Add some glue to the corner joints. One of the other nice advantages of the drawer-lock joint is that the drawers can be clamped together with only a couple of clamps across the drawer width. The joint itself will hold everything tightly in place.

After assembly, slide the bottom in place to square up the drawer before nailing the bottom in place to the back.

Not Just Paint
While poplar is a good, sturdy and inexpensive wood for building this type of shop cabinet, it's not exactly attractive. I build a lot of Shaker-style furniture, so I've become fond of

BENCHTOP ROUTER TABLE STAND

	NO.	ITEM	DIMENSIONS (INCHES)			MATERIAL	COMMENTS
			T	W	L		
❑	1	Top	$^3/_4$	$18^1/_2$	24	Poplar	
❑	2	Sides	$^3/_4$	$17^1/_2$	$25^1/_4$	Poplar	$^1/_4$" x $^1/_4$" rabbet at back
❑	1	Bottom	$^3/_4$	$17^1/_4$	21	Poplar	
❑	3	Braces	$^3/_4$	$4^1/_4$	$20^1/_2$	Poplar	
❑	1	Back	$^1/_4$	$21^1/_2$	$25^1/_4$	Plywood	
❑	4	Drawer fronts	$^3/_4$	5	$20^1/_2$	Poplar	Drawer-lock joints
❑	4	Drawer backs	$^1/_2$	$4^1/_2$	$20^1/_2$	Poplar	Drawer-lock joints
❑	8	Drawer sides	$^1/_2$	5	$15^3/_4$	Poplar	Drawer-lock joints
❑	4	Drawer bottoms	$^1/_4$	19	$15^1/_2$	Plywood	
❑	2	Fixed mounting strips	$^3/_4$	$2^3/_4$	17	Poplar	
❑	2	Short mounting strips	$^3/_4$	$2^3/_4$	4	Poplar	
❑	2	Removable router table mounting strips	$^3/_4$	$2^3/_4$	13	Poplar	

milk-paint finishes. They brush on easily and look like a finish on the piece, rather than a coat of paint. My sister painted the outside surfaces (including the still-unattached back) and the drawer fronts.

I installed the drawer hardware by following the instructions supplied with the full-extension, 100-pound-capacity drawer slides I bought. When installing, the drawer fronts are held flush to the front edges of the cabinet.

Mounting a Table

Except for adding the Shaker knobs on the drawers, the cabinet essentially is complete. But to make it a router table stand, I still needed to add cleats to the top to secure the router table.

The cleats are a variation on a couple of very good ideas: the sliding dovetail and a French cleat. By mounting two strips of poplar cut lengthwise at a 45° bevel opposite one another on the top, you create the female part of

a sliding dovetail. The mating strips then are mounted to the bottom of whatever portable router table already is in your shop.

To make a stop to keep the table from sliding front-to-back, I cut the second set of strips 4" shorter, then attached the 4" blocks to the rear of the cabinet, tight against the bevel of the longer, attached strips. Now the router table slides into place and stops where I want it.

OK, I have a confession to make. While I like the usefulness of being able to make my portable router table stationary and vice versa, it wasn't my only reason for making this stand. I'm guilty of owning more than one router table and leaving a set of routers ready-to-use for some joinery at all times. My router table stand allows me to switch out tables effortlessly. I know it's extravagant, but I like routers!

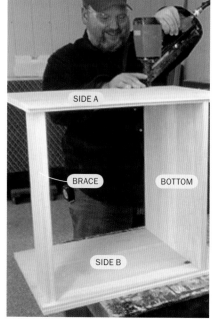

To assemble the bottom and sides, use one side to hold the bottom upright in the dado, put glue in the other side and install it. One of the braces makes a temporary support for the side piece as I nail it to the bottom.

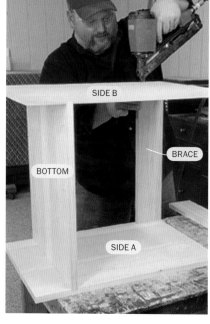

After flipping the assembly and attaching the other side the same way, I take the brace I've been using as a support and shoot it in place at the upper back corner of the cabinet using my nailer.

Nail the other two braces in place below the bottom. The braces help square up the cabinet as you attach them – assuming they're cut square.

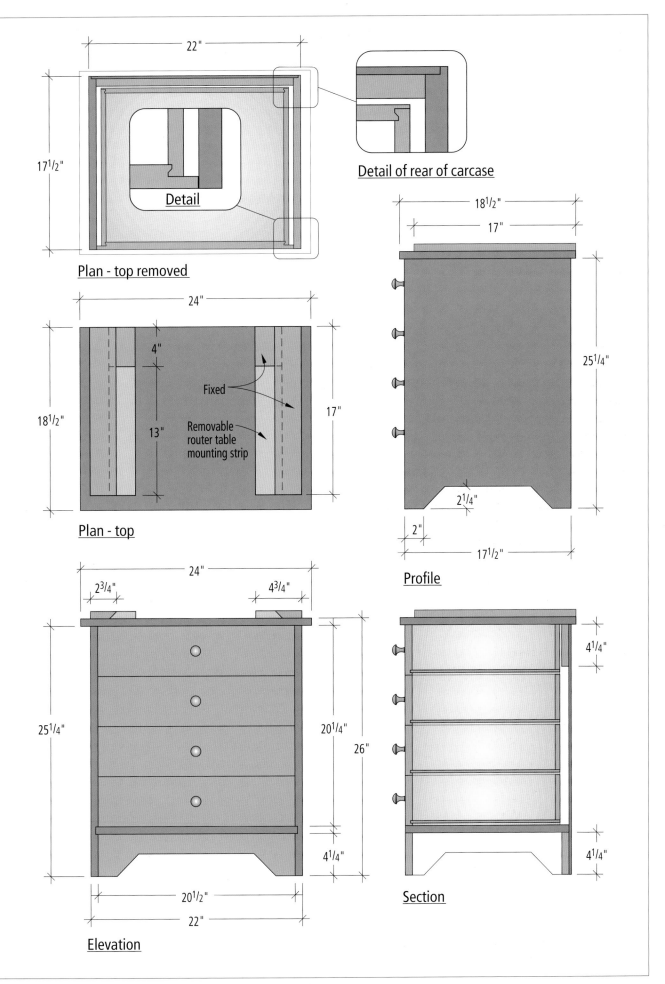

22"

17 1/2"

Detail

Plan - top removed

Detail of rear of carcase

18 1/2"

17"

25 1/4"

2 1/4"

2"

17 1/2"

Profile

24"

4"

Fixed

13"

Removable
router table
mounting strip

18 1/2"

17"

Plan - top

24"

2 3/4"

4 3/4"

25 1/4"

20 1/4"

26"

4 1/4"

20 1/2"

22"

Elevation

4 1/4"

4 1/4"

Section

The carcase is essentially complete. All that's missing is the back, which I leave off until after I paint it and install the drawers.

LARGE RABBET CUT BEFORE DRAWER-LOCK JOINT

With the bottom grooves cut and the back trimmed for length, shoot the drawers together. The drawer-lock joint (inset) pulls the parts tighter, so there's less need to clamp during assembly.

Once the cabinet is assembled, use the dimensions provided in the illustrations to mark and cut the "feet" on the front and back braces, and on the sides. A jigsaw makes quick work of these cuts.

THE DRAWER-LOCK BIT

If you're shopping for a clever router bit for making drawers, add the drawer-lock bit to your list.

I used it to make the drawers for the router table stand, and I'm going to be using it a lot more. The cut created by the bit is a variation on a tongue-and-dado joint that is used a lot in commercial drawer-making. But the bit is quicker and looks nicer, too.

The photo below left shows the router table setup with the bit ready to cut. You should note that the drawer front I'm about to cut has a notch cut in it already. Because I'm using drawer slides, I needed to allow 1/2" clearance on either side of the drawer. This means the drawer front extends beyond the drawer to hide the slide hardware. So the drawer-lock cut is deeper on the front than it would be on a drawer without slides.

Rather than try to hog off all that wood with the drawer lock bit in one pass (which would not be good for the router), I notched the drawer fronts and backs on my table saw first.

The photo below right shows the cut being made in the front. I run all the drawer fronts and backs with this setup. (Though the backs are thinner, I don't have to reset the bit height.) You also should note that I've added a build-up to the router table fence. This helps protect my hands during the cut, and it's also the setup needed for the next cuts on the drawer sides. By simply running the sides vertically against the fence, the mating half to the drawer lock joint is complete! It's a pretty slick system.   – TS

If everything worked out right, you'll have 1/2" clearance on either side of the drawer for the drawer slides. With the back off, it's a lot easier to attach the slides to the cabinet sides. Then it's some final fitting, paint and adding a back.

PRE-CUT NOTCH

BUILD-UP ON FENCE

SUPPLIES

Woodworker's Supply
800-645-9292 or
woodworker.com

4 pair • 16" drawer slides
#860-835, $13.79/pair

4 • Walnut Shaker knobs
#938-503, $1.89

1 qt. • Federal Blue milk paint
#895-130, $21.99

Prices as of publication deadline.

ROLLING CLAMP RACK

BY DAVID THIEL

David is Executive Editor of Popular Woodworking books

When you've got so many clamps that it's a problem getting them to where the work is being done, build this rolling clamp rack! It holds about 50 clamps, takes up a little more than four square feet of floor space and can honestly be built in an afternoon. The construction of the frame is simple, but the "hanging" part of the rack depends a great deal on the type and variety of clamps you own.

Construction

Cut the ends of the four uprights and the two base support pieces at a 10-degree angle as shown. Assemble the two side frames by screwing two cross supports between the pairs of uprights, holding the top inside edge of the support flush to the inside of the upright, and flush to the top or bottom 10-degree angles. Attach the two frames together to form the "A" by screwing the base supports and the top supports to the sides of the frames, holding them flush to the bottom and top of the frames. Now attach the casters to the outside ends of the two lower cross supports. Consider your clamps and how they can best be stored on the two slanted sides of the rack, and notch the clamp supports accordingly. Then screw the supports between the uprights. I used an extra cross support screwed to the top of the rack for storing hand screws and spring clamps. I also added two notched strips to the sides for storing smaller clamps.

Each ³/4" x 1 ¹/2"notch is equally spaced from the given inset. Your clamps may require different notch sizes.

Plan of clamp holder "B"

1 ³/8" 1 ¹/4" ³/4" 1 ³/8" 1 ¹/2"

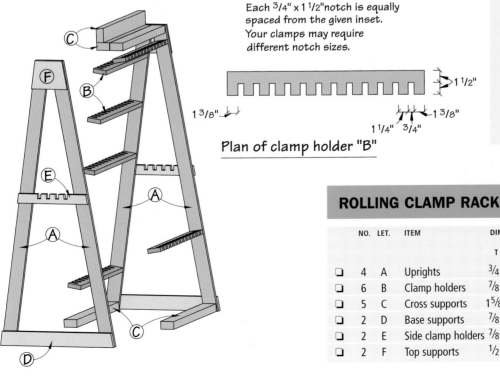

SUPPLIES

From Lee Valley, www.leevalley.com:

4- casters - #00K20.01 We recommend using 2 rigid and 2 locking casters for ease of "steering" your rolling clamp rack.

ROLLING CLAMP RACK

NO.	LET.	ITEM	DIMENSIONS (INCHES)			MATERIAL
			T	W	L	
❏ 4	A	Uprights	³/4"	3"	61¹/2"	Poplar
❏ 6	B	Clamp holders	⁷/8"	3"	25¹/2"	Poplar
❏ 5	C	Cross supports	1⁵/8"	3"	25¹/2"	Poplar
❏ 2	D	Base supports	⁷/8"	3"	26"	Poplar
❏ 2	E	Side clamp holders	⁷/8"	2"	16"	Poplar
❏ 2	F	Top supports	¹/2"	8"	6"	Plywood

SAW BENCH AND SHOP STOOL

BY JOHN WILSON

John Wilson currently writes and operates The Home Shop in Charlotte, Michigan, where he teaches classes and sells Shaker box supplies.

My simple plywood two-step in the old tool shed had reached the end of the road. Looking at it you could see a pile of old wood ready for the burn pile. I saw in it a project that recalled 45 years of working life. It was more than just memories that came to mind. If it was time to recycle the old stool then it was important to document what had been a most useful object, and perhaps make a successor to it before its last rites.

My time in home building and remodeling went back to four summers during college. I learned the trade of carpentering before the modern era of specialization, the days when a small carpenter crew did everything from the first framing to a completed house ready for painters. It was a good education. The shop stool represented a sort of rite of passage into the world of construction.

That first summer I was too busy learning the ropes as the new kid to understand the significance of a shop stool. I borrowed someone else's when a task was at ceiling height. The second summer I was more confident of what was required on the job. After all, they had hired me back.

One day the boss suggested I stop by his shop to make a shop stool. It sounded helpful to me, but looking back on it from the perspective of years later I can see its significance. It marked my acceptance as a man who could use an on-site bench to do his work. From now on along with my growing box of tools, the back of my car held my very own work stool, something some newer member of the crew would ask to borrow. That pile of old plywood ready for the burn pile was to me a badge of rank, hard won during months of work on the job.

So what was so special about the shop stool on the job? The place at which you work is an important extension of the tools you use. This is as true of home building and remodeling as it is in the workshop. In fact this shop stool is an asset in either your shop or on the building site.

- It serves as a stable two-step work platform.
- It's a mobile work surface for cutting and assembly.
- It holds doors on edge for planing tasks.
- Two stools will replace the need for sawhorses.
- It keeps tools in one place where they are easier to find and transport to a new work site.

All of this is from a half sheet of ³⁄₄" plywood and some deck screws. Recalling all the ways the shop stool gives good service made me realize how important it was to record its dimensions. I inherited mine from men of experience on the job. There is no better school of design than experience. So here it is for you, too.

Construction Tips

While plywood is a stock construction item, I found that its quality varied considerably and that taking time to shop for a sheet with reasonable finish, free from major voids, and not warped, paid off. Some of the best plywood these

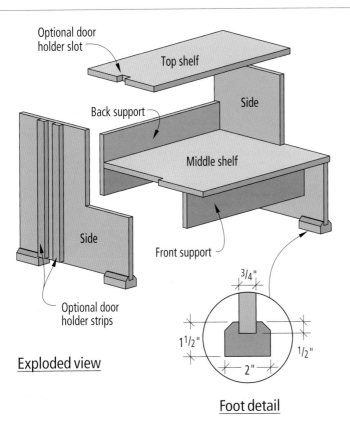

Optional door holder slot

Top shelf

Side

Back support

Middle shelf

Side

Front support

Optional door holder strips

Exploded view

3/4"

1 1/2"

1/2"

2"

Foot detail

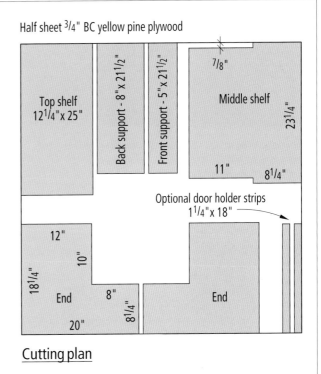

Half sheet 3/4" BC yellow pine plywood

Top shelf 12 1/4" x 25"

Back support - 8" x 21 1/2"

Front support - 5" x 21 1/2"

7/8"

Middle shelf

23 1/4"

11"

8 1/4"

Optional door holder strips 1 1/4" x 18"

18 1/4"

12"

10"

End

8"

8 1/4"

End

20"

Cutting plan

Construction Steps:

1. After cutting all the plywood pieces, round over all the exposed edges in the stool using a 1/8"-diameter roundover router bit.
2. Assemble pieces using tapered drill and countersink to pre-drill for 1 5/8" deck screws. Start with the front and back supports on the middle shelf.
3. Cut 4'-long hardwood blocks for the feet with a groove to fit 3/4" plywood. Adjust the thickness of the blocks to make the stool level and glue them in place.
4. Finish with a sealer coat of polyurethane and thinner mixed 50/50.

days comes from yellow pine and is the BC grade with one good face. Pick the best you can.

The illustrations and cutting plan give you direction. Start by screwing the 8" back support to the middle shelf, and then screw the 5" front support under the middle shelf leaving it centered with 7/8" exposed at each end. With these in place, the sides will screw to the middle shelf more easily. The top step goes on and you are done. It's that simple.

The door holder slot, if desired, is added to one side. And there is one more addition that will add years of life to your shop stool. I found that the plywood feet abraded away with use, as you can see in the picture below. As that happens, the stool loses stability as well. So I made some simple hardwood blocks. The blocks are made from a piece of 1 1/2" × 2" with a groove 3/4" wide by 1/2" deep routed into the wider face. Cut these into four pieces 4" long and glue them onto the sides.

One further use of the stool comes at noon – all the guys sitting around the work site with their lunch pails open!

Here is the old stool after a life of usefulness, now on the burn pile to be returned to basic elements of the universe and to be recombined into a new generation of materials. Note the badly worn corners where the plywood feet gave out. The attachment of the hardwood "shoes" as I describe in the article will extend the life of your stool.

SUPPLIERS

ADAMS & KENNEDY —
THE WOOD SOURCE
6178 Mitch Owen Rd.
P.O. Box 700
Manotick, ON
Canada K4M 1A6
613-822-6800
www.wood-source.com
Wood supply

ADJUSTABLE CLAMP COMPANY
404 N. Armour St.
Chicago, IL 60622
312-666-0640
www.adjustableclamp.com
Clamps and woodworking tools

THE BURGESS EDGE
Michael Burgess
P.O. Box 32 Route 125
Ripton, Vermont 05766
802.233.1489
www.burgessedge.com
*A revolutionary edge-banding
system using specially designed
router bits*

B&Q
Portswood House
1 Hampshire Corporate Park
Chandlers Ford
Eastleigh
Hampshire, England SO53 3YX
0845 609 6688
www.diy.com
*Woodworking tools, supplies and
hardware*

BUSY BEE TOOLS
130 Great Gulf Dr.
Concord, ON
Canada L4K 5W1
1-800-461-2879
www.busybeetools.com
Woodworking tools and supplies

**CONSTANTINE'S WOOD CENTER
OF FLORIDA**
1040 E. Oakland Park Blvd.
Fort Lauderdale, FL 33334
800-443-9667
www.constantines.com
Tools, woods, veneers, hardware

**FRANK PAXTON LUMBER
COMPANY**
5701 W. 66th St.
Chicago, IL 60638
800-323-2203
www.paxtonwood.com
Wood, hardware, tools, books

THE HOME DEPOT
2455 Paces Ferry Rd. NW
Atlanta, GA 30339
800-430-3376 (U.S.)
800-628-0525 (Canada)
www.homedepot.com
*Woodworking tools, supplies and
hardware*

KLINGSPOR ABRASIVES INC.
2555 Tate Blvd. SE
Hickory, N.C. 28602
800-645-5555
www.klingspor.com
Sandpaper of all kinds

LEE VALLEY TOOLS LTD.
P.O. Box 1780
Ogdensburg, NY 13669-6780
800-871-8158 (U.S.)
800-267-8767 (Canada)
www.leevalley.com
*Woodworking tools and
hardware*

LOWE'S COMPANIES, INC.
P.O. Box 1111
North Wilkesboro, NC 28656
800-445-6937
www.lowes.com
*Woodworking tools, supplies and
hardware*

**ROCKLER WOODWORKING
AND HARDWARE**
4365 Willow Dr.
Medina, MN 55340
800-279-4441
www.rockler.com
*Woodworking tools, hardware
and books*

**TREND MACHINERY &
CUTTING TOOLS LTD.**
Odhams Trading Estate
St. Albans Rd.
Watford
Hertfordshire, U.K.
WD24 7TR
01923 224657
www.trendmachinery.co.uk
*Woodworking tools and
hardware*

WATERLOX COATINGS
908 Meech Ave.
Cleveland, OH 44105
800-321-0377
www.waterlox.com
Finishing supplies

WOODCRAFT SUPPLY LLC
1177 Rosemar Rd.
P.O. Box 1686
Parkersburg, WV 26102
800-535-4482
www.woodcraft.com
Woodworking hardware

WOODWORKER'S HARDWARE
P.O. Box 180
Sauk Rapids, MN 56379-0180
800-383-0130
www.wwhardware.com
Woodworking hardware

WOODWORKER'S SUPPLY
1108 N. Glenn Rd.
Casper, WY 82601
800-645-9292
www.woodworker.com
*Woodworking tools and
accessories, finishing supplies,
books and plans*

INDEX

MORE GREAT TITLES FROM POPULAR WOODWORKING!

MEASURE TWICE, CUT ONCE

By Jim Tolpin

From design and layout to developing a cutting list, Jim Tolpin's easy-to-follow style introduces a variety of tools (new and old) used to transfer measurements accurately to the wood. You'll learn the best cutting techniques, how to prevent mistakes before they happen, and for those unavoidable mistakes, you'll learn how to fix them so no one will know!

ISBN 13: 978-1-55870-809-9
ISBN 10: 1-55870-809-X
paperback, 128 p., #Z0835

ISBN 13: 978-1-55870-816-7
ISBN 10: 1-55870-816-2
paperback, 128 p., #Z0991

I CAN DO THAT! WOODWORKING PROJECTS

Edited by David Thiel

You can do that, quickly, easily and save money. Each project requires a minimum of tools, inexpensive materials found at your local home center. You'll also learn how to use each tool, which makes this book perfect for the beginning woodworker. The projects are fun and easy to make and are practical.

WOODSHOP LUST

Edited by David Thiel

While the woodshop is most frequently a private place, every woodworker is happy to show another woodworker around his shop, and, he's just as happy to visit someone else's. This book lets you take a trip through some normal and not-so-normal woodshops around the U.S. See how woodworkers have adapted their space to their hobby and how they overcome space issues.

ISBN 13: 978-1-55870-822-8
ISBN 10: 1-55870-822-7
paperback, 128 p., # Z1079

THE COMPLETE CABINETMAKER'S REFERENCE

By Jeffrey Piontkowski

This indispensable resource for cabinetmakers includes cutting and assembly instructions, along with lists of types and quantities of materials needed for all standard-sized cabinets. You'll also learn how to adapt the projects to build custom-sized pieces.

ISBN 13: 978-1-55870-757-3
ISBN 10: 1-55870-757-3
hardcover w/ concealed wire-o
128 p., #70710

These and other great woodworking books are available at your local bookstore, woodworking stores or from online suppliers.

www.popularwoodworking.com